# ONE DAY AT A TIME

## Devotions for Today's Teen

MICHAEL SHANKS

One Day at a Time:

Devotions for the Teens of Today



Grace Notes Publishing



ISBN: 978-0-578-82768-1

## DEDICATION

This book is for you, dear teen! Along with all who contributed to this book, I want you to know that you are a precious generation. God can and will use you for His glory!

## SPECIAL THANKS GOES TO:

The friends who joined me in the writing of this book. Each of these men are (or were) in teen ministry. With the exception of February, their contributions are found in the foreword and final day of each month. These men include Cory Fehr (Senior Pastor of Cornerstone Church, Argos, IN); Dr. Bill Higley (Vice President for Academics, Clarks Summit University); Wayne Morgan (Missionary to the Northeast at National Network of Youth Ministries); Eddie Newton (Bible teacher at The King's Christian School, Cherry Hill, NJ); Carl Pesesky (Family Ministries Pastor of Fellowship Bible Church, Troy, PA); Andy Shanks (Youth and Worship Pastor of Breesport Baptist Church, Breesport, NY); Mel Walker (Youth Pastor of Wyoming Valley Church, Plains, PA; also serves as Youth Author, Speaker, Consultant and Coach); and Alf Wilkes (Missionary and Ministry Leader Coach for Word of Life Fellowship). I'm so thankful to call them my friends and brothers!

The teens who took the time to help me edit this book. This was a big project, and they took it on! These teens included Nathan Gorsline, Kaden Gorsline, Daniel Teeter, and Madelynne Wrisley. Their influence made such a difference to me.

Jess Rainer and Craft Book Publishing. You gave me the confidence that this book could become a reality. I appreciate all of your encouragement and terrific work.

My church (Independent Baptist, Towanda, PA). I'm grateful for the privilege of serving you. Thank you for allowing me to write as part of my ministry to our teens.

My family. My incredible wife (Lisa) and children (Lydia, Lincoln, and Landon). Each one chipped in with their thoughts, and they even helped me to edit the index page of Bible passages at the end of this book. I love you all so much! May this book encourage you, dear children, when you become teenagers yourselves one day.

# CONTENTS

In this book, every month begins or ends with a set amount of devotions dedicated to specific themes. The remaining days of the month are a collection of topical passages geared for your growth.

## FOREWORD

How do we get to know someone? Nowadays, we might start with a friend request on Snapchat, or Facebook, or Instagram. If they happen to live near us, we might find a time and place to go hang out with them. Whatever the means, making friends and developing relationships takes both time and intentional effort on our part.

So it is with God. I contend that one of the greatest needs of our time is to get to know the God who loves us and cares for us. In many ways, He is the ultimate friend. Since this is true, I would think that all of us would want to know Him, and know Him well, better than any other friend we may have on social media. But how do we develop a relationship with Him? Let me offer some help to this question.

There's an age-old debate among theologians that goes like this: "Does the Bible set out to 'prove' that God exists, or does the Bible 'assume' that God exists?" I personally believe the latter. After all, what does Genesis 1:1 say? "In the beginning, God created the heavens and the earth." This verse seems to be a rather straightforward assumption: there is a God, and this God created. The writers of the Bible take it for granted that there is a God. And more importantly, they claim that He knows us, and that we can know Him.

In some ways, it sure would be nice if we could just Snapchat with God, or send Him an Instagram post, or message Him on Facebook. I admit that this would be way more convenient! However, God doesn't speak directly to us through social media. Instead, His way of communicating with us is through the Bible. If we want to get to know God, we must do it through the Word of God.

Since this is so, we have to develop a habit of reading, studying, and learning the Bible. Let's be honest... that's not easy! Like those friends we're connecting with on social media or hanging out with on the weekends, it takes time and effort to build good relationships.

Relationships take a certain level of commitment to stick. But here's the thing: if we really like our friends, and if we really want to hang out with them, then we'll make the time. We even look forward to that time. If they are really our friends, we don't think of it as work at all. We do it because we want to be with them. That's not work; that's the reward and joy of a good relationship with true friends. Likewise, if we want to know God, and if we want to develop a better relationship with Him, we will make the time and effort.

Speaking of a relationship with God, let me be clear: The Bible is the story of God's relationship-building with us. That may sound a bit weird, so let me explain.

The Bible is a grand story of God's work in this world. It starts at creation. That creation included the presence of the perfect relationship God shared with His greatest of creatures (Adam and Eve). Our earthly parents shared the kind of relationship with God that He desired with all of humanity. But Adam and Eve were tempted by Satan, and they fell to sin. Their sin caused a major break in their relationship to God. In one sense, the rest of the Bible is the story of their descendants, seeking restoration with God.

However, even through our best efforts, we cannot restore the broken relationship. Why? It goes back to Adam and Eve. The sin they committed affected every person who would come after them. We can never be fully restored in our relationship with God through our own efforts, because sin prevents it. This relationship is only restored by God Himself. As a matter of fact, God took the initiative to send His Son Jesus to give us the way back to Him. In the end, our human efforts will always come up short, and it is only God who can restore all things to His original design. By His power, He will! In a nutshell, that is the purpose and story of the Bible: His creation, our fall, our redemption through Jesus, and His final restoration.

Let me talk to you about this from a very personal perspective. As I referenced above, the way that we can be restored in our relationship to God is through His Son, Jesus Christ. Jesus came to earth as a baby. He was God, but he was also a human. As both God and man, he was qualified to be offered as a sacrifice for our sin. The Bible tells us that the way that we can be restored in our relationship to God is by believing in Jesus. This belief is called faith.

This faith is not blind. It's the belief that recognizes Jesus as God. As God, he lived a perfect life, he went to a cross and died to pay the price for our sins, he was buried, and he was resurrected. This was an act of perfect love! His death paid the penalty for our sins, and his resurrection proved his victory over sin.

*When we accept the truth that Jesus was who he said he was, and that his death on the cross paid the price for our sins, we can have a personal and restored relationship with God.*

If you have never done this, I challenge you to think about it. Find someone in your life who follows Jesus, and allow this person to talk you through the truth that I just laid out. He or she would be thrilled to show you the truth from the Bible.

But that is just the beginning. Like with any friends, connecting with them on our favorite social media sites doesn't necessarily mean that we really know them. The connection is just the beginning of the relationship. Quality time together is what allows us to build a real relationship with them.

This brings us full circle and back to my point: The Bible is the communication from God that allows us to truly get to know Him. If we really want to know God, we've got to figure out how to read, study, and learn about Him in His Word.

This is where my friend (Mike Shanks) has given us a wonderful tool. I first got to know Mike when he was a college student. Mike enrolled in a few courses I taught, and over time, our relationship moved from "Professor-Student" to real friends. Mike is a gifted person. He loves people, and he loves God. Through different circumstances in his life, and in God's perfect timing, Mike and his wife (Lisa) have been given the opportunity to serve the youth of their church for several years. In that time, Mike has realized that students want to know God and desire to have a relationship with Him. He has led and coached many through that process.

Midway through his ministry, Mike began writing teen devotions. The devotions became a core tool for his youth ministry. In time, Mike was challenged to share those devotions with other teens. This book comes from those efforts and is the result of his desire to help teens learn how to study the Bible. It is a gift to anyone who reads it. Why? Because in these devotions, Mike skillfully and creatively helps the reader begin to know God's Word, and thus, to know God Himself.

If you are reading this, I will assume that you have an interest in reading devotions. You've come to a good place. This book, through its various themes and topics, will walk you through the Bible. In it, you will learn about the key people, places, events, and most importantly, about the key person of the Bible, Jesus Christ. In the end, Mike's desire is to point you to Jesus, and the relationship you can have with God through him.

By His grace, I trust that you will grow in your relationship with the God who loves you.

For His glory,
**Bill Higley**
**Vice President for Academics, Clarks Summit University**

## HOW SHOULD I READ A BOOK OF DEVOTIONS?

But as for you, continue in what you have learned and have firmly believed, knowing from whom you learned it and how from childhood you have been acquainted with the sacred writings, which are able to make you wise for salvation through faith in Christ Jesus. All Scripture is breathed out by God and profitable for teaching, for reproof, for correction, and for training in righteousness, that the man of God may be complete, equipped for every good work. (2 Timothy 3:14-17)

As a Christian, it took me many years to get into a regular habit of daily reading my Bible. I was discouraged by my lack of commitment, and I knew that something had to change. That change came once I committed to more personal accountability. I discovered that any biblical resource which kept me on track each day was a tremendous help for my spiritual growth.

Dear teenager, here is my hope for you:

- If you miss a day or two (or more!), please don't get discouraged, and please don't give up! Lifelong habits take time to develop. The discipline of reading God's Word is the best discipline to embrace.
- Take your time. God is in no hurry to teach you! Carefully ponder and pray as you read. Your life will be transformed.
- If you can only read a portion of the devotion, choose the daily Bible passage (found at the bottom of each page). The words of the Bible are far more important than the words of this book's contributors!

*I am so excited that you have this book in your hands!* May God bless you as you grow and go.

# JANUARY

## YOUTH OF THE BIBLE

LET NO ONE DESPISE YOU FOR YOUR YOUTH, BUT SET THE BELIEVERS AN EXAMPLE IN SPEECH, IN CONDUCT, IN LOVE, IN FAITH, IN PURITY. (1 TIMOTHY 4:12)

1 Timothy 4:12 is a command from the Apostle Paul to Pastor Timothy. I don't know how young Timothy was at the time. However, as we see in the Bible, he was young enough to deal with the challenges that came from being a "rookie." Paul did not focus on the fact that he was not the most experienced, or the most knowledgeable, or perhaps not even the most popular leader in his church. Age is not an issue when you show everyone a consistent example of godly living.

The Bible becomes even more exciting to read when we learn how it shatters assumed barriers. God does not share our presuppositions about age and value; He uses both young and old! In the Bible, the young ones were often teenagers. How cool is that? People like Joseph, Daniel, David, Josiah, and Mary... all teens that changed the world.

If God chose someone in your town to do a mighty work, who would it be? Many would look for a dashing leader who has proven to be successful. Yet the Bible reveals many believers who were not "wise according to worldly standards, not many were powerful; not many were of noble birth" (1 Corinthians 1:26).

We're going to spend some time this month looking at various "youth of the Bible" (including many teens!). Maybe, just maybe, you will be blown away at what God can do in you, as well.

CONSIDER WHAT TIMOTHY WAS ASKED TO DO IN 1 TIMOTHY 4:9-16.

## YOUTH OF THE BIBLE - DAVID

THEN SAMUEL SAID TO JESSE, "ARE ALL YOUR SONS HERE?" AND HE SAID, "THERE REMAINS YET THE YOUNGEST, BUT BEHOLD, HE IS KEEPING THE SHEEP." AND SAMUEL SAID TO JESSE, "SEND AND GET HIM, FOR WE WILL NOT SIT DOWN TILL HE COMES HERE." AND HE SENT AND BROUGHT HIM IN. NOW HE WAS RUDDY AND HAD BEAUTIFUL EYES AND WAS HANDSOME. AND THE LORD SAID, "ARISE, ANOINT HIM, FOR THIS IS HE." (1 SAMUEL 16:11-12)

David was a young man at this time of his life. A teenager? Probably! We do know he was the youngest son, and as the baby of the family, and he was not treated very kindly by his brothers. This teen would soon become the second king of Israel. One day, he was an unknown boy to most of the world, spending time alone caring for the sheep; the next, he was defeating a giant and his army. Indeed, God does not see things in the way that we do (1 Samuel 16:8)!

Greatness, as defined by God, is not based upon the standards of man. Our nation honors people by a very different set of rules. We like people that are incredibly attractive, or extremely gifted, or very athletic. However, *the Lord defines greatness as a lifetime of obedience.* Even as a teenager, David was recognized by God as a man after His own heart. Can you think of a greater compliment from the Almighty? As we read through David's teenage years in history and psalm, we begin to understand how this shepherd boy was shaped by the Master into a man who was like no other king in Israel.

What is God doing in your life? How is he shaping you? Is it away from the public eye, in an unknown valley, where you have to depend upon him and no one else? If so, good! Like David, may the Lord also form you into a man or woman who is like no other.

↑ READ ABOUT A YOUNG DAVID IN 1 SAMUEL 16:1-13.

## YOUTH OF THE BIBLE – JOSEPH

THESE ARE THE GENERATIONS OF JACOB. JOSEPH, BEING SEVENTEEN YEARS OLD, WAS PASTURING THE FLOCK WITH HIS BROTHERS. HE WAS A BOY WITH THE SONS OF BILHAH AND ZILPAH, HIS FATHER'S WIVES. AND JOSEPH BROUGHT A BAD REPORT OF THEM TO THEIR FATHER. (GENESIS 37:2)

Does anyone like a tattle-tale? Not anyone I have ever met! You know who especially hates the tattle-tale? The ones who are about to get in big trouble!

Joseph the teenager was a half-brother to the sons of Bilhah and Zilpah. Their mothers were wives of Joseph's father Jacob, only because Jacob's original two wives struggled with infertility issues. Joseph's mother passed away, but she had always been Jacob's true love, so Jacob loved Joseph and his little brother Benjamin more than all the rest of the boys. What a recipe for disaster!

The Bible does not condemn Joseph for the bad report. Those brothers were probably acting very wickedly. Genesis 37:2 is our introduction to the life of Joseph, and we quickly discover the kind of life this teen would face. He was a truth-teller among men who could not stand the truth. He was a loved son among sons who were not loved. He was given dreams for his life that caused his siblings to lose sleep.

According to His plan, God allowed those hardened brothers to abuse Joseph and sell him to slavery. As a teen, Joseph would become a slave in Egypt, thrown in prison on trumped up charges of rape, and forgotten by a man who could have freed him from prison.

But you know what? This teen would also become second in command to the Pharaoh, and he would save not only his brothers from a famine, but the whole nation of Egypt. Not bad for a teen, wouldn't you say?

LET'S READ ABOUT JOSEPH THE TEEN IN GENESIS 37.

## YOUTH OF THE BIBLE - DANIEL

THEN THE KING GAVE DANIEL HIGH HONORS AND MANY GREAT GIFTS, AND MADE HIM RULER OVER THE WHOLE PROVINCE OF BABYLON AND CHIEF PREFECT OVER ALL THE WISE MEN OF BABYLON. (DANIEL 2:48)

There are many amazing teens in the Bible! God used them to influence the course of history. Today's teen is one of the best. In fact, this teen has nothing bad written about him. His name is Daniel.

King Nebuchadnezzar wanted the brightest and best of Israel to be trained in Babylon. Naturally, smart leaders would advance the progress of his kingdom. What Nebuchadnezzar could not have anticipated was his future humility in the presence of Daniel's God.

Though the boy was taken out of the land, the land was not taken out of the boy. Daniel lived by his conscience (he refused to be defiled by eating food that was against God's law), and he lived by his faith (he trusted the Lord to interpret the king's dream, even with a sentence of death upon his head). What courage! What character! What a teen!

It was never God's desire to see His people held captive in a distant land. However, He never left them, nor forsook them, even though they deserved their Babylonian imprisonment. Daniel would end up living out the entire prophesied 70 years of captivity. Through it all, this one-of-a-kind teenager lived faithfully to the end. Incredible!

How wonderful it is that God does not use age as a defining factor for service, but rather the willing heart?

READ DANIEL 1 TODAY! I AM SO THANKFUL FOR THIS YOUNG MAN.

## YOUTH OF THE BIBLE - MARY

AND MARY SAID, "BEHOLD, I AM THE SERVANT OF THE LORD; LET IT BE TO ME ACCORDING TO YOUR WORD." AND THE ANGEL DEPARTED FROM HER. (LUKE 1:38)

You know her story. The miracle of miracles - a baby born to a virgin. Mary (a teenage girl, in all likelihood), pregnant with the Son of God. Pregnancy is usually a wonderful thing... except when it isn't; and to those around her, she had allegedly committed an awful sin by sleeping with another man before the proper time. People didn't understand that she was pregnant virgin; but how would they? Would you or I understand? So this poor girl and her soon-to-be husband left town, based upon the faith that God really knew what He was doing.

Oh, the thoughts that must have rushed through her head when she was told she would conceive by the Holy Spirit! Yet Mary only asks one question: "How can a virgin get pregnant?" This is a pretty legitimate question, I do believe! Many people in the Bible had asked questions of God and His angels concerning his miraculous works. Mary had a question that dealt with a miracle of unheard proportions. What happened to her had never occurred before, nor ever will again!

And along with that one question, Mary had just one reply: "Behold, I am the servant of the Lord; let it be to me according to your word." This short verse reveals so much about her character! Luke 1:38 is the proper response of any servant to his or her master; it is also the response that released the Savior of the world to come and rescue mankind. Yes, it's amazing what a humble and obedient response to the Lord will do to change the world.

As her cousin Elizabeth would later proclaim, "Blessed are you among women, and blessed is the fruit of your womb!" (Luke 1:42).

↑ WE SEE MORE OF MARY'S CHARACTER IN LUKE 1:46-56.

## YOUTH OF THE BIBLE - JOSIAH

"GO, INQUIRE OF THE LORD FOR ME, AND FOR THE PEOPLE, AND FOR ALL JUDAH, CONCERNING THE WORDS OF THIS BOOK THAT HAS BEEN FOUND. FOR GREAT IS THE WRATH OF THE LORD THAT IS KINDLED AGAINST US, BECAUSE OUR FATHERS HAVE NOT OBEYED THE WORDS OF THIS BOOK, TO DO ACCORDING TO ALL THAT IS WRITTEN CONCERNING US." (2 KINGS 22:13)

Josiah was the last good king of Judah. He was the ripe old age of 8 years old (!) when he took the throne. His dad was King Amon, and his grandfather King Manasseh. Both were terribly wicked men. What an awful heritage to pass on to this boy! Yet, defying the odds, "he did what was right in the eyes of the LORD and walked in all the way of David his father, and he did not turn aside to the right or to the left" (2 Kings 22:2). Wow! Teens, what do you think when you see a child doing the right thing? Does it impact you to do the same?

2 Chronicles 34 and 35 also cover the life of Josiah. In 34:3, we read this: "For in the eighth year of his reign, while he was yet a boy, he began to seek the God of David his father, and in the twelfth year he began to purge Judah and Jerusalem of the high places, the Asherim, and the carved and the metal images." The king would have been 16 years old when God opened his eyes! At the age of 26, Josiah was cut to the heart when he heard the words of the Law. Immediately, he restored God's commanded method of worship, and he got rid of the false idols that were in the land. His spiritual clean-up project earned Judah several decades of reprieve before the exile.

What is God preparing you for in this life? If you live to be 80, then you are not even one quarter of the way done on this earth. So much of what God can do in you as an adult is being shaped in you as a teen. Ask the Lord to work on you! Live out His plans, not yours!

LEARN MORE ABOUT JOSIAH IN 2 KINGS 22.

## YOUTH OF THE BIBLE – REBEKAH

AND THEY CALLED REBEKAH AND SAID TO HER, "WILL YOU GO WITH THIS MAN?" SHE SAID, "I WILL GO." (GENESIS 24:58)

How old was Rebekah when she got married? No one knows for sure. When Abraham's servant came to look for her, we read that he prayed for God's help to meet "a girl", or damsel. The Hebrew word that describes Rebekah reveals that she is in her childhood or adolescence. The word for "woman" is a different word altogether. In all likelihood, Rebekah was a teenager. Though this may be rather unique to us, a teenage wife is not unusual to societies, both past and present.

What was so amazing about Rebekah the teen? Well, how about her willingness to marry a man she had never met, and who lived 500 miles away from her? She wasn't told that she had to go; she was asked. Though she heard the incredible story given by Abraham's servant in Genesis 24, she could have said "no" and stayed comfortably at home. The response of "I will go" is extraordinary! It reveals faith in a future that was unknown. And she wasn't given weeks to decide – the servant was ambitious to get back to Abraham ASAP (we read in Genesis 24:56 that he planned to leave one day later). No time to figure out if Isaac was cute, or strong, or smart, or anything else. She just went... and trusted... and ultimately, became a significant figure in the history of both Israel and the line of Christ.

Teens – like Rebekah, you don't need to have it all figured out. Life is full of important choices. Even when we make plans, God holds the future. Sometimes He calls us to step forward when we don't have a clue what will happen next. That's not a bad thing; He has all the answers! Life is so much better when we say "yes" to God. In turn, God says "yes" to His magnificent blessings.

↑ WHAT A LOVE STORY! READ GENESIS 24 TODAY.

# YOUTH OF THE BIBLE - SAMUEL

AND SAMUEL GREW, AND THE LORD WAS WITH HIM AND LET NONE OF HIS WORDS FALL TO THE GROUND. AND ALL ISRAEL FROM DAN TO BEERSHEBA KNEW THAT SAMUEL WAS ESTABLISHED AS A PROPHET OF THE LORD. (1 SAMUEL 3:19-20)

The story of Samuel is a special one. His mom wondered if he would ever come. The LORD heard Hannah's cry for a child, and like many "surprise" children in the Bible, Samuel was given a special mission. We read that Hannah dedicated him to God's work from the beginning. Because of this, little Samuel went off to live with the priest Eli when he was just a kid. During those early years of his life, Samuel was spoken to by God. We are not sure of his exact age in 1 Samuel 3, but he was not yet a man when God gave him a message that altered Israel.

The message was not a blessing, but a curse. It was a message of doom for Samuel's mentor and family. What a tremendous burden for this boy to carry! Samuel must have deeply grieved as he told Eli about God's judgment upon his priestly family, but nonetheless, he did exactly what God told him to do.

The boy would grow up to be a teenager, and the teenager a man. Samuel would remain a faithful prophet for the rest of his days.

Teens, God is calling us to be truth-tellers. As a prophet, Samuel would spend his life as a proclaimer of truth. To tell the truth is to speak God's language, for God Himself is the Truth. Yes, telling the truth can be awfully uncomfortable! But we can believe the promise Jesus gave in John 8:31-32: "If you abide in my word, you are truly my disciples, and you will know the truth, and the truth will set you free."

Lies enslave; truth sets us free!

↑ READ ABOUT SAMUEL'S FIRST PROPHECY IN 1 SAMUEL 3.

## YOUTH OF THE BIBLE – JEREMIAH

THEN I SAID, "AH, LORD GOD! BEHOLD, I DO NOT KNOW HOW TO SPEAK, FOR I AM ONLY A YOUTH." BUT THE LORD SAID TO ME, "DO NOT SAY, 'I AM ONLY A YOUTH'; FOR TO ALL TO WHOM I SEND YOU, YOU SHALL GO, AND WHATEVER I COMMAND YOU, YOU SHALL SPEAK." (JEREMIAH 1:6-7)

Was Jeremiah a teenage prophet? It's very possible. The sources I read suggest that he was a young adult looking for a way out of God's call for his life (similar to Moses' response when God called him back to Egypt). Though we are not sure of his age, Jeremiah was young enough to feel like a teenage prophet, even if he was an adult.

If you were Jeremiah, how would you respond to God's command? How would you feel about bringing down the hammer on the leaders in your life? Sounds scary to me! We naturally recognize that some experience comes with years, so even if we disagree or disrespect older people, we should be careful in correcting them.

However, God is not bothered by Jeremiah's youth. In fact, in one incredible mind-blowing verse (Jeremiah 1:4), He tells Jeremiah that He knew him *before* he was in his mother's womb! God's omniscience is not limited by time – He is all-knowing, which spans eternity past to eternity future. He chose Jeremiah, end of story. And since this was the will of the Lord, the proper response for Jeremiah was to obey.

As a youth pastor, I recall times in the past when a teen has spoken words of correction to me. The names Amber, Stephen, and Shelly may mean nothing to you, but these teens had the courage to speak up when I needed to hear it. I am a better man because of them!

Jeremiah did obey the Lord. Though he had a very difficult ministry, he trusted the Lord, and God blessed him for it. What a young man!

↑ CHECK OUT JEREMIAH 1:1-10. GOD CAN USE YOU!

## YOUTH OF THE BIBLE – ESTHER

"Go, gather all the Jews to be found in Susa, and hold a fast on behalf, and do not eat or drink for three days, night or day. I and my young women will also fast as you do. Then I will go to the king, though it is against the law, and if I perish, I perish." (Esther 4:16)

As is the case with many other teenagers in the Bible, we are guessing at the age of Esther (she is called a "young woman" in Esther 2, and the king would certainly be given a virgin to marry). Considering these criteria, she easily could have been a teenager at her wedding. Regardless of her exact age, her story is incredible. Even though His Name is not mentioned even once in this story, the Lord was ever with His people, and He used Esther in a mighty way.

Esther put her life on the line by going to visit the king. Why is that? Ahasuerus had a "I call you, you don't call me" policy. Even though she was the queen, there were different rules at work in those days, and she did not have the right to go see the king unless she was called upon. But Esther approached the king nonetheless, doing it for the sake of her people. Satan is always at work, and he was using the wicked Haman in his plans to commit mass genocide of the Jews. Esther needed tremendous courage to stop this from happening. The king did invite her to come and speak with him... and the rest is history!

*God is always at work!* The story of Esther teaches us about His perfect control over all matters. Even in a foreign land, He is Lord of all. Don't you love the fact that He chose a young girl to save thousands of God's people? The Jews would not forget this (and still celebrate the deliverance in a Jewish holiday called "Purim").

God is always at work – in history, and in you.

🡅 THE WHOLE BOOK IS SO CAPTIVATING! THE CLIMAX IS IN ESTHER 7.

# YOUTH OF THE BIBLE – SHADRACH, MESHACH, ABEDNEGO

"If this be so, our God whom we serve is able to deliver us from the burning fiery furnace, and he will deliver us out of you hand, O king. But if not, be it known to you, O king, that we will not serve your gods or worship the golden image that you have set up." (Daniel 3:17-18)

I've played out the scenarios in my head more than once. I always come to the same conclusion. The worst way I can think of to die is a death by fire. So when I think about the courage of the three men who were thrown into a fiery furnace, I am in awe. And guess what? In all likelihood, the three men were probably teens!

All they had to do was bow down. Couldn't they just pretend to worship Nebuchadnezzar so that they could live? Sure, they could have done that, if they had no faith in their God. Instead, they chose the Lord over life. We see a miracle – they survived the furnace without even being singed – but remember, these men had *no idea* if they would survive. According to the verses above, they were at peace if God spared them, and they were at peace if He did not.

Teens, we cannot underestimate the power of faith. The faith of Shadrach, Meshach, and Abednego was not a faith of chance. It comes from a disciplined love for the Lord.

There comes a point in our Christian walk when we realize that a life lived away from God is no life at all. His promised future for us makes everything worth it!

I appreciate the chorus of the old hymn, "God Leads Us Along." It says, "Some through the waters, some through the flood, some through the fire, but all through the blood; some through great sorrow, but God gives a song, In the night season and all the day long." Lead on, Lord!

READ DANIEL 3 AND DISCOVER THE REST OF THIS TERRIFIC STORY.

# YOUTH OF THE BIBLE - AZARIAH

In the twenty-seventh year of Jeroboam king of Israel, Azariah the son of Amaziah, king of Judah, began to reign. He was sixteen years old when he began to reign, and he reigned fifty-two years in Jerusalem. His mother's name was Jecoliah of Jerusalem. (2 Kings 15:1-2)

In the Old Testament, the kings of Judah are twice reviewed: once in the books of the Kings, and once in the books of the Chronicles. When we study these books, we can see that the books of the Kings place an emphasis on the political, while the Chronicles focus more upon religious life. Yes, the Bible is not afraid to discuss politics and religion!

U.S. law states that an elected president must be at least 35 years old. However, we read that a few kings in the O.T. were teens or children. Azariah (also known as Uzziah) was one of them. His reign lasted a long time (52 years), and "he did what was right in the eyes of the LORD," to a degree (2 Kings 15:3-4). The account in the Chronicles gives us some helpful insight into his life. Israel was strong under Azariah, but pride led to his fall. In his rebellion, the king tried to be the priest. God struck him with leprosy, and Azariah's remaining years were lived away from society. What a shameful way to end his reign.

Before pride took over, the king "set himself to seek God in the days of Zechariah, who instructed him in the fear of God, and as long as he sought the LORD, God made him prosper" (2 Chronicles 26:5).

Teens, I want to challenge you to seek the LORD today. Make that your daily purpose. Azariah did not have to fail, but somewhere in his life, he decided to follow his own advice. He failed to finish his race well.

Who wants to be remembered as the person who fell to sin, and as a result, died with a disease? Not me! Let's seek Him for all of our days!

↑ CHECK OUT THE LIFE OF AZARIAH (UZZIAH) IN 2 CHRONICLES 26.

# YOUTH OF THE BIBLE - DINAH

NOW DINAH, THE DAUGHTER OF LEAH, WHOM SHE HAD BORNE TO JACOB, WENT OUT TO SEE THE WOMEN OF THE LAND. AND WHEN SHECHEM THE SON OF HAMOR THE HIVITE, THE PRINCE OF THE LAND, SAW HER, HE SEIZED HER AND LAY WITH HER AND HUMILIATED HER. (GENESIS 34:1-2)

Today's teenager is only a guess - we are not sure how old Dinah was in Genesis 34. She is also a difficult case to discuss. Dinah's tragedy reveals her very dysfunctional family. In this chapter, we read about a young lady that was raped. This is not the only time that rape is mentioned in the Bible. It is a terrible crime, both then and now.

You'll have the opportunity to read Genesis 34 today, but before you do, here are some things that make me shake my head in disbelief. First, the guy who raped Dinah is then the guy who proposes to her father (Jacob) for her hand in marriage. Second, Jacob is passive about the crime against his daughter (Genesis reveals that he was not the model of fatherhood in the Bible!). Third, Dinah's brothers decide to go along with the proposed marriage, as long as all the men of the village get circumcised (bummer for them!). And fourth, a couple of Dinah's brothers go on a killing spree, taking out all of the newly circumcised Shechemites with their swords. Still think that the Bible is boring?

Teens, when you think about Dinah, remember that her life mattered deeply to God. Women should never be treated as objects for the pleasures of men. Rape is a crime against humanity, and the Lord will punish the offender. Thankfully, God does not look at those who have been through sexual assault as second-class citizens. Our bodies may suffer at the hands of men, but our spirit remains safe and secure.

"Heal me, O LORD, and I shall be healed; save me, and I shall be saved, for you are my praise" (Jeremiah 17:14). Amen... and thank you, God.

↑ THE COMPLETE STORY OF DINAH IS FOUND IN GENESIS 34.

## YOUTH OF THE BIBLE – THE FIRST GENERATION OF ISRAEL

"SAY TO THEM, 'AS I LIVE, DECLARES THE LORD, WHAT YOU HAVE SAID IN MY HEARING I WILL DO TO YOU: YOUR DEAD BODIES SHALL FALL IN THIS WILDERNESS, AND OF ALL YOUR NUMBER, LISTED IN THE CENSUS FROM TWENTY YEARS OLD AND UPWARD, WHO HAVE GRUMBLED AGAINST ME, NOT ONE SHALL COME INTO THE LAND WHERE I SWORE THAT I WOULD MAKE YOU DWELL, EXCEPT CALEB THE SON OF JEPHUNNEH AND JOSHUA THE SON OF NUN.'" (NUMBERS 14:28-30)

It would take 40 years for millions of adults to die, but none of Israel's first generation (save two - Joshua and Caleb) would enter the Promised Land. Let that settle in for a moment. The teens who left Egypt would make it to their new home. Their parents and grandparents, however, would be buried in the wilderness, due to their sin and rebellion. What a terrible price to pay for not trusting God.

I look at the families of our own communities. There is a real need for adult leadership. A lot of parents just don't have a clue how to navigate through life. So many moms and dads live for themselves. So many of them are wrapped up in things that are destructive. The natural results of sin are passed from one generation to the next, unless God intervenes. I spoke with a former teen recently who is dealing with a heritage of drug abuse. His parents have had serious problems in this area. The only way he will break the chains of his past is to cling to the God of freedom.

But here's the good news. That first generation of teens? They succeeded! They did not commit the sins of their fathers, but instead followed Joshua into the Promised Land. They defeated the enemy nations and made a home for themselves.

When teenagers take God at His word, they turn into victorious adults.

MOSES REMINDS THESE FORMER TEENS OF THEIR PARENTS' PAST IN DEUTEROMONY 1:26-46. HIS WARNING IS THEIR GAIN.

## YOUTH OF THE BIBLE - MANASSEH

MOREOVER MANASSEH SHED VERY MUCH INNOCENT BLOOD, TILL HE HAD FILLED JERUSALEM FROM ONE END TO ANOTHER, BESIDES THE SIN THAT HE MADE JUDAH TO SIN SO THAT THEY DID WHAT WAS EVIL IN THE SIGHT OF THE LORD. (2 KINGS 21:16)

Manasseh was twelve years old when he became king. He was a very bad king – the worst of the worst. The Bible makes mention of this on several occasions. In many ways, he put the final nail in the coffin of Judah's doomed fate; his evil decisions paved the way for the prophesied exile to occur. In the history of Judah, a number of kings left a good legacy. Hezekiah (his father) was one of them. However, Manasseh chose the path of evil. What in the world went wrong?

When we stop and consider the consequences of Manasseh's reign, it gives us a couple of warnings. First, for those of you who will be parents one day, be the kind of dad or mom that God wants you to be. You know the saying: "Actions speak louder than words." Don't let your actions compromise the words you teach! Hezekiah had some issues with compromise (which makes we wonder what kind of a dad he was to Manasseh).

Second, you are responsible for your own choices. You are fully capable of making a right decision, no matter what your mom or dad does. Manasseh was steeped in evil because he rebelled against the God of Israel. The Lord always provided counselors and prophets for the kings of His nation, but many (Manasseh included) refused to listen.

Teens, you will destroy yourself if you live like Manasseh. So why copy him? Be the one that people can say, "He (She) did what was right in the eyes of the LORD."

🡅 READ ABOUT THE WICKED KING MANASSEH IN 2 KINGS 21:1-18.

## YOUTH OF THE BIBLE – THE EXILED

"THUS SAYS THE LORD OF HOSTS, THE GOD OF ISRAEL, TO ALL THE EXILES WHOM I HAVE SENT INTO EXILE FROM JERUSALEM TO BABYLON: BUILD HOUSES AND LIVE IN THEM; PLANT GARDENS AND EAT THEIR PRODUCE." (JEREMIAH 29:4-5)

My boys hate the discipline of getting a "time-out". Sitting in the corner for fifteen minutes seems worse for them than taking Christmas away! After two minutes, they usually start asking if their time is up. I remind them that I will let them know, and if they ask again, I will add another five minutes to their torture. Oh, the joys of parenting!

The prophet Jeremiah wrote to the exiles about settling down in Babylon. God had made up His mind; they would be in captivity for 70 years. 70 years - no more, and no less. If you were a teen that went into captivity at the fall of Jerusalem, you would be in your eighties when the prophesied time came to an end. For that reason, many Jews decided to stay put in Babylon; not many returned to the land when King Cyrus of Persia gave the order.

Teens, we cannot set an amount of time over the consequences of our sin. For example, if someone cheats on their spouse, it may take years, even decades, to recover. But God offers that unfaithful spouse the grace to rely on Him while he or she waits "in captivity". Ezekiel was one prophet who encouraged the exiles to wait upon the Lord. His message largely went unheeded, though he proclaimed God's goodness to His people in the hardest of times.

We need to learn to trust the Lord as He works us through the consequences of a wrong decision. He will not release us until His work is finished, even though the work may be very painful.

READ JEREMIAH'S LETTER IN JEREMIAH 29:4-14.

# YOUTH OF THE BIBLE - JEHOIACHIN

AND HE CARRIED AWAY JEHOIACHIN TO BABYLON. THE KING'S MOTHER, THE KING'S WIVES, HIS OFFICIALS, AND THE CHIEF MEN OF THE LAND HE TOOK INTO CAPTIVITY FROM JERUSALEM TO BABYLON. (2 KINGS 24:15)

He was 18 when he became king. His reign lasted around 3 months. He was evil in evil times. He was deported to a powerful enemy, carried off to a distant land. He really never stood a chance as king of Judah in those days.

You are looking forward to graduation. You have a future ahead of you (perhaps college, or a good job?). Jehoiachin "graduated", and then he was carried off to Babylon as a prisoner of war. Not the way most of us envision starting life after we don the cap and gown!

In some ways, the reality of Jehoiachin's horror is being played out today. Being the prisoner of a Middle Eastern nation that hates Christianity is an unspeakable nightmare. Babylon is modern day Iraq, smack center in an intolerant area of our world. Muslims claim to worship the one true God, but all false religions are against Him.

Can you imagine being kidnapped and taken away to Iraq, or Iran, or Afghanistan? It would be terrible! Yet Jehoiachin was not executed, and hope endured. Unbelievably, in the last few verses of 2 Kings, he was released to dine with the king of Babylon for the rest of his days. This teenager finds redemption from prison as an old man... and the Jews are given a symbol of hope while they wait in exile.

READ ABOUT JEHOIACHIN IN 2 KINGS 24:8-17 AND 25:27-30.

# YOUTH OF THE BIBLE – JESUS

AND JESUS INCREASED IN WISDOM AND IN STATURE AND IN FAVOR WITH GOD AND MAN. (LUKE 2:52)

Read this verse carefully and slowly. Look at it word by word. Jesus... increased? It makes my jaw drop. After all, we are talking about the Christ here – the King of kings and Lord of lords, the Creator of the world, the sinless Savior, the Alpha and the Omega, The Holy One, the God-Man, Immanuel. *He* grew in wisdom? *He* grew in stature? *He* grew in favor with God above and men below? How is that so?

We never read any details about Jesus' life as a teenager, but this verse sums up what happened in the days after he was twelve years old. From the time he was 12 until he was 30, he grew. Growing is something that Jesus would not have needed to do in heaven. Yet in a human body, amongst his brethren, this was necessary and right.

It's hard for me to put my mind around Luke 2:52, because I automatically connect the need for growth with overcoming sin. Yet we know that Jesus did not sin. So his growth was based upon another standard. If he needed to learn the trade of being a carpenter, it was not his sin that kept him from doing the perfect job the first time he tried. And he did not study his Bible to keep himself from future sin. Since Jesus is the "God-Man", it must be that growing in wisdom, stature and favor was all planned for him. As a teenager, he fulfilled God's will for his life by growing as deity clothed with flesh. Amazing!

As a Christian, do you desire to grow like Christ? I hope so! To grow in wisdom and stature and in favor is to grow like our Savior did – both as a teen and as a man.

↑ CHECK OUT A MATURE TWELVE YEAR-OLD JESUS IN LUKE 2:41-52.

## YOUTH OF THE BIBLE - THE UNSPOKEN OTHERS

OUT OF THE MOUTHS OF BABIES AND INFANTS, YOU HAVE ESTABLISHED STRENGTH BECAUSE OF YOUR FOES, TO STILL THE ENEMY AND THE AVENGER. (PSALM 8:2)

How many other teenagers are a part of biblical history? Only God knows! We can guess at the age of the disciples, or the boy with the loaves and fishes, or Paul's nephew (who helped rescue him from a murder attempt), or the young pastor Timothy. Honestly, we do not know how old they were at the time each book was written. Only on occasion does the Bible gives us the ages of certain individuals.

Sometimes I wish we had more details like this, but then I come to realize how good it is to *not* know some things. The fact that age is usually a biblical unknown teaches us that it is not a determining factor for service. You can make a world of difference simply through obedience, whether you are age 5 or 95. God calls us to live for Him at any age, and by His strength, we can always accomplish His will.

Precious teen, never forget that God revels in using the supposed weak things of this world to confound the wise. We read of this many times as we learn about the heroes of the faith.

When you feel weak, unable to match up, or less than worthy, remember God. He knows all things, and He knows you! We cannot fully grasp what He can and will do through any willing teen who loves Him above all.

🡅 READ PSALM 8!

# DEFLECTION TO RECEPTION

NOW WHEN THEY HEARD THIS THEY WERE CUT TO THE HEART, AND SAID TO PETER AND THE REST OF THE APOSTLES, "BROTHERS, WHAT SHALL WE DO?" (ACTS 2:37)

Deflect. Synonyms of this word include "avert, cover up, divert, ricochet, swerve, and veer." It's what we often do when someone gets too close to matters of the heart. Who likes it when a friend comes up and talks to us about our sin? Who wants to be asked about how our prayer life is *really* going? Who wants someone looking over our shoulder as it pertains to our Bible study habits?

Because we deflect, we learn to give answers that are false. We don't want people to dig too deep, since we desire to avoid the pain associated with change. We don't want to deal with the embarrassment of our past, so we keep our private world private. By doing all of this, our souls slowly starve, and we dry up inside.

When Peter spoke for the first time after Christ returned to heaven, he made his message personal. Any former attempts to deflect went out the window. His preaching worked; in Acts 2, the men responded. By making it personal, thousands came to know the truth they desperately needed to hear. God changed "deflection" to "reception".

The gospel is personal. Teens, if you have not done so yet, let's make it personal in your own life!

↑ HAGGAI NEEDED TO ADDRESS SOME "DEFLECTION" ISSUES WITH HIS COUNTRYMEN – READ THIS TWO CHAPTER BOOK.

## THE LOVE OF "NO"

ONE MAN OF YOU PUTS TO FLIGHT A THOUSAND, SINCE IT IS THE LORD YOUR GOD WHO FIGHTS FOR YOU, JUST AS HE PROMISED YOU. BE VERY CAREFUL, THEREFORE, TO LOVE THE LORD YOUR GOD. (JOSHUA 23:10-11)

Some of the leaders found in the Bible gave farewell speeches. Joshua was among them. Israel was now a young nation that had begun to settle the Promised Land. He gave a stirring speech to the people, challenging them to serve the LORD (tragically, they did not listen, and many generations of Jews would suffer the awful consequences).

At the end of his life, Joshua reminded his brethren of what they should and should not do. They were to say "yes!" to obeying God's word, and "no!" to embracing the nations around them. Like so many of us, we find out soon enough that Israel also hated the word no. It is a word that suggests a wall, chains, fences, and limitations. Who wants to be told not to do something?

But here's the thing: God's "no" to the Christian is a good thing. It should be understood in the context of "I love you!". "Don't date that unsaved boy, because I love you, and I know what is best for your future! Don't lust after that pretty girl, because I love you, and I don't want to see you hurt yourself! Don't waste so much time on social media, because I love you, and want you to make the most of your life!" When we do say yes to God's no, we discover what a great God He truly is. His love is loyal, and He fights for us. He will never leave us. He will never forsake us.

Let us remember His best "no" of all – the "no" found in Christ Jesus, who proclaimed no death and hell for the believer. Since this is true, we can certainly trust Him with all other noes that come our way.

CHECK OUT THE REST OF JOSHUA 23!

# BORDERS

"FEAR OF MAN WILL PROVE TO BE A SNARE, BUT WHOEVER TRUSTS IN THE LORD IS KEPT SAFE." (PROVERBS 29:25)

Borders. My wife and I have them for our kids. Inside the house, some of those borders include not yelling unless there is an emergency, not touching the oven while it is hot, and not putting your fingers in the hinges of a revolving door (ouch!). Outside, it means staying away from the road, watching for the occasional traffic that comes into the parking lot next to us, and not petting the black and white-striped "cats" we occasionally see waddling around in the summer.

Borders. God has them, too. We see them expressed through The 10 Commandments; the entire law as given to His holy nation Israel; the commands given by our Savior while he was on earth; and statements given by Paul to the churches. The Lord has made his borders abundantly clear to the human race.

Borders. Whether we want to admit it or not, we need them. Behind God's "don't do this!" is a "I don't want you to get hurt!". And the purpose for God's "make sure you do this!" is a "I want you to live in freedom, both for my glory and to your fullest potential!"

Our Sheltie is learning about borders. He has a problem with chasing squirrels. Since he has not learned his borders, he sometimes needs to be "bordered" back in the house (which he finds very sad!).

Dear teens, don't shun borders. We all must live by them. Earthly borders have a way of changing, but God's borders remain the same. *Inside of His borders, we are free!*

↑ THE SLAVE ONESIMUS FLED HIS BORDERS. WHAT DID PAUL SAY TO ENCOURAGE PHILEMON (THE MASTER)? READ PHILEMON TODAY.

## MADLY IN LOVE

"My beloved is mine, and I am his; he grazes among the lilies."
(Song of Solomon 2:16)

There is a reason that people get excited about engagements and marriages – in the purest form, they represent the hope for a future of joy and happiness expressed in the greatest of human relationships. Teens, listen carefully: *when God is the center of a marriage, this hope will come true.*

If you take the time to read the Song of Solomon, you will find a couple madly in love. Solomon understands that he has found a wife suitable for him ("she is the perfect match!"), and as he personally wrote, "He who finds a wife finds a good thing and obtains favor from the LORD" (Proverbs 18:22). The two lovers can hardly stay away from each other. The language of this romantic book can be difficult to understand (the same would be true if you picked up one of my old love letters to Lisa; you might scratch your head over some things you read!). Yet the book overflows with tremendous expressions of love that intertwines the physical, emotional, sexual, and spiritual.

Is true love even possible today? Could it happen to you? Oh, how the world is seeking it – just turn on the radio and listen to one of a countless number of love songs. But truly, being madly in love with a spouse is possible. The condition? God must be the center. That's it!

A few weekends ago, I attended a celebration of a couple that have been married for 70 years. God is the center, and they are still "madly in love". What a testimony they have… and what a God we have!

↑ TAKE THE TIME TO READ SONG OF SOLOMON 2 TODAY.

## SURPRISED BY THE TEST

COUNT IT ALL JOY, MY BROTHERS, WHEN YOU MEET TRIALS OF VARIOUS KINDS, FOR YOU KNOW THAT THE TESTING OF YOUR FAITH PRODUCES STEADFASTNESS. (JAMES 1:2-3)

In his letter to the believers, James barely says "Hi!" before he jumps into a heavy topic: the reality of trials. This reality is not an "if", but a "when". And not only that, but James talks about trials in the plural (yes, more than one). Since he's on a roll, James also adds that trials will come in all kinds of ways. Really, James? He might not be the best candidate for a "lift me up" moment!

So why are we surprised at the testing that comes from trials? I feel embarrassed at being surprised about it, especially when the purpose is given to us in the Bible. I should know this by now!

Here's my problem: I'd really like to think that I am good to go as a Christian. I am ready to admit that I need some changes in my life, but I want to believe that those changes are minor (needing only a smooth-grit sand paper to get rid of a few rough edges). I care not to look at the sin issues that have dogged me for most of my life. I'd really rather not think hard about my shortcomings. If I focus on the positive alone, it makes me feel a whole lot more comfortable.

James 1:4 tells us that perseverance needs to complete its work. If it does, I will be mature and complete. Trials bring on the opportunity to persevere. They effectively fix my wrong reliance upon self.

Truly, I have a long way to go. I need God to grow me. Trials will do just that. We can trust that God knows exactly what He is doing.

"Lord, help me to not be surprised by the test, but to rejoice in it."

🡅 CHECK OUT JAMES 1:1-8.

# PLAYING HOUSE TOGETHER

YOU HAVE WEARIED THE LORD WITH YOUR WORDS. BUT YOU SAY, "HOW HAVE WE WEARIED HIM?" BY SAYING, "EVERYONE WHO DOES EVIL IS GOOD IN THE SIGHT OF THE LORD, AND HE DELIGHTS IN THEM." OR BY ASKING, "WHERE IS THE GOD OF JUSTICE?" (MALACHI 2:17)

Living together. It used to be looked down upon, but it is now widely accepted in our culture. Why is that so? Does God really have a problem with it?

"Playing house together" is very prevalent in our nation. Some would say it is wrong, based upon their belief that sex before marriage is forbidden. Indeed, the Bible calls premarital sex a sin, but there is more than sex here that needs to be considered.

Teens, living together before marriage is an attempt to dismiss the marriage boundaries found in Genesis 2. When a man and woman are commanded to "leave and cleave", the cleaving deals with all aspects of the relationship - not just the physical, but also the emotional (our feelings), the mental (our intellect), the volitional (our will), and the spiritual (our soul). To ignore the God-given laws of marriage is to rebel, and to rebel is to shun His blessing upon our relationship with Him. We are completely bombarded with TV shows and movies where couples live together. It is so prevalent that we have forgotten how to be ashamed of it. Yet God Himself has not forgotten how He feels about it! To remain pure in our culture takes real steps of faith. Purity is more than the sexual; it also covers the area of the mind, the will, and the soul.

I pray that you will desire God's blessing upon your whole life. He cannot, and He will not, bless the home of the couple who tries to act married outside the parameters of marriage.

↑ HEED THE WORDS OF MICAH 6:8-16.

## CHURCH: IT'S ALL OR NOTHING

I KNOW YOU ARE ENDURING PATIENTLY AND BEARING UP FOR MY NAME'S SAKE, AND YOU HAVE NOT GROWN WEARY. BUT I HAVE THIS AGAINST YOU, THAT YOU HAVE ABANDONED THE LOVE YOU HAD AT FIRST. (REVELATION 2:3-4)

Today, we will be seeing a lady that means so much to our family. She has a lot going for her, she has been good to us in a number of ways, and she wants to make a difference with her life. But last I knew, she has not been committed to a church for years.

She is now in a position where she needs to make a major life decision. If she says "yes", I believe she will be making one of the worst mistakes of her life. She has continued to push this decision off for years, but I fear the inevitable.

I know I need to talk to her. I do fear the repercussions, but talking to her is the loving thing to do. I have wrestled with what I would tell her. She claims to be a Christian, yet she has little to no desire to meet and worship with God's family. That is a problem!

Teens, what do you think? Can this lady make the right choice while saying "no" to church in her life? Let's put it another way. Can we tell Christ the husband (as expressed in Ephesians 5) that we love him, yet tell the church (his bride) that we hate her? One answer can be found in Revelation 2:1-7. God tells the church at Ephesus that they have some good things going for them, but they had forsaken their first love. As a result, He threatened to take the church right out of the picture.

No, He is not ok with attempts at simultaneously doing the right thing and wrong thing. It cannot work.

↑ CHECK OUT THE INTRO TO THE BOOK OF ZECHARIAH IN 1:1-6.

# WORK NOW, EAT LATER!

For even when we were with you, we would give you this command: If anyone is not willing to work, let him not eat. (2 Thessalonians 3:10)

Recently, I volunteered to help some friends of ours get their farm ready for sale. I have a blister on my left index finger to prove that I worked hard! My work included a ton of weed whacking, and I also power-washed farm equipment and a cattle trailer. Once again, I have the greatest respect for those who farm (I married into a farming family!). It is certainly challenging work.

I was glad to help our friends, and hard work on a farm is good for a guy that often spends most of his time in his office. But in the midst of whacking weeds and cleaning equipment, I must admit that the thought of food and drink kept me going! My desire to be replenished drove me forward on that hot day.

We all know that food is essential to life. The Bible says that if we have food and clothing, we can be content. It also teaches us that our hunger can help us to finish the job.

Let me give you some advice that is simple but often forgotten: *Allow yourself to eat only when the task is done.* Eating is a natural reward for the body as a result of hard work being accomplished. It also causes us to take further control of the body when we make ourselves wait to eat. If you can control your body in this manner, you might be surprised how many other things can wait, as well.

↑ PAUL WARNS AGAINST GENERAL IDLENESS IN 2 THESSALONIANS 3:6-14. WORKING BEFORE EATING IS A GOOD THING!

## WE ARE SAFE IN HIS EMBRACE

HE WILL TEND HIS FLOCK LIKE A SHEPHERD; HE WILL GATHER THE LAMBS IN HIS ARMS; HE WILL CARRY THEM IN HIS BOSOM, AND GENTLY LEAD THOSE THAT ARE WITH YOUNG. (ISAIAH 40:11)

What a tender verse! How comforting for the suffering people of Israel, and how comforting for us, for we too are His sheep.

I think about a former teen in our youth group, a young lady who was courageous enough to talk to me about her pain. She expressed appreciation for many in our youth group who were not afraid to give her a hug, since she does not receive physical affection at home. In her words, "No one wants to touch me and show me love." As a youth pastor, this is a cause for concern (for her and for all teens who do not receive physical affection from their parents). I begged her, "Please do not find yourself in the arms of another man with evil intentions."

Dear teens, the Sovereign Lord is a Shepherd who cares for His sheep. He is a Master who knows everything. He knows just how deeply He loves you. He knows that you are a helpless little lamb. He tends to you, He gathers you, He carries you, and He leads you. That is personal, loving, and intimate, my friend!

When you feel lonely, tired, and frustrated, remember that God offers His unmatchable love for your soul. Don't allow yourself to be fooled into accepting a cheap replacement. One day, the physical touch will come from God Himself, as we read in the book of Revelation (21:4).

The Lord is not afraid to hold us; truly, we are safe in His embrace!

🡅 JESUS WAS NOT AFRAID OF PHYSICAL TOUCH, AND JOHN KNEW IT. READ JOHN 13:18-30 TO SEE HOW JESUS EXPRESSED HIS LOVE.

## THE PSALMS: MUSIC FOR GOD'S NATION

O SING TO THE LORD A NEW SONG, FOR HE HAS DONE MARVELOUS THINGS! HIS RIGHT HAND AND HIS HOLY ARM HAVE WORKED SALVATION FOR HIM. (PSALM 98:1)

Hey teens... try to go a whole day without listening to music. Think you can do it? If so, how about a whole week? Perhaps a few of you could pull it off, but I'm thinking it would drive most of us crazy!

In the days of David, the nation of Israel did not have access to a constant stream of music. I'm not sure how many songs were at their disposal, but the songs they did have were written to glorify God. These songs were full of truth, and they expressed that truth in many ways (praise, laments, instructions, prayers, etc.). Followers of the Lord would embrace this music, recognizing that the truths of the songs would influence their everyday lives.

Today, we often pick music according to how we feel. This usually means that the lyrics are not a high priority. We feel good when we hear our favorite singer or band, and gradually, we start to believe what they sing. This does not happen overnight, but given time, the message of the song will embed itself deep into our minds. Inevitably, our actions will follow those song lyrics.

However, what if we picked music not according to how we feel, but what we know? And what if you took charge of your thoughts so that you determined to fill your head with truth? What if you believed that the Bible is the only source for truth? How would that change your music choices, and in turn, your life as a whole?

The psalms were Israel's best "set list" - and these "Top 150" songs change the hearts of all who serve the Lord!

↑ THINK ABOUT SONGS YOU LIKE, THEN CHECK OUT PSALM 98 TODAY.

# NO, YOU ARE NOT ALONE!

YET I WILL LEAVE SEVEN THOUSAND IN ISRAEL, ALL THE KNEES THAT HAVE NOT BOWED DOWN TO BAAL, AND EVERY MOUTH THAT HAS NOT KISSED HIM. (1 KINGS 19:18)

As a freshman, I felt very alone in high school. Not only was I in a different building, but I also had moved into classes with many people I had never met. The one girl that I thought was a Christian didn't really act like it. I tried to fit in where I could. I did excel in music, and gradually made friends in our band and choir. But life was so awkward! Years later, I have still not met any adult who has said to me, "I wish I could go back and do my freshman year of high school all over again!"

In reality, I had much growing up to do. This included not relying on my peers for my comfort and stability. I also needed to walk with the Lord so that others could see the real me. When that new reality began to take hold in my life, I discovered that I was not the only Christian in my school. All it took was some humility in understanding God's bigger picture for me as His child.

Elijah got to a place in his life that He believed he was the only one left who served God. However, that was not the case. Seven thousand others were also doing the right thing. Apparently Elijah never knew this before ("I, even I only, am left, and they seek my life, to take it away"). Or perhaps Elijah doubted the power of the LORD, not only with Jezebel's rage, but also in His ability to spare a remnant of believers. Either way, he was convinced that he was alone in his predicament. But truly, he was not.

Do you feel like you are the only Christian around? I hope not! But if you do, there are probably more believers than you may know at this moment. Ultimately, you are never alone when God is on your side!

READ 1 KINGS 19:1-18.

## HOW DO YOU LIVE BY THE SPIRIT? (BY CORY FEHR)

If we live by the Spirit, let us also keep in step with the Spirit. (Galatians 5:25)

Do your parents ever leave you notes about chores? You had a day off of school, and thought you had your day to yourself and... BAM! A slap in the face with some job to do. You've probably handled it both ways. You either chose to do it or not. If you did it, when you saw them next, wasn't it nice and easy? You just say, "I did it," and no big deal. What about if you didn't? There's all kinds of ways that conversation goes. Sometimes, your parents may not even handle it correctly. Maybe you don't, either. One thing is for certain: life gets more difficult!

In Galatians 5, Paul already made his case that the only way for us to live is by the Spirit. It's so easy to live by what's popular, whatever our friends do, feelings, FB posts, and YouTube videos. We think they're funny and entertaining. So do I, but I've learned something. When I don't follow my Father's note (His Word), life always gets more difficult. Every time. But in your relationship with God, He's perfect in everything He asks. He even gives us the strength to do it.

The Bible says that the Spirit wrote the Word of God. It's His note to me to follow. I know... "BIG NOTE!" All I know is when I don't follow it, life gets more difficult. I'm glad you're reading this devotion, because you are choosing to follow His note to you. God always blesses that. That's keeping in step with the Spirit. The more I choose that, the more love, joy, and peace I have. I'm all for that!

In my 38 years of trying to read my Bible each day, there's lots of times I didn't feel like it. Every time I've done it, I've never thought to myself, "That was a waste of time." It's always worth it. Good job today. ?

↑ LET'S READ GALATIANS 5:22-26!

# FEBRUARY

# ATTACKS ON THE BIBLE

Blessed are those who keep his testimonies, who seek him with their whole heart, who also do no wrong, but walk in his ways! (Psalm 119:2-3)

I have a pastor-friend that has much in common with me. I value our friendship, and I pray for him often. Yet this friend and I do not share the same biblical approach. After many conversations with him, I know that he believes the Bible is true, yet he also leaves room for his experiences to help him define its truth.

Why would I have a problem with his approach? Using the experiences of life to understand truth may sound reasonable, but the minute we allow them to define truth itself, we open the door for compromise. Our experiences take place in a world of sin, so it makes them flawed and untrustworthy. Before we fully realize what is happening, we began to accept the wisdom of the world, which starts our drift away from the Bible. We veer off of the safe path into the unknown, where the roaring lion (Satan) awaits us.

King David loved his God, so he naturally loved His truth. In fact, he wrote an amazing song about God's Word (Psalm 119, the longest chapter in the Bible). Brilliantly penned, this psalm is broken up into 22 sections of 8 verses; each section is started by a consecutive letter of the Hebrew alphabet.

This month, we'll make our way through Psalm 119. Teens, my hope for you is that you will grow in your love and wonder of the Bible. I also hope that you will learn to trust God's Word as the complete authority for your life. Finally, I pray that you will know how to handle the many attacks on the Bible with assurance and confidence.

🡅 HERE WE GO! PLEASE READ PSALM 119:1-8.

# ATTACKS ON THE RELIABILITY OF THE BIBLE (1 OF 2)

WITH MY WHOLE HEART I SEEK YOU; LET ME NOT WANDER FROM YOUR COMMANDMENTS! (PSALM 119:10)

*"How can I believe a book that is so old? Some of the accounts don't match up; in certain places, there are questions on which words are the correct ones; we don't know all of the authors of the books; much of it had to be written later than the given dates; some of the authors have serious character issues. Also, there are many versions of the Bible, so which one is correct? And who decided which of the books really belong in the Bible as we have it today?"*

Teens, these are questions that educated people use to attack the reliability of God's Word. In all sincerity, they are good questions! The question sums them up: "Can we trust the Bible?". Is it reliable, even when there seems to be contradictions everywhere?

Let's consider one answer today in this two-part devotion. I want to ask you to step outside and look around. This world in which we live... it's a pretty incredible place, wouldn't you say? The wonder of how creation works, from the intricacies of a single cell in your body, to the furthest reaches of this universe, and so far beyond - how incredibly awesome! It *must* be the work of a Mastermind, a Being that is far greater than us. And to think that this God would care enough to love me, just one of the countless numbers of souls who have lived on this earth? Can it be? And that His love would know no limits, but would be fully expressed by the sacrifice of His Son? Wow – that is amazing grace!

If the gospel is true (and it certainly is!), why wouldn't we believe that God can also give us a reliable book to live by in this life?

🡅 PLEASE READ PSALM 119:9-16. TRUST THESE VERSES!

# ATTACKS ON THE RELIABILITY OF THE BIBLE (2 OF 2)

YOU REBUKE THE INSOLENT, ACCURSED ONES, WHO WANDER FROM YOUR COMMANDMENTS. (PSALM 119:21)

Teens, when people in your lives express doubt about the reliability of the Bible, ask questions.

***"The Bible is too old to be relevant!"*** **Oh really? Since when does the age of a book make it irrelevant?**

***"There are places in the Bible where stories contradict each other."*** **Are you sure about that? Perhaps the writers decided to include different facts for their audience? Or is this a case two separate accounts?**

***"Some verses have different words, depending on the manuscript."*** **That's true! But since we don't have the original copies, are you open to the fact that copyists might have made an error? More importantly, do these mistakes change the eternal truths found in the book?**

***"Men must have written the Bible later than indicated by the dates, since some events occurred many years later after a book was completed."*** **So... you're telling me that God cannot reveal the future to His people?**

***"Some of the authors were untrustworthy men; I can't trust what they wrote!"*** **Yeah, some of them made terrible choices (David and Jonah come to mind), but does this disqualify them? Are any of us worthy of writing Scripture?**

***"The many versions of the Bible that exist cast doubt on its reliability."*** **Do you know how to read Hebrew and Greek? If not, does God have the power to lead men in translating His Word into the language of our day?**

***"The various books in the Bible don't complement each other very well."*** **Is that so? Have you read the Bible from cover to cover to understand its theme of salvation and redemption?**

THE BIBLE IS RELIABLE; MANKIND IS NOT! READ PSALM 119:17-24.

# ATTACKS ON THE BOOK OF GENESIS (1 OF 2)

I HAVE CHOSEN THE WAY OF FAITHFULNESS; I SET YOUR RULES BEFORE ME. (PSALM 119:30)

If you are new to the Bible, then you will need to know a few quick facts about the book of Genesis.

There are 66 books that make up the Bible, and Genesis is the first one. The title *Genesis* is a word that means "the beginning". It is a book of beginnings, from how this world was created to how the nation of Israel began. It easily answers some of our biggest questions, such as "Where did I come from?" and "What is my purpose in life?".

Genesis is also one of the most maligned books by those who do not take it as truth. The first eleven chapters not only talk about the beginning of all that is created, but also about the perfect Garden of Eden; how sin entered the world through the first humans; critical information on the earliest genealogies; how Noah and the worldwide flood changed history; and how mankind spread across the globe, due to their rebellion against God.

If you are willing to doubt the book of beginnings (which is the very foundation of the Bible), then how can you trust the remaining 65 books? Satan certainly works on our uncertainties, so he craftily introduces many false ideas about Genesis. As a result, countless people have been fooled into doubting or dismissing the truth.

Teens, do you believe what God tells us in Genesis? How does your answer shape your world view?

CHECK OUT PSALM 119:25-32 TODAY. SEE HOW THE GOOD KING DAVID WAS SHAPED BY THE WORD OF THE LORD.

# ATTACKS ON THE BOOK OF GENESIS (2 OF 2)

TURN MY EYES FROM LOOKING AT WORTHLESS THINGS;
AND GIVE ME LIFE IN YOUR WAYS. (PSALM 119:37)

Genesis chapters 1-11 is not the only part of the book under attack. The theory of evolution is just one example of how the enemies of the Bible seek to undermine it.

Teens, keep this in mind: if someone can get you to doubt the foundation of anything in your life, then everything else is on shaky ground. You would not purchase a house with cracks in the foundation, would you? You better not! The same goes for anyone selling you beliefs that contradict the Bible - don't buy what they are selling!

Just so you know, there are plenty of good organizations that exist for the purpose of proclaiming and defending the truth of the Bible. Personally, I most appreciate the work of the organization "Answers in Genesis". Men like Ken Ham have devoted their entire lives to help us all learn about the book of Genesis. You can only learn so much about God's truth in a short devotion from me; you can learn so much more about Genesis by diving into the resources of AiG.

In Psalm 119:37, David asks the Lord to turn his eyes "from looking at worthless things." He knew that these ways only lead him on a path to death. Anything that takes our minds away from the truth is worthless; anything that brings us toward the truth is life-giving.

So let me ask you this. Is it wise to follow wandering men? Ken himself is famous for saying, "The answers are found in Genesis!". Take the time to read Genesis 1-11, and you'll be amazed how the truth of the beginning makes complete sense from a biblical perspective!

🡅 PLEASE READ PSALM 119:33-40 TODAY.

# ATTACKS ON THE BOOK OF REVELATION

I WILL KEEP YOUR LAW CONTINUALLY, FOREVER AND EVER, AND I SHALL WALK IN A WIDE PLACE, FOR I HAVE SOUGHT YOUR PRECEPTS. (PSALM 119:44-45)

There are 66 books in the Bible, and the book of Revelation is the final one. We already know that people attack the Bible by mishandling Genesis. As it is with the beginning, so it is with the end – the last book is often treated with the same disregard as the first.

Admittedly, Revelation can be difficult to understand. But with that said, it is a book that *can* be understood! It greatly helps us when we choose to read the Bible in order, as it is written. By the time we get to the last book, the difficulties are not insurmountable.

When it comes to the Bible, we have no right to derive our own interpretations. Revelation is a primary target for misinterpretation.

Teens, we need to approach Revelation the same way we would handle any other biblical book. We must carefully observe, interpret, and apply the text. When we don't understand something ourselves, we go to other mature Christians who carefully observe, interpret, and apply! The truth will become evident, if we take time in our discovery.

David promises to "keep your law continually, forever and ever." It's a promise that can only be kept by a proper understanding of these laws. To purposely mishandle the Word is to miss the "walk in a wide place."

2 Timothy 3:16-17 says, "All Scripture is breathed out by God and profitable for teaching, for reproof, for correction, and for training in righteousness, that the man of God may be complete, equipped for every good work." Revelation is included here... so let's be diligent!

↑ BE CHALLENGED BY PSALM 119:41-48.

# ATTACKS ON TOPICAL TRUTHS OF THE BIBLE

When I think of your rules from of old, I take comfort, O LORD. (Psalm 119:52)

The death penalty. Our sexuality. Euthanasia. The definition of marriage. Gender identity. Life in the womb.

These are some of the many topics that have caused controversy in our nation. They are also some of the topics addressed in the Bible. Many centuries before we arrived, God gave us His truth on what we are to think, say, and do. In fact, not one soul has ever lived on this earth minus the knowledge of God's holy expectations!

Those who are against what the Bible says will often attack it in two ways: one, they attempt to dismiss it in places they deem controversial, and two, they twist its words and meanings to fit their beliefs. So, if I am for homosexual rights, then I will refuse to believe any place in the Bible that speaks against it. I will also define that practice in such a way that makes it acceptable to God and humanity.

Homosexuality is one of many important topics today. However, there are ways that it is simply an issue of our current times. Not long ago, it was the legalization of abortion. Before that, it was alcohol and women's rights. And before that, it was slavery. *Our issues change, but God does not change!* The Bible has the answers, even if we don't like what we read.

Here's the scary thing with sin (including the sin of this nation): when we do not repent, sin builds upon itself. One domino falls after another, and destruction is inevitable. However, history teaches us that the Lord is gracious when a nation chooses to repent.

↑ THE BIBLE IS UNCHANGING! READ PSALM 119:49-56.

# ATTACKS ON THE GOD OF THE OLD TESTAMENT (1 OF 3)

"I AM A COMPANION OF ALL WHO FEAR YOU, OF THOSE WHO KEEP YOUR PRECEPTS." (PSALM 119:63)

As Americans, we tend to struggle with the God of the Old Testament as we read through the Bible. He is anything but Santa Claus, which is the kind of god we so often desire. In His revealed character, we see judgment, wrath, and anger. In His commands, we read about destruction, killing, and strict cultural laws. Oh, how this goes against our sense of all that is fair! We don't want to hear it, but Americans have created a god in our own image, and it is not the God of the Bible.

As a result of wrong thinking, people attack the Bible by attacking the God of the O.T. The Lord told His people to wipe out wicked nations, so they decide that this God is a monster, not worthy of our worship. God commanded Israel to have nothing to do with those who are against Him. If God commanded this, isn't He putting us in a place to judge others? Again, we don't like that! This God of the Old Testament is very "unpatriotic", to say the least!

Once again, I challenge you to think about the Bible as a whole. We're terribly guilty of taking verses out of context. If we would actually read God's Word from the beginning, and study what is revealed to us, our eyes would be opened. Teens, allow God to reveal Himself to you! Understand that *we have no right to question Him!* Can we ask questions? Sure! Can we wonder if He is wrong? No way.

The Bible reveals a God who will not be boxed. Remember what Job said: "Therefore I have uttered what I did not understand, things too wonderful for me, which I did not know" (Job 42:3). Such a wise statement when Job humbly considered the God of Israel.

↑ PLEASE READ PSALM 119:57-64!

# ATTACKS ON THE GOD OF THE OLD TESTAMENT (2 OF 3)

TEACH ME GOOD JUDGMENT AND KNOWLEDGE, FOR I BELIEVE IN YOUR COMMANDMENTS. (PSALM 119:66)

Many believe that the Bible cannot be true because the God of the Old Testament cannot be real. To those people, He is too unfair, unloving, and unkind. However, we need to allow ourselves an open mind to know the eternal character of God. He completely transcends our limited thoughts about Him!

I believe it is critically important to know that God worked through a nation (Israel), and not a church, in the O.T. This greatly affects our theology (which is the knowledge we possess of God). The nation itself consisted of many unbelievers. The Lord was their God and king. A king has all the rights to do what he sees fit, and a king is in a position to execute justice. A good king rids his kingdom of the evil that exists both inside and outside of his realm.

God claimed the Promised Land as the special place where His people would dwell. It was His will to remove unrepentant evil-doers out of His kingdom. The Canaanites, who lived in the land when God's people left Egypt, were given every ability to repent, but most did not. They were guilty of the murder of innocents, sexual perversion of every kind, the burnt sacrifices of infants, and all kinds of horrendous acts that covered many centuries. A holy God cannot put up with this! When the time of their evil came to the tipping point, God said "Enough is enough!", and he commanded Israel to wipe out all unrepentant nations.

If you were God, what would you do with violence, drunkenness, sexual deviation, murder, etc.? Can you understand that God absolutely must judge sin, even if this judgment means death?

READ PSALM 119:65-72 TODAY.

# ATTACKS ON THE GOD OF THE OLD TESTAMENT (3 OF 3)

LET THOSE WHO FEAR YOU TURN TO ME, THAT THEY MAY KNOW YOUR TESTIMONIES. (PSALM 119:79)

If a flag is flying in Heaven, then keep in mind that the flag is not the colors of red, white, and blue. If anything, it is the flag of the cross, since that is the flag of victory! God is under no obligation to run His kingdom as if it were the United States. I say this as one who dearly loves my country; but like Abraham, I look forward to a heavenly one.

Not only did the God of the Old Testament rule His nation, He did so with complete control over all other nations, as well. The Holy Lord orchestrated every detail and event to His glory.

Let me be quick to admit that I don't understand everything about our God in the O.T. But who am I, that I would think I could tell God just how He should conduct His business? The godly Job thought about the things he would say to God if they would meet face to face, and even he was shown how thoroughly incompetent he was when compared to the Eternal One (read about it in Job 38-41).

When you read about the actions of the Lord, and your sense of all that is right and fair is violated, remember that the Bible teaches us to think beyond ourselves. God is immortal, and we are not. He cannot sin; not even once. He knows how to communicate to us in ways that we can understand, even if that understanding comes later in life.

As you read the Bible, ask Him to open your eyes. It's amazing how things just start to make sense. God gets bigger, and I get smaller, and life gets richer! So study the Bible – don't be afraid of it, it is God's love letter to His children – and watch His Spirit work as He transforms you.

🡅 KEEP READING THIS GREAT CHAPTER: PSALM 119:73-80.

# ATTACKS ON THE PROPHECIES OF THE BIBLE (1 OF 2)

ALL YOUR COMMANDMENTS ARE SURE; THEY PERSECUTE ME WITH FALSEHOOD; HELP ME! (PSALM 119:86)

There are moments in our lives when we realize that something we had previously believed is not true. One of those moments in my life as a kid was when I learned the shocking truth about game shows. They are not videoed for a live audience – they are taped weeks or months in advance. I was stunned! All those times I had been rooting for that contestant to spin the wheel and solve the puzzle for big money, and it was not happening right at that moment? If this reality is also news to you, I'm sorry that I am the one to burst your bubble!

Game shows taught me that I cannot trust everything I see and hear. The false teachers of our day have also taught me that the devil is out to get anyone who will listen to his lies.

I think people don't trust the prophecies of the Bible because we have learned to believe that a "prophet" is untrustworthy. We compare men like Jeremiah, Hosea, and Micah to today's fortunetellers. We also try to fit meanings from the biblical prophets into the 21st century, so their words do not make a lot of sense. As a result, we end up dismissing significant portions of the Word.

If we are going to understand the present and the future as God has purposed in His will, we must believe the entire Bible, including all of the prophets and their messages. Teens, biblical prophecy is not a mere prediction of what could happen; it is a "forth telling" of what will happen. We need to be a humble student in our approach, looking to understand the Bible as truth written for all of time.

🡅 LET'S READ PSALM 119:81-88.

# ATTACKS ON THE PROPHECIES OF THE BIBLE (2 OF 2)

FOREVER, O LORD, YOUR WORD IS FIRMLY FIXED IN THE HEAVENS. (PSALM 119:89)

The prophets of the Bible spoke often about things that were not categorized as future events. However, every prophesied event in the Bible has accurately come to pass thus far. How do we know that the remaining future events (which include the Rapture, the Tribulation, the Millennium, and the Eternal State) will occur? Because God keeps His word! Again, every prophecy meant to be fulfilled at this point of history has indeed been fulfilled.

Teens, biblical prophecy is so fascinating! The prophet Habakkuk foretold of how a powerful nation would overtake Israel. An unknown prophet mentioned a future king by name (King Josiah, foretold in 1 Kings 13). We read about the future world kingdoms in Daniel 7-12 (it shares how Babylon would be followed by Persia, then Greece, then Rome). Many prophets were given the privilege of telling us about the Messiah and his coming. The prophets wrote both about his first coming (his birth, his life, his death, and his resurrection) and his second coming (the Battle of Armageddon and the Kingdom of Christ).

People attack the prophecies because they see God as very small. Mankind is proud in nature, and we think we have things figured out in this modern era. As a result, there is no room in our minds for the Bible to be accurate in revealing the future. "Seeing is believing", they say; but prophecy calls us to believe by faith.

Teens, my prayer for you is the same as Elisha's prayer for his servant: "O LORD, please open his eyes that he may see" (2 Kings 6:17). What the servant saw changed his thinking. May the same be true for you!

↑ KEEP WORKING THROUGH THIS PSALM! READ PSALM 119:89-96.

# ATTACKS ON DIFFICULT PASSAGES OF THE BIBLE

I HAVE MORE UNDERSTANDING THAN ALL MY TEACHERS, FOR YOUR TESTIMONIES ARE MY MEDITATION. (PSALM 119:99)

Those who seek to undermine the Bible like to look for passages that seem to compromise its authority. One of these passages is Mark 16:9-20. In this section of Mark, we read that "in my name they will cast out demons; they will speak in new tongues; they will pick up serpents with their hands; and if they drink any deadly poison, it will not hurt them; they will lay their hands on the sick, and they will recover." Is this true? How do we process this information?

Well, let me ask you this: if I questioned you about your family, but only learned about one member of your family, how much would I know about your entire family? I might learn a lot, or I may learn a little. But knowing only one family member keeps me very limited in my knowledge of your whole tribe!

I use this example to make us think more about the passage in Mark. By itself, Mark is an important writer. However, he is only one contributor to our Bible. If we took time to dig deeper, we would find that many early copies of Scripture did not even include this section of the book. We would also find that the word "they" in these verses refers to the disciples. And we would see that doing things like drinking poison and picking up snakes was not a command. Mark 16 is hard to digest when we separate it from the rest of the "family'!

God lives inside of every believer, which means you have the Holy Spirit to show you what is true and what is false. So when it comes to difficult passages, just pray, ask for wisdom, and talk to mature believers who love God's Word. May God lead and guide you in the difficult passages!

GO TO PSALM 119:97-104 TODAY.

# ATTACKS ON THE VIRGIN BIRTH

YOUR WORD IS A LAMP TO MY FEET AND A LIGHT TO MY PATH. (PSALM 119:105)

*If the Bible is proven wrong at just one point, then the Bible cannot be trusted.* It can be no other way. So, if the Bible is wrong on the virgin birth of Jesus, then indeed, we cannot trust the rest of Scripture.

Famous TV personality Larry King is one person who has not accepted Christianity. He is one who questions the reality of the virgin birth. On one hand, he is brilliant in recognizing that everything about Jesus hinges on the miraculous conception. If it's true that Jesus was conceived by the Holy Spirit, then everything else about him is also possible. But if he was born like of us, then our faith in Christ is vain.

Why did Jesus come from the virgin Mary? Those who believe the Bible know that sin is passed from the parents to the child at the point of conception. This has been happening since the days of the first sinners (Adam and Eve). Yes, the beauty of conception is marred by the ugliness of the curse. We all are born with a sin nature... except for one. Jesus was not, since he is the sinless God. That is why the Spirit impregnated a virgin; it is the only way Christ could come in the flesh!

Psalm 119:105 is one of the most recognized verses in this lengthy psalm. If it were not for the word, we would certainly fall and lose our way. God's Word gave us both Psalm 119 and Luke 1. Knowing that the virgin birth is true is part of the lamp and the light. The more that I believe all that God has told me, the more I see where I need to go.

The greatest truths in life cannot be explained by the fallen minds of men. Trust God, who is perfect in every way! And trust Jesus, who has come for us by the most marvelous of miracles.

↑ READ PSALM 119:105-112. MAY THESE VERSES LIGHT YOUR WAY.

# ATTACKS ON THE CANONICITY OF THE BIBLE

You are my hiding place and my shield; I hope in your word. (Psalm 119:114)

The Bible is a collection of all kinds of writing – letters, poetry, law, songs, chronologies, historical accounts, prophecies, and more. It was written over the course of many centuries. Together, the collection of biblical books is called a canon. 66 books were chosen to make up this canon. Why these specific books? The names of those who compiled the finished canon are unknown, but here's what we can conclude.

First, they were looking for human authors that were legit. Men like Moses, David, and Jonah were all sanctioned in God's will as Old Testament authors. They either lived or wrote the message, as each one was directly used for the Lord's purposes. In the New Testament, it was men that had seen or been with Jesus Christ. This even includes Paul, who was not a Christian when Jesus was on earth, but was given the privilege of seeing his Savior nonetheless (1 Corinthians 15:8). Only trustworthy eyewitnesses produced writings that were included in the biblical canon.

Second, those who collected our completed version of the Bible left out any questionable writings that would conflict with the rest of Scripture. The Apocrypha is a collection of writings connected to Bible times and themes, but it also contains untrustworthy material that contradicts God's truth to mankind.

Finally, God had no problem in supernaturally guiding believers in the early church years. He did not allow Satan to gain the advantage, which certainly included the completion of the Bible. The believers went to great lengths in discerning the validity and necessity of the early manuscripts. God used them to give us the gift of the completed Word.

THE WORD OF GOD IS AWESOME! READ PSALM 119:113-120.

# ATTACKS ON THE RESURRECTION (1 OF 3)

DEAL WITH YOUR SERVANT ACCORDING TO YOUR STEADFAST LOVE,
AND TEACH ME YOUR STATUTES. (PSALM 119:124)

My son came home from school the other day and shared with me about an encounter with his friend. Lincoln told him about Jesus, that he had died for us and that we need to believe in him to be saved. Let me tell you something: this evangelizing son of mine humbly teaches me more than he realizes! However, Lincoln's friend informed him that since Jesus died, this means that "God is dead", and there is no need to believe in Christ.

In his encounter, Lincoln stumbled upon a most significant truth: Jesus is "a stone of stumbling, and a rock of offense" (we read this in both Isaiah 8:14 and 1 Peter 2:8). Sinners stumble over the gospel, which boldly claims that after Jesus died, he came back to life.

To many people, the resurrection is foolishness. And the apostle Paul recognized this. Referring to those religious Jews who were against Christianity, he wrote, "What do I gain if, humanly speaking, I fought with beasts at Ephesus? If the dead are not raised, 'Let us eat and drink, for tomorrow we die.'" (1 Corinthians 15:32). Paul knew that everything he taught hung on the hope of the resurrection.

Christ's resurrection is something that forces us to make a decision. Do we believe it happened? If so, what is the proof? How do I answer the critics that say otherwise? If he remained dead, what would be the implications? Can someone *really* be resurrected from the dead?

PLEASE READ PSALM 119:121-128.

# ATTACKS ON THE RESURRECTION (2 OF 3)

THE UNFOLDING OF YOUR WORDS GIVES LIGHT; IT IMPARTS UNDERSTANDING TO THE SIMPLE. (PSALM 119:130)

The resurrection is the foundation and the hope of our faith. The Bible provides plenty of proof for it. When people attack the truth of Christ's resurrection, here are five reasons you can give to enlighten them:

1. *The transformation of the early disciples, as seen in the early part of the book of Acts (they were changed men!).*
2. *There was a willingness to die for what is known (many of the followers of Christ were martyred. They were willing to die as martyrs based upon their knowledge that their Savior was alive).*
3. *The church was born (we read about this in Acts 2. The church began just weeks after the crucifixion).*
4. *The response of the Roman and Jewish leaders (those who crucified Christ tried to cover up the discovery of an empty grave!).*
5. *There were multiple post-resurrection eyewitnesses (Jesus stayed on earth many days after he rose again, and a number of individuals saw him, including those who were not among his 12 apostles).*

Do these reasons make sense? I hope so! Teens, we need not fear those who are spiritually ignorant. We have ample proof that Jesus is alive. Don't be afraid to share these reasons; you many find that the attackers are really seeking after truth - and you have the truth!

↑ DO YOU PERSONALLY BELIEVE IN THE RESURRECTION? I HOPE SO! PLEASE READ PSALM 119:129-136.

# ATTACKS ON THE RESURRECTION (3 OF 3)

YOUR PROMISE IS WELL TRIED, AND YOUR SERVANT LOVES IT. (PSALM 119:140)

Teens, if a person is to become a Christian, they absolutely have to believe in the resurrection of Christ. There is just no way around this fact! When you hear of anyone attacking the reality of his resurrection, you can be assured that he or she is not a believer.

There are verses in the Bible that we should memorize, and chapters that we should know very well. 1 Corinthians 15 is one of those chapters. In it, Paul convincingly writes about the resurrection. It's so powerful! If I had to come over to your house and read it to you, I would! But instead, why don't you read it yourself?

An intellectual argument can be a good thing, but it is not "the whole thing." The bridge that brings the grace of God to us is the presence of faith. The greatest minds of this world can respond in faith, as well as the simplest and most ignorant of all people. Believing in what I cannot see is not exclusively a mark of being a Christian – people practice acts of faith all the time. Rather, faith in Christ is the belief that God really did raise him from the dead, for His glory and for our salvation.

One day, we will all meet Jesus. We'll know him by his scars, which will be a vivid reminder of his victory. We will gladly bow down in worship. Unbelievers will be ashamed, since they rejected the gospel. The ones who attacked the resurrection will answer for their lack of faith.

"I am the resurrection and the life. Whoever believes in me, though he die, yet shall he live, and everyone who lives and believes in me shall never die" (John 11:25-26). Jesus is our resurrection; he is our life!

↑ WE ARE NEARING THE END OF PSALM 119! READ VERSES 137-144.

## ATTACKS ON THE SONG OF SOLOMON

BUT YOU ARE NEAR, O LORD, AND ALL YOUR COMMANDMENTS ARE TRUE. (PSALM 119:151)

It's an awful moment when everyone notices something embarrassing about you that you hoped would remain hidden (like a ketchup stain you got on your shirt at lunch). Ugh! Unfortunately, this is how many critics treat the book of Song of Solomon. Sex is a wonderful gift from God, and He is not afraid to express this truth in His Word. But the rest of us seem scared to talk about this book (I think most Christians secretly hope they will never have to lead a discussion about it!).

Oh, how we have greatly mishandled sexuality in our society! The Bible recognizes married sex as an act of purity. Those against the Bible attack the Song of Solomon, for in their minds, this sensual book has no place in the rest of Scripture. Many Christians tend to allegorize it (they "give it another meaning"). Their thinking is that the Bible would not focus so heavily upon the physicality of romance and love-making.

Listen, dear teens: God is "pro-sex". He created it, so why wouldn't He be for it? His first command to Adam and Eve was to "be fruitful and multiply." In other words, "Have sex and make babies!"

We need to believe that God treats this gift to us in the same way that He handles everything else – with perfect holiness. Wonderful things have protective boundaries. For example, driving a car is fun, but not when we go off the road into a ditch! There are lines on the road to guide us. Sex is always best when we believe that God set the lines.

The Song of Solomon is a gift to us – it's a great "back and forth" dialogue between a husband and wife madly in love – and it doesn't blush in sharing the wonder of sexuality in marriage.

↑ READ PSALM 119:145-152.

## ATTACKS ON THE BIBLICAL COMMAND TO JUDGE

THE SUM OF YOUR WORD IS TRUTH, AND EVERY ONE OF YOUR RIGHTEOUS RULES ENDURES FOREVER. (PSALM 119:160)

Recently, I helped a man in need of some gas for his vehicle. As we talked, he informed me that he had recently visited some churches that had (in his opinion) judged him, and because of that, he did not want to go to church anymore.

Sadly, it's true – many churches judge both their members and visitors alike. We ignore verses like Matthew 7:1, which clearly tell us not to do so. However, many also believe that we are never to judge others under any circumstance at all.

If it's true that we are never allowed to judge others, then we have a problem, because there are verses in the Bible that do tell us to judge! Do we have a dilemma here?

Remember Psalm 119:160. No matter what man says, all that God commands is forever. There are times when we are to judge, and there are times when we are to refrain from it. The times we are to judge are based upon the commands God has given to us (we must recognize murder as wrong, for example). The times we are not to judge deal with a person's life choices outside of God's commands (such as the decision to consume alcohol). To call murder a sin is to correctly judge. To call drinking alcohol a sin is to incorrectly judge. The Bible condemns drunkenness, but not the consumption of alcohol. I may not be a fan of drinking, if I call it a sin, I should rightly be rebuked for judging others.

So what's the verdict? God says that we should *both judge AND not judge.* Since that's the case, let's do both in wisdom and grace!

🡅 LET'S READ PSALM 119:153-160.

# SCIENTIFIC ATTACKS ON THE BIBLE (1 OF 2)

GREAT PEACE HAVE THOSE WHO LOVE YOUR LAW;
NOTHING CAN MAKE THEM STUMBLE. (PSALM 119:165)

In life, we often have the same facts to work with, but we come up with different conclusions (you see a glass as half full, I see a glass as half empty). When this happens, who is right? You or me?

When the Bible and science are discussed in conversation, it's often treated as "The Bible vs. Science". What a shame! If people would be open to the truth, they could see that science, at its best, wonderfully supports God's Word.

Though I was never very good at science class in my school years, I loved discovering how God made His creation work. I also love to read the many terrific science books written by knowledgeable Christians.

Those who attack the Bible have a way of dismissing it as invalid because it does not meet the standards of science. For example, scientists who hold to the authority of the Bible believe that genetic makeup cannot lead us to sin. However, worldly scientists claim that some have certain genetic predispositions that cannot be suppressed. It has led to such beliefs as the freedom to alter the gender of an individual. This belief goes against the God's Word; however, His Word does not have the final say. As a result, it must give way to science.

In a world where the Bible is not the authority, confusion reigns. Science is wonderful when it is guided by truth, and every Christian ought to know that the Bible is the truth. But when we doubt the truth, things get very muddy. The result is disorder, which will destroy us - as individuals and as a nation.

🡅 PLEASE READ PSALM 119:161-168!

# SCIENTIFIC ATTACKS ON THE BIBLE (2 OF 2)

LET MY SOUL LIVE AND PRAISE YOU, AND LET YOUR RULES HELP ME. (PSALM 119:175)

Teenagers take a lot of classes in school (no kidding, right?). You have all kinds of history, math, science, and reading classes, let alone the extras like music, food, technology, foreign languages, gym, etc. Some of these classes lend themselves to easily recognizable truths (like 2+2=4). Others are very much open to debate (like "what did the author mean in this poem?").

For those who believe in the authority of science, the approach is often one that teaches an understanding of scientific law as truth. When the Bible serves to prove the law, it is a good book. When it does not, it is dismissed. Teens, you need to question both scientific theories and laws. Should the Bible really be disregarded if it does not match up?

There is only one full proof way to know when science is wrong. It's the knowledge of God's Word! Because the Lord allowed me to grow up in a Bible-believing church, I was able to recognize when I was being taught something that was false. The teachers of my church taught me to "go and read the Bible for yourself". I'm so glad that they did.

As we wrap up this series about attacks on the Bible, I realize that science is a primary tool being used today to form your thinking. I urge you not to believe the word of men – they all will die or have already died – instead, turn to the Word of God. Countless people have been transformed simply because they picked up a Bible and read it. Many have testified that they went to Scripture looking to prove it wrong, only to discover that they were wrong themselves. Now they are free! Teens, you can be free, as well.

↑ CONGRATULATIONS, YOU MADE IT TO THE END OF THIS PSALM! READ PSALM 119:169-176 TO FINISH UP THE CHAPTER.

# THE FREEDOM OF KNOWING THE TRUTH

So Jesus said to the Jews who had believed him, "If you abide in my word, you are truly my disciples, and you will know the truth, and the truth will set you free." (John 8:31-32)

The day is coming when Lisa and I will need to sit down with our adopted daughter and talk to her about how she came into our lives. I'm not sure when that day will be. I'm not sure how she will handle the truth. I'm not sure how much we should tell her. I guess you could say that there are lots of things I'm not so sure about! We will need to pray about this day and lean upon good counsel before we have this conversation.

There is one thing I'm sure about - she needs to know that she is adopted, because I believe God will use this truth to grow her faith.

We often associate pain with bondage. That is not always the case. To the contrary, the painful realization that our sin put Jesus on the cross has led many to believe that he died to set us free. Lydia will experience some sense of loss when she comes to understand that her birth parents chose to abandon her rather than to keep her. Our prayer is that she will know God planned this all along for her good. She was always meant to be a member of the Shanks family.

Knowing the truth about God's great grace in her life has all the power to set Lydia free.

And knowing the truth of God's great love in our lives has all the power to do the same for our souls!

↑ GREAT VERSES OF FREEDOM CAN BE READ IN ZECHARIAH 8. SEE HOW TRUTH AND FREEDOM CORRELATE FOR THE FUTURE JERUSALEM.

## HE FINALLY CAME!

But when the fullness of time had come, God sent forth his Son, born of woman, born under the law, to redeem those who were under the law, so that we might receive adoption as sons. (Galatians 4:4-5)

When the Lord brought our first child into our lives, my wife and I cried many tears of joy. It was wonderful to finally have a baby! For Lisa and I, it was the end of a difficult journey. Why? Because we did not know if our son Lincoln would ever come. Many years of infertility left us wondering, wondering, and wondering some more. It was a valley in our lives that carried much grief and pain.

Once Lincoln was born, it got me thinking about why things were so hard when we were childless. I finally came to see the reason: we desired a special relationship to come *from* us. It made me think about all the kinds of relationships we can have as people. When we lack a special relationship, there is a natural void in our lives. When a child loses a parent (perhaps to death or a divorce), they are missing a relationship. When an adult finds themselves well into their 30's and still not married, they are missing a relationship. When older people do not experience the joy of having grandchildren to play with, they are missing a relationship. And teens, as you see your friends dating while you're still not, you get a sense of missing a relationship. Indeed, we were made for relationships!

God certainly knows all of this. He would know, since He is our Creator. Thankfully, when a human relationship does not develop as we expected it would, He reminds us that Christ is all we ever needed. God's greatest act to fulfill our relationships – with Him and with each other – happened when Jesus conquered the grave, reconciling us ("restoring the relationship") to Himself. When our Savior finally came, we would have the relationship we both needed and desired.

➜ CHECK OUT 2 CORINTHIANS 5:11-20!

# HOW DO WE PRAY?

O LORD, LET YOUR EAR BE ATTENTIVE TO THE PRAYER OF YOUR SERVANT, AND TO THE PRAYER OF YOUR SERVANTS WHO DELIGHT TO FEAR YOUR NAME, AND GIVE SUCCESS TO YOUR SERVANT TODAY, AND GRANT HIM MERCY IN THE SIGHT OF THIS MAN. (NEHEMIAH 1:11)

Nehemiah is an inspirational book of the Bible on leadership. Nehemiah was also a man who knew how to pray.

There are many prayers in the Bible. Each one is unique in its own right, but godly prayers have a pattern. Take the time right now to open your Bible to Nehemiah 1:5-11 and see the progression of Nehemiah's prayer. His prayer opens with *recognition and praise* to God (using descriptions such as "great" and "awesome", and reminding God that He is a keeper of His promises). He then makes an immediate *request* ("Hear me!" and "See me!"). This same request is brought up again at the end of the prayer. After the original plea, he *confesses* the sin of his life and his nation ("we have acted wickedly"; "we have not obeyed"). But Nehemiah does not give up hope, as he *quotes Scripture* as a call to the Lord to act upon His goodness (he reminds God of a promise He gave through Moses to Israel in verses 8-10). Often, a prayer will end in another proclamation of praise, but we see his request repeated here because it was urgent in nature.

Nehemiah was an incredible leader. His leadership was predicated on his prayer life. Yes, there are many inspirational leaders today who are not Christians, but for a believer to be a real leader, he must pray knowledgeably and faithfully. The pattern of prayer is not a magic formula; rather, it is a proper way to approach a holy God.

So... how do *we* pray?

↑ LET'S READ NEHEMIAH 1.

# INTERNAL SCARS

AND SHECANIAH THE SON OF JEHIEL, OF THE SONS OF ELAM, ADDRESSED EZRA: "WE HAVE BROKEN FAITH WITH OUR GOD AND HAVE MARRIED FOREIGN WOMEN FROM THE PEOPLES OF THE LAND, BUT EVEN NOW THERE IS HOPE FOR ISRAEL IN SPITE OF THIS." (EZRA 10:2)

If you approached the main entrance of our church and looked closely at the right pillar, you will see white marks on the bricks. Sometimes these marks are very visible, and sometimes they are hard to see. They exist as a result of vandalism; years ago, someone sprayed paint on this pillar. Much of the paint has been removed, but it has not completely disappeared. The marks remind me that people are cursed, but also that God has protected us from crimes that are far worse.

This vandalism left "scars" on the church building. As I write today's devotion, I think about the scars of a former youth helper. She told us that we should seriously listen to the Bible, because she did not want our teens to commit the same mistakes she did. Her past left her with many internal scars. She is healed, but the scars serve as a reminder of what should not have occurred in her life.

Teens, the worst scars in life don't appear on the outside. The person who cuts may have marks on their wrists, but the real pain is in the heart. The one who sleeps around is susceptible to sexual diseases, but this wrongdoing reveals a sickness of the soul. In Ezra 10:2, many Jews had married foreign women, and now they needed to separate from them. There are spiritual wounds that result from marrying unwisely!

By God's grace, it does not have to be this way for you. Teens, always listen to the adults that call you away from sin. Internal scars are avoidable to the one who listens and obeys the Lord.

READ SOLOMON'S PRAYER FOR ISRAEL IN 2 CHRONICLES 6:22-39!

## HOW DOES THE DEVIL ATTACK OUR SENSES?

When my life was fainting away, I remembered the LORD, and my prayer came to you, into your holy temple. (Jonah 2:7)

We recognize five senses in the human body. But what if these senses also show us a reality that is beyond this world? God teaches us about the spiritual by using the physical, and we can learn more about the "spiritual senses" when we understand how Satan attacks them:

1. **Our Sight. 2 Corinthians 4:3-4: "And even if our gospel is veiled, it is veiled to those who are perishing. In their case the god of this world has blinded the minds of the unbelievers, to keep them from seeing the light of the gospel of the glory of Christ, who is the image of God."**
2. **Our Smell. 2 Corinthians 2:15-16: "For we are the aroma of Christ to God among those who are being saved and among those who are perishing, to one a fragrance from death to death, to the other a fragrance from life to life. Who is sufficient for these things?"**
3. **Our Hearing. 2 Timothy 4:3: "For the time is coming when people will not endure sound teaching, but having itching ears they will accumulate for themselves teachers to suit their own passions, and will turn away from listening to the truth and wander off into myths."**
4. **Our Taste. Hebrews 6:4-6a: "For it is impossible, in the case of those who have once been enlightened, who have tasted the heavenly gift, and have shared in the Holy Spirit, and have tasted the goodness of the word of God and the powers of the age to come, and then have fallen away, to restore them again to repentance,"**
5. **Our Touch. Job 9:24: "The earth is given into the hand of the wicked; he covers the faces of its judges – if it is not he, who then is it?"**

Satan is out to destroy the human race! Can you sense it?

↑ GOD USED ALL OF JONAH'S SENSES WHEN HE WAS SWALLOWED BY THE GREAT FISH! READ JONAH 2 TODA

## WHO DO YOU FEAR? (BY ANDY SHANKS)

OH THAT THEY HAD SUCH A HEART AS THIS ALWAYS, TO FEAR ME AND TO KEEP ALL MY COMMANDMENTS, THAT IT MIGHT GO WELL WITH THEM AND WITH THEIR DESCENDANTS FOREVER! (DEUTERONOMY 5:29)

One summer, I took a group of teens on a campout trip. We hiked, we swam, and we hung out around a fire pit making hotdogs and s'mores. We had a great day of fellowship and fun. However, some of my teens found a Gardner snake and decided that it would be fun to put it in my sleeping bag. I am afraid of snakes (poisonous or not)! Thankfully, a kindhearted soul removed it before I went to bed that night. Had I come across that snake in my sleeping bag, my fear would have caused me to react. The reaction would have likely included screaming, running, not sleeping the rest of the night, and severe consequences!

Speaking of fear, did you know that God calls us to fear Him? This fear is not one that motivates us to scream and run, but one that motivates us to follow Him. This fear is one of reverence and awe. This fear is founded upon an understanding of our God.

How is the fear of God similar to my fear of snakes? If I had encountered the snake in my sleeping bag, it would have moved me into action, and I would never look at sleeping bags the same again. Fearing God, or being in awe of him, must motivate us to respond. The proper response is obedience to His commands.

What is the result of fearing God? Consider Deuteronomy 5:29! When we keep His commands, it will go well for us. This does not necessarily mean riches and comfort, but rather joy and purpose in our lives.

May you fear the "Who" (God) and not the "what" (the snake)!

🡅 CONSIDER OUR PROPER REPONSE TO GOD IN EZEKIEL 36:22-32.

## AN EXTRA DAY!

AND GOD SAID, "LET THERE BE LIGHTS IN THE EXPANSE OF THE HEAVENS TO SEPARATE THE DAY FROM THE NIGHT. AND LET THEM BE FOR SIGNS AND FOR SEASONS, AND FOR DAYS AND YEARS, AND LET THEM BE LIGHTS IN THE EXPANSE OF THE HEAVENS TO GIVE LIGHT UPON THE EARTH." AND IT WAS SO. (GENESIS 1:14-15)

February 29th! What a unique day. I often thought it would be fun to have been born on that day; then I changed my mind when I realized loved ones might forget my birthday. I actually know of someone who got married today, simply because it is February 29th. Crazy!

History tells us that Caesar Augustus is responsible for this day. He decided to make sure that August had two extra days (see the name connection in this month?), so the Romans robbed February. Sounds like insecurity issues to me!

Speaking of dates on the calendar, the Old Testament Jewish calendar actually starts with the Passover in mind (that occurs in March or April). Even the hours that make up a 24-hour day began differently than what we are accustomed to in the 21st century. Knowing this helps us to understand the Bible even more, especially as it pertains to significant dates or religious holidays.

If you knew that you would be given one extra day, and it was at the end your life, what would you do? Have a big party? Spend some time with your best friends? Make things right with God? Go and witness your faith? I believe your answer here will reveal your heart.

That is exactly why I encourage you, right now, to think hard about your answer. We're talking about one extra day before you see God face to face. Would you be ready for that meeting?

↑ READ DANIEL'S HUMBLE PRAYER IN DANIEL 2:17-23.

# MARCH

## WHO HAS THE FINAL SAY?

He said to them, "But who do you say that I am?" Simon Peter replied, "You are the Christ, the Son of the Living God." (Matthew 16:15-16)

There are many days I wish I had Peter's guts. Sure, he put his foot in his mouth more than once, but at least he had the courage to actually say something. On the other hand, my lack of willingness to step out and say something has left me on the outside missing blessings that could have been mine.

As we consider some of the big questions in life, we often lean upon two influences: our self and others. Our self, for we were made to be thinking creatures with the ability to make decisions. Others, for we were also made to interact with these same intellectual beings. But what about God? Does He play a role in the big questions of life? Indeed, He does! Since we are the creatures and He is the Creator, God plays more than a role. He is, and always will be, the star of His show.

"Who has the final say?". When it comes to all things pertaining to life, the answer is Jesus, for he is "The Final Word."

Many of the devotions for both April and August will be in this format:

1. WHAT DO THEY SAY?
2. WHAT DOES GOD SAY?
3. WHAT DO YOU SAY?

In your mind, who has the final say? That answer will impact everything you believe and live for on earth.

↑ LET'S READ MATTHEW 16:13-20.

# WORLD PEACE: WHAT DO THEY SAY?

"BUT THE WICKED ARE LIKE THE TOSSING SEA;
FOR IT CANNOT BE QUIET, AND ITS WATERS TOSS UP MIRE AND DIRT.
THERE IS NO PEACE," SAYS MY GOD, "FOR THE WICKED."
(ISAIAH 57:20-21)

In world history, peace between two nations has always been a temporary commodity. Fortunately, we Americans have enjoyed peace with much of the world, unlike any other nation before us. Yet even so, we have still seen our share of conflicts and battles through the years.

The world wants to believe that people are good in nature. Yes, there are some terrible men out there, but by and large, each person has something good about them, because they were good at birth. So if we allow people to do what makes them happy and make beneficial compromises, world peace should be attainable. If a group of people stand in the way of this goal, they should be ignored or eliminated.

Despite what the Bible says, there are even some Christians who believe it is our great responsibility to usher in God's future kingdom by pursuing world peace. We often spot those believers avidly working in politics toward that very end. They remind me of a song I sang in school years ago, called "Let There Be Peace On Earth". Here is the first verse:

***"LET THERE BE PEACE ON EARTH, AND LET IT BEGIN WITH ME.***
***LET THERE BE PEACE ON EARTH, THE PEACE THAT WAS MEANT TO BE.***
***WITH GOD AS OUR FATHER, BROTHERS ALL ARE WE.***
***LET ME WALK WITH MY BROTHER, IN PERFECT HARMONY."***

Is world peace possible through the efforts of man?

↑ CHECK OUT ISAIAH 57:14-21.

## WORLD PEACE: WHAT DOES GOD SAY?

Of the increase of his government and of peace there will be no end, on the throne of David and over his kingdom, to establish it and to uphold it with justice and with righteousness from this time forth and forevermore. The zeal of the LORD of hosts will do this. (Isaiah 9:7)

Is there a problem with desiring world peace? No! But a problem exists when we want to bring peace to this world through our own efforts. So we make fragile treaties with enemy nations that have absolutely no interest in peace. And we become friends with other nations that do not share our historical values. And often, we'll take the easy way out when it comes to service and sacrifice, the very elements that have kept peace within our own borders.

By the way, if you believe what God says about history and peace, there will be no world peace until certain biblical events take place. There is a tribulation period that stands between us and God, in which the world will see everything but peace. I hope you will not be around on earth during these unprecedented years! However, once God rightly finishes His outpouring of judgment upon the earth, the Prince of Peace will take his place as the King, and He will reign for 1,000 years.

As we await the Kingdom, Jesus tells us to focus upon our inward peace: "I have said these things to you, that in me you may have peace. In the world you will have tribulation. But take heart; I have overcome the world" (John 16:33).

Ponder this: peace has *always* been God's plan. We will not go into eternity before experience the Prince of Peace on his throne. There is nothing that Satan can do to keep this from happening!

🡅 GOD'S PROMISE OF PEACE TO ISRAEL IS FOUND IN ISAIAH 9:1-7.

## WORLD PEACE: WHAT DO YOU SAY?

Too long have I had my dwelling among those who hate peace. I am for peace, but when I speak, they are for war! (Psalm 120:6-7)

Is it wrong to hope for world peace? Absolutely not! If you are one that pursues peace in all aspects of life, good for you! What a godly thing to do. However, I encourage you to study what God has to say about peace. His Word is the place to find all of the answers, including the reality of world peace.

On a *personal* level, you can only find peace in Christ alone. For all believers, peace is a fruit of the Spirit. Also, we are to live at peace with all men. And when we obey the Lord, the Bible says we can even be at peace with our enemies.

But as we learned yesterday, on a *public* level, peace will not happen until God says it will happen. We are uncertain of when this will occur, because we do not know when the Tribulation period will start.

With this knowledge, what is your response? How will you now live? I hope you will personally take ownership for what you believe. If you still think that world peace is possible, why is that so? Does this belief come from your perceptions of mankind? Or perhaps it originates from what you have been taught in school, by your family, or from your friends? Is peace possible because we are good beings, or is it just the opposite? Hint: Romans 3 contains God's thoughts on this last point!

Perhaps the bigger question is this: Does world peace even matter to you? I hope so. But don't let your desire for this peace sweep the truth under the rug. We will not live to see the day of peace until all that God has first proclaimed is accomplished.

🡅 CHECK OUT JEREMIAH 6:9-15.

## HAPPINESS: WHAT DO THEY SAY?

If you know these things, blessed are you if you do them. (John 13:17)

Happiness is a big deal in our culture. How often have you heard variations of the phrase, "Whatever makes you happy!"

Maybe I can humor you by sharing some "advice" I was given by television commercials when I was a teen.

*"Good times, great taste, that's why this is our place.*

*Good times, great taste! At McDonalds" (McDonalds)*

*"Have it your way!" (Burger King)*

*"Snickers really satisfies!" (Snickers)*

*"Who could ask for anything more?" (Toyota)*

*"They're grrrrrrrrreat!" (Frosted Flakes)*

*"I want a clean as real as Ivory. It's gotta be 99.44" (Ivory Soap)*

Oh, how I miss the advertising musical jingles of my teenage years (haha!). It wasn't until I got older when I realized how EVERY SINGLE ADVERTISEMENT offered some form of promised happiness. Hey, these companies have every right to sell their product. However, there is a real problem if we buy into the idea that something physical will satisfy the spiritual.

What do they say? They say that sex will make you happy, regardless of your gender and identity. They say that alcohol will make you happy, so forget the law. They say that getting a good degree to make lots of money will make you happy, so set the church aside and get ahead in life. They say that people will always betray you, so live together for awhile and see if a future marriage will actually work. They say _____ (you fill in the blank!). However, "they" aren't truly happy!

↑ WHAT THE WORD "THEM" REFER TO IN JOHN? READ JOHN 13:1-17!

## HAPPINESS: WHAT DOES GOD SAY?

BLESSED IS EVERYONE WHO FEARS THE LORD, WHO WALKS IN HIS WAYS! YOU SHALL EAT THE FRUIT OF THE LABOR OF YOUR HANDS; YOU SHALL BE BLESSED, AND IT SHALL BE WELL WITH YOU. (PSALM 128:1-2)

This might be breaking news to you, but *God is not against happiness!* In fact, I found the word "happy" mentioned dozens of times in the Bible. So, if the Bible talks about happiness in a positive light, why does it seem like He wants us to not do the things that make us happy?

For starters, we need to understand that the Lord defines happiness different than we do. Today, I was "happy" when I ate a peanut butter chocolate cupcake that my wife brought home. I ate it nearly two hours ago. Now, I am no longer happy about the cupcake. Why? Because that yummy delicious thing is gone! My happiness was fleeting. It was based on the emotions I have for all things chocolate and peanut butter.

God's definition of happiness is far better. It's focused more on the idea of "blessed", and it does not rely solely upon our emotions. In fact, several verses mention the word "happiness" in the same verse as "suffering". How can this be? It must be that God does not always equate happiness with our will. If we had our way, most of us would live a life of ease. The Lord knows that kind of life is not a happy one.

Listen, teens: God really does take pleasure in our happiness! We need to understand that our happiness is tied in with His blessings. That's a good thing!

↑ CONSIDER HAPPINESS IN PSALM 128.

# HAPPINESS: WHAT DO YOU SAY?

BLESSED IS THE ONE WHO FINDS WISDOM, AND THE ONE WHO GETS UNDERSTANDING, FOR THE GAIN FROM HER IS BETTER THAN GAIN FROM SILVER AND HER PROFIT BETTER THAN GOLD. (PROVERBS 3:13-14)

The Bible has much to say about happiness, but there is an even greater word that is mentioned in the Scriptures: the word joy. As I consider the meaning of happiness and joy, I believe that *happiness* is focused upon our shot-term emotions, while *joy* is found upon our knowledge and understanding. In Proverbs, happiness is celebrated ("blessed" and "happy" are interrelated words in this context). God is gracious and gives us happiness on earth, allowing us to appreciate this special gift from Him. But joy *transcends* happiness. Joy is finding God's best for us in all circumstances. Joy never depends upon our emotions. Joy comes with every intention to stay! Joy can be found anywhere, anytime (even in the worst imaginable circumstances).

Teens, there is a constant call for you to pursue happiness. And yet, more people in our nation are unhappy than ever before. Why is there such a disconnect?

Happiness is not found in pleasing ourselves. We are only blessed when we please our Creator. He made us, so He certainly knows how we work. He calls us to joy, no matter how we feel. Our best option in life is to pursue the goal of pleasing God. By doing so, we reap the benefits of happiness and joy.

Teens, I'm challenging you right now: choose joy. Happiness is fleeting. Don't make it the highest purpose of your life.

↑ WHAT DO YOU SAY ABOUT ALL OF THIS? GOD TELLS US TO SEEK WISDOM, AS WE READ IN PROVERBS 8:1-11!

## ALCOHOL: WHAT DO THEY SAY?

I SEARCHED MY HEART HOW TO CHEER MY BODY WITH WINE – MY HEART STILL GUIDING ME WITH WISDOM – AND HOW TO LAY HOLD ON FOLLY, TILL I MIGHT SEE WHAT WAS GOOD FOR THE CHILDREN OF MAN TO DO UNDER HEAVEN DURING THE FEW DAYS OF THEIR LIFE.
(ECCLESIASTES 2:3)

Many topics that cannot be addressed well in a short devotion. The topic of alcohol is one of them. So, let's narrow our attention to underage drinking. "What do they say" about teens and alcohol?

As teens, you know the answer to this question better than I do. This is what I have heard: "The law is stupid!"; "Cultures around the world allow their kids to drink wine or beer"; "What difference does your age make?"; "Try it now while you are safe in the confines of home!"; "It's fine as long as you don't get caught"; "It's fine as long as you don't get drunk"; "Alcohol has some benefits for the body"; "Just make sure you do not drive when you drink. Always have a designated driver!".

Because they buy into the excuses, many teens drink. Perhaps you are one of them. America loves its alcohol and has made it attractive to consume. The commercials are usually hilarious. Open up a menu at an upscale restaurant, and the drink varieties are colorfully pleasing to the eyes. You don't want the calories? Try some lite beers. As long as you are responsible, it's not a problem... right?

Solomon wrote the verse above as the wisest man who ever lived, but also as a man who missed out on God's great blessings in life, due to his sin. Read the context of verse 3 in the passage below, and think about life from the view of a man that tried it all (alcohol included), yet left this life very empty and unfulfilled.

READ ECCLESIASTES 2, AND LEARN FROM A WISE BUT BROKEN MAN.

# ALCOHOL: WHAT DOES GOD SAY?

WINE IS A MOCKER, STRONG DRINK A BRAWLER,
AND WHOEVER IS LED ASTRAY BY IT IS NOT WISE. (PROVERBS 20:1)

The Bible says plenty about alcohol and drinking, and it makes me realize that I need to sit up and pay attention as I seek His will in this area of my life. Does Proverbs 20:1 put alcohol in a positive light? Not here! In a book that is all about wisdom, Proverbs warns us about drunkenness; alcohol can easily lead us away from being wise.

If you studied the references to alcohol in the Bible, you would find other warnings, as well as examples of fools who embraced it. However, in some cases, you would also find it spoken of as a positive. Jesus did perform his first miracle by making more wine. And Proverbs itself recommends it on the occasion of being in the throes of death.

So... what about us? Does God allow room for drinking? You alone must pursue an answer to this question; however, It is important that we always remember what the biblical context teaches us. Teens, you will not discover a verse the promotes underage drinking (rather, we are to obey our authorities in this matter). Certainly, drunkenness is condemned for all ages in Scripture.

Let's take a step back to see what God says about another subject: our bodies. In 1 Corinthians 6:12, Paul address sexual immorality, but the verse itself is helpful when handling the topic of alcohol. It states, "'All things are lawful for me,' but not all things are helpful. 'All things are lawful for me,' but I will not be dominated by anything."

Now think hard, dear ones. Is teenage drinking beneficial? Is it controlling? Is it lawful? What would God have you to do?

↑ WOULD YOU COMMIT EPHESIANS 5:17-18 TO MEMORY TODAY?

# ALCOHOL: WHAT DO YOU SAY?

I REMEMBER YOUR NAME IN THE NIGHT, O LORD, AND KEEP YOUR LAW.
(PSALM 119:55)

At the time of this writing, there was a crash that claimed the lives of two teenage boys. It came out that alcohol was a contributing factor. What a tragedy!

Now, with that in mind, please let me ask something to make you reflect. After the crash, do you think we heard anyone speak up for the rights of teenage drinking? It's so sad that it takes an awful situation to awaken us to the truth. Drunkenness has real consequences, and teens are especially not immune.

Long ago, when I was a teenager, I decided that alcohol would not play a role in my life. Certainly, that decision was based in part upon my parents' convictions about the matter. But eventually, I was set loose, and I decided to adopt my parents' standards on this belief.

For me, the decision not to drink is about what is best for my body, which is owned by the Lord. By not drinking, I am also not placing myself in a position to be tempted by drunkenness. I am not leading my kids to question what they should do with alcohol, since they don't see it present in my house. I am not causing my weaker brothers and sisters to wonder what they should do in this area. I have found that there is much freedom to be had by letting the bottles sit on the shelves at the store. Honestly, there are plenty of other things to drink!

But that's me. What do you say? Drinking is illegal for you… right now. Is it worth it when you turn 21? Is it what God wants for your life? if you are bought by Christ, He does own you. Never forget this!

↑ IN LIGHT OF TODAY'S DEVOTION, CONSIDER ROMANS 14:19-23.

# DATING: WHAT DO THEY SAY?

FINALLY, BROTHERS, WHATEVER IS TRUE, WHATEVER IS HONORABLE, WHATEVER IS JUST, WHATEVER IS PURE, WHATEVER IS LOVELY, WHATEVER IS COMMENDABLE, IF THERE IS ANY EXCELLENCE, IF THERE IS ANYTHING WORTHY OF PRAISE, THINK ABOUT THESE THINGS. (PHILIPPIANS 4:8)

My kindergartener walks in the door one day, telling me that he has a girlfriend. Ummmm, I don't think so, son! Let's just hold up on that for a few years (few = 20!).

So, it seems that being a teenager today means that *you must have a boyfriend or girlfriend*, or there is something wrong with you. What happened to the concept that being single is a good thing?

Teens, I know that the pressure is real. You watch your other friends date. That's where all the fun is, right? And after three days of dating, they are very much in love (so they say!). And the questions start to come your way: *"Oh, you do not have a boyfriend (or) you cannot find a girl yet? Something must be different about you! If you cannot find a someone, then maybe you have an identity issue? Hurry up and do something about it, or you will be alone for the rest of your life!"*

It amazes me how little patience we humans possess. As a result, dating is embraced with little to no regard for God's will.

What do they say about dating? "Find happiness with a significant other, no matter who it is!" This view slaps purity in the face.

🡅 READ PHILIPPIANS 4:4-9, AND THINK ABOUT HOW THE WORD "PEACE" IS EMPHASIZED IN VERSE 7.

## DATING: WHAT DOES GOD SAY?

DO NOT REBUKE AN OLDER MAN BUT ENCOURAGE HIM AS YOU WOULD A FATHER, YOUNGER MEN AS BROTHERS, OLDER WOMEN AS MOTHERS, YOUNGER WOMEN AS SISTERS, IN ALL PURITY. (1 TIMOTHY 5:1-2)

Dating is very much a cultural practice. The Bible speaks to what is commonly understood as courtship, and in times past, many marriages were arranged. Courtship had the purpose of marriage in mind, and an arranged marriage often revealed the will of the parents (all the more reason for the teens of that time to stay on their good side!).

The verses above give us terrific relationship counsel. In the context, the Apostle Paul is talking to Pastor Timothy in familial terms. He recognizes that people love their moms, dads, brothers, and sisters. Yes, we have fights with them at times, but at the end of the day, we know that we love them. We stick together. We defend each other. We are on this together journey called life. We don't cross the line with one another, and if we do, we must make it right. That is how a good family is supposed to work!

Specifically, in reference to dating, Paul tells Timothy to treat his Christian sisters "in absolute purity". That word "purity" is related to words of "being clean", "innocence", "modesty", and "perfection". Fellas, this command is to be taken very seriously. Dating, courtship, arranged marriage, or whatever the pursuit, we are to be pure in the sight of the Lord!

Even though we are not in his eternal presence right now, Jesus calls the church "his bride" (see Ephesians 5). The way he treats us is a perfect example of how we should treat each other, even as it pertains to preparing for our own marriage.

↑ READ A BIBLICAL MODEL OF DATING IN SONG OF SOLOMON 1.

# DATING: WHAT DO YOU SAY?

HE WHO FINDS A WIFE FINDS A GOOD THING AND OBTAINS FAVOR FROM THE LORD. (PROVERBS 18:22)

Unfortunately, dating in our culture is often pursued with an unworthy purpose: to find short term happiness with another, no matter who it is. God's purpose is quite the opposite. Dating ought to be purposeful. It should seek out a future spouse for life. It has God's view of marriage in mind: "one man and one woman." It centers all hope on the Lord, the only One who can give us what we need.

The Bible's way of "dating" challenges our thinking. It calls for patience. You could be waiting for a future spouse for years. You could have to say "no" altogether to a boyfriend or girlfriend in high school. You could miss out on fun times with other friends, or lose friends who think you are not worth their time. Not what you want to hear, I know! But godly adults can guarantee you that dating and marrying the wrong person is far more painful than the alternative.

You know what I like about that Proverbs verse above? It mentions the word "finds". Finding is not an accidental pursuit (like "falling head over heels for her" or "he is just so cute!"). It is not a surprise discovery. Finding a wife has a purpose in mind, and God gives the husband His favor when he finally marries his bride.

What do you say? Let me remind you that the best things in life take time. Marriage is one of those best things. Let's handle it right. Don't rush into dating; in fact, don't date at all unless God is in it. Trust Him! He knows how to care for you, and believe me, He does not need the help of a boyfriend or girlfriend to do it.

🡅 LET'S READ SOME WORDS OF WISDOM TODAY IN PROVERBS 18.

## SUCCESS: WHAT DO THEY SAY?

AGAIN, THE DEVIL TOOK HIM TO A VERY HIGH MOUNTAIN AND SHOWED HIM ALL THE KINGDOMS OF THE WORLD AND THEIR GLORY. AND HE SAID TO HIM, "ALL THESE I WILL GIVE YOU, IF YOU WILL FALL DOWN AND WORSHIP ME." (MATTHEW 4:8-9)

Tom Brady. Will Smith. Bill Gates. Oprah Winfrey. Queen Elizabeth. Angelina Jolie. Michael Jordan. All are names you probably recognize. All are acclaimed in the eyes of the world. All are people that are emulated. They've had so much success. They must be happy... right?

Satan tried to make Jesus the offer of a lifetime when he "showed him all the kingdoms of the world and their glory". Were they really his to offer? In one way, yes. Satan has tremendous influence on the cursed kingdoms of this world (this includes our own nation). In this moment of temptation in Matthew, the devil proposes a transfer of power over to Jesus. This would have included the Roman Empire, as well as all the other kingdoms that existed 2,000 years ago. However, in order to accept this offer, Jesus would have disobeyed his Father – something he could not and would not do.

Teens, you are under tremendous pressure to find success. Satan uses the same tactics with you as he did when he tempted Jesus. Somehow, we are led to believe that choosing the right college, career, husband or wife, house, car, etc. will make you successful. Expensive vacations in the Caribbean, having a fancy car, eating out at 5-star restaurants, having lots of kids that you don't have to watch yourself - all signs of success, according to the world.

If status and possessions are the signs of success, then Jesus would have been one of the most unsuccessful people that ever lived.

CHECK OUT WHAT HAPPENED TO A VERY "SUCCESSFUL" KING WHO DID NOT KNOW GOD – READ DANIEL 4!

## SUCCESS: WHAT DOES GOD SAY?

THE BOOK OF THE LAW SHALL NOT DEPART FROM YOUR MOUTH, BUT YOU SHALL MEDITATE ON IT DAY AND NIGHT, SO THAT YOU MAY BE CAREFUL TO DO ACCORDING TO ALL THAT IS WRITTEN IN IT. FOR THEN YOU WILL MAKE YOUR WAY PROSPEROUS, AND THEN YOU WILL HAVE GOOD SUCCESS. (JOSHUA 1:8)

Joshua was given a very specific set of instructions. Success for him would lead to conquering Canaan (God's Promised Land). By and large, Israel was successful, though remnants of wicked civilizations would remain (and sadly, come back to haunt them later).

In Joshua 1:8, we notice something very interesting to consider today. Joshua would not have prospered by studying methods on how to take down big walls, nor was he given the book "Warfare for Dummies" to read. He was told to know the Bible! He would be successful in his leadership by studying and living by "The Book of the Law". And as we read various accounts of Israel's victories, God's way of fighting leaves us speechless. He is undefeated, since He is undefeatable. If Joshua was going to be successful, victory depended upon the Lord, and Him alone.

The blueprint for Joshua is the same blueprint for us. Oh, we may not lead a people into a promised land, but the Bible lays out all that we need for life and godliness. God calls us to study it and live by it. It is a call to faith.

When all was said and done, Joshua was definitely one of the most successful saints of the Bible. Was it because he received a college degree from "The University of Egypt", or rode the finest 8-cylinder chariot, or hung out with Moses? No! That's just nonsense. He succeeded because his life revealed a man who knew the Book of the Law. God wants us to meditate on it day and night, as well!

↑ READ ABOUT JOSHUA'S SUCCESS AT THE FAMOUS BATTLE OF JERICHO IN JOSHUA 5:13 - 6:27.

## SUCCESS: WHAT DO YOU SAY?

BUT AS IT IS, THEY DESIRE A BETTER COUNTRY, THAT IS, A HEAVENLY ONE. THEREFORE, GOD IS NOT ASHAMED TO BE CALLED THEIR GOD, FOR HE HAS PREPARED FOR THEM A CITY. (HEBREWS 11:16)

The "they-their-them" pronouns in Hebrews 11:16 are the saints that God recognized as people of faith. In fact, Hebrews 11 has been given the nickname "The Hall of Faith". The Lord proclaims these saints as successful (though the world martyred many of them!).

Teens, let's just ponder something for a moment. Some of the most popular people that you know, recognized as successful by the world, living in fame and wealth... if they died without Christ, what would they have really gained? All that fame, all that money, all that worldly success... what did it mean? I believe you know the answer, and so do I. It all adds up to nothing. Popularity and money and fame and possessions collected on a cursed earth awaiting a future destruction? This is not God's definition of success.

But what if we thought about success in a "better country?" What if we considered the words "Well done!" as successful? Our Savior will speak those words to the believers who live by their faith. What if our eyes were so fixed on Jesus that we could care less about our own success on earth? What if our sole passion was to see Jesus increase and us decrease (John 3:30)?

I hope you find yourself doing the things in life you were created to do, and that you will take great joy in doing it. But know this: your success will be based upon living by faith. Faith and success are synonymous. What do you say to that?

↑ CHECK OUT HOW THE SUCCESSFUL MOSES CONCLUDED HIS LIFE IN DEUTERONOMY 34.

# COMMUNICATION: WHAT DO THEY SAY?

LET NO CORRUPTING TALK COME OUT OF YOUR MOUTH, BUT ONLY SUCH AS IS GOOD FOR BUILDING UP, AS FITS THE OCCASION, THAT IT MAY GIVE GRACE TO THOSE WHO HEAR. (EPHESIANS 4:29)

Teens, have you noticed that some people have an "anything goes" mentality when it comes to their speech? Most of us are usually careful about what we say out loud and to whom we say it, but sooner or later, what we really believe comes out of our lips (or on to a keyboard!).

Social media is a serious culprit of "corrupting talk". Some examples of what I've seen of late include the following:

- Vicious fighting in a long text conversation.
- A "coming out" party for those who support homosexuality.
- Horrendous language.
- Sexual references to body parts.
- Threats against one another.

Tell me: when did all of this become so acceptable as the norm?

People act bravely when they don't have to see each other face to face. Somehow, they justify saying things that they can type or text because they don't have to deal with personal interaction. The consequences of this, however, are dealt with on a very real level. It is not unusual for the ugliness found in social media to spill over into our daily lives. How many acts of abuse, bullying, or violence have occurred due to harmful communication on the internet?

No matter the mode of communication, what we say always matters!

🡅 READ ABOUT WICKED COMMUNICATION FROM JEZEBEL AND THE CONSEQUENCES OF IT IN 1 KINGS 21.

# COMMUNICATION: WHAT DOES GOD SAY?

LET YOUR SPEECH ALWAYS BE GRACIOUS, SEASONED WITH SALT, SO THAT YOU MAY KNOW HOW YOU OUGHT TO ANSWER EACH PERSON. (COLOSSIANS 4:6)

Don't you love how the Bible uses terrific illustrations in order to teach us important lessons? Salt has been valued by many nations throughout history. You don't need a devotion from me to tell you how salt makes food taste better. Most of us use at least a little bit to bring out the flavor of our meat, vegetables, fries, or other foods we enjoy.

*Grace* is the salt of our communication. Grace may be defined as "giving goodness to someone who does not deserve it". We all need grace, don't we? God commands it in our conversations. Grace makes us recognize that we need to be careful about what we say – both in choosing words of goodness to say to others, as well as using humble words to say about ourselves.

The verses that lead up to Colossians 4:6 teach us about prayer. Concerning prayer and our communication with others, here's a thought: what if we actually prayed before we hit "send" on a controversial text? What if we held our tongue and let things settle down before we spoke to the one that angered us? What if we stopped and asked God about what to do before we expressed our emotions to everyone else? What if all of our messages were "seasoned with salt"? God knows exactly what we need to say to each other. Our communication should have the word *grace* sprinkled into it. If it does not, use your "delete" button!

Truly, isn't it great to receive uplifting words from others? Since you know it is, then be that person! The Lord is very concerned about what we communicate; indeed, every word matters.

↑ CHECK OUT COLOSSIANS 4:2-6.

# COMMUNICATION: WHAT DO YOU SAY?

LET THERE BE NO FILTHINESS NOR FOOLISH TALK NOR CRUDE JOKING, WHICH ARE OUT OF PLACE, BUT INSTEAD LET THERE BE THANKSGIVING. (EPHESIANS 5:4)

Take a moment, and think about what you said yesterday. Think about the words, the sentences, and the conversations that took place in your life. Was it encouraging? Was it pure? Was it "seasoned with salt"? Our character has a way of being revealed by our mouths (or fingers).

I have often gone to bed at night, replayed the day in my head, and thought to myself, "Why in the world did I say that today?" In disobedience to Ephesians 5:4, I have participated in my share of obscenity (filthiness, foolish talk, and crude joking). It's embarrassing. I wish I could replay those days and get rid of that worthless and evil communication. Ugh!

You may already know this, but James 1:19 tells us to be "slow to speak" and "quick to hear". In our world, I would add, "slow to text!" In this context, James is dealing with anger, and when I do slow my speech and quicken my ear, I have often saved myself from saying something out of place.

It seems like many people think that worthless communication is acceptable. Guess what? God isn't laughing. He desires words of thanksgiving to come out of our mouths. Is that so hard to believe?

So teens, what do you say? Seriously, what (words) do you *say*? May God help us! As the little children's song teaches, "Oh, be careful little mouth what you say. Oh, be careful little mouth what you say. For the Father up above is looking down in love! Oh, be careful little mouth what you say."

↑ READ EPHESIANS 5:3-14 TODAY!

## THE END OF OUR PATIENCE?

BETTER IS THE END OF A THING THAN ITS BEGINNING, AND THE PATIENT IN SPIRIT IS BETTER THAN THE PROUD IN SPIRIT. BE NOT QUICK IN YOUR SPIRIT TO BECOME ANGRY, FOR ANGER LODGES IN THE HEART OF FOOLS. (ECCLESIASTES 7:8-9)

Can I be real with you? Right now, I am struggling to be patient with someone in my life. I'm at the "Enough is enough!" stage, and everything inside me wants to justify doing what it takes to stop this individual from causing me more pain.

Do I have this right? God has a limit upon His patience – He takes action in His perfect timing – so what about me? What am I allowed to do?

Then I start to look at verses concerning patience, and I realize that He calls me to practice it, regardless of the outcome. I cannot find any verses that would allow me to react negatively against this person. Instead, I discover Paul telling us that patience will transform me. Peter tells us that it is a good thing to suffer patiently. James tells us to patiently hang in there, because Christ is coming. There are many psalms about waiting patiently for the LORD to act according to His will. Again, I find nothing that says, "You can put up with it until this point, and after that, you can move on."

Maybe you would pray with me today? "Father, you know my situation. You know all things. You know when I am hurt. Your tender mercies are all I need. Please help me to remember that Your hand is extended toward me at all times. In your love, I can crawl upon your lap and feel better. In your grace, I can put up with this suffering, even if it means for the remaining years of my life. Help me not to respond in my feelings, but to trust in the knowledge of your goodness. In Jesus' Name, Amen."

🡅 CONSIDER MORE WORDS OF WISDOM IN ECCLESIASTES 7:1-14.

# A SINKING SHIP AND A SLITHERING SNAKE

THEREFORE LET IT BE KNOWN TO YOU THAT THIS SALVATION OF GOD HAS BEEN SENT TO THE GENTILES; THEY WILL LISTEN. (ACTS 28:28)

Perhaps you have heard stories about conquerors who overcame the worst of circumstances, only to have something unusual or bizarre take them out of play. This happened to Alexander the Great, the famous Greek king and military leader. Though he had conquered much of the civilized world at the time, he died at the age of 32 due to unknown circumstances (poisoned, perhaps?). He survived many battles, yet surprisingly left the world at a very young age.

A few centuries later, the Apostle Paul would experience many hardships himself. At the start of Acts 28, we read that he just survived a shipwreck, only to be bitten by a viper when he arrived on shore! Talk about a series of unfortunate events!

Yet to the amazement of the islanders, he survived. In fact, he went on to heal many others before he left Malta. Paul's story could not end on that island, for God had given him a mandate: "So you must testify also in Rome" (Acts 23:11). Rome would be his final mission.

What is your mandate? What is your mission? Do you walk close enough with the Lord to know what He has in mind for you? As I learn more from the Bible, I learn that God reveals his will to those who seek Him with their whole hearts.

Dear ones, the Lord has great plans for His children! Neither sunken ships nor slithering snakes can stop Him. Know your God, and you will know your mission.

🡅 THIS INCREDIBLE ACCOUNT IS FOUND IN ACTS 28:1-10.

# DO I REALLY WANT GOD'S DISCIPLINE?

MY SON, DO NOT DESPISE THE LORD'S DISCIPLINE AND OR BE WEARY OF HIS REPROOF, FOR THE LORD REPROVES HIM WHOM HE LOVES, AS A FATHER THE SON IN WHOM HE DELIGHTS. (PROVERBS 3:11-12)

Amazing how God works! Just minutes ago, my new neighbor came over and asked for some advice. His stepdaughter is giving them all kinds of trouble, and he is exasperated. He doesn't know what to do. From what he told me, it sounds like he is disciplining her correctly, but she is not responding to it. I promised him that I would pray for the family, and I also offered my help. This happened just minutes before I planned to write on the subject of discipline!

Did you know that God is "pro-discipline"? That's right! You can read all about it in Hebrews 12. Just like our earthly parents, He does it because He chooses to do what is good for us. And even though I am an adult, I still need His discipline. Without it, I would certainly run astray. The Father's correction keeps me from finding all kinds of trouble. His discipline = His love.

With that said, I don't want to purposely bring discipline upon myself. Paul asked the question, "Are we to continue in sin so that grace may abound?". He answers his own question: "By no means! How can we who died to sin still live in it?" (Romans 6:2). If I decide to jump back into the pit of sin, then my loving Father cares enough to pull me out of it again. However, it is so much better when I decide to steer clear of the pit. By doing so, I please my Father. As His child, I sincerely want to please my Father!

May we appreciate His loving discipline for the gift that it is to us.

🡅 THE NATION OF ISRAEL RECEIVED GOD'S DISCIPLINE MANY TIMES IN HER HISTORY. READ NUMBERS 14:26-45 TODAY.

## IT'S SO NOT LIKE THE MOVIES!

When Pharaoh heard of it, he sought to kill Moses. But Moses fled from Pharaoh and stayed in the land of Midian. And he sat down by a well... And Moses was content to dwell with the man, and he gave Moses his daughter Zipporah. (Exodus 2:15, 21)

Moses spent 40 years in Midian (a land east of Egypt). You would think that 40 years would cover a lot of biblical information on the life of Moses. However, it does not. We read some verses about his marriage and transition of prince to shepherd, and that's about it until Exodus 3.

What if the Bible covered those 40 years in detail? We would probably have read details about his daily life in caring for sheep – feeding them, walking with them, finding new pasture, protecting them from predators, breeding them, taking care of the sick ones, etc. He'd be doing this same thing year after year after year. Sound a bit boring to you? Moses had an amazing life, but he dealt with the daily routine, just like you and me. And it was the daily routine that greatly shaped the man into becoming the leader of Israel.

Can you imagine if people followed you around with a video camera for the whole world to see? If they got the uncut version, people would quit watching because they would be bored to death. No offense, but it's the truth! Oh yes, we all have exciting moments, but most of our moments are very similar, because they are routine. And that's fine! In fact, it is exactly what God planned in the first place. Inside of the routine, He is working all things together for our good (Romans 8:28).

Moments that shape us are often moments shared with God alone. He turns the routine into the wonderful. Just like Moses, His work is slowly and surely shaping us, little by little.

↑ CONSIDER PAUL, WHO SPENT THREE YEARS IN THE DESERT TO GROW. READ GALATIANS 1:13-24 TO LEARN HOW GOD USED THIS IN HIS LIFE.

# OUR LAMENT (CONCERNING OUR PAINFUL YEARS OF INFERTILITY)

*"Oh, that you would answer our prayers!*
*Oh, that you would listen as we cry in pain!*
*By now, we thought he would be here, and he is not.*
*We have cried day and night, trusting in your word.*
*We have sought out help, but to no avail.*
*You promised that you would take care of us. Will you?*
*Our friends and families are seeing their hopes come to life,*
*Yet still we wait.*
*Our hearts are losing hope,*
*And we wonder about the sins of our past.*
*Is this right? Is this fair? Are you listening? What more can we do?*
*Nevertheless, we trust in You, for there is nowhere else to turn.*
*And in the pain, we will continue to pray, to seek, and to trust You to meet our needs.*
*No matter what, You are God.*
*We praise You, Lord. You are our peace and our rest."*

🡅 GOD HEARS! GOD UNDERSTANDS! HE CAN HANDLE OUR CRIES TO HIM. READ ANOTHER LAMENT - PSALM 142.

# AM I ACCEPTED?

FINALLY, BROTHERS, WHATEVER IS TRUE, WHATEVER IS HONORABLE, WHATEVER IS JUST, WHATEVER IS PURE, WHATEVER IS LOVELY, WHATEVER IS COMMENDABLE, IF THERE IS ANY EXCELLENCE, IF THERE IS ANYTHING WORTHY OF PRAISE, THINK ABOUT THESE THINGS. (PHILIPPIANS 4:8)

"Am I accepted?". I imagine some of you ask this question every day. *"What do my friends think of my outfit? Did they hear about my older brother going to jail? Do they know that my mom ran off with another man? How many know that I failed that math test? Are they turned off by how I look?"*

Oh, the struggles of being a teenager! It makes me want to take all of you in a time machine and move ahead 10 years. I myself have learned the truth of what I was told by wise people as a teen – those classmates of yours eventually set aside the silliness and fights that were so awful in school. So, hang in there!

The concern for acceptance can dominate. The Bible tells us that our thoughts are actions of the mind, and since we are responsible for our actions, we can control our thoughts as we are led by the Holy Spirit. What if we took our minds off of our friends and focused on what is true, honorable, just, pure, lovely, and commendable? Putting our thoughts on these things is like taking our brain out for a good walk or run – it is so spiritually healthy!

As you ponder all things that are excellent and worthy of praise, you will discover your acceptance in Christ. At that moment, what others think of you no longer matters at all. Talk about freedom!

↑ A BIBLE EXAMPLE OF ACCEPTANCE FOR OTHERS THROUGH FORGIVENESS: GENESIS 50:15-21.

# I WANT ANOTHER ANSWER!

KING ZEDEKIAH SENT FOR HIM AND RECEIVED HIM. THE KING QUESTIONED HIM SECRETLY IN HIS HOUSE AND SAID, "IS THERE ANY WORD FROM THE LORD?" JEREMIAH SAID, "THERE IS." THEN HE SAID, "YOU SHALL BE DELIVERED INTO THE HAND OF THE KING OF BABYLON." (JEREMIAH 37:17)

King Zedekiah ended up being the last king of Judah. He was on the throne when the nation fell in 586 B.C. If you read the book of Jeremiah, you will find out that the king was given a ton of chances to surrender and live. He chose to ignore the prophet, and by doing so, ended up paying for that decision with his life.

Zedekiah's question in Jeremiah 37 was not the first time he asked it to the prophet. Jeremiah had told him exactly what would happen – Jerusalem would fall to Babylon – but the king didn't want to hear it. He kept hoping for a different answer, so he surrounded himself with liars who told him what he wanted to hear. Obviously, this did not work out so well! The truth is the truth; God's foretold punishment had come, and there would be nothing the king could do to stop it. He could only surrender. Tragically, he chose not to do so.

Just like the king, we often want another answer that relieves us from the consequences of sin. We will wiggle and squirm and ask again and sometimes pout and sometimes cry and sometimes lash out, while hoping for something different. Yet the truth does not change: if we sin, we have to deal with the results. God cannot say "It's ok!" to the very actions that caused His Son to be killed. In Him, my sin is forgiven (praise God!); but remember, He will not dismiss the effects of my sin on my life while I am on this earth. I must face His discipline.

"Lord, thank you that You have kept me from paying the full amount for my sin – an eternity separated from You."

HOW PAUL HANDLED A "NO" IN HIS LIFE: 2 CORINTHIANS 12:1-10.

# HER REAL NEED

AND HE SAID TO HER, "YOUR SINS ARE FORGIVEN." THEN THOSE WHO WERE AT THE TABLE WITH HIM BEGAN TO SAY AMONG THEMSELVES, "WHO IS THIS, WHO EVEN FORGIVES SINS?" AND HE SAID TO THE WOMAN, "YOUR FAITH HAS SAVED YOU; GO IN PEACE." (LUKE 7:48, 50)

This woman - this sinner - shows up in the least likely of places (the home of a Pharisee). On a normal day, this would have been the last place she would ever come; but today was not a normal day. You see, Jesus was there, and she did not want to miss this. Despite all of her known despicable "activities", she willed herself to go inside. She would, for *he* was inside!

What she did next is both authentic and amazing. With a heart beating wildly, with gratitude beyond words, and with emotions flooding openly, she cleans the feet of the Savior with her multitude of tears. Being without a towel, she uses her own hair to wipe away the dirt from his feet. Knowing the depth of his love for her, she then kisses those feet nonstop. She goes the sacrificial distance by pouring her own perfume on his feet – a very costly gift.

The Pharisee was repulsed. This woman, in his home, touching this teacher. If Jesus only knew, he would have banished her from his presence! But oh, he knew! And instead of banishment, he offered her salvation and peace.

Teens, what we have in front of us is a picture of true forgiveness. Forgiveness was her real need. You and I? We're no better than this woman. But you and I? We are offered the same gift. It's our real need!

Have you accepted the gift of forgiveness for your sin?

🡅 READ ABOUT THIS FORGIVEN WOMAN IN LUKE 7:36-50.

# TREASURES IN HEAVEN

DO NOT LAY UP FOR YOURSELVES TREASURES ON EARTH, WHERE MOTH AND RUST DESTROY AND WHERE THIEVES BREAK IN AND STEAL, BUT LAY UP FOR YOURSELVES TREASURES IN HEAVEN, WHERE NEITHER MOTH NOR RUST DESTROYS AND WHERE THIEVES DO NOT BREAK IN AND STEAL. FOR WHERE OUR TREASURE IS, THERE YOUR HEART WILL BE ALSO. (MATTHEW 6:19-21)

If you met me as a teenager, you would have soon discovered that I was involved in academics, soccer, and music. I enjoyed these activities very much. However, each one also taught me some of life's realities.

As an academic student, I started high school ranked eighth in my class, but slipped to fourteenth by the time I graduated. My goal of finishing in the top ten did not happen. In soccer, I had a very promising junior season (making 5 goals) on a solid team that made the playoffs. I became a captain during my senior year, but I only made two goals; I lost my starting position partway into the season; and we did not make the playoffs. It was humbling. In both choir and band, I made it to the district level each of my last three years, but never cracked the regional level, finishing as a runner-up twice. Music was definitely my thing, so that certainly left a bitter taste in my mouth.

But what I learned back then is the very thing I want to teach my children today: earthly treasures are nice, but they are ultimately worthless compared to the treasures of heaven. Missing regionals, losing a starting position in soccer, and not finishing in the top ten did not ruin me in the least. All of those accomplishments were desirable, but they were also open to moths, rust, and thieves.

The things which are done for heaven's sake are the treasures that I will enjoy forever.

↑ CHECK OUT MATTHEW 6:19-24!

## LIVING WITH REGRET?

FOR YOU, O LORD, ARE GOOD AND FORGIVING, ABOUNDING IN STEADFAST LOVE TO ALL WHO CALL UPON YOU. GIVE EAR, O LORD, TO MY PRAYER; LISTEN TO MY PLEA FOR GRACE. IN THE DAY OF MY TROUBLE I CALL UPON YOU, FOR YOU ANSWER ME. (PSALM 86:5-7)

*"I can't believe I did that! What was I thinking? I will never forget it for as long as I live. I'm sure that God will punish me for this. I am such an idiot! If I could go back in time and fix this, I would do it in an instant. How in the world am I going to live this down? My thoughts, oh how they haunt me! I hurt a lot of people by making this stupid decision! I am so worthless."*

Have you ever felt like this? I'm sure you have - you and me both! We all have done some serious wrongdoing, and it makes us guilty before God. Sometimes our sin causes us to think about ways to fix the problem (as if we can possibly *work* our way back into His will).

But God does not work that way. Thank the Lord for that! Here are His rules (summed up in my words): *"I know you have sinned! Indeed, it has caused me grief and sadness. But here is what you need to do: I want you to tell me about it; admit that you are wrong and that you are truly sorry (this needs to be done in sincerity, mind you!); then get up and move forward! I have not given up on you, for I am accomplishing a good work in you. Don't wallow in regret. My forgiveness is real, and it is complete. I will not be done with My work in you until the day you see Me. So let's go, My child!"*

How does this sound to you?

🡅 READ PSALM 86. MAY THIS PSALM ENCOURAGE YOU TODAY!

# GAINING FROM THE EXPERIENCED

BUT HE ABANDONED THE COUNSEL THAT THE OLD MEN GAVE HIM AND TOOK COUNSEL WITH THE YOUNG MEN WHO HAD GROWN UP WITH HIM AND STOOD BEFORE HIM. (1 KINGS 12:8)

Most of the Old Testament kings were not so great. There were only a few who stood out as good men. Some of them started out that way, then turned bad. A majority were wicked from the start.

Rehoboam was on "the naughty list" of kings. His father was Solomon, and if you know anything about the wisest man of all, you know that he acted unwisely in his later years. His foolish decisions left the kingdom on the brink of a split. So you would think that Rehoboam would make careful decisions early on, right? Alas, he did not. As prophesied, the kingdom split into the North (Israel) and the South (Judah), never to regain the glory it formerly enjoyed under his father.

As a new king, Rehoboam was given advice by two groups of men: one group was older, and one was younger. In reading the context of 1 Kings 12, it doesn't seem like the king gives much thought at all to what the elders had to say. He should have strongly considered the words of men who had been there with Solomon. Perhaps that split would have been delayed? In the past, God had been known to hold off on judgment when His people decided to repent.

Today, I challenge you to consider what the experienced have to say. Yes, they can be wrong! And yes, experience does not equal truth. However, God uses experiences in our lives not only to mold the individual, but to mold others that come later in life. To reject the voice of the experienced is to follow in the path of Rehoboam. In short order, he realized the great mistake he had made – it nearly cost him his life.

↑ CHECK OUT PART OF KING REHOBOAM'S STORY IN 2 CHRONICLES 10.

# HE WILL WIPE THOSE TEARS AWAY (BY WAYNE MORGAN)

HE WILL WIPE EVERY TEAR FROM THEIR EYES, AND DEATH SHALL WILL BE NO MORE, NEITHER SHALL THERE BE MOURNING, NOR CRYING, NOR PAIN ANYMORE, FOR THE FORMER THINGS HAVE PASSED AWAY. (REVELATION 21:4)

One spring, when my kids were little, we took them outside to play. They both climbed, crawled, ran... FELL, got back up and did it all again. They were COVERED with dirt when it was all done. After getting immersed in uncleanliness, my two-year old son had his feelings hurt and had the guts to come over to me, lift both arms, and say, "UP!"

Did he know how gross he was?

Didn't he realize I JUST saw him CRASH in the slimy mud?

NO! He didn't care and NEITHER DID I. He knew that his father would pick him up and wipe away the tears. This is the beauty of love, and of being loved - there was no fear of rejection.

Jesus will also not reject us, no matter how messy we are. He did not keep his distance from a naked and demon-possessed man. He was not turned off by a lady who suffered from a severe bleeding condition. He did not shun the woman at the well who had been married five times. And he did not decommission his disciples after they all left him before his death. What a picture of his beautiful love!

I was wondering what God was doing with me all this week as I stumbled around with my stress. He was watching me climb, crawl, run... and fall in the mud, starting to cry. He was just waiting for me to come over and have the guts to lift up both grimy arms and say, "UP!"

🡅 READ PSALM 30 TODAY.

# APRIL

# A LOT LIKE US

AGAINST YOU, YOU ONLY, HAVE I SINNED AND DONE WHAT IS EVIL IN YOUR SIGHT, SO THAT YOU MAY BE JUSTIFIED IN YOUR WORDS AND BLAMELESS IN YOUR JUDGMENT. (PSALM 51:4)

The common cold. You would think, after all these years, we would have come up with a cure by now. God has allowed us to overcome many diseases, yet every year, most of us come down with a cold. Colds are also unpredictable – they care not what season it is, and they last as long as they desire. So unfriendly, these colds!

Sin. You would think, after all these years, I would stop doing it by now. Yet here I am, in my 40's, needing to fight the flesh and flee from the devil. Sin is still a problem; but thanks be to God, who always offers His grace to overcome!

This month, we will look at how King David succeeded and failed in his life. He lived about 3,000 years ago, but he was a man a lot like us. David faced the same temptations of us all, which are "the desires of the the flesh and the desires of the eyes and the pride of life" (1 John 2:16). As we learn about his successes and failures, I pray we will all grow from this knowledge!

Teens, the Bible gives us plenty of examples in how to live, so that we would learn to be obedient, and in doing so, we would be blessed. King David was an amazing individual – a "man after God's own heart" – but in so many ways, he was no different than you and I.

In the Lord's strength, may we learn what it takes to conquer sin, live by faith, and trust God all the days of our lives.

READ 1 JOHN 2:9-17 TODAY!

# DAVID AND HIS COURAGE

WAIT FOR THE LORD; BE STRONG, AND LET YOUR HEART TAKE COURAGE; WAIT FOR THE LORD! (PSALM 27:14)

What would it take for you to fight someone who is a lot taller and stronger than you? Back in the days of David, there were giants in the land. Goliath was one of them, and he just happened to be on the side of the enemy. David was anything but a giant, yet he still fought him one-on-one. What courage!

When we read 1 Samuel 17, we learn that David the shepherd took out a lion and a bear. That is very impressive, but did he have what it takes to fight this Philistine warrior? King Saul tried to put his own armor on David, but Saul was missing the big picture – he lacked the faith that God would grant a victory. You see, David knew he could win in the same way that he won against the lion and the bear. His victories were not through skill and luck, but with a courageous confidence that his life belonged to God, no matter the outcome. And when Goliath dared to mock the Name of the Holy One? Well, David made sure that he wasn't going down without a fight!

Teens, this is a time in David's life when he was barely older than you. Courage does not belong to adults alone. Our world stands in awe when a young person displays courage in the Lord. History has been altered when a teenager charged forward with reckless abandon, with faith leading the way. Heaven watches in great excitement when God wins another victory through the likes of the young and willing.

Teens, may you stand strong! If you know Christ, you know victory. Live in courage, and watch the giants fall!

READ A NARRATIVE (1 SAMUEL 17) OR A SONG (PSALM 27).

# DAVID AND HIS FEAR

HEAR MY VOICE, O GOD, IN MY COMPLAINT; PRESERVE MY LIFE FROM DREAD OF THE ENEMY. (PSALM 64:1)

Yesterday, we learned about David and his courage. Today, we read about his fear (specifically, in the days before he became king).

Are the two in direct contrast to one another? Was David in sin when he ran away from other "giants"? I don't believe so. He had a close relationship with his God in the days leading up to his reign. David knew when to fight, and he knew when to "flight"; he knew what do do, because he knew how to pray.

David was given plenty of reasons to fear for his life. Sometimes, he could fight back (as he did with Goliath). Other times, God led him to flee from those who would kill him. If you had a murderous king hunting you down, but you knew that you were not supposed to fight back, you'd be scared, too!

David was threatened and attacked by Saul many times, but he trusted in his God, and took to writing psalms to express how he felt. Psalm 64 is one of many psalms that reveal David's trust in God while enduring trials. His fear drove him to find safety in his Rock and his Fortress.

Teens, when you are afraid, remember the words of Jesus. "And do not fear those who kill the body but cannot kill the soul. Rather fear him who can destroy both soul and body in hell" (Matthew 10:28).

"God, please teach me when to stay or when to run. Either way, hold me fast in peace and safety!"

READ A NARRATIVE (1 SAMUEL 23:7-29) OR A SONG (PSALM 64).

# DAVID AND HIS ADULTERY

IT HAPPENED, LATE ONE AFTERNOON, WHEN DAVID AROSE FROM HIS COUCH AND AND WAS WALKING ON THE ROOF OF THE KING'S HOUSE, THAT HE SAW FROM THE ROOF A WOMAN BATHING; AND THE WOMAN WAS VERY BEAUTIFUL. AND DAVID SENT AND INQUIRED ABOUT THE WOMAN. AND ONE SAID, "IS THIS NOT BATHSHEBA, THE DAUGHTER OF ELIAM, THE WIFE OF URIAH THE HITTITE?" (2 SAMUEL 11:2-3)

Lust defined: "I want it, and I must have it, so I will go and get it!" So different from "I need it, so please give it to me." Lust is not limited to what a man sexually desires in a woman (or a woman in a man). We can lust for food, or drugs, or cars, or all kinds of things. Unchecked lust leads to rampant sin. Sin itself leads to death (see James 1:13-15). For the believer in Christ, lust must be taken seriously.

David lusted after a woman (and a married woman, at that). Somehow, David severely dropped his guard and dove headlong into the awful sin of adultery. As king, the "I want it, and I must have it, so I will get it!" mentality took over in his life, and this man of God gave Satan the victory. Oh, how I wish 2 Samuel stopped at chapter 10, so we would not have to read about his terrible sin and the consequences to follow.

Lust can be stopped. We do not have to act upon what we feel. If lust is unchecked, it will only lead to other sins. For David, his lust led to deception, lying, and murder. What happened to this shepherd boy that killed a giant? How sad!

Teens, we cannot overstate the need for self-control in all areas of our lives, including lust. David would be forgiven, but his sin would permanently affect his family and kingdom. It didn't have to be this way. Sin always, *always* takes us farther than we wanted to go.

Let's learn from David and get control over lust in our own lives!

↑ READ A NARRATIVE (2 SAMUEL 11:1-5) OR A SONG (PSALM 51).

# DAVID AND HIS RIGHTEOUSNESS

THE LORD JUDGES THE PEOPLES; JUDGE ME, O LORD, ACCORDING TO MY RIGHTEOUSNESS AND ACCORDING TO THE INTEGRITY THAT IS IN ME. (PSALM 7:8)

When do we see our integrity at its best? When we have the opportunity to do what is wrong, but we choose what is right. In his life, David was given plenty of chances to choose sin. Sometimes he did. But when he did what was right, he added to his godly legacy.

The Bible gives us many examples of David's righteousness (as we'll see in 2 Samuel 16 today). In this chapter, David is on the run, and his rebel son is attempting to overtake the capital. On the way out, a descendant of his predecessor (Saul) treats him with disdain. "You are getting what you deserve!" is Shimei's cry. He proceeds to throw both insults and rocks at the king. David's eager body guard wants to kill the guy, but David won't let him. Instead, he says, "It may be that the LORD will look on the wrong done to me, and that the LORD will repay me with good for his cursing today" (verse 12).

David was a man determined to do what was right. When he was wrong, he also determined to make things right. We rarely see such a man living like this today.

We need Christians who know they will stand before God one day and answer for their actions. No believer has the defense of a sinless existence; yet he or she will be able to stand before God as righteous.

Teens, by God's grace, let us do what is right, no matter what may come! Righteousness is the way to go.

READ A NARRATIVE (2 SAMUEL 16:5-14) OR A SONG (PSALM 7).

# DAVID AND HIS DECEPTION

In the morning David wrote a letter to Joab and sent it by the hand of Uriah. In the letter he wrote, "Set Uriah in the forefront of the hardest fighting, and then draw back from him, that he may be struck down, and die. (2 Samuel 11:14-15)

As I read these verses again, it's hard to comprehend that the Lord called David a man after God's own heart (1 Samuel 13:14). God knows everything, and in his omniscience, He knew David would commit murder. Even so, He still gives David this recognition. How can this be? We are talking about killing another human being, here!

Teens, I believe we are often snookered into thinking that our sin stands by itself; when I choose to sin, it's "one and done." In believing this, we are deceived in two ways. First, our sin does not affect others. Second, I may sin by doing ________, but it does not mean that I will do ________. If we believe this, we are wrong on both accounts.

My sin *always* affects at least one other person, even if that person is myself. Also, when we disobey God, it is easy to do commit all kinds of sin. David's one-night stand turned into a pregnancy, which turned into lies and deceit, which turned into murder. I have to think that David thought it would end that night with Bathsheba. It didn't. Without God's forgiveness, our sin ultimately ensnares and kills us.

When we deceive, we not only lie to others, but we also deceive ourselves. Let me add my voice to others in your life that urge you to *always tell the truth!* Don't let the fear of painful consequences stop you from doing what is right.

Remember this: deception is of the devil – he is the father of lies, and his goal is to get you to live for yourself. Live for eternity instead!

🡅 READ A NARRATIVE (2 SAMUEL 11:6-13) OR A SONG (PSALM 143).

## DAVID AND HIS MURDER

"WHY HAVE YOU DESPISED THE WORD OF THE LORD, TO DO WHAT IS EVIL IN HIS SIGHT? YOU HAVE STRUCK DOWN URIAH THE HITTITE WITH THE SWORD AND HAVE TAKEN HIS WIFE TO BE YOUR WIFE AND HAVE KILLED HIM WITH THE SWORD OF THE AMMONITES." (2 SAMUEL 12:9)

No, David did not kill Uriah with his own hands - he allowed the enemy to do it in battle - but the king orchestrated the event. As directed, Commander Joab pulled back the front line in the heat of a battle, and Uriah was exposed as a target. A good man died that day, murdered by the very one to whom he had committed his loyalty.

David... what happened to you?

Some say that murder is an unforgiveable sin. The Bible does not state this - and if we believe what Jesus said, we are all guilty of murder (see Matthew 5:21-26). Not only that, we are also the ones who put Jesus on a cross. Though we were not present, our sin killed the Savior.

The consequences for David? "Now therefore the sword shall never depart from your house, because you have despised me and have taken the wife of Uriah the Hittite to be your wife" (2 Samuel 12:10).

However, a true child of God is never beyond His love. In David's life, this meant judgment from the Lord, but also forgiveness and grace. The Bible gives us accounts like this so that we can understand how God works. Murder is one of the worst things we can do, and it comes with grave consequences, but murder cannot eternally keep us from the Father. Always, always, He seeks those who will repent.

"Lord, the sum of my sins is far deeper than a single act of murder. Christ took them away for me at Calvary. I repent... please forgive me!"

↑ READ THE NARRATIVE (2 SAMUEL 11:14-26) OR A SONG (PSALM 38).

## DAVID AND HIS KINDNESS

AND DAVID SAID TO HIM, "DO NOT FEAR, FOR I WILL SHOW YOU KINDNESS FOR THE SAKE OF YOUR FATHER JONATHAN, AND I WILL RESTORE TO YOU ALL THE LAND OF SAUL YOUR FATHER, AND YOU SHALL EAT AT MY TABLE ALWAYS." (2 SAMUEL 9:6-7)

Before we learn about David's disastrous sin in 2 Samuel 11, we read about Mephibosheth. It's a great story! In fact, the best stories are often the ones that deal with the theme of redemption. Welcome to the redemption of Mephibosheth.

For starters, let's remember that in ancient times it was not unusual for a conquering king to stamp out the family of the conquered. Can you imagine if that happened in America today? A new president wiping out the family of the previous leader? That's a crazy thought... and one that makes me thankful for the type of government we have in the U.S.

It's no reach to think that Mephibosheth would have been afraid for his life. Not only was he one of King Saul's only family survivors, he was also crippled. Why would *he* be allowed to live? But good King David had other plans. He loved Mephibosheth's father Jonathan, and he wanted to do the right thing. Not only did Mephibosheth get to keep his life, but he "ate at David's table, like one of the king's sons" (2 Samuel 9:11). By sparing this cripple, the king kept a promise he made to Saul himself (see 1 Samuel 24:21, 22).

Tell me, teens – who else received our worst, yet gave us his best? That would be Jesus, the kindest of them all. We spat on him, and mocked him, and ultimately, we killed him; but he came back to life and offered us eternity with him. What amazing love! David did a Jesus thing by extending his kindness to a "dead dog" (2 Samuel 9:8). Likewise, may our kindness also reveal the Savior, who kindly gave us all things.

READ THE NARRATIVE (2 SAMUEL 9) OR A SONG (PSALM 101).

# DAVID AND HIS MORAL ABSENCE

THUS ABSALOM DID TO ALL OF ISRAEL WHO CAME TO THE KING FOR JUDGMENT. SO ABSALOM STOLE THE HEARTS OF THE MEN OF ISRAEL. (2 SAMUEL 15:6)

Absalom, the deceiving son of David, wanted the kingdom for himself. Rather than taking the king head on, he chose the passive-aggressive approach. At a time when David himself was passively ruling, his son stepped in and took matters into his own hands. The day finally came when Absalom felt it was time to make his move, and his father had to flee the capital to save his life.

Keep in mind that 2 Samuel 11-14 comes before 2 Samuel 15 (obviously!). Why is that important? Because in chapter 11, we read about adultery, lies, and murder; in chapter 12, we have the death of an infant; in 13, we have rape and murder; and in 14, we have a guilty son weaseling his way back into Jerusalem. Imagine if one of our presidents had this drama taking place in his family. Can anyone say "impeachment"?

The father (David) did something terribly wrong, and his kids stopped listening to him. The boys lost their faith in their dad; David lost his moral high ground because he gave into lust and so much more.

Dear teens, you are so close to adulthood. The older you get, the more it becomes crucial that you choose right over wrong. When we cross the line into what is evil, we cannot control the outcome. Though David's sons were responsible for their own actions, we know that David had to live with his failure for the rest of his life. If he could do it all over again, he would have not crossed that line.

Teens, be morally present! Sin always comes with a high price tag.

🡅 READ THE NARRATIVE (2 SAMUEL 15:1-14) OR A SONG (PSALM 3).

## DAVID AND HIS SORROW

AND THE KING WAS DEEPLY MOVED AND WENT UP TO THE CHAMBER OVER THE GATE AND WEPT. AND AS HE WENT, HE SAID, "O MY SON ABSALOM, MY SON, MY SON ABSALOM! WOULD I HAD DIED INSTEAD OF YOU, O ABSALOM, MY SON, MY SON!" (2 SAMUEL 18:33)

The greatest fear of any parent is to see the loss of a child. As terrible as Absalom was to his father, King David was crushed by the death of his son. When you read the verse above, can you just hear the anguish in his voice? Not only is David dealing with the loss of Absalom, I believe he also recognized that his own sin led to the rebellion of his son. Would Absalom have tried to take over Israel from a morally present father? It makes you wonder.

David had many sorrows in his life, and he wrote about them in the form of songs. His many psalms are a gift to us, as they teach us how to handle our sorrow.

Teens, many of you have dealt with tragedy and suffering in your young lives. Have you ever taken the time to write down your thoughts? Take this a step further: have you ever written them to God above?

When we suffer pain and agony in our own lives, we can relate with David. We discover that God does not ask us to just "deal with it"; no, he wants us to work through the pain with the knowledge that He is the answer to it.

The wonderful thing with the laments we read in the Psalms is that they end in hope. Whether it is the loss of a child, or the pain of being bullied, or the plight of being an orphan, or anything else lamentable, God understands - and He acts in our behalf. "O LORD my God, I cried to you for help, and you have healed me" (Psalm 30:2).

↑ READ THE NARRATIVE (2 SAMUEL 18:29-19:8) OR A SONG (PSALM 56).

# DAVID AND HIS DISCERNMENT

AND DAVID SAID TO THE GIBEONITES, "WHAT SHALL I DO FOR YOU? AND HOW SHALL I MAKE ATONEMENT, THAT YOU MAY BLESS THE HERITAGE OF THE LORD?" (2 SAMUEL 21:3)

The Gibeonites were a protected people group. Originally, they were a people group that would have been targeted for destruction in the days of Joshua, but they deceptively made a treaty to ensure their safety (the story is found in Joshua 9). Fast forward to the days of King Saul, and we learn that he killed an unknown amount of Gibeonites. God did not forget the evil done by Saul; He saw fit to bring a judgment upon Israel for it during the reign of David.

The judgment for Saul's wickedness was a three-year famine. None of this was David's fault, yet he had to deal with it. I'm not sure what I would have done, but David responded to the Gibeonites with great discernment. He asked the questions in the verse above, and the response is a demand for an execution – the death of seven male descendants of Saul. The Bible does not say that David wrestled with this request, but I'm sure it would have been hard to say yes.

However, David did the right thing. These descendants of Saul would be put to death. The Gibeonites would be avenged, and the famine would be stopped.

We recognize David's tremendous character when he made this tough decision. Time and time again, David chose pain and suffering over doing what was easy. In his discernment, he determined that doing the right thing was the right thing to do! In my own life, I know I admire the men and women in my life who put the bigger picture ahead of their own agenda. They are the ones who have shown me what it means to "count the cost." May God grant us discernment to do the same.

🡅 READ THE NARRATIVE (2 SAMUEL 21:1-14) OR A SONG (PSALM 11).

# DAVID AND HIS PRIDE

SO THE KING SAID TO JOAB, THE COMMANDER OF THE ARMY, WHO WAS WITH HIM, "GO THROUGH ALL THE TRIBES OF ISRAEL, FROM DAN TO BEERSHEBA, AND NUMBER THE PEOPLE, THAT I MAY KNOW THE NUMBER OF THE PEOPLE." (2 SAMUEL 24:2)

Pride - it's so devastating! It sneaks up on us like a lion in the jungle. It causes us to think that we are the humblest person in the world... and we are proud of it! David had added pride to his kingly resume when he decided to count of soldiers in his army.

Why was numbering the army such a big deal? Don't we want to know the number of personnel in our own armed forces today? David's decision was in direct contrast to what he wrote himself in Psalm 20:7 ("Some trust in chariots and some in horses, but we trust in the name of the LORD our God.") We may need to know how many men and women we have in the U.S. military, but David was supposed to rely completely on God for the protection of Israel. If God told David to take a count, that would be one thing; but since He did not, we clearly see that the king is doing it in his pride. There really was no need to number the fighting men – even his army commander questioned it – but the king failed the test, and the nation would suffer as a result.

Satan's problem with pride got him kicked out of Heaven. Formerly known as Lucifer, he was quite an amazingly creature (some would refer to Ezekiel 28:11-19 here as a description of Satan before his fall). His chosen weapon against mankind is often pride. It is one of three categories that sums up our sin ("the pride of life" is a direct reference from 1 John 2:16). He used it to cause our own fall in Adam and Eve.

If pride was the original sin that condemned the devil to eternal darkness, dare we practice the same thing?

↑ READ THE NARRATIVE (2 SAMUEL 24) OR A SONG (PSALM 32).

# DAVID AND HIS HOLY DESIRE

AND YOUR HOUSE AND YOUR KINGDOM SHALL BE MADE SURE FOREVER BEFORE ME. YOUR THRONE SHALL BE ESTABLISHED FOREVER. (2 SAMUEL 7:16)

If you could pick a place on earth for God to live, where would you choose? A castle? A palace? A beautiful island? A high mountaintop?

How about a tent?

*A tent?* Really? No way! But indeed, a tent was God's accommodations for several centuries. David wanted to see this changed, so he talked to Nathan the prophet about what could be done. Nathan told him, "Go for it!" But God told Nathan, "Wait just a minute!" It would not be David who built a glorious temple for God to live amongst His people (his son Solomon would have the honor). David's desire was to be the man who gave God a "proper home", but God's desire did not match David's. He told him, "You may not build a house for my name, for you are a man of war and have shed blood" (1 Chronicles 28:3).

Yet God understands our hearts, and He blessed David for his desire to serve the Lord. David had a physical structure in mind, but the Lord gave him something far better: "When your days are fulfilled and you lie down with your fathers, I will raise up your offspring after you, who shall come from your body, and I will establish his kingdom. He shall build a house for my name, and I will establish the throne of his kingdom forever" (2 Samuel 7:12-13). David's offspring was none other than Jesus himself. That's awesome!

Teens, I encourage you today to pray over your desires. Do they please God? His plans are going to be accomplished, no matter what. How great it is when our desires align with His sovereign will.

READ THE NARRATIVE (2 SAMUEL 7) OR A SONG (PSALM 45).

## DAVID AND HIS FINAL DAYS

THEN DAVID SLEPT WITH HIS FATHERS AND WAS BURIED IN THE CITY OF DAVID. AND THE TIME THAT DAVID REIGNED OVER ISRAEL WAS FORTY YEARS. HE REIGNED SEVEN YEARS IN HEBRON AND THIRTY-THREE YEARS IN JERUSALEM. (1 KINGS 2:10-11)

Whether we like it or not, we are often defined by certain events in our lives. For some, that defining moment will be during their final days on earth. The struggle against sin is still very real for those who make it to the later years. Case in point - we can read of many good kings in the Bible that failed at the end of their lives. In spite of all the failures that David experienced in his life, I am thankful that his life ended well.

At the beginning of 1 Kings, the king is very frail. He cannot keep his body temperature up, and in his weakness, one of his sons tries to take the kingdom by force (not the first time it happened to him!). Yet David rallies himself to make sure that Solomon takes his promised position as king, according to the will of God. He also gives his son some final instructions in dealing with matters that he would leave behind.

Teens, in this life, we will never arrive at perfection. We never even get to an age where we are "good enough." The battle against sin is an ongoing battle, and we will lose if we decide to take off our spiritual armor. It scares me to think that I could choose to stop fighting as an older man. I don't want to drag my feet to the finish line!

I challenge you, in the strongest of terms, to follow the example of David, and also that of Paul: "I have fought the good fight, I have finished the race, I have kept the faith" (2 Timothy 4:7). The good king could say this as he breathed his last in his final days.

↑ READ THE NARRATIVE (1 KINGS 2:1-12) OR A SONG (2 SAMUEL 22).

# DAVID AND HIS LEGACY

"AND AS FOR YOU, IF YOU WALK BEFORE ME, AS DAVID YOUR FATHER WALKED, WITH INTEGRITY OF HEART AND UPRIGHTNESS, DOING ACCORDING TO ALL I HAVE COMMANDED YOU, AND KEEPING MY STATUTES AND MY RULES, THEN I WILL ESTABLISH YOUR ROYAL THRONE OVER ISRAEL FOREVER, AS I PROMISED DAVID YOUR FATHER, SAYING, 'YOU SHALL NOT LACK A MAN ON THE THRONE OF ISRAEL.'" (1 KINGS 9:4-5)

What a wonderful promise to the son of Israel's greatest king! David left an incredible legacy to Solomon. When we read about the reign of Solomon, we see a king who was given the gift of wisdom, and he led well for a good part of his life. Sadly, he would not leave the same kind of legacy as did his father (he allowed himself to embrace idolatry); yet Solomon's failures could not annul God's promises to David.

This is not the first time that God speaks about the character of David after his death. When we read about the life and times of Israel's kings, his name often pops up. The Lord chose to honor David with a promise of being the kingly root for the King of kings. He also spared Israel from certain destruction based upon this promise. When Jesus came into the world, we read that the Jews still recognized David's prominence in their history. His name shows up a lot in the four gospels (and Jesus himself was referred to as "the son of David").

Teens, at this point of your lives, it's hard to grasp the importance of a legacy. Old age seems so far away. So perhaps you can think about your immediate family instead. Consider your parents and grandparents. Generally speaking, you are who you are because of them. What kind of legacy are they leaving you? Do you want to be the same person? Why, or why not? Even now, as a teenager, you are building a legacy!

The beauty of David's legacy is not one of a sinless life – it's one of a forgiven life.

🡅 READ THE NARRATIVE (1 KINGS 9:1-9) OR A SONG (PSALM 25).

## PRAYING FOR OUR ENEMIES?

"AND SHOULD I NOT PITY NINEVEH, THAT GREAT CITY, IN WHICH THERE ARE MORE THAN 120.000 PERSONS WHO DO NOT KNOW THEIR RIGHT HAND FROM THERE LEFT, AND ALSO MUCH CATTLE?" (JONAH 4:11)

Nineveh would have been the Berlin of WWII, or the Moscow of the Cold War era, or perhaps the Tehran of the current war on terror. Cities in history, feared and hated, because of their tremendous power to wield evil. If Jonah were alive and knew the kind of weapons we have today, he would have asked God to "nuke 'em!"

However, God gave the wicked Assyrians a reprieve. Why? Well... because they actually repented! They realized that God was going to judge them for their wickedness, so they sought forgiveness. The city that was known for skinning its prisoners alive was given a chance to change their ways. And Jonah, who eventually showed up to share a message of hope (his journey to Nineveh is a whale of a story!), hated God's offer of compassion.

How about us? Think of the world we live in. Would we pray for the terrorists? Would we ask God to forgive them? It is easy to say, "They don't deserve God's forgiveness!" Well, that's true. They don't! Here's the problem, though... I don't deserve it, either. I'm also guilty, as charged. Thank God that someone(s) prayed for me.

Let's make this personal. What about those who have hurt you? Can you forgive them, as your heavenly Father has forgiven you?

Romans 5:10 reminds us that we were once the enemies of God, but He still reconciled us through the death of His Son. That says it all!

↑ READ OF THIS RECONCILIATION IN ROMANS 5:9-11, THEN READ OF JONAH'S PREDICAMENT IN JONAH 4.

# WHEN OUR PARENTS SIN BEFORE THE LORD

THE SOUL WHO SINS SHALL DIE. THE SON SHALL NOT SUFFER FOR THE INIQUITY OF THE FATHER, NOR THE FATHER SUFFER FOR THE INIQUITY OF THE SON. THE RIGHTEOUSNESS OF THE RIGHTEOUS SHALL BE UPON HIMSELF, AND THE WICKEDNESS OF THE WICKED SHALL BE UPON HIMSELF. (EZEKIEL 18:20)

The people of Israel had the saying, "The fathers have eaten sour grapes, and the children's teeth are set on edge." Basically, they claimed that the wrongdoing of the parents led to equal or worse judgment upon the children. It was a saying that God denied (look at Ezekiel 18:1-4). We alone are responsible to do what is right, for "the soul who sins shall die" (vs. 20).

As a youth pastor, I have heard a number of stories about how parents have legitimately wronged their teenage children. We are talking about some serious stuff here – as in *deliberate* acts of wickedness. Some of you may be carrying the weight of that heavy burden. I grieve for you.

However, please do not believe that you are responsible for the God-ordained consequences of their decisions. When parents purposely decide to do what is wrong, they stand alone before God and answer for their actions. The Bible says that He does not hold you accountable for the sin of your parents. Knowing this truth is freedom; you are free to do what is right and good, since your parents' sin does not condemn you to a life of guilt and punishment.

In the Lord, you are free! May He help you to honor your parents (remember, it is one of the Ten Commandments), and may He help you overcome any resulting hardship as you seek His will in your life.

CHECK OUT THE CONTEXT OF THESE THOUGHTS IN EZEKIEL 18:19-32.

# NICE

"But the fruit of the Spirit is love, joy, peace, patience, kindness, goodness, faithfulness, gentleness, self-control; against such things there is no law." (Galatians 5:22-23)

Once upon a time, some nice words were given by a popular world leader. His thoughts included an offered prayer for blessing upon the work of his nation and courage to do what was right. He shared a belief that men were created for God's will and purpose. He expressed that he was powerless outside of the blessing from the Lord above.

Sounds like a man that we could follow, right? The man who said these nice words of inspiration was Adolf Hitler. If you were to study the history of the man, you also recognize that he was a liar and deceiver, and he went on to do the unthinkable to the Jews during WWII.

Did you know that the word "nice" is not even found in the Bible? The word "kindness" is used, but the two words do not have the same meaning. *Kindness* refers to moral excellence, whereas *nice* is focused upon a demeanor, or a set of culturally-recognized positive actions (regardless of morality). "Nice" is a term that is changeable in nature. God does not change; thus, it cannot be a word that best describes Him. His children are to be known by the fruits of the Spirit. Don't be fooled; "nice" is not one of those fruits!

Teens, don't place your trust in "nice." Too many young people are led astray by nice people. Instead, trust God, who cannot and will not lead us astray. He will not fool you!

↑ RECOGNIZE THE FRUITS OF THE SPIRIT. READ MORE ABOUT KINDNESS VS. NICE IN 2 SAMUEL 2:1-7!

# THE COURAGE TO WALK AWAY

REPAY NO ONE EVIL FOR EVIL, BUT GIVE THOUGHT TO DO WHAT IS HONORABLE IN THE SIGHT OF ALL. (ROMANS 12:17)

Which takes more courage - to stand up and fight, or to turn and walk away?

We are commanded to flee temptation. It is easy to give in and fight against an enemy. It isn't easy to allow God to take vengeance in His own time.

Most of our fights are not physical in nature, but instead, they are a war of words. How many battles are fought on social media? How many punches are thrown in texts and messages? These online fights are ways that people repay evil for evil. Rather than speak face to face, many choose the easy way out, and they get all tough and nasty behind the safety of their technology. Through social media, the consequences may be delayed, but the consequences are still very real.

Teens, it's time to stop being cowards. The right thing to do is to always walk away. Mature people hold their tongues by controlling their fingers (Proverbs 21:23 tells us, "Whoever keeps his mouth and his tongue keeps himself out of trouble"). Be courageous; just walk away! Two wrongs don't make a right. Your decision to fight back is that second wrong choice, and it is just as sinful as the first. "Do what is honorable in the sight of all."

Trust the Lord to handle your reputation. He knows what He is doing!

↑ THE BIBLE TALKS ABOUT AMAZIAH'S LACK OF COURAGE TO WALK AWAY IN 2 KINGS 14:1-21.

## THE POSTURE OF PRAYER

THEN SOLOMON STOOD BEFORE THE ALTAR OF THE LORD IN THE PRESENCE OF ALL THE ASSEMBLY OF ISRAEL AND SPREAD OUT HIS HANDS TOWARD HEAVEN. (1 KINGS 8:22)

Sitting. Lying down. Kneeling. Standing up, with arms outstretched. Laying prostrate, face down. All completely acceptable positions for prayer. None is holier than the other. All are meant to reflect a heart that is humble in the knowledge of this wonderful privilege.

As we read the Bible, we see many postures of prayer. With that said, how do we know when it is appropriate to sit, or kneel, or stand? We can take our cues from the contexts we read in the Bible. As a king and mediator of a nation, King Solomon stood on his feet to speak to the Lord. As a recipient of overwhelming revelation, John prostrated himself before God and the angels who delivered the messages. As a humble servant who looked for the redemption of Israel, Daniel got on his knees three times a day to pray toward Jerusalem.

Our habits in prayer reflect our relationship with God. So let's consider these questions when we pray: "What do we think of God? How well do we know Him? Should our prayer posture reflect that knowledge? How does one approach our Lord, or our King, or our Savior, or our Brother, or our Friend, or our Father?" Do we remember that God is all of these, and is that important enough to guide our posture in prayer?

May we meditate on how God is revealing Himself to us each day, and may this knowledge move us to respond accordingly.

↑ DANIEL IS AMAZING! SEE HIS COURAGEOUS PRAYER IN DANIEL 6.

## ON THE ROAD TO NOWHERE (1 OF 2)

BUT MY PEOPLE HAVE FORGOTTEN ME; THEY MAKE OFFERINGS TO FALSE GODS; THEY MADE THEM STUMBLE IN THEIR WAYS, IN THE ANCIENT ROADS, AND TO WALK INTO SIDE ROADS, NOT THE HIGHWAY, MAKING THEIR LAND A HORROR, A THING TO BE HISSED AT FOREVER. (JEREMIAH 18:15-16A)

Are you a "let's see where this road goes!" kind of person? I am! And I still love figuring out how to get to certain places by using an old-fashioned atlas. At first, it was a bit hard for me when technology was developed to follow a map via satellite, but now, I usually type in the destination and listen to the directions. It's boring for me, but for some reason, my wife does not like it when I get lost following the atlas!

Spiritually, we were also given a map. God gave us one path to follow; His Bible is the compass of our lives. Yet, like Israel, we often follow exit signs to roads that lead to nowhere. They are the "ancient roads" and "side roads" spoken of in Jeremiah. Yet here we are, ready to explore them anyway. Drive on them long enough, and you'll discover that they all will take you on a path to destruction.

By following wisdom, we follow the right road. Listen to Proverbs 3:17: "Her (wisdom) ways are ways of pleasantness, and all her paths are peace." Oh, that we would live in wisdom! Truly, we were made to enjoy pleasure and peace. Only a fool would run away from this offer.

Dear teens, I pray you will not turn to travel on the road to nowhere. "In all your ways acknowledge him, and he will make straight your paths" (Proverbs 3:6). The Lord knows the way – follow His map!

↑ PLEASE READ PROVERBS 3:1-18.

## "ON THE ROAD TO NOWHERE" (2 OF 2)

LET NOT YOUR HEART TURN ASIDE TO HER WAYS; DO NOT STRAY INTO HER PATHS, FOR MANY A VICTIM HAS SHE LAID LOW, AND ALL HER SLAIN ARE A MIGHTY THRONG. (PROVERBS 7:25-26)

You are driving on the interstate. It's a long drive, and you are becoming bored. You want to get off, even though you know you really should press on. Then you notice a big green exit sign up ahead. This one says, "ALCOHOLISM, 2 MILES". What?!! No way will you take that exit! A few minutes later, there is another sign: "PORNOGRAPHY, ½ MILE". Are you kidding? You need to stay on the main road, that's for sure! Yet the end of the journey is so, so far away. Maybe there is another exit that you can take?

As you consider that option, a third sign appears: "BAD NEWS GIRLFRIEND, 5 MILES". Hmmm. What should you do? In the past, you've never considered where this road might take you.

Before you know it, the exit is upon you. Not knowing what to do always leads the soul away from the main road, so you take the exit. At first, you are happy ("Wow, check out this road! There is so much to do! Good-bye, boredom!"). And so you drive fast, and it's really fun, and the interstate becomes a spec in the rearview mirror. You lose all track of time, and you throw common sense out the window. But soon enough, "BAD NEWS GIRLFRIEND" leaves you with no fuel in a broken-down vehicle on the wrong side of the tracks. Welcome to the town of "NOWHERE".

Teens, God's paths are not always the easiest, but they are not meant to be easy. The long drive on HIs road shapes our lives. So please (I beg you!) stay on wisdom's path. It is the only road that leads to home.

🠝 READ PROVERBS 3:19-35 TODAY.

## SILENT BEFORE THE SOVEREIGN LORD

BE SILENT BEFORE THE LORD GOD! FOR THE DAY OF THE LORD IS NEAR; THE LORD HAS PREPARED A SACRIFICE AND CONSECRATED HIS GUESTS. (ZEPHANIAH 1:7)

"Wait until your father gets home!" were not my favorite words growing up. Sometimes my mom handled the discipline, but most of the time, my dad did it. When I did something wrong and had to wait for dad to come home from work... not good!

By the time King Josiah came to the throne of Judah, the kingdom was all but conquered. Josiah was one of the good kings; as a result, God gave Judah a short reprieve. Zephaniah was written in those days. Like most of the prophets, he had to pronounce harsh words to the people. Sadly, they would not listen... once Josiah died, the remaining kings were evil, and their reigns were short-lived.

There have been times in my life when I did something so bad, I just knew that I needed to be quiet and face the music. Judah should have known the truth about their sin and what their Almighty God would do. "The day of the LORD" was not something these Jews could look for with hope and joy, for their evil and wickedness had reached its limit. That day would be one of judgment: a removal of the people from their promised land.

To various degrees, we all struggle with sin. So join me in times when we choose to stop talking and just listen. To recognize God's justified wrath means we put a hand over our mouth and remain silent before the Sovereign Lord. It is a "shhh, be quiet!" kind of moment.

🡅 ZEPHANIAH 1:1-13 – REAL, JUSTIFIED, AND COMPLETE JUDGMENT FROM GOD AGAINST JUDAH.

# I'M DEPRESSED!

YOU WILL KEEP IN PERFECT PEACE WHOSE MIND IS STAYED ON YOU, BECAUSE HE TRUSTS IN YOU. (ISAIAH 26:3)

Depression. I have much to learn about the topic. But I know it is prevalent, as I seen my share of teenagers go through it. We are richly blessed as a nation, yet there are so many depressed Americans.

Sometimes we use the meaning of the word *depression* too lightly. In today's reading, we're talking about clinical depression (not "I can't see my boyfriend today, so I'm depressed!"). Real depression leaves us in a dark place where we've lost our way, believing we'll never make it out.

A devotion is a short piece of writing, and it cannot possibly cover all the attention this subject deserves. However, would we be willing to consider today that depression can be caused by our sin? It seems that people are very quick to dismiss their sin as a possible root cause for depression. Other solutions are introduced to overcome depression, and the real problem may never be dealt with in our lives. Sadly, we are often convinced that addressing a sin problem is the worst thing that could ever happen to us, so we eliminate this as a possibility.

What if we prayed and asked God about any sin in our lives, confessing it to Him? At the end of Psalm 139, David asks God to search him. He also sought a mind stayed on the Lord, desiring His perfect peace.

If you are depressed, there is hope in the Lord! If you think that your sin may be the cause of your depression, please ask Him to reveal this to you. How sweet it is when we have a close relationship with God. In the context of spiritual healing, "The prayer of a righteous person has great power as it is working." (James 5:16).

READ PSALM 23.

# DOES TIME HEAL ALL WOUNDS?

MOREOVER, THE LIGHT OF THE MOON WILL BE AS THE LIGHT OF THE SUN, AND THE LIGHT OF THE SUN WILL BE SEVENFOLD, AS THE LIGHT OF SEVEN DAYS, IN THE DAY WHEN THE LORD BINDS UP THE BROKENNESS OF HIS PEOPLE, AND HEALS THE WOUNDS INFLICTED BY HIS BLOW. (ISAIAH 30:26)

Time is a powerful reality! However, does time have healing powers?

We have heard it said, "Time heals all wounds". In my experience, the ones who say this are usually good people. Often, they are also people who have "been there, done that" in their lives. I get the gist of their advice - allow time to take place, because the worst of our pain is at the beginning of a loss (like the initial days after losing a loved one).

Yet in Christ, we are new creations. Our healing is directly tied to the Healer. I cannot put my faith in the passing of days, months, or years to get feeling better inside. I must go to Him for what ails my soul. He knows all things, and His medicine of peace, comfort, and hope are just what the doctor ordered (or, in this case, the Great Physician). Time itself can be fickle; we wait and wait and hope for the best, when really, we are just burying symptoms of the sickness we carry. Only God knows how to heal the hurting, and only God can give the hurting the rest they need.

You may have been abused, or beaten, or disregarded as worthless. As time goes on, you discover that you don't feel any better; in fact, you feel worse, even though the source of pain was so long ago. You have a choice - you can go and do something that will numb the pain, or you can go to the only One who can heal you. What will you do?

Every saved soul is given the privilege of healing in God's arms.

↑ WHAT DOES MALACHI 4 SAY ABOUT HEALING? READ IT TODAY!

# WHAT'S KEEPING YOU FROM BELIEVING?

MANY OF THE JEWS THEREFORE, WHO HAD COME WITH MARY AND HAD SEEN WHAT HE DID, BELIEVED IN HIM, BUT SOME OF THEM WENT TO THE PHARISEES AND TOLD THEM WHAT JESUS HAD DONE. (JOHN 11:45-46)

SO THE CHIEF PRIESTS MADE PLANS TO PUT LAZARUS TO DEATH AS WELL, BECAUSE ON ACCOUNT OF HIM MANY OF THE JEWS WERE GOING AWAY AND BELIEVING IN JESUS. (JOHN 12:10-11)

What will it take for you to believe that Jesus died for your sins? What has to happen for you to repent? What requirements do you have in order to follow him?

Would you be satisfied if Jesus did the following?

1 Showed up at your doorstep and performed a miracle for you alone.
2. Made everything that is painful in your life go away.
3. Let you live your life the way you want, with the expectation that you would gain entrance into heaven.
4. Brought vengeance upon all the people who hurt you.
5. Did something amazing for the public, like walk on water, provide a feast from a lunch box, heal the blind and the deaf, or perhaps even raise a dead person to life.

Jesus did all of this; there is nothing more that he needs to do. Nothing! In his life, He performed many signs, wonders, and miracles, and finally conquered death at the cross. After even all of this, there were many who still did not believe.

What about you? What's keeping you from believing?

↑ NOT EVEN THOSE FROM CHRIST'S HOMETOWN BELIEVED HIM FOR HIS MIRACLES. READ MARK 6:1-6 TO SEE HOW THEY REACTED TO JESUS.

# OUR RELATIONSHIP WITH THE CHURCH

LET NOT YOUR HEARTS BE TROUBLED. BELIEVE IN GOD; BELIEVE ALSO IN ME. IN MY FATHER'S HOUSE ARE MANY ROOMS. IF IT WERE NOT SO, WOULD I HAVE TOLD YOU THAT I GO TO PREPARE A PLACE FOR YOU? AND IF I GO AND PREPARE A PLACE FOR YOU, I WILL COME AGAIN AND TAKE YOU TO MYSELF, THAT WHERE I AM YOU MAY BE ALSO. (JOHN 14:1-3)

In the Bible, our relationship with God is revealed in many levels. Each level is wonderful and undeserved. As you search the Scriptures, you will find that we are slaves to the Lord, servants of God, a holy nation unto the King, children of the heavenly Father, brothers and sisters to God's Son, and the bride of Jesus Christ. That final description is expressed in John 14:1-3; you also can read about the bride of Christ in Ephesians 5 and Revelation 21, 22.

The marriage of a husband and wife offers the greatest relationship opportunity that two humans can share. Sadly, many marriages fail, and many more never make it to their greatest fulfillment. Yet every man and woman that says "I do" places their hope in a future that resembles the one described between Christ and his church. He loves her dearly, and she is called to love him in return.

What do you think of God's church? We know what God thinks – she is the bride of His Son. Do you see her in the same way?

If I said to one of my married friends, "You're a great guy, but I really don't like your wife!", how would that make him feel? I would deserve to get punched! Keep in mind that people do this when they reject the church. Essentially, we tell God that His Son is not good enough.

I challenge us today to love His church, for when we hold this relationship in its rightful place, we are also loving our own souls.

🡅 BELIEVERS WILL EXPERIENCE THE HOLY CITY AS A BRIDE – READ ABOUT IT IN REVELATION 21!

# THE PURPOSE OF THE TEST

AND SO IN THE MATTER OF THE ENVOYS OF THE PRINCES OF BABYLON, WHO HAD BEEN SENT TO HIM TO INQUIRE ABOUT THE SIGN THAT HAD BEEN DONE IN THE LAND, GOD LEFT HIM TO HIMSELF, IN ORDER TO TEST HIM AND TO KNOW ALL THAT WAS IN HIS HEART. (2 CHRONICLES 32:31)

King Hezekiah was a good king. However, he also made some very poor choices. On one occasion, he decided to show some messengers from Babylon the riches of his kingdom. Judah had just come off a God-given victory over Assyria, their enemy and ruling empire of that time. Shortly afterward, Babylonian visitors arrive. Rather than protecting the sanctity of God's temple and nation, we read in the verse above that the king shows off to the future destroyer of Jerusalem. In the alternate account found in 2 Kings 20, the Bible records that Hezekiah was at peace with the fact that God would bring destruction at a later date, since it would not happen in his lifetime. How sad... and how selfish! Hezekiah, what were you thinking?

Why did the LORD test men like Hezekiah? For that matter, why does He test us? The Bible teaches us that the Lord is omniscient – He knows everything. In that omniscience, He knew what Hezekiah would decide to do. But God also allows Himself to "know" through experiences with us within the realm of time. He interjects Himself into our world in such a way that He goes through the situation AND controls the outcome.

Testing is ultimately not for God's benefit. It is for ours. Like many kings before him, Hezekiah would learn that he was weak in the area of pride. He would have the choice to grow from his failed test. His subjects would also be given the opportunity to learn from his failure. And as the readers of the text, we have the same opportunity!

May we humble ourselves and learn from the tests of life.

↑ READ A SUMMARY OF HEZEKIAH'S LIFE IN 2 CHRONICLES 32:24-33.

# I'LL SERVE YOU, GOD! WHATEVER YOU WANT!

AND HE SAID TO HIM, "YOU SHALL LOVE THE LORD YOUR GOD WITH ALL YOUR HEART AND WITH ALL YOUR SOUL AND WITH ALL YOUR MIND." (MATTHEW 22:37)

*"I'll serve You, God! Whatever You want! Just right now, though, I am kind of busy. I'm just a teenager! I've got to work on getting my license, figure out where to go to college, play soccer for my school, and hang out with friends. But when I graduate, I'm all Yours!"*

*"I'll serve You, God! Whatever You want! But you know that I've been married a couple years... and now we have a baby! This apartment we live in is way too small. The house we are looking at is going to mean jobs for both of us. I'm sure You're ok if I sleep in Sundays, right? But once we get our house, I'm all Yours!"*

*"I'll serve You, God! Whatever You want! Our kids are about to graduate, and life will be different! Though I'm not sure when they will move out of the house, or how they are going to pay for college, or how they can afford a car. Somehow, when the kids are settled and I know their ok, I'm all Yours!"*

*"I'll serve You, God! Whatever You want! However, being retired means traveling, and oh, how we've been waiting for years now to go on long road trips! Anyway, what would the church think if we just started to show up after all this time? We would feel really embarrassed! But once we stay at home for good, I'm all Yours!"*

*"I'll serve You, God! Whatever you want! But how can I now, since the doctor says I have cancer and only a matter of weeks to live? Does it have to end this way? My kids and grandkids want nothing to do with You. Tragically, I served me, God. It was 'Whatever I want'."*

↑ CHECK OUT THE PARABLE OF THE RICH FOOL IN LUKE 12:13-21.

# WHEN SOMEONE MAKES FUN OF YOU (BY ALF WILKES)

AND HEROD AND HIS SOLDIERS TREATED HIM WITH CONTEMPT AND MOCKED HIM. THEN, ARRAYING HIM WITH SPLENDID CLOTHING, HE SENT HIM BACK TO PILATE. (LUKE 23:11)

I'm sorry. I really am. "Sorry? For what? You don't even know me." You're right, I don't know you. But what I do know is that if you are living and breathing, at some point in your life, someone has made fun of you. Even the best of friends can hurt us with their words.

When I was in school, I was not one of the popular kids. I never had the newest and coolest sneakers. Most of my clothes were hand-me-downs from others. And when my mom was able to buy me some new clothes, they came from the "husky boys" section of the store. I wasn't exactly a small kid. So trust me, I know what it is like to be made fun of.

Our verse today from the Gospel of Luke shows us that Jesus Himself was teased, mocked, made fun of, and bullied. Use whatever term you want to use, but the pain is still there. Make sure you read the Bible passage below from the book of Hebrews. There you will see that Jesus totally understands what you are going through when people make fun of you. People made fun of Jesus, too.

Unfortunately, we have little control over what other people think and say about us and to us. But like Jesus, we can control how we react to what others say. I encourage you to take time to read through the Gospels of Matthew, Mark, Luke and John. They will help you see how Jesus dealt with people who made fun of Him and rejected Him.

Let me also encourage you to treat others with kindness and speak only good things about others. Remember this: if words of OTHERS can hurt YOU, then YOUR words can hurt OTHERS, if you're not careful.

↑ PLEASE READ HEBREWS 4:12-16. TRULY, HE UNDERSTANDS.

# MAY

## "I WILL"

I WILL PUT ENMITY BETWEEN YOU AND THE WOMAN, AND BETWEEN YOUR OFFSPRING AND HER OFFSPRING; HE SHALL BRUISE YOUR HEAD, AND YOU SHALL BRUISE HIS HEEL. (GENESIS 3:15)

God. He is the Almighty One, the Creator of the Universe. He has made many promises in the Bible. In spite of God's many "credentials", people still question: "Can He keep *all* of those promises? Will He do *all* that He said He would do?"

When we question God's power to keep His word, we also question the future as revealed in Scripture. We doubt God, though He has fulfilled all things according to plan. When we doubt Him, it affects everything. Just think about the fear that exists concerning the end of the world. The Bible spells out how the end will come; yet countless theories abound outside of the Bible.

Teens, when we really study the Scriptures, we discover that the number of God's promises that are fulfilled are staggering! if you believe in God as "The Keeper of All Promises", I believe you will have no doubts about the future according to the Bible.

When God says "I will" in His Word, listen up! He makes an "I will" promise right off the bat to Adam and Eve during their final moments in the Garden of Eden. Much of this promise deals with the awful effects of sin (like painful child-bearing, difficulty in making a living, and challenges in the marriage). But there is also a statement of hope and redemption for mankind. The fulfillment of God's "I will" is found in Jesus Christ. Satan struck his heel (at the cross), but Jesus crushed his head (at the resurrection). If God can save the world through His Son, can He not fulfill the rest of His promises given to us?

🡅 CONCERNING THIS PROPHESIED "I WILL", READ GENESIS 3:14-24.

# I WILL MAKE HIM A HELPER

(THE PROMISED "I WILL"): THEN THE LORD GOD SAID, "IT IS NOT GOOD THAT THE MAN SHOULD BE ALONE; I WILL MAKE HIM A HELPER FIT FOR HIM." (GENESIS 2:18)

(THE FULFILLED "I WILL"): AND THE RIB THAT THE LORD GOD HAD TAKEN FROM THE MAN HE MADE INTO A WOMAN AND BROUGHT HER TO THE MAN. (GENESIS 2:22)

If our goal is to know the truth, then it is necessary for us to believe the Bible. Jesus believed it. In John 17:17, he prayed, "Sanctify them in the truth; your word is truth." God never uses words flippantly; His words are perfect, ordered, and measured.

Genesis 2:18 includes some of God's first words about man. Some details that I noticed include the following: 1. Man came first. 2. He should not be alone! 3. God provided a solution for man. 4. The solution was "suitable" (meaning, "exactly what the man needed").

Makes sense, right? However, you and I know that the relationship involving this first married couple is being redefined today. The attacks against marriage as a gift for a husband and wife come from outspoken unbiblical voices. As a result, we live with divorce, role identity issues, cohabitation, adultery, same-sex marriages, and many other problems.

But what if we just believed God? What if we believed that He provided the perfect solution for the best relationship of all? What if the traditional view is actually the timeless command? We watch the world around us run from God and His laws; at the same time, we also see the world falling apart, and we can't seem to figure out the problem.

"I will" give humanity the deepest of relationships, God tells us! So... do we believe it?

↑ READ MORE ABOUT THE MARRIAGE TRUTHS IN GENESIS 2:15-25.

# I WILL BLOT OUT MAN

(THE PROMISED "I WILL"): SO THE LORD SAID, "I WILL BLOT OUT MAN WHOM I HAVE CREATED FROM THE FACE OF THE LAND, MAN AND ANIMALS AND CREEPING THINGS AND BIRDS OF THE HEAVENS, FOR I AM SORRY THAT I HAVE MADE THEM." (GENESIS 6:7)

(THE FULFILLED "I WILL"): HE BLOTTED OUT EVERY LIVING THING THAT WAS ON THE FACE OF THE GROUND, MAN AND ANIMALS AND CREEPING THINGS AND BIRDS OF THE HEAVENS. THEY WERE BLOTTED OUT FROM THE EARTH. ONLY NOAH WAS LEFT, AND THOSE WHO WERE WITH HIM IN THE ARK. (GENESIS 7:23)

You may be surprised to discover that many of God's promises deal with matters of judgment. Since God must deal with sin, He has given promises that deal with the consequences of sin.

During the days before the flood, "The LORD saw that the wickedness of man was great in the earth, and that every intention of the thoughts of his heart was only evil continually" (Genesis 6:5). In His holy judgment against mankind, God deemed it necessary to flood the earth. We see proof of this flood today, from fossils on top of a mountain to the existence of the Grand Canyon. In His creation *and* destruction of that creation, God is awesome in power and might!

The time that it took God's spoken "I will" in Genesis 6 to the fulfillment of it in Genesis 7 included many years. People lived longer lives before the flood (Noah's ancestry itself recorded men living well over 900 years old!). Unbelievers would have had plenty of time to repent of their sin before the flood took place. Sadly, only Noah and his family boarded the ark in that final hour.

How much time do you have before God tells you that it's over? It's always less time than you think, even if you do live to be a ripe old age! Teens, if you are not saved, I beg you to repent, before it is too late.

↑ READ GENESIS 6:1-8 AND 7:11-24.

# I WILL REMEMBER MY COVENANT

(THE PROMISED "I WILL"): I WILL REMEMBER MY COVENANT THAT IS BETWEEN ME AND YOU AND EVERY LIVING CREATURE OF ALL FLESH. AND THE WATERS SHALL NEVER AGAIN BECOME A FLOOD TO DESTROY ALL FLESH. (GENESIS 9:15)

(THE FULFILLED "I WILL"): WHEN THE BOW IS IN THE CLOUDS, I WILL SEE IT AND REMEMBER THE EVERLASTING COVENANT BETWEEN GOD AND EVERY LIVING CREATURE OF ALL FLESH THAT IS ON THE EARTH. (GENESIS 9:16)

A rainbow. It's the sign of a promise. It's a promise from God to never, ever destroy the earth again by a flood. It is a symbol of peace for a world that deserves to be flooded. People may use the rainbow as a symbol for it's own purposes, but it will never cease to be a beautiful reminder of God's grace for us.

A covenant. By nature, it is serious, it is binding, and it comes with a promise. The Lord's covenant in Genesis 9 is not one that depends upon us to keep (thanks be to God for that!).

Do you think that God has the right to wipe out what He created? He sure does, and He used a world-wide flood changed everything. Name me another physical event like Noah's flood that altered the course of the entire planet. You won't find one! Yet, His rainbow reminds us that He remains patient and true to His covenant.

Do you believe in the truths of Genesis 1-11? It is the foundation upon which we build our faith. I know that it can be difficult to believe in a flood that was many centuries ago, but the proof is all around us. In fact, there is so much proof that it takes more faith *not* to believe.

May God cause us to believe in all of His promises. He is a covenant keeper, and we can trust Him.

🡅 STUDY GENESIS 9:1-17.

# I WILL MAKE OF YOU A GREAT NATION

(The promised "I will"): And I will make of you a great nation, and I will bless you and make your name great, so that you will be a blessing. (Genesis 12:2)

(The fulfilled "I will"): But the people of Israel were fruitful and increased greatly; they multiplied and grew exceedingly strong, so that the land was filled with them. (Exodus 1:7)

What an incredible book we have in Genesis! And what an incredible story we have in Abraham. We have the blessing of seeing how God made Israel into a great nation – both in quantity (many descendants of Israel have lived upon this earth) and quality (specifically, it is the nation that gave us our Savior). It started with Abraham.

Yet, this patriarch struggled with the "I will" of God in Genesis 12. And frankly, we would have, too. The promise of verse 2 came to a man who was childless for decades. The Bible makes it clear that he and his wife Sarah were past the time of childbearing (Hebrews 11:11-12 shares this truth). Yet in spite of their age (both were in their 90s!), faith finally won the day. The "I will" turned into Isaac, which turned into Jacob, which turned into 12 sons, which turned into tribes that together numbered in the millions, which turned into a nation that left Egypt and conquered the Promised Land.

The account of Abraham is yet another reminder to me that I should never doubt God. If He can do such great things in the life of one man, why can't He guide the history of the world to its intended end? He can, and He will!

Teens, live your life by faith in the Lord, and you will find His promises both true and transformative.

READ GENESIS 21:1-7 AND HEBREWS 11:11-12.

# I WILL STRIKE EGYPT

(THE PROMISED "I WILL"): SO I WILL STRETCH OUT MY HAND AND STRIKE EGYPT WITH ALL THE WONDERS THAT I WILL DO IN IT; AFTER THAT HE WILL LET YOU GO. (EXODUS 3:20)

(THE FULFILLED "I WILL"): THEN HE SUMMONED MOSES AND AARON BY NIGHT AND SAID, "UP, GO OUT FROM AMONG MY PEOPLE, BOTH YOU AND THE PEOPLE OF ISRAEL; AND GO, SERVE THE LORD, AS YOU HAVE SAID." (EXODUS 12:31)

It is quite incredible to think of how God brought about the birth of the United States. She was the ultimate underdog against England (a very powerful nation at the time). Yet, the Lord has allowed her to exist as a nation for nearly two and a half centuries! I'm thankful to be an American. With that said, we were not established in the midst of signs, miracles, and wonders (as seen in Exodus). Only Israel can say that!

Miracles, signs, and wonders all display the mighty work of God, but more was at stake than just Israel's deliverance. When the Lord sent Moses and Aaron to confront the Pharaoh, He Himself would dismantle the gods of the Egyptians. One by one, the plagues upon Egypt would signify a defeat of every single false deity.

When Egypt lost all of her first-born sons, Pharaoh could not get the Israelites out of the land fast enough. In his ignorance and pride, he decided to chase them down, only to face defeat when he lost his army in the Red Sea. The Egyptians would never enslave Israel again.

So... did the plagues really happen, or is this another historical fable? The burden of proof lies with those who reject the Bible. In their unbelief, scoffers make God out to be very small. However, God will not be placed in a box. He is bigger than we could ever imagine, and He cannot be beaten. Just ask Pharaoh!

↑ PLEASE READ EXODUS 12:29-42.

# I WILL BLESS ISRAEL

(The promised "I will"): So shall they put my name upon the people of Israel, and I will bless them. (Numbers 6:27)

(The fulfilled "I will"): So you shall know that I am the LORD your God, who dwells in Zion, my holy mountain. And Jerusalem shall be holy, and strangers shall never again pass through it. (Joel 3:17)

Teens, you have been given unique opportunities to bless others, even at your young age. A blessing is not limited to gifts or money; rather, it is the gift of yourself for the betterment of others. The Lord gave Israel the gift of Himself - He came to live among His people in both a tabernacle and a temple. Truly, God's presence was the greatest blessing that He could ever give to His people! However, they would only enjoy this blessing based on one condition: their obedience.

Sadly, Israel chose to disobey (a lot!). So they rarely experienced the joy and peace of God's presence. For several centuries, the Lord remained in the midst of His people, but Israel missed out on so much. The day came when He would leave His land, but as that terrible day approached, prophets foretold of another blessed day yet to come. It is a day when this promised "I will" will ultimately find its completion. That day is the start of the Millenium, which is the 1,000-year period when Christ will reign as king. Finally, the many prophecies about this day will come true. God will never leave, ever! All will be made right.

I have no idea what amount of earthly blessings are left for me. Honestly, it doesn't even really matter. My greatest desire is one and the same with Israel: to live in the presence of my King. Only sin can make me forget how blessed I really am.

*"Enough of you, world! Since I am a saved man, I am a blessed man!"*

🡅 GOD OFFERED BLESSINGS TO ISRAEL IN LEVITICUS 26:1-13.

# I WILL CURSE ISRAEL

(THE PROMISED "I WILL"): SEE, I AM SETTING BEFORE YOU TODAY A BLESSING AND A CURSE... AND THE CURSE, IF YOU DO NOT OBEY COMMANDMENTS OF THE LORD YOUR GOD, BUT TURN ASIDE FROM THE WAY I AM COMMANDING YOU TODAY, TO GO AFTER OTHER GODS THAT YOU HAVE NOT KNOWN. (DEUTERONOMY 11:26, 28)

(THE FULFILLED "I WILL"): THE LORD HAS SWALLOWED UP WITHOUT MERCY ALL THE HABITATIONS OF JACOB; IN HIS WRATH HE HAS BROKEN DOWN THE STRONGHOLDS OF THE DAUGHTER OF JUDAH; HE HAS BROUGHT DOWN TO THE GROUND IN DISHONOR THE KINGDOM AND ITS RULERS. (LAMENTATIONS 2:2)

"Johnny, if you ________, then I am going to have to ________!" And Johnny does it anyway. And Johnny gets in trouble, as promised. Johnny, Johnny, Johnny... what's up with you? Why did you do it?

Oh, the rebellion that lives inside the human heart! We know what is right, don't we? Then we go ahead and do the opposite. God promised His curse upon Israel if they decided to rebel, and over the course of their history, they chose to experience all of the terrible consequences found in Leviticus 26. The day came when their rebellion led to defeat and captivity, and the final curse was fulfilled (this occurred in 586 B.C., at the hands of the Babylonian Empire).

Israel was literally given everything they needed to succeed, and yet they chose the way of pain. But let me ask us this question: "How are we just like them?" Too much, I'm afraid.

Teens, the curse-breaker is Jesus Christ. This is true for both Israel and us. Haven't we had enough of the awful effects of sin? I know I have!

O sinner, repent! Cry out for forgiveness. Then watch your cursed life become one that is blessed forevermore.

↑ GOD SAID "I WILL" CURSE ISRAEL IN LEVITICUS 26:14-39.

# I WILL REMEMBER ISRAEL

(The promised "I will"): (t)hen I will remember my covenant with Jacob, and I will remember my covenant with Isaac and my covenant with Abraham, and I will remember the land. (Leviticus 26:42)

(The fulfilled "I will"): (w)ho says of Cyrus, "He is my shepherd, and he shall fulfill all my purpose"; saying of Jerusalem, "She shall be built", and of the temple, "Your foundation shall be laid." (Isaiah 44:28)

Teens, there is some amazing things happening between these two verses of Scripture! After the days that Isaiah spoke the prophecy above, Israel was taken captive and deported in three waves (occurring in 605, 597, and 586 B.C.). Several centuries before, Moses recorded in Leviticus that Israel would be out of the land for all the Sabbath years she missed. That added up to 70 years (!). And then, Cyrus, the king of Persia, told them they could go back and rebuild their temple. Yes, a pagan king told them to get worshipping their own God. How about that?!! And what's even crazier? God told Isaiah that this would happen a few centuries before it took place!!! If the people in 535 B.C. had a copy of Isaiah's prophecies on hand, they would have marveled at the command of Cyrus. What an incredible account!

But, in order for God to remember his covenant, the people would need to "confess their iniquity and the iniquity of their fathers" (Leviticus 26:40). God was looking for a sincere "I'm sorry!". Paul writes in the New Testament that confession remained necessary: "For godly grief produces a repentance that leads to salvation without regret, whereas worldly grief produces death" (2 Corinthians 7:10).

Thankfully, men like Daniel confessed and asked forgiveness for Israel (check it out in Daniel 9). They give us a firm example of the power of confession – it moves the Lord to remember His promises.

↑ READ ABOUT GOD'S REMEMBRANCE OF ISRAEL IN LEVITICUS 26:40-46.

# I WILL BE WITH YOU

(The promised "I will"): No man shall be able to stand before you all the days of your life. Just as I was with Moses, so I will be with you. I will not leave you or forsake you. (Joshua 1:5)

(The fulfilled "I will"): And now I am about to go the way of all the earth, and you know in your hearts and souls, all of you, that not one word has failed of all the good things that the LORD your God promised concerning you. All have come to pass for you; not one of them has failed. (Joshua 23:14)

As a nation, Israel's first generation experienced an exodus from Egypt and the accompanying 40-year detour in the wilderness. Her next generation would conquer much of the Promised Land. Joshua, that long-time faithful servant of the Lord, as well as Moses' right hand man, was the leader of this second generation.

As promised, God never left Joshua. He was guilty of making some poor decisions, yet he remained committed to the Lord. This was such a critical time in Israel's history. They were not given an open-door invitation into Canaan, and many battles took place in order to wipe out the evil and secure the land. You may have heard of the Battle of Jericho; this battle took place in Joshua's time. By the time he was ready to die, a good portion of the land was claimed by Israel's tribes.

In these important times, can you imagine if God made His promise to Joshua conditional? What if He said, "Josh, I will be with you, IF you do everything exactly right. No mistakes allowed! The moment you slip up, My people will need to go back to the wilderness and start all over. I'm watching now; no goofs! Not even a little!" No, God had awesome plans for Joshua – he just had to be a willing servant – and thankfully, he was! What a great way to end a book named after himself.

CHECK OUT JOSHUA 24. ALSO, SEE HOW HEBREWS 13:5 COMPARES GOD'S PROMISE GIVEN TO THIS LEADER.

# I WILL NOT DRIVE THEM OUT

(The promised "I will"): So now I say, I will not drive them out before you, but they shall become thorns in your sides, and their gods shall be a snare to you. (Judges 2:3)

(The fulfilled "I will"): (I)n those days there was no king in Israel. Everyone did what was right in his own eyes. (Judges 21:25)

A significant purpose of these "I will" devotions is to help us understand the past, so that we can understand the future. As we study the past in the Bible, we see that all of God's "I will" statements are proven to be true. Some have not yet happened, but the rest have been completed or fulfilled, exactly as God said they would. Much of the biblical past deals with the nation of Israel. This history is completely relevant for us today, as our Savior came from the Jews. In so many ways, our past, present, and future is linked to God's nation.

Judges is a book about generational idol worship. About the time one generation got right with God, their children chose to revert back to idolatry. The land could have been conquered, but the tribes did not finish the job, choosing instead to embrace the ways of the enemy. The vicious cycle that followed was one of captivity, sorrow, repentance, deliverance, peace, sin, and finally, a return to captivity. How awful!

If only Israel had obeyed the first time! Their failure reminds me of our half-hearted efforts today. "I'll get a 'C'... that's good enough!" or "If I put away my clothes, I can go out with my friends (never mind that the rest of my room is a wreck!)" or "I don't want to do these dishes... I'll let the dog lick the plates and call it good (yuck - don't do that!)".

Unfinished soul work leaves room for Satan to thrive. Teens, humble yourselves, and allow God to drive out any wickedness inside of you.

↑ READ ABOUT GIDEON'S FAILURE IN JUDGES 8:22-35.

# I WILL ESTABLISH HIS KINGDOM

(The promised "I will"): When your days are fulfilled to walk with your fathers, I will raise up your offspring after you, one of your own sons, and I will establish his kingdom. He shall build a house for me, and I will establish his throne forever. (1 Chronicles 17:11-12)

(The fulfilled "I will"): Then the seventh angel blew his trumpet, and there were loud voices in heaven, saying, "The kingdom of the world has become the kingdom of our Lord and his Christ, and he shall reign forever and ever." (Revelation 11:15)

In the days of King David, Israel flourished, but God remained in a tent. That did not sit well with David. He wanted to build a temple for God, but the Lord told him to wait. His son Solomon was appointed to do the job. However, David received an "I will" of great importance. Not only would he be in the ancestry that produced Jesus Christ, he was also blessed to be the "trunk of the royal tree." We trace Jesus rightful position as King because God proclaimed this promise in to David.

Teens, here is yet another example of a promise that was foretold hundreds of years before it actually happened. Amazing!

David was a terrific king, yet we read that he made some terrible decisions, which cost him dearly. It was proof that Israel's greatest king was not the One who would be the Savior of the world. David needed one of his descendants to come and rescue him from sin. This "son of David" came 1,000 years later. The Pharisees and other religious leaders didn't want to recognize Jesus as the Promised One (read about that in Matthew 22:41-46), but in David, the line was established.

Oh, how we look to the day when Christ sets up his kingdom on this earth for good. It is coming – and he shall reign forever and ever!

↑ CHECK OUT WHAT GOD TOLD DAVID IN 1 CHRONICLES 17:1-15.

# I WILL SURELY TEAR THE KINGDOM

(The promised "I will"): Therefore, the LORD said to Solomon, "Since this has been your practice and you have not kept my covenant and my statutes that I have commanded you, I will surely tear the kingdom from you and will give it to your servant." (1 Kings 11:11)

(The fulfilled "I will"): And when all of Israel saw that the king did not listen to them, the people answered the king, "What portion do we have in David? We have no inheritance in the son of Jesse. To our tents, O Israel! Look now to your house, David." So Israel went to their tents. (1 Kings 12:16)

What would it take for you to decide that it was time to separate from your family? Perhaps you have had to deal with the awful reality of living through a divorce and seeing your family split. If this is the case, I grieve for you. Please know that God is our Healer, no matter what happens. He sees, and He cares!

After three kings reigned over Israel, God's nation split in two. Ten of Israel's twelve tribes would make up a kingdom to the north, and the remaining two in the south. Who was to blame for this? King Solomon was the main culprit; his love for women and their idols changed the course of Israel's history. Yes, he was the wisest man to ever live, yet his sin led the nation to a civil war, ending the unity of the 12 tribes.

Yet in this fulfilled "I will", we still see God's patience and perfect timing. He did not wipe Israel off the map and start over. He did not leave the future kings without prophets, who faithfully shared God's message to the leaders and the people. For the sake of His servant David, He kept the southern kingdom (Judah) intact, with the big plan still in place – the King of kings would come one day to save His people.

If your world is being torn in two, His plans for you are still in effect!

↑ READ HOW THE KINGDOM WAS DIVIDED IN 1 KINGS 11:1-24.

# I WILL REMOVE JUDAH AND REJECT JERUSALEM

(The promised "I will"): And the LORD said, "I will remove Judah also out of my sight, as I have removed Israel, and I will cast off this city that I have chosen, Jerusalem, and the house of which I said, My name shall be there." (2 Kings 23:27)

(The fulfilled "I will"): He took into exile in Babylon those who had escaped from the sword, and they became servants to him and to his sons until the establishment of the kingdom of Persia, to fulfill the word of the LORD by the mouth of Jeremiah, until the land had enjoyed its Sabbaths. All the days that it lay desolate it kept Sabbath, to fulfill seventy years. (2 Chronicles 36:20)

I believe in God on the mountain, and I believe in God in the valley.

I believe in God at creation, and I believe in God at destruction.

I believe in God when He is gracious, and I believe God when He is wrathful.

I believe in God in times of peace, and I believe in God in times of war.

I believe in God during the best of life, and I believe in God during the worst of life.

When my soul is crushed from the weight of sin, and when judgment is executed fairly and righteously, I will continue to believe God. My faith rests in Him. I cannot control the times in which I live, but I can pray for myself, my family, my church, my friends, and my nation.

I will ever believe God, who is my Hope and my Savior. And I will ever sing the words of the hymn, "I need no other argument, I need no other plea. It is enough that Jesus died, and that He died for me!"

↑ THE FALL OF JUDAH AND JERUSALEM: READ 2 KINGS 25:1-26.

# I WILL SEND MY MESSENGER

(THE PROMISED "I WILL"): BEHOLD, I WILL SEND MY MESSENGER, AND HE WILL PREPARE THE WAY BEFORE ME. AND THE LORD WHOM YOU SEEK WILL SUDDENLY COME TO HIS TEMPLE; AND THE MESSENGER OF THE COVENANT IN WHOM YOU DELIGHT, BEHOLD, HE IS COMING, SAYS THE LORD OF HOSTS. (MALACHI 3:1)

(THE FULFILLED "I WILL"): HE SAID, "I AM THE VOICE OF ONE CRYING OUT IN THE WILDERNESS, 'MAKE STRAIGHT THE WAY OF THE LORD,' AS THE PROPHET ISAIAH SAID." (JOHN 1:23)

Isaiah wrote about him. So did Malachi. There would be a frontrunner for the King, and his name was John the Baptist. Malachi mentioned this prophet around 400 years before it happened, and Isaiah 300 years before Malachi. Another "I will" has come to pass. In a world where people are quick to believe a single rumored prediction come true, the Bible offers hundreds of fulfilled promises, and we still don't believe.

Timing is everything, right? God, who is not bound by time, fulfills His promises in His perfect time. Can you imagine waiting over 400 years for the Lord to finally speak again? This is exactly what happened in the historical years between the Old and New Testaments. We really don't understand that kind of patience, do we? The response of the world is to mock those who wait for God to do His perfect work.

However, once again we see "good things come to those who wait." John the Baptist would make way for the Son of God - the fulfillment of God's many "I will's" - and the world would finally have the Savior.

And when the messenger finally came, so did God's message - the gospel of Jesus Christ. Hallelujah!

"God bakes with ovens, not microwaves." I'm glad He is not in a hurry!

↑ READ THE SOBERING WORDS OF MALACHI 3:1-5.

# ALL THREE, FROM THE START

IN THE BEGINNING, GOD CREATED THE HEAVENS AND THE EARTH. THE EARTH WAS WITHOUT FORM AND VOID, AND DARKNESS WAS OVER THE FACE OF THE DEEP. AND THE SPIRIT OF GOD WAS HOVERING OVER THE FACE OF THE WATERS. (GENESIS 1:1-2)

Here's a question for you: "Of all the families that you know, which family do you admire the most?" I am willing to bet that this family is good about doing life together. I imagine that they love each other; they generally get along well; they are unselfish and willing to serve others. Overall, they are not perfect (who is, right?), but they are the picture of unity.

I know a number of good families, and I see many of those same character traits. When a Christian family displays unity, it reflects the Trinity – God the Father, God the Son, and God the Holy Spirit. They were united even before time began (what an amazing thought!). At the beginning of time, the Bible refers to all three Persons, creating this universe together.

There's a good chance you already have the very first verse of the Bible memorized. When we read that God did the creating, it might be easy to think that God the Father was the only One involved. But then we read the second verse, and we see that God the Spirit was hovering. Some adjectives that describe this Hebrew word are "flutter", "shake", and "move". In this verse, we see the Spirit in action, on the brink of making amazing things happen. And finally, let's not miss God the Son. Colossians 1:16 tells us, "For by him all things were created, in heaven and on earth, visible and invisible". So, when we read that God created, we learn that all three Persons were involved.

We worship a unified Creator. Wow!

↑ CHECK OUT GENESIS 1:1-13 TO SEE THE TRINITY IN ACTION.

# US

THEN GOD SAID, "LET US MAKE MAN IN OUR IMAGE, AFTER OUR LIKENESS. AND LET THEM HAVE DOMINION OVER THE FISH OF THE SEA AND OVER THE BIRDS OF THE HEAVENS AND OVER THE LIVESTOCK AND OVER ALL THE EARTH AND OVER EVERY CREEPING THING THAT CREEPS ON THE EARTH." (GENESIS 1:26)

We learned yesterday that God – the "Three in One" - worked together in perfect unity to bring about the creation of this universe. Good to know that this world didn't just arrive from a cosmic explosion, huh? The universe itself is amazing; however, the height of God's creation is found later in Genesis 1, where we find a marvelous verse that tells us precisely who created mankind. His greatest creation is you!

In the verse above, the word "us" reveals the wonderful work of the Trinity. Us includes the Father, the Son, and the Spirit. They already had been working together, but now the Bible shows us the importance of the final act of creation by referring to the Holy Trinity. You see, we are the only created beings that are made "in our image, after our likeness." As the Three-in-One, God not only made us, He stamped Himself upon us. What a thought!

This is a big deal here. When you feel like you are just another worthless person, remember that "us" created you. When you think that life is not really worth living, don't forget that "us" made you in his image and likeness. "Us" has also given you an important task (Genesis 1:28-29). Our worth is not based upon anything separate from the Trinity. You can believe it!

↑ READ ALL ABOUT IT IN GENESIS 1:14-31.

# BULLYING: GOD KNOWS, AND GOD CARES

BE GRACIOUS TO ME, O LORD, FOR I AM LANGUISHING; HEAL ME, O LORD, FOR MY BONES ARE TROUBLED. MY SOUL ALSO IS GREATLY TROUBLED. BUT YOU, O LORD – HOW LONG? (PSALM 6:2-3)

Bullying is wrong in many ways. Awhile ago, one of our teens expressed her concern for a friend who was being bullied at school. Looking around the room that night, I could tell that those present sympathized with her. We all know that it is wrong to treat another person with disrespect at any level, bullying included.

Did you know that Israel's second king was bullied by the first king? Saul hated the fact that David, and not his son Jonathan, was to be the next king of Israel. So he bullied David in a number of ways. How so? He threw spears at him; he chased him all over the countryside with his army; he tried to turn David's wife (who was also Saul's own daughter) against him. The bullying turned into a vengeance for murder, as Saul made numerous attempts to kill the heir to the throne.

In spite of it all, David decided to trust God. In the midst of the bullying, he ran to God to plea for help. As we read the biblical narrative, we know that God indeed delivered David from Saul. The Lord did not let the bully win the day.

Are you being bullied? Do you know of someone who is dealing with a bully? GET HELP! Be there for your friend; the Lord wants us to defend the weak. And most of all, know that God understands and answers prayer. The helpless of this world are close to His heart.

MAY PSALM 6 ENCOURAGE YOU. GOD KNOWS, AND GOD CARES!

# HEY! I REALLY NEED TO TELL YOU SOMETHING!

FAITHFUL ARE THE WOUNDS OF A FRIEND; PROFUSE ARE THE KISSES OF AN ENEMY. (PROVERBS 27:6)

You want to know something that is not fun at all? Needing to tell a friend that they are way out of line!

Understand here that we are talking about friends, the very ones we love. I don't think it's that hard for people to pour out condemnation against their enemies (we see this often in the world of social media). But when it comes time to tell your friend that they are really messing up? That's tough.

Proverbs 27:6 is a terrific verse on this subject. Notice that the wounds are "faithful"; they are present, but they don't hurt us without a purpose. These kind of wounds drive us to do what is right, and they turn us from the path that leads to destruction.

If you have a good friend, and they have the guts to tell you that you are wrong, then you really do have a good friend! The fact that your friend would rather see your feelings hurt than for you to continue down the wrong road is true friendship.

As you think about the verse above, I'm guessing someone comes to mind that you should "wound". Would you ask God to help you love that person by talking to them about the sin in his or her life?

🡅 CHECK OUT HOW PAUL "WOUNDED" PETER IN GALATIANS 2:11-21.

## BAPTIZED BY THE SPIRIT

AND PETER SAID TO THEM, "REPENT AND BE BAPTIZED EVERY ONE OF YOU IN THE NAME OF JESUS CHRIST FOR THE FORGIVENESS OF YOUR SINS, AND YOU WILL RECEIVE THE GIFT OF THE HOLY SPIRIT." (ACTS 2:38)

How do you prefer to get into a swimming pool? I take the "jump in and don't ask questions" approach. As long as I don't see boiling bubbles or frozen glaciers, I dive in... no questions asked! My wife is far more conservative, ever so slowly making her way into the pool, so that her body gradually gets acclimated to the temperature. To me, that seems like torture, yet I have not been able to change her mind about this approach (though I've tried many times!).

Being baptized by the Holy Spirit is our "jump in and get completely wet" reality. *Baptism* is simply another word for "immersion"; we are completely covered by Him when we are saved. As there is no way to remain dry when we are swimming in a body of water, there is also no way to remain unsaved when we are immersed in the Spirit. It's God's way of telling us, "We've got you covered!".

As I write this devotion, I have a bottle of water on my desk. When I drink the water, it will find its way inside of me to do all the good things that water does. That's a simple picture of the Spirit at work. My spirit is immersed; I am the recipient of His living water.

Speaking of that, you may recall that another Person mentioned in the Bible offers us "living water". With Jesus Christ, we will never thirst again. He told the woman at the well, "Whoever drinks of the water that I will give him will never be thirsty again. The water that I will give him will become in him a spring of water welling up to eternal life." (John 4:13-14). Amen to that!

➜ CHECK OUT ACTS 2:29-41.

# EXCUSES, EXCUSES!

AND I HEARD THE VOICE OF THE LORD SAYING, "WHOM SHALL I SEND, AND WHO WILL GO FOR US?" THEN I SAID, "HERE I AM! SEND ME." (ISAIAH 6:8)

*"WHY ME?"*
*"I'M NOT SMART ENOUGH TO DO IT!"*
*"WHAT IF NOBODY BELIEVES ME?"*
*"I'M NOT CAPABLE TO DO IT!"*
*"DON'T MAKE ME DO IT!"*

Does this sound like a child making excuses to his parent? It does to me. But it is also the way Moses responded to God when he was told to return to Egypt and lead his people out of slavery. You'll read more about his response today in Exodus 3.

What if God said to Moses, "OK, fine, stay with the sheep. I don't want to use anyone that has such a 'baaaaaaad' attitude!" If God dismissed Moses for making excuses, He could have easily used another, more willing servant. But if that happened, Moses would have missed out on all the blessings that come through obedience.

When people say "no" to God, they miss out, big time! The Almighty God has mighty plans for the man or woman who follows him. Isaiah knew how to respond ("Here I am! Send me."), and the prophet never looked back.

*"God, help me to quit making excuses. When I do, I am simply choosing to live by sight, rather than by faith. In You, there are no excuses. In Christ, I can do all things, for it is You who gives me strength!"*

↑ READ MORE ABOUT MOSES IN EXODUS 3.

# WHAT IS LOVE?

In this is love, not that we loved God but that He loved us and sent His Son to be the propitiation for our sins. (1 John 4:10)

It was "love at first sight". Dennis caught Jennifer's eye in the school cafeteria a week ago. He was the star running back for the varsity football team; she was a popular cheerleader. Their friends knew it was only a matter of time before they hit if off. When Dennis asked her to go to the prom, Jennifer was ecstatic! She would finally have a boyfriend again, and they already had so much in common. Both did well academically; they loved the same music; they only lived a few blocks apart; and both sets of parents were very wealthy.

Brad and Jennifer are all set to "live happily ever after." Right?

Teens, if there ever was a word that we mishandle, it's the word "love". Dennis and Jen have a certain attraction for each other, and you know what? There is nothing wrong with that. In fact, most of us would probably be jealous of them. However, if Dennis and Jen have no sense love's character and meaning, then it is *impossible* for them to really love each other. Be attracted? Yes. Love? No.

If we consider how love is defined by the verse above, we see that love is centered upon the Father's act to willingly send His Son for our salvation. This kind of love is "agape" (one of the Greek words for love). Agape love is selfless, sacrificial, and unconditional.

What is love? At it's fullest, love is displayed by God Himself. Don't be fooled into thinking otherwise.

🡅 CHECK OUT 2 JOHN. IT'S SHORT, BUT IT'S A WONDERFUL LETTER!

# I WANT OUT OF THIS TOWN!

I KNOW HOW TO BE BROUGHT LOW, AND I KNOW HOW TO ABOUND. IN ANY AND EVERY CIRCUMSTANCE, I HAVE LEARNED THE SECRET OF FACING PLENTY AND HUNGER, ABUNDANCE AND NEED. I CAN DO ALL THINGS THROUGH HIM WHO STRENGTHENS ME. (PHILIPPIANS 4:12-13)

"I *want out of this town!"*

Ever heard that said? Ever say it yourself?

I heard it a lot growing up. It seems like most of my classmates wanted to move away and never come back. In their minds, a better future did not reside in their hometown.

I grew up in the very rural community of East Smithfield, PA. It is one of many very tiny towns that make up that part of Pennsylvania. We are generally conservative in this area of the state. In fact, my hometown is still without any traffic lights!

On the other hand, there is a sense of safety in those rural hills. There is natural beauty all around us. Once you make a friend here, they are usually a friend for life. People know how to be generous, in spite of the fact that most of them do not have much to give.

Ultimately, we need to recognize that God has every right to decide where *and* how we ought to live. He can give us incredible riches, or He can allow us to experience desperate poverty. Regardless of our location, we need to remember Paul's words in the verses above.

No matter where you live, remember this: God is good! He knows exactly what He is doing with your life.

↑ CHECK OUT THE CONTEXT IN PHILIPPIANS 4:10-20.

## GODLY SORROW

For godly grief produces a repentance that leads to salvation without regret, whereas worldly grief produces death. (2 Corinthians 7:10)

When I was in college, I worked for the United Parcel Service (UPS). My job was to load packages into tractor trailers and those famous brown trucks that pull into driveways. For a short time at UPS, I worked with a guy named Louie. I felt like Louie had the desire to annoy everyone. I remember getting into an argument with him one night, and I left work wanting to unload some of my "packaged" anger upon him! Over the course of the next day, I knew that I needed to apologize to him for the argument. The next night on the job, I did so, and he nearly fell over! After that point, I had no issues with him.

It's one thing to feel sorry; it's another thing to actually do something about our sorrow. When we understand that we have offended God, feel sorry for our offenses, and rightly respond to that sorrow, it's called "repentance". As the verse states above, this kind of repentance "leads to salvation without regret."

It's not easy to say "I'm sorry!". It usually leaves a bad taste in our mouth, like eating a combination of fruit cake, spinach, worms, and black licorice. Gross! I guess if we never sin, we would never need to say that we're sorry. But since we do sin, sorrow is very necessary! Here's the good news: not only does godly sorrow produce salvation for the unbeliever, it is a spiritually healthy exercise for those who already believe... as I learned once again at UPS those many years ago.

↑ READ 2 CORINTHIANS 7:8-16. MAY THERE NEVER BE A TIME IN YOUR LIFE WHEN YOU ARE ABOVE REPENTANCE!

## THE UNFAIR PRESSURE UPON OUR LADIES

DO NOT LET YOUR ADORNING BE EXTERNAL – THE BRAIDING OF HAIR, THE PUTTING ON OF GOLD JEWELRY, OR THE CLOTHING YOU WEAR – BUT LET YOUR ADORNING BE THE HIDDEN PERSON OF THE HEART WITH THE IMPERISHABLE BEAUTY OF A GENTLE AND QUIET SPIRIT, WHICH IN GOD'S SIGHT IS VERY PRECIOUS. (1 PETER 3:3-4)

Ladies, this one is for you!

The pressure you face about how you look is INTENSE. As a teen, I remember feeling awkward myself as I physically changed (glasses, pimples, braces, etc.). I survived (hey, at least I knew that my mommy loved me!), but what I faced then is far less difficult than what you cope with today.

As a young lady, you deal with an awful lot of pressure to dress a certain style, weigh a certain amount, put on certain make-up, talk a certain way, and on and on. It seems to me that all this "certain" stuff ends up leaving most girls feeling more uncertain than ever before!

So, what does God (your Creator) think about how you look?

When God says that your inner self is incredibly important to Him, and the rest of the world tells you to spend time focusing on your outward beauty, we have a conflict here! Ladies, I want to tell you something. As surely as men will notice if your focus is on your looks, we will also notice if you place greater importance on your soul. The good guys out there (the ones you will want as a husband one day) are greatly impressed with a lady who nurtures "the hidden person of the heart", and who has a "gentle and quiet spirit". I'm not kidding - this speaks volumes to godly men. It also keeps you out of the unnecessary pressure that comes from what the world thinks of you.

↑ CHECK OUT 1 PETER 3:1-7. MAY YOU "IMPRESS" THE LORD!

# OUR CHAMPION HAS ARRIVED!

MAKE A JOYFUL NOISE TO THE LORD, ALL THE EARTH! SERVE THE LORD WITH GLADNESS! COME INTO HIS PRESENCE WITH SINGING! (PSALM 100:1-2)

You're at the big game! Your team is ready to run out on to the field. They won it all last year. You love these guys; this is *your team*. They have worked hard all season, and once again, they are undefeated. They put fear in the hearts of all their opponents. You know the players, and they are simply the best!

And here they come, running and clapping and leaping and yelling all at once. They are an unstoppable force, an incredible ball of energy, and a show of determination and strength! You rise up as one with the crowd; you are screaming for them at the top of your lungs; your heart races in excitement at the very sight of them; you cannot wait to see them take the field and earn the victory! You feel your adrenaline rise as the crowd shakes the stadium in raucous delight! This is YOUR TEAM! These are YOUR CHAMPIONS!

Take in this scene above. For all Christians, this is simply a prelude for what is yet to come! In the future, whenever the believers meet together in "Heaven Stadium", we will wait in hushed anticipation for the moment our Savior walks on the stage. The response to his arrival will be mind-blowing! Chants of "JESUS CHRIST" will fill the air. The decibel level will be unmatched! Everything that has breath will praise the Lord. It is a moment that is worth waiting for; yes, it is *the* moment that is worth living for!

Forever our champion: JESUS CHRIST! "Let all the earth fear the LORD; let all the inhabitants of the world stand in awe of him" (Psalm 33:8).

↑ CHECK OUT PSALM 33. WHO IS LIKE OUR GOD?!!

# THERE IS ONLY ONE

HEAR, O ISRAEL: THE LORD OUR GOD, THE LORD IS ONE. YOU SHALL LOVE THE LORD YOUR GOD WITH ALL YOUR HEART AND WITH ALL YOUR SOUL AND WITH ALL YOUR MIGHT. (DEUTERONOMY 6:4-5)

There are many theories on how the came into existence. Since history began, cultures have embraced all kinds of beliefs about our origins. Millions have been led to think that we came into being by something less than an act of God; but THERE IS ONLY ONE CREATOR.

Rulers have come and gone. Mighty men have conquered nations, imposing their will upon the masses, yet they have all died. Driving people in fear, torturing and killing those who stand in their way, relishing the power and control, the wicked dominate for a time; but THERE IS ONLY ONE KING.

Humanity needs someone, so we become convinced that the next elected leader will spare us the awful consequences of our nation's sin. If only we had the right person in place; if only I had more money; if only people treated me the way that I should be treated; but THERE IS ONLY ONE SAVIOR.

They say that insanity is doing the same thing over and over again, expecting a different result. Men insist upon serving gods of their own making, when God Almighty tells us that He is in control. "I am the master of my fate: I am the captain of my soul", they say; but THERE IS ONLY ONE LORD.

He is a jealous God; He loves His own; He will not put up with the idols in our lives. There is only One, and He is Creator, King, Savior, and Lord! Every knee will bow and every tongue will confess this truth.

🡅 GO TO DEUTERONOMY 6. HE IS THE ONLY ONE!

# THE MASTER DECEIVER

GOD MAY PERHAPS GRANT THEM REPENTANCE LEADING TO A KNOWLEDGE OF THE TRUTH, AND THEY MAY COME TO THEIR SENSES AND ESCAPE FROM THE SNARE OF THE DEVIL, AFTER BEING CAPTURED BY HIM TO DO HIS WILL. (2 TIMOTHY 2:25-26)

You probably know people who say that there is no such thing as the devil. If that ever comes up in a conversation, I challenge you to ask them what they believe about the Bible. If they claim it as the truth, show them that there are references about Satan all over its pages. *Denying his presence doesn't change the reality of his existence.*

Satan's most devastating work is in taking your attention away from the truth. He likes to provide ways that keep us busy, as well as leave us thinking that we have no time for God. Through his deception, he has us convinced that "busy-ness" is good for us (and when things are busily going well, we tend to believe we have God's approval).

Right now, the devil is making an all-out assault on America. How so, you ask? He is deceiving us into believing that happiness lies in our possessions. Though the Bible says possessions will rot, break down, and be destroyed, we have an unhealthy obsession in "stuff". Just consider technology alone. How many devices do you own that keep you occupied? They absolutely dominate us, don't they? God will have no idols before Him, technology or otherwise.

When we forget that the devil is our enemy, then the master deceiver has accomplished one of his deadliest goals.

↑ FIGHT MATERIALISM. HEED 1 TIMOTHY 6:6-10!

# HIS GRADUATION SPEECH

THE THIEF COMES ONLY TO STEAL AND KILL AND DESTROY. I CAME THAT THEY MAY HAVE LIFE AND HAVE IT ABUNDANTLY. (JOHN 10:10)

What if Jesus was the main speaker at your graduation? What would he say? Perhaps the following?

*"Dear school board, faculty, parents, and students: I am here to congratulate this class of graduates! To graduate from high school is quite an accomplishment. You worked hard and have persevered. You have fought the good fight and have finished the race. Now, the future will take you away from this school. What will you do?*

*"The world will have you believe that happiness is found in your future pursuits. I am here to tell you otherwise. Many centuries ago, I was on this earth for another purpose: to make sure that you could have a future and a hope. If you want to discover your purpose in life, then understand that I AM that future and that hope. I AM the way, the truth, and the life. I AM the resurrection and the life. I AM the bread of life and I AM the living water. I AM; and since I AM, this is all that matters! You may not fully grasp it at this point, but all of your hopes, goals, and dreams are wrapped up in me. I should know; I am the one who created you in the first place. In the world, you will find trouble. But fear not, for I have overcome the world!*

*"Dear graduates, follow me, and find out what it really means to live. Know my truth, for it will set you free. 2000 years ago, I came that you might have life, and have it abundantly. I offer a future that includes eternity with me. When your life is over, believe me... they'll be quite a party at your heavenly graduation!"*

↑ DEAR "SHEEP", READ WHAT JESUS OFFERS US IN JOHN 10:7-21.

# STINGS, SIN, AND DEATH

The sting of death is sin, and the power of sin is the law. But thanks be to God, who gives us the victory through our Lord Jesus Christ. (1 Corinthians 15:56-57)

Years ago, I watched my son Lincoln pull his first dandelions of the season for his appreciative mother. It reminded me of the day I learned about nature and a lesson in life. As a kid, I enjoyed lying in the grass and watching God's creation at work. The ants all had places to go; the clover was plenteous (though it seemed the four-leaf kind never grew in our backyard); and the smell of the earth was captivating. The bees certainly enjoyed the dandelions in my backyard, and in an effort to learn more about bees, I put my finger up to one as she was busy at work. The bee crawled upon my pointer finger, and God's beautiful little creature did a most unbeautiful thing: it stung me. Ouch! So much for trying to "bee-friend" that buzzing insect!

Death also has a sting. The name of death's sting is "sin". If it were not for sin, then death would not be able to sting us. If it were not for sin, we would all be living uncursed lives. Everyone from the beginning of time would still be alive and in perfect health. You would get to visit your Grandpa Adam and Grandma Eve. But sin and its sting ruined the beautiful picture of what could have been at the beginning of time. Thankfully, the antidote for the sting is the blood of Jesus, who conquered sin and death. At the cross, Satan was sure that he would win the day, and that our sin placed upon Christ would be the death sting that gave him the ultimate victory. Yet God "gives us the victory through our Lord Jesus Christ". No, not even my own sin can cause my demise, because Jesus took away the sting of death in my life.

I am thankful that a little ole' bee reminded me of that truth!

LET'S READ HOSEA 13:14-14:9.

# WHO IS JESUS CHRIST TO YOU? (BY MEL WALKER)

"Simon Peter answered and said, 'You are the Christ, the Son of the living God.'" (Matthew 16:16)

By this point, His followers, the twelve disciples, had spent some significant time with Jesus. They had listened to Him preach life-changing messages, they had watched Him do incredible miracles, and they heard Him confront and confound the religious leaders of their day. It was time for another important lesson.

Matthew 16:13-20 contains the account of how the Lord asked them this essential question, "*Who do you say that I am?*"

Some of the disciples had already given Him their answers. In doing so, they shared what others in that culture were saying about Him. Basically, they responded by saying something like this: "Most people think you are just another religious leader" (see Matthew 16:14).

It is at this point when Jesus asked His pointed question. "But, *who do you say that I am?*" (see Matthew 16:16). The Apostle Peter, who was normally the first disciple to speak, spoke up. "*You are the Christ, the Son of the living God*", he answered. Peter didn't always act like He believed his answer, but at this point in the narrative, he got it right! He boldly claimed that this Teacher, this Prophet, this Healer, was the Christ – the Messiah and the Savior of the world. Jesus was truly God – not just one more voice in a long line of religious leaders.

In a sense, the Lord is also asking all of us that same question today. "*Who do YOU say that I am*?" If our answer is the same as Peter's was – that we believe that Jesus is God and is the Savior of the world - then we must give our lives whole-heartedly to Him and follow Him as well!

READ THE TESTIMONY OF JOHN THE BAPTIST IN MARK 1:1-8.

# JUNE

## SATAN'S "ADVICE"

But the serpent said to the woman, "You will not surely die. For God knows that when you eat of it your eyes will be opened, and you will be like God, knowing good and evil." (Genesis 3:4, 5)

Advice from Satan? Sounds scary. Does he try to advise Christians? If so, would we recognize it when we heard it? Do we ever get fooled into taking his advice? Can we differentiate it from the truth?

The Bible does not record the devil speaking that often, but here in Genesis, at the beginning of time, he comes to Adam and Eve as a serpent. In this encounter, he introduces all of humanity to sin and death. Satan is a lot of terrible things, but an idiot he is not. Rather than revealing anything about the disastrous consequences of sin, he invites them to place their faith in his ways. "Knowing good and evil" sounds perfectly reasonable to the innocent; but as a fallen child of Adam, I sure wish I never knew evil. Obviously, it was not worth the bite of that forbidden fruit!

Look carefully at the invitation in Genesis 3. Read it again like it was the first time you read it. Would you also have been fooled? Truly, I answer that question every time I choose to sin. I have the power to choose God, yet I choose what Satan wants instead. Yes, I would have fallen, just like my earthly parents.

For the majority of this month, we will learn about the lies of Satan, and learn that he cannot be trusted.

My advice to you? Never take Satan's "advice!"

SATAN THRIVES ON CAUSING BELIEVERS TO DOUBT GOD'S GOODNESS. READ ABOUT HABAKKUK'S DOUBTS, AND GOD'S ANSWER TO HIM, IN HABAKKUK 1:12-2:20.

# SATAN'S APPROACH TO HIS ADVICE

YOU ARE OF YOUR FATHER THE DEVIL, AND YOUR WILL IS TO DO YOUR FATHER'S DESIRES. HE WAS A MURDERER FROM THE BEGINNING, AND DOES NOT STAND IN THE TRUTH, BECAUSE THERE IS NO TRUTH IN HIM. WHEN HE LIES, HE SPEAKS OUT OF HIS OWN CHARACTER, FOR HE IS A LIAR AND THE FATHER OF LIES. (JOHN 8:44)

Let's remember that Satan will ultimately twist everything that comes from God. Whatever the Lord has said or done, the devil will counter with the exact opposite. However, our God uses everything for our good, no matter how much the evil one attempts to enforce his will.

As the father of lies, Satan's approach includes all forms of lying. Think about the time he spoke to Eve in Genesis, and let's dissect the way he lied to her. In general, all of his "advice" was a lie. But specifically, he questioned what God said (leading her astray); he deceived Eve into doubting the promise given from God; he misled her about the real outcome of eating the forbidden fruit; he denied that death was a possibility; he painted a rosy picture of the ability to know good and evil; he appealed to her on a physical (fleshly) level, disrespecting the innocence of her soul.

Oh, how deadly are all of his ways!

Satan's advice was a packaged lie so complete that Adam and Eve fell head over heels for it. The temptation to sin was made even stronger when he misquoted the command of God. He twisted the Creator's words just enough to lure humanity into a result of damnation.

The original lie is the pattern of Satan's approach to all of his lies to us. Beware!

READ JOHN 8:42-47.

# SATAN'S ADVICE ON DATING

DO NOT BE UNEQUALLY YOKED WITH UNBELIEVERS. FOR WHAT PARTNERSHIP HAS RIGHTEOUSNESS WITH LAWLESSNESS? OR WHAT FELLOWSHIP HAS LIGHT WITH DARKNESS? (2 CORINTHIANS 6:14)

Satan's "advice" on dating:

*"Did God really say, 'Do not be unequally yoked together with people?' Well, if you are just dating, you're not exactly married, are you? God knows that it is hard to find a good Christian out there to date. Don't you think that it might be a little unreasonable to wait and wait and wait until someone shows up? You know, there are people out there who don't find love until they are 30, or 40, or even 50. Seriously, how long can you wait? Besides, almost all of your friends are dating! Some of them have found happiness in same-sex relationships. Be open to the possibilities!*

*"Listen to me. What God wants for you is hard. How can He understand, since He has never dated? Since you know this is true, why don't you go ahead and let yourself get involved with someone that's available? I'm sure your character will rub off on them. The good will make the bad go away, and the person you love will change for the better! Enjoy yourself, and don't worry, you are just friends – it doesn't have to be serious. Don't mind the adults in your life who tell you otherwise; honestly, as they have aged, they have lost track of reality. Have fun, get what you can out of your relationship, and don't wait around – you only live once!"*

Satan's advice may sound good to you. However, his end game is *always* destruction and death. Always! Dear teens, I pray that you will not be fooled by his lies in this area of your life.

↑ BE DISCERNING! READ AN EYE-OPENING ACCOUNT IN EZRA 10:9-17.

## SATAN'S ADVICE ON TAKING DRUGS

But when the archangel Michael, contending with the devil, was disputing about the body of Moses, he did not presume to pronounce a blasphemous judgment, but said, "The Lord rebuke you." (Jude 9)

Crazy stuff going on in the book of Jude! First, let's realize something: like Michael, we depend upon God to fight our battles with Satan. Also, for reasons I do not completely understand, the body of Moses is very important, enough so that the devil wanted to claim it.

Now, what does any of this have to do with using drugs? We don't know God's exact purpose for the body of Moses, but nonetheless, our bodies themselves are very important to Him (Psalm 139:14 tells us, "I am fearfully and wonderfully made"). Drugs destroy what is fearfully and wonderfully made. You already know this, but perhaps you don't know just how precious your body is to the Lord. Right now, your body is imperfect and appointed for death; however, if you are a believer, it will someday be restored to uncursed state. Hooray for that!

Satan has no concern for your body, so he tricks us into believing drugs are ok. Here is one example of his "advice." Rather than come out and say, "Pot will destroy your future!", he says, "Try it! Marijuana is becoming legal all over the country, so what's the problem? How many people have done drugs and never been caught? It's fun, and there is only a small chance that you will ever get hooked. Besides, it will prove that you are not afraid, and you will fit in with many of your friends. Remember – it is *your* body – no one owns it but you!" The father of lies never mentions that death is near to all who rebel against God's commands. He never designed our bodies as a vessel for impurity.

↑ OUR BODIES ARE MEANT TO BE ENSLAVED TO RIGHTEOUSNESS, NOT DRUGS. READ ROMANS 6:15-23!

# SATAN'S ADVICE ON CHEATING

WE TAKE THIS COURSE SO THAT NO ONE SHOULD BLAME US ABOUT THIS GENEROUS GIFT THAT IS BEING ADMINISTERED BY US, FOR WE AIM AT WHAT IS HONORABLE NOT ONLY IN THE LORD'S SIGHT BUT ALSO IN THE SIGHT OF MAN. (2 CORINTHIANS 8:21)

You sit down to take that big test. You need to get a good grade if you are going to pass the class this year. Your seat is close to one of the smartest people in your grade. Your teacher is occupied with correcting papers at his desk. You know that you put very little time into studying for the test, and the pressure to cheat is mounting for you.

What should you do? God has given you a conscience about what is right and wrong, so you know that cheating does not please Him. But Satan is also whispering into your ear, working to convince you that cheating is not a big deal. His advice? *"Many people do it! It's just this once. You need to do it for the 'better good!' You won't do it again. Besides, there are far worse things you could do."*

I've been there myself. I wish I could tell you that I have never cheated on a test. I have cheated a few times (and though I was usually one of the smarter kids in my class, cheating was one of the dumbest things I ever did in school). It left me feeling guilty, and in the long run, what did it really accomplish? Basically, I was telling God that I did not trust Him to take care of me. My wrong decision opened the door for the possibility of cheating to be a problem in my life. And if I got caught, I would have certainly lost my testimony.

What a terrible decision... just because I took Satan's advice.

🡅 "SET YOUR MINDS ON THINGS THAT ARE ABOVE, NOT ON THINGS THAT ARE ON THE EARTH." READ COLOSSIANS 3:1-11 TODAY.

# SATAN'S ADVICE ON YOUR PAST

THIS SAYING IS TRUSTWORTHY AND DESERVING OF FULL ACCEPTANCE, THAT CHRIST JESUS CAME INTO THE WORLD TO SAVE SINNERS, OF WHOM I AM THE FOREMOST. (1 TIMOTHY 1:15)

I think one of Satan's most successful tactics has been to "advise" Christians about their past. He cannot deny the presence of the Holy Spirit inside the life of every believer, but He will still attempt to cast doubt onto us (like He did from the beginning, when he whispered his lies into Eve's ear).

I've heard him whisper more than once in my own ear. *"Mike, how can you be a pastor? If everyone knew what I know about you, you'd be done. Your sin has disqualified you from being anything worthwhile. God won't bless you. He's seen what you have done, and I've seen it, too. It's bad, man... it's bad!"* Believing what Satan tells us about our sin will keep us from spiritually thriving. It hinders our witnessing, our willingness to forgive, our commitment to remain pure, and a host of other problems.

But here's the beautiful thing about God: He does not keep a score card! Oh yes, our sin has significant consequences, but God isn't into dwelling on our past. As the Potter, His goal is to form His clay into the image of His Son. He tells us, *"Look ahead, child! The past is done; a new day is upon you! Come, enjoy sweet fellowship with Me! I have forgiven you and cast your sins as far as the east is from the west!"*

Don't you think it's time to believe God's Word, rather than Satan's advice, as it pertains to our past?

↑ PETER RECOGNIZED HIS SINFULNESS, AND CHRIST CHOSE HIM ANYWAY. READ LUKE 5:1-11!

# SATAN'S ADVICE ON YOUR FUTURE

DO NOT BE CONFORMED TO THIS WORLD, BUT BE TRANSFORMED BY THE RENEWAL OF YOUR MIND, THAT BY TESTING YOU MAY DISCERN WHAT IS THE WILL OF GOD, WHAT IS GOOD AND ACCEPTABLE AND PERFECT. (ROMANS 12:2)

Satan's "advice" on your destiny:

*"So, your dad is an alcoholic. Your mom is distant, always on the computer. Your older brother is into drugs, and neither of your parents even know it. Your younger sister is failing school, even though you are trying to help her pass her classes. You have no money to your name, so your parents want you to get a job... without having a car to do so. And last week, you found out that your best friend is pregnant.*

*"Listen, I have some advice. You are who you are, so make the best of it. People cannot change. Do your best to control your situation, but don't count on the fact that your family and friends will change. Remember: you are all born with certain genetic predispositions, which cannot be altered. Take care of yourself first of all. Happiness comes when you focus upon your own life, so just get what you can, now!"*

So many teens end up becoming just like the adults they wished they were not. They follow the pattern of their parents, not believing that real change is possible.

Satan will never tell you the truth about Jesus Christ. He is the One who changes the heart! You are not condemned to a future that cannot be altered. In Christ, individuals are not conformed; instead, they are transformed! How great is that?

Believe in Jesus, and watch your future unfold indescribably!

↑ THE POWER OF GOD TO CHANGE US: READ EZEKIEL 11:16-25.

# SATAN'S ADVICE ON WHAT WE DESERVE

You save a humble people, but your eyes are on the haughty to bring them down. For you are my lamp, O LORD, and my God lightens my darkness. (2 Samuel 22:28-29)

Perhaps one of Satan's deadliest tricks is getting us to believe that we deserve a pain-free life. We believe Satan's advice when we complain about the small things ("I hate these hot days!" is another way to say, "I don't deserve this!"). And we believe Satan's advice when we complain about the big things ("Why can't my mom be like my friend's mom?" is another way to say, "I deserve a better parent!").

Here is a sobering thought: "What do we deserve?" To say I deserve good is to make the claim that I have done enough right in my life, and I should get my way in return. Since God is in control of everything, He should see fit that I get all the "good" that is coming to me.

Satan was directly involved in the book of Job, and Job's "friends" reveal that they believe Satan's advice. Certainly, since Job was dealing with horrific trials, he must have been very bad somewhere along the line. However, we read that Job was righteous. In life, the good is not always met with good, and the bad is not always met with bad.

What do we deserve? There is only one answer for that. *We deserve hell.* Our sin put the Son of God on the cross. The fact that we don't get what we deserve is called *mercy*. And the fact that we are given what we don't deserve - the gift of eternal life - is called *grace*.

Don't buy Satan's lie. *We deserve nothing that is good!* So when we do receive anything that is good from the loving hand of God, may it cause us to worship Him!

↑ CHECK OUT EZRA 9:10-15, ESPECIALLY VERSE 13.

# SATAN'S ADVICE ON DEBT

BE NOT ONE OF THOSE WHO GIVE PLEDGES, WHO PUT UP SECURITY FOR DEBTS. IF YOU HAVE NOTHING WITH WHICH TO PAY, WHY SHOULD YOUR BED BE TAKEN FROM UNDER YOU? (PROVERBS 22:26-27)

If you want a depressing reality check, go to usgovernmentdebt.us, where you will discover our current federal deficit. As you ponder this astronomical number, ask yourself the question: "Do you think we might have followed some of 'Satan's financial advice'?"

Teens, if you want a clue as to how Satan advises millions of people about their money, just open a credit card offer in the mail. According to form, you will never see Satan leading people to write letters that tell us, *"Come use this card, and you will struggle to stay financially afloat! You'll feel sick to your stomach at the crazy-high interest you must pay! It will take most of the best working years of your life to overcome your future mountain of debt. You will probably give up on giving money to the church. You'll sacrifice your children's future so that you can have fun today. Yeah, baby! Let's go places!"*

*"What's in your wallet? NOTHING, that's what! Ha!"*

Those cards always offer a future that looks too good to be true - because it is! Yet, we fall for it anyway. What starts out as one missed monthly payment often turns into a lifelong commitment to financial slavery. And while we try our hardest to throw off those chains, we miss wonderful opportunities to use our resources for God's glory.

Oh, how Satan has many people fooled - hook, line, and sinker. But teens, you personally can determine to avoid debt at any cost. You will not regret it – nor will your spouse and kids, someday!

LET'S READ PROVERBS 22:17-29 TODAY.

## SATAN'S ADVICE ON MARRIAGE

HE WHO FINDS A WIFE FINDS A GOOD THING AND OBTAINS FAVOR FROM THE LORD. (PROVERBS 18:22)

If God is for marriage, it is not hard to conclude that Satan is against it. Indeed, marriage is a very important topic in the Bible; it pops up early in Genesis and late in Revelation.

So, if Satan wants to completely reverse God's design for marriage, what do you think he would advise? How about some of the following lies that many have been led to believe:

"TRY LIVING TOGETHER FIRST - SEE IF YOUR FUTURE MARRIAGE WILL WORK OUT!"

"LIKE ALL MARRIAGES, YOURS WILL GET TO A PLACE WHERE IT IS DULL AND ROUTINE."

"DOES MARRIAGE REALLY NEED TO BE LIMITED TO ONE MAN AND ONE WOMAN?"

"A DIVORCE IS NOT UNUSUAL, SO IF YOU DO NOT LOVE HIM OR HER ANYMORE, THEN ALLOW YOURSELF TO FIND FREEDOM."

"DON'T LET TRADITIONAL VIEWS STOP YOU FROM MARRYING SOMEONE OF THE SAME SEX."

"MAKE SURE YOUR SPOUSE GIVES YOU EVERYTHING THAT YOU DESERVE!"

Don't be fooled, teens. Satan hates marriage because he hates God, and marriage was God's first gift to humanity, just moments after Adam met Eve. The lies listed above are not new, but they are in full force today. If we follow Satan's advice, marriage will be so desecrated that God will have no other option but to punish us.

*"GOD, WE NEED YOUR MERCY - YES, WE DESPERATELY NEED YOUR MERCY!"*

↑ A MOST BEAUTIFUL PICTURE OF SOLOMON AND HIS BELOVED: READ ABOUT THEIR MARRIAGE CEREMONY IN SONG OF SOLOMON 3.

# SATAN'S ADVICE TO JESUS (1 OF 2)

SUBMIT YOURSELVES THEREFORE TO GOD. RESIST THE DEVIL, AND HE WILL FLEE FROM YOU. (JAMES 4:7)

The books of Matthew, Mark, and Luke address a time when Satan came to tempt Jesus. This happened shortly after Christ began the work of his public ministry. It's amazing to think that the devil believed he could win Jesus over to his side. Didn't he know whom he was up against? But that's just the thing about Satan - his pride is his downfall, and in his pride, he tried to cause the Son of God to sin.

How did he "advise" Jesus? After miraculously fasting for 40 days and nights, Jesus was understandably vulnerable. Ever the deceiver, Satan did not swoop in and declare, "Hello, Jesus. I am going to kill you now." Instead, the devil presents three conditions for Christ. Three "ifs." "If you are the Son of God" covers the first two, and "if you bow down and worship me" is the last. After fasting for that long, who among us would have been able to withstand the devil?

As is typical of his approach, Satan twists the truth, hoping to trip up Jesus. "Was Jesus the Son of God?" Of course he was. There was no "if, and, or but" about it. And as we read through the temptations, could Jesus have turned a stone into bread, be rescued from harm by angels, and choose to worship Satan? Yes, he had the power to make any of those choices. Yet, he did not. We also see Satan using his original tactics by appealing to "the cravings of sinful man, the lust of his eyes, and the boasting of what he has and does" (1 John 2:16). But, as he always does, he lost to God again on that day.

Praise God that His Son did not follow the advice of Satan! His victory is our victory. And like Jesus, we can also withstand the wiles of the devil.

↑ MATTHEW 4:1-11 RECORDS THE TEMPTATION OF JESUS.

# SATAN'S ADVICE TO JESUS (2 OF 2)

AND WHEN THE DEVIL HAD ENDED EVERY TEMPTATION, HE DEPARTED FROM HIM UNTIL AN OPPORTUNE TIME. (LUKE 4:13)

Starving. Lonely. Thirsty. Afraid. Exposed. These words described Jesus on the cross, but they also accurately portray his plight in the desert, during the days that Satan came to tempt him.

How did Jesus handle the temptation of Satan? If I were Jesus, I think I would have picked him up and chucked him somewhere beyond the Nile River. However, Jesus always obeyed his Father. In this case, he quoted Scripture. He simply told Satan what the Bible said, which was the most powerful thing he could have done. In truth, Jesus gave him his very words, since Jesus is God himself. And on that authority, the devil had to high-tail it out of there. That's just awesome!

Each time Satan "advised" Jesus on what to do, Christ came back with commands that God had given His people from the books of the Law (in this case, it was Deuteronomy). Satan attempted to use God's word against Christ (when he told Jesus to jump from the top of a tower, the devil quoted Psalm 91:11-12). Yet the devil only uses the Bible when it suits his purposes; even at that, he only knows how to twist the truth.

Teens, this is a huge wake-up call for all of us who know very little about what the Bible says. When (not *if*, but *when*) Satan comes to tempt us, those who are clueless about God's commands will fall to temptation. Ignorance of the truth leaves us vulnerable to sin.

However, when "I have stored up your word in my heart", I will "not sin against you" (Psalm 119:11). What a great way to be like Jesus!

↑ READ ANOTHER ACCOUNT OF THE TEMPTATION: LUKE 4:1-13.

## SATAN'S ADVICE ON RULES

As Jehudi read three or four columns, the king would cut them off with a knife and throw them into the fire in the fire pot, until the entire scroll was consumed in the fire that was in the fire pot. (Jeremiah 36:23)

Jehoiakim... what a wicked king he was! Things are desperate in the land of Judah - judgment and exile are close at hand - and this hardened man is burning up a message from the LORD. His heart was so dull that he had no regard whatsoever for God's words. His reign would not last long; he would die in his sin.

Satan must have been very pleased with Jehoiakim, as he is with all who set aside the law of the Lord. He has tricked mankind into thinking that rules are associated with slavery, pain, boredom, etc. So he advises us in finding ways to ignore and disregard them. In his book, rules are always negative.

Rules do not make us Christians. But as a Christian, I am here to tell you that God's rule give me freedom! By not using foul language, his rule over my tongue has led me to have respect with those I am free to influence. By not flirting with other women, his rule over my marriage has led to deeper intimacy with my wife. By consistently reading His Word, his rule over my time has given me the freedom to live eternal moments. It is for reasons like these that I love His law over my life (which David expressed splendidly in Psalm 119).

God's rules stand in opposition to Satan's advice - His rules are the very definition of freedom!

READ THIS ACCOUNT OF JEHOIAKIM'S LIFE IN JEREMIAH 36:20-32.

# SATAN'S ADVICE ON BEER

WINE IS A MOCKER, STRONG DRINK A BRAWLER, AND WHOEVER IS LED ASTRAY BY IT IS NOT WISE. (PROVERBS 31:6-7)

Spending five years of my life living near the city of Scranton reminds me of beer on St. Patrick's Day. This is a big holiday for the thousands of Irish who live in that city. There is much green, and much beer, and even much green beer! There are also the consequences that come from drunkenness. Indeed, that day is not just about a nice parade winding through the streets of this city.

Some Christians like to spend hours debating if alcohol is acceptable to God. The Bible does not say a lot on this subject, but it says enough to convince me of my need to stay away from drinking.

Here's something to think about: what if Satan visited this St. Patrick's Day parade, and he was interviewed about all the beer? What would he say? Maybe the following..?

*"Beer helps me to relax, man! And did you know that there are actually some health benefits in alcoholic drinks? Besides, this parade is just once a year. It's a blast! How boring would it be without the alcohol flowing? A good beer takes a load off, and we all deserve to get rid of some stress now and then. Look at the people out here! We're having a great time! Besides, there are lots of great causes to come and support. Some of the bars have given back to the city. How could they do this without selling their product?"*

It all sounds good... but is it? When considering alcohol, may God give you wisdom as you choose to love Him *and* hate sin.

↑ CONSIDER PROVERBS 31:1-9 AND EPHESIANS 5:18. WHAT IF WE TOTALLY ABSTAINED FROM BEER? WOULD THAT BE WISDOM FOR US?

# SATAN'S ADVICE ON SEXUAL BOUNDARIES (1 OF 2)

I ADJURE YOU, O DAUGHTERS OF JERUSALEM, THAT YOU NOT STIR UP OR AWAKEN LOVE UNTIL IT PLEASES. (SONG OF SOLOMON 8:4)

I remember some talks I had with my youth pastor when my future wife and I started dating. He was a man I trusted, so I asked him the question of "how far is ok?" in a relationship. What I was looking for was a green light to kiss my girlfriend! Instead, he gave me his thoughts on how to handle self-control. What wisdom!

Satan does not hold back in his efforts to bombard us with lies about our sexuality. He desires to be the only "sex education" teacher in your life. He would never want you to go to the Bible to learn about sex, so he works hard to make God look like the bad guy (when in actuality, God created sex and celebrates it as a part of marriage. If you are not convinced about this, read the Song of Solomon).

Sex outside of marriage is on display everywhere. There is little to no respect for what God calls holy. We have lost track of what it means to be pure. As we stumble in the dark, many have lost the ability for a richer, fuller life. Truly, these are evil days.

Listen, teens: *we can have control over our sexuality!* Unlike what you might hear today, God did not make us animals who lack self-control. Instead, we are charged to "not stir up or awaken love until it pleases." I believe that command covers everything from the simple confession of "I love you!" to the cleaving of a man and his wife. We *can* have control; indeed, we *must* have control.

Guard your heart! Set boundaries! Don't listen to Satan's advice!

↑ JUDAH (JACOB'S SON) DID NOT DEFINE HIS SEXUAL BOUNDARIES, AND IT LEFT A REAL MESS BEHIND. READ GENESIS 38 TO LEARN MORE.

# SATAN'S ADVICE ON SEXUAL BOUNDARIES (2 OF 2)

FOR PEOPLE WILL BE LOVERS OF SELF, LOVERS OF MONEY, PROUD, ARROGANT, ABUSIVE, DISOBEDIENT TO THEIR PARENTS, UNGRATEFUL, UNHOLY, HEARTLESS, UNAPPEASABLE, SLANDEROUS, WITHOUT SELF-CONTROL, BRUTAL, NOT LOVING GOOD, TREACHEROUS, RECKLESS, SWOLLEN WITH CONCEIT, LOVERS OF PLEASURE RATHER THAN LOVERS OF GOD, HAVING THE APPEARANCE OF GODLINESS, BUT DENYING ITS POWER. AVOID SUCH PEOPLE. (2 TIMOTHY 3:2-5)

Sometimes it's hard to know the limits of sexual boundaries, since Satan has made such a mess of what is supposed to be beautiful and pure. In thinking back to my dating years, I know I focused on these boundaries in terms of what was lawful ("how far can I go?"), rather than seeing sex as a gift to be enjoyed for those who are patient.

Teens, it takes faith to control our bodies, trusting that God knows best. When it comes to sex, the Bible says, "Wait for it. If you do, you will be blessed by just how good it is!" Remember, waiting includes more than sexual intercourse; it also includes everything else that leads to the "stirring and awakening of love" (Song of Solomon 8:4).

Paul tells Timothy to relate to younger women as "sisters", and this is done "in all purity" (1 Timothy 5:2). Think about this: What are you wiling to do with your biological sister or brother? Would you hold their hand? Would you brush their hair? Would you kiss them? Would you touch them inappropriately, or "go all the way" with them? If the answer is "no way!" to any of these, then why would you do such a thing with a brother or sister in Christ? Perhaps this will give some perspective on what is appropriate, wouldn't you say?

If you respect the protective walls that God has put in place, you will not regret listening to Satan's advice.

GOD SAYS, "IN MARRIAGE, I REMOVE THE BOUNDARIES." TODAY, LET'S READ SONG OF SOLOMON 6.

# SATAN'S ADVICE ON HARD WORK

GO TO THE ANT, O SLUGGARD; CONSIDER HER WAYS, AND BE WISE. (PROVERBS 6:6)

On the subject of hard work, here is Satan's "advice":

*"Hey there! I see you, trying to drag yourself out of bed again this morning! You have to shower, and brush your teeth, and put some deodorant on, and all that stuff. Then you go to school and listen to teacher after teacher, all of whom give you tons of homework. Ugh!*

*"What a poor way to spend your day. However, since you have to do it, I have some advice for you. The less work, the better your life will be, right? Study just enough to pass your classes. You don't have to get an 'A'. Too much studying will keep you from doing what you want to do. Let's just focus on the fun times outside of school. You've got your friends, and your games, and your phone, and a status to update, and messages to send, and a party to attend later this week. The homework can wait. Also, skip whatever chores you can get out of... your mom will eventually do them, if you wait long enough.*

*"Hey, what's this? That new movie you've been waiting for is now playing at the theater? Get on down there; you deserve it! Let's do your work another time (maybe after you have slept in this Sunday morning?). Take it easy! Like I've told you before, you live just once!"*

Satan's goal for you is to eliminate all hard work. If you choose to be lazy, you will fail, and by doing so, you will accomplish his goal for him.

Teens, let's be an ant, and not a sluggard!

EMBRACE HARD WORK! BE CHALLENGED BY PROVERBS 6:1-11.

## SATAN'S ADVICE ON THINGS TO COME

BUT THE DAY OF THE LORD WILL COME LIKE A THIEF, AND THEN THE HEAVENS WILL PASS AWAY WITH A ROAR, AND THE HEAVENLY BODIES WILL BE BURNED UP AND DISSOLVED, AND THE EARTH AND THE WORKS THAT ARE DONE IN IT WILL BE EXPOSED. (2 PETER 3:10)

God desires that we take care of the earth (He told us to have dominion over it in Genesis 1:26-28), However, He never told us to save our planet. That's right; He never said anything about our responsibility to keep this world moving into the unforeseeable future.

Wait a minute... if not us, then who will make sure the earth is going to be ok? Well, let's see. How about the One who created it in the first place! God is in control. Since this is true, who has been telling us that we humans must save the earth? Hmm...

Remember, Satan will advise us by slowly leading us away from the truth until we completely buy the lie. In reality, this world can *never* be saved by us. It does not have millions of years left (as it never had millions of years beforehand). Our efforts to take care of the environment may help in the immediate, yet it is only delaying the inevitable consequences of the curse.

At our church, we do ministries like the "Adopt-a-Highway" program; it helps us to be an example to our community. Yet we realize that picking up 40 bags of trash a year does not add centuries to the existence of humanity. We trust God in things to come, *and* we live responsibly by taking care of His creation.

God knows how the future will unfold. He has reveal much of that information with us. Satan is not interested in you learning about it!

↑ CHECK OUT THE FUTURE "DAY OF THE LORD" IN 2 PETER 3.

# SIN IS DISGUSTING!

LIKE A DOG THAT RETURNS TO ITS VOMIT IS A FOOL WHO REPEATS HIS FOLLY. (PROVERBS 26:11)

The Bible is often surprising! It isn't afraid of using vivid illustrations to get a point across. If you have ever owned a dog in your life, you have probably seen Proverbs 26:11 in action. Perhaps you are not so quick to get kisses from Fido when he decides to take the action above. Yuck!

We have a beautiful Sheltie named "River." He's a lot of fun, makes us laugh, protects the yard from squirrels, and loves to sit on our laps. However, he is still a dog; at times, he also lives out the proverb!

For God, choosing what is wrong over and over again is like a dog and his vomit. Sin disgusts Him. When Jesus bore our sin at the cross, God the Father had to turn away. He could not stand it. Our sin was so revolting that He needed to take drastic measures against it, which meant the death of His Son.

Why do people return to their sin? According to Scripture, a constant return to folly is the mark of a fool. His conscience tells him that sin is wrong, yet he denies it and plays some more in the mud. As you consider the fool, maybe someone comes to your mind, but when we ourselves run to sin, we play the the fool. God has given us a banquet of delicacies, yet we somehow think that our vomit will taste better. It is spiritually gross, and it leaves us so unfulfilled.

Do you hate sin? Does it disgust you? The hatred of sin is a true mark of a Christian. Don't be like a dog!

🡅 PROVERBS 26:11 IS QUOTED LATER IN THE NEW TESTAMENT - READ ABOUT FOOLISH TEACHERS IN 2 PETER 2:17-22.

# LAMENTING WITH HOPE

"THE LORD IS MY PORTION," SAYS MY SOUL, "THEREFORE I WILL HOPE IN HIM." (LAMENTATIONS 3:24)

It's the young lady that quit doing homework a long time ago, only to find out that now she won't graduate. It's the young man who pressured his girlfriend into having sex, only to discover he will be a father in a matter of months. It's the girl who started smoking when she was fourteen, and now has cancer with only days to live. It's the man who just cannot quit drinking, and now has no family at home.

Each one of these people has cause for lament. They now live their days full of heartache, misery, and regret.

Jeremiah lived in the days when his nation fell. Israel's own evil finally conquered them, so He rightfully poured out His wrath upon His people. The prophet knew that their demise was coming, but like the death of a loved one, it did very little to take away the pain he experienced. As he looked upon his beloved city of Jerusalem – the city of the Lord, where God dwelt in His holy temple – all he could do was weep. He poured out his emotions in the book of Lamentations.

Can you relate to Jeremiah? Personally, I have never experienced loss to that magnitude. But when I hurt, I know where I can go to find an understanding ear. God has included many laments in His Bible, for He knows that we live in a lamentable world, where sin causes terrible pain and suffering. Thankfully, *a biblical lament always provides hope in the worst of circumstances.* In the midst of his deep grief, Jeremiah proclaimed, "The steadfast love of the LORD never ceases; his mercies never come to an end; they are new every morning; great is your faithfulness" (Lamentations 3:22-23).

PLEASE READ LAMENTATIONS 3 TODAY.

# QUALIFIED BY GOD

HE SHALL BE TO YOU A RESTORER OF LIFE AND A NOURISHER OF YOUR OLD AGE, FOR YOUR DAUGHTER-IN-LAW WHO LOVES YOU, WHO IS MORE TO YOU THAN SEVEN SONS, HAS GIVEN BIRTH TO HIM. (RUTH 4:15)

I am not qualified to play in the National Football League. When I was a kid, I dreamed of playing in the NFL. However, I'm not strong enough, skilled enough, in shape enough, and sadly, I'm now not young enough!

In the days of Ruth, one could also say that she was not qualified to be in the line of Christ. The Bible tells us that Ruth is the great-grandmother of King David, who is well-known for his place in the kingly lineage of our Savior. But Ruth was also a woman of Moab (an enemy nation of Israel). She was married once before, but she lost her husband not long afterward. To think that she would fit into God's big plan would be hard to imagine during the ugly days of Israel's judges. Ruth would have certainly "muddied" the Messianic line... right?

Funny how God ignores the presumptions of men! This godly woman left Moab to care for her widowed mother-in-law. In faith, she went out into a stranger's field empty and came home full... with food *and* the hope of a future husband. Her decision to propose to him was nothing less than courageous. When all was said and done, Ruth became both a wife and mother, who earned an honored position in biblical history. What a wonderful story in the midst of hopeless days!

Are you qualified? This answer does not really depend upon what you do, but rather Who you belong to. If you belong to the Lord, you are perfectly qualified to do His great work. What that work might be, only God knows; but whatever it is, do it in faith! A life lived in faith qualifies you for the rewards you will receive in heaven one day.

READ RUTH 1, 2, 3, OR 4... OR THE WHOLE BOOK! IT'S SO GOOD!

# WHAT HE WANTED TO SAY, AND WHAT HE SAID

BELOVED, ALTHOUGH I WAS VERY EAGER TO WRITE TO YOU ABOUT OUR COMMON SALVATION, I FOUND IT NECESSARY TO WRITE APPEALING TO YOU TO CONTEND FOR THE FAITH THAT WAS ONCE FOR ALL DELIVERED TO THE SAINTS. (JUDE 3)

Not long ago, it was my duty to call someone about our church's decision to exercise discipline upon her. Thankfully, she didn't give me a hard time during our brief conversation, but when I hung up, I felt sick. When a member of the family refuses to turn away from sin, God tells the church that discipline is in order. It's not easy to do so!

I would have rather talked about the faith that we share together. In fact, we shared many wonderful experiences together as members of our church. I look back fondly on those memories.

The book of Jude is a little letter in the Bible, found right before the last book of Revelation. In verse 3, Jude shares what he originally wanted to write about. However, the rest of his letter is focused upon those who wanted to destroy God's people. He wrote about this topic, not out of desire, but out of necessity. He addressed the elephant in the room - evil people were infiltrating the ranks, intent upon dismantling the church. Their work was nasty business, so Jude wasted no words in condemning them for who they really were.

Teens, as long as the devil is on the move, we have a fight on our hands! Unfortunately, he takes no vacation time. We can celebrate the fact that all believers have eternal life, as we should. But our lives are under spiritual attack. Unless we put on the full armor of God (see Ephesians 6), we will fall. Let's not hide our faces from the present reality. When we turn to God, we turn from sin; and in order to do this, we need to "contend for the faith."

↑ READ THE SHORT BOOK OF JUDE TODAY.

## WHAT WERE THEY THINKING?

SO WHEN THE WOMAN SAW THAT THE TREE WAS GOOD FOR FOOD, AND THAT IT WAS A DELIGHT TO THE EYES, AND THAT THE TREE WAS TO BE DESIRED TO MAKE ONE WISE, SHE TOOK OF ITS FRUIT AND ATE, AND SHE ALSO GAVE SOME TO HER HUSBAND WHO WAS WITH HER, AND HE ATE. (GENESIS 3:6)

It only took seconds... but oh, the things that go through our minds in seconds.

You know the story. You know how Adam and Eve fell. And whenever we struggle with sin, we are reminded that they ate from the wrong tree. Sometimes I wonder what was going on inside the heads of our original parents. What were they thinking?

Eve: *"Wow, I've never been shopping at this tree before! How beautiful is the fruit on it! It must be as tasty as it looks! You know what? This strange-talking snake has a point. I can take this fruit for myself! What's the big deal, anyway? Why would God hold anything back from me? And look, Adam is not saying anything to stop me."*

Adam: *"Wow, what an amazing place! What an amazing woman! But who is she talking to? A serpent? That seems a bit odd. What he is saying makes sense, though that is not at all what God told me. What should I do? I'll just watch and see what happens and... oh, she took a bite. She looks fine to me! Guess I will take a bite, too."*

So sad. So tragic. So long, Garden of Eden. Don't kid yourselves - we would have done the same thing. To win us back, God would make the ultimate sacrifice, and it would come at a great price.

Always be thankful to God for sending Jesus Christ as our Savior. At the fall, when we thought about ourselves, He thought about our salvation.

↑ HOW DID THEY FALL? READ GENESIS 3:1-13.

## YOUR RESPONSE

BUT HE WAS PIERCED FOR OUR TRANSGRESSIONS; HE WAS CRUSHED FOR OUR INIQUITIES; UPON HIM WAS THE CHASTISEMENT THAT BROUGHT US PEACE, AND WITH HIS WOUNDS WE ARE HEALED. (ISAIAH 53:5)

The Lord is always teaching His children, and lately, He has been teaching me about the gravity of our sin. Isaiah 53 is a clear chapter on how "The Suffering Servant" had to die for us. Yes, it was for us! His death was personal to God, and it demands a response from us.

What are some words that describe what Jesus experienced in our behalf? Here are some found in Isaiah 53: **despised, rejected, sorrowful, suffering, stricken, smitten, afflicted, pierced, crushed, oppressed, judged, guilty (by association).**

What is your response? For an unbeliever, sadness alone will not do. Feeling guilty does not cut it. Understanding the weight of our sin is not enough. There is only one course of action; there is only one proper response. *We must repent!* Turn to God. Get on the floor, face down, and beg Him for forgiveness. Ask Him to save you from certain doom. Believe that Jesus died for you. It was *your* sin that put him on the cross. Your response must be personal, or it is not true repentance.

*"Dear Father, I only came to you because you loved me first. Thank you for bringing me to my knees. You came calling for this poor sinner, and You caused me to respond in faith. I will worship You, forever!"*

🡅 READ ISAIAH 53. WHAT THOUGHTS COME TO MIND? WHY THOSE SPECIFIC THOUGHTS? HAVE YOU RESPONDED TO THE ONE WHO DIED IN YOUR BEHALF?

## WHAT MAKES A GOOD PRESIDENT?

AND BEHOLD, A MAN CAME UP TO HIM, SAYING, "TEACHER, WHAT GOOD DEED MUST I DO TO HAVE ETERNAL LIFE?" AND HE SAID TO HIM, "WHY DO YOU ASK ME ABOUT WHAT IS GOOD? THERE IS ONLY ONE WHO IS GOOD. IF YOU WOULD ENTER LIFE, KEEP THE COMMANDMENTS." (MATTHEW 19:16-17)

What makes a good president? Ask 100 different people, and I think you will get 100 different answers! I am thankful for the men who have served our office well (in particular, I have always admired Abraham Lincoln as my favorite president).

The word "good" has been used in a number of ways. What does this word even mean? Well, take a look again at Matthew 19:16-17.

Notice how "good" is mentioned multiple times in just two verses? It's an important word here! My Bible concordance says that *good* has an intrinsic value; in other words, it focuses on what is internal. In these verses, we can properly conclude that God alone is good; He *alone* does all things well. With that definition of "good", a president is only good if God lives within him/her. It is not the external acts that makes the president a good person; no, goodness is based upon the fact that God is working through him/her.

We may like the policies of the president, and his/her efforts might put us in a better position. I'm thankful when this happens. However, we also need to consider this: "Would God Himself say that our president is good?" His thoughts matter far more than my opinions!

Here's the bottom line: we have a good president when that president puts God first. It is then that the people are served well.

↑ LEARN MORE ABOUT "PRESIDENTS" (KINGS) IN PROVERBS 25:1-8.

## WHAT A LONG TIME!

THEN THE LORD SAID TO ABRAM, "KNOW FOR CERTAIN THAT YOUR OFFSPRING WILL BE SOJOURNERS IN A LAND THAT IS NOT THEIRS AND WILL BE SERVANTS THERE, AND THEY WILL BE AFFLICTED FOR FOUR HUNDRED YEARS." (GENESIS 15:13)

When we consider the story of Moses and the deliverance of Israel, we are faced with a difficult question: "Why did God allow the tribes of Israel to be in slavery for 400 years before Moses delivered them?" It's a stunning amount of time, and honestly, I have no idea why the Lord decreed four centuries (!) to pass before He delivered them. Think about it - at least 10 generations of people never knew freedom from slavery. That's hard to grasp!

At the surface level, it doesn't seem fair. But what else do we know about God? 1. His ways are not our ways (Isaiah 55:8-9). 2. He puts all of us in a position to respond in faith, regardless of the circumstances around us (Hebrews 11). 3. He will not leave us nor forsake us, and trials are only for a season (Revelation 6:9-11). 4. He has a purpose in mind; sometimes He tells us, and sometimes He doesn't (in the context above, God tells Abram in verse 16 that the wickedness of the people in the Promised Land had "not yet reached its full measure", meaning that He would punish them when it was time to do so).

You know what? The Israelites who believed in God during those years of slavery now stand complete before Him. They praise God right now as you read this devotional. They have no regrets about how the Lord handled their lives on earth. They know that we are all saved by grace!

Let's praise God for the freedoms that we have here on earth. Even more so, let's praise Him that we are not slaves to sin and death.

↑ READ ABOUT THE SLAVERY OF GOD'S PEOPLE IN EXODUS 1.

# THE PRAYER OF A RIGHTEOUS MAN

THEREFORE, CONFESS YOUR SINS TO ONE ANOTHER AND PRAY FOR ONE ANOTHER, THAT YOU MAY BE HEALED. THE PRAYER OF A RIGHTEOUS PERSON HAS GREAT POWER AS IT IS WORKING. (JAMES 5:16)

WHY DO I HAVE A TREASURE OF A WIFE? SOMEONE PRAYED.

WHY DO I HAVE THREE AMAZING KIDS? SOMEONE PRAYED.

WHY AM I IN THE MINISTRY? SOMEONE PRAYED.

WHY DO I HAVE GOOD HEALTH? SOMEONE PRAYED.

WHY ARE MY NEEDS MET EVERY DAY? SOMEONE PRAYED.

WHY DOES ANYTHING GOOD HAPPEN TO ME AT ALL? SOMEONE PRAYED.

WHY AM I SAVED? SOMEONE PRAYED.

With my whole heart, I believe in the power of prayer. And for God to have done the things that He has done for me, I understand that righteous people were praying in my behalf. There is no way I would be anything close to a good man if it were not for the prayers of the righteous. I would have been dead in the water, I know!

*"God, thank you for those who have prayed for me. I'm guessing You have answered many prayers for my life. I know you delight in the prayers of the righteous. May I be found worthy to be a prayer warrior for my brothers and sisters. It's all for your glory! In Jesus' Name, Amen."*

↑ FIND CLUES ABOUT DANIEL'S RIGHTEOUS CHARACTER IN DANIEL 10.

# EITHER IT'S TRUE, OR IT'S NOT

SANCTIFY THEM IN THE TRUTH; YOUR WORD IS TRUTH. (JOHN 17:17)

*"The Pittsburgh Steelers belong to the National Football League. Founded in 1933, they are the oldest team in their conference. Their early decades were fraught with losing seasons, but in the 1970's, they turned into a winning team. At this date, they have more Super Bowl victories than any other team, with six Lombardi trophies in their possession. They have been owned by members of the Rooney family since the team's inception. Their colors are black and gold. The name of their stadium is Heinz Field. Their head coach is Mike Tomlin. They play their home games in Pittsburgh, Alaska."*

Well, it's nice to know a few things about the best NFL team ever (my humble opinion!), but something seems amiss. This mini-biography is exactly 100 words long, but one word is not correct. Can you guess which word it is? (Hint: look at the last word!).

So, if I told you that you could believe this paragraph about the Steelers because it is the truth, would I be correct? No, I would be lying. *"But wait! One word is wrong. The other ninety-nine words are correct. So this paragraph is 99% true!"* You know, as well as I do, that one word changes everything. A lie is a lie is a lie.

How about the Bible? It contains thousands of verses in hundreds of chapters in sixty-six books. If God's Word was 99% true, could you trust it? If not, which part is untrustworthy? And if that part is wrong, then what about other parts? Either the Bible is true, or it is not. We cannot have it both ways.

↑ JESUS PROCLAIMED GOD'S WORD TO BE TRUTH. LOOK AT THE EMPHASIS ON TRUTH IN JESUS' PRAYER IN JOHN 17:12-19.

# DUDES, WE NEED TO MAN UP!

IN THE SAME WAY HUSBANDS SHOULD LOVE THEIR WIVES AS THEIR OWN BODIES. HE WHO LOVES HIS WIFE LOVES HIMSELF. FOR NO ONE EVER HATED HIS OWN FLESH, BUT NOURISHES IT AND CHERISHES IT, JUST AS CHRIST DOES THE CHURCH, BECAUSE WE ARE MEMBERS OF HIS BODY. (EPHESIANS 5:28-30)

Today's devotion is geared to our guys!

Recently, I read about part of Jacob's life in Genesis 29 and 30. His life took many crazy twists and turns, for sure! He wanted to marry one girl, but ended up marrying her sister first, then married the girl he liked, then married the younger sister's maidservant, and then married the older sister's maidservant. Why did he have all these wives? Because the sisters fought with each other to see who could have more children, and they ended up using their maidservants in this contest. He really only loved one of his wives, but she was the one who had a hard time having kids. So... you thought your family had issues?!!

One thing that sticks out to me in this story is Jacob's ineffectual leadership. We watch the women of his life control him. He didn't necessarily ask them to do it; he just didn't step up to the plate and lead like a man is supposed to lead. His passive approach led to much pain in his life and in his family.

Young men, the Bible is not afraid to teach husbands about God's design for leadership. Men are far from perfect, and we often marry women smarter than us (I sure did!). However, by God's design, you are to lead your future wife. We just need to follow Christ's example.

"Loving" is a word of action. Guys, *be men of action!* Learn to "man up" now in your life. Love and serve well! Allow God to lead you, so that you will be "the man" for a future wife and family.

↑ CONSIDER THIS LEADERSHIP ROLE IN COLOSSIANS 3:18-25.

# FALL IN LOVE WITH GOD OVER EVERYTHING AND EVERYONE ELSE (BY CARL PESESKY)

I HAVE NO GREATER JOY THAN TO HEAR THAT MY CHILDREN ARE WALKING IN THE TRUTH. (3 JOHN 4)

John, the last living apostle, wrote this great verse to Gaius, a friend that he mentored. Gaius was faithful to Jesus by loving God and loving others! You can read throughout John's letters (1, 2, & 3 John) that loving God and loving others is a huge theme, which is something that John practiced and mentored to others. Love is a word that we use freely. I love coffee. I love French fries. I love this TV show. But if we take a moment to stop and consider the word "love", all other loves really do fall short when we consider the great love of God for us.

So great is His love for you and me that he sent his only Son (Jesus) to die, that we might live through him (John 3:16). It has been said that the person or thing that you spend the most time focused upon will become your god. So I encourage you to pursue an intimate relationship with God alone, and begin to learn for yourself how amazing and indescribable His love truly is for us!

The father in the story of the prodigal son (Luke 15:11-32) ran out to meet his son, even before anything had been set right. He didn't know that his son came back to express his sorrow. The father's lack of knowledge did not stop him from running to his son, because of the overwhelming love he had for him. God feels the same way about you.

God runs to you, right as you are! The Father longs for you to love Him and have the same oneness as His Son, had with Him when he walked the earth. So, spend time in God's Word; get to know the Father; and fall in love with God over everything and everyone else!

↑ CHECK OUT JOHN 17:20-26 TODAY.

# JULY

## THE PREAMBLE AND CHRIST'S KINGDOM

"We the People of the United States, in Order to form a more perfect Union, establish Justice, insure domestic Tranquility, provide for the common defence, promote the general Welfare, and secure the Blessings of Liberty to ourselves and our Posterity, do ordain and establish this Constitution for the United States of America."
(The Preamble for the Constitution of the United States of America)

The Vision. Core Values. A Mission Statement. The Strategy. These are conceptual terms meant to capture the heart of an organization. At our church, we are "Building Up and Reaching Out." Everything else we do falls under this vision. For a new nation that began in 1776, a constitution would be written one day, with it's vision expressed in the form of a preamble.

For the next several devotions, we are going to consider the Preamble of the U.S. Constitution in light of the future Kingdom of Christ. It will give us an opportunity to understand the natures of our physical and spiritual citizenship. We'll learn that there are many similarities between the two, but also some important differences. If you are an American, my hope is that these devotions will make you proud of your citizenship, but even more, that you will be thankful of your position as a child of God.

As a citizen of the United States, I might experience a full life (let's say 80 years, if I manage to live that long). As a citizen of the Kingdom, we will live 1,000 years and forever after. So if you live to be 100 years old on this earth, you will live 10 times as long in His Kingdom. That certainly makes the Millennial period worthy of study, don't you think?

🡅 CONSIDER THE EMPHASIS OF THE KINGDOM IN THE LORD'S PRAYER: READ MATTHEW 6:5-15.

# THE "PREAMBLE" OF ISRAEL'S CONSTITUTION

"HEAR, O ISRAEL: THE LORD OUR GOD, THE LORD IS ONE. YOU SHALL LOVE THE LORD YOUR GOD WITH ALL YOUR HEART AND WITH ALL YOUR SOUL AND WITH ALL YOUR MIGHT." (DEUTERONOMY 6:4-5)

In order for a nation to remain intact, it needs a set of laws that are respected and obeyed. God's laws for Israel are found are generally found in the second through fifth book of the Bible (Exodus, Leviticus, Numbers, and Deuteronomy). The reference above in Deuteronomy is known to the Jews as *The Shema*. We could liken the statement to our own preamble, as the Law itself rests upon this foundational command.

We know that God's command here is the greatest commandment, because Jesus himself told us so. Matthew 22:37-40 is one place we learn of this; he states that "on these two commands depend all the law and the prophets" (in this passage, the other command is, "You shall love your neighbor as yourself").

In the kingdom period, God will give His people a new heart, so that they will naturally love the Lord their God. It will be a peaceful time in which to live! I believe that everything commanded in Exodus through Deuteronomy will finally be carried out to perfection in the Millenium. There was never anything wrong with God's original "constitution"; it was His subjects that failed to obey. Israel had the 10 commandments; they had Moses, Aaron, and a whole priesthood to help them carry out their duties; and they had a set of rules that gave them freedom to live with God in their presence. But through sin, they repeatedly failed.

Not so in the kingdom. At the start of the millenium, "Thy kingdom *comes*, thy will *is* done on earth as it is in heaven." My U.S. citizenship cannot compare to the promised kingdom of Christ!

↑ PLEASE READ MATTHEW 22:34-40.

# "WE, THE PEOPLE OF THE KINGDOM OF CHRIST"

"BLESSED ARE THOSE WHO ARE PERSECUTED FOR RIGHTEOUSNESS' SAKE, FOR THEIRS IS THE KINGDOM OF HEAVEN." (MATTHEW 5:10)

(From The Preamble) *"We, the People of the United States."* It's a bold and powerful beginning! In these first few words, the focus is upon the establishment of a democracy. Teens, I trust you understand that most nations on earth are not governed "of the people, by the people, for the people," as Abraham Lincoln proclaimed in Gettysburg. The great experiment of these United States is based upon that first word: "We!" By God's grace, "We" are still here. What a privilege to live in this country. Never take it for granted!

(In The Kingdom) *"We, the People of the Kingdom of Christ."* We are a people that are known for being poor in spirit and persecuted for righteousness. God reminded Israel that their nation did not belong to Him because they were the best (see Deuteronomy 9:6). And Paul reminded the Corinthians that they were not "all that", either (see 1 Corinthians 1:26). Our nation's forefathers shared some of these very same qualities (they were also poor and persecuted), yet most of them recognized that only God can give the kind of freedom we enjoy today.

Make no mistake: in the Kingdom, we will not be led by "President Jesus". He is the King (sorry, Elvis and LeBron!). He will only lead one kind of government: a kingdom. A king is given all authority to rule, in whatever manner he sees fit. Most worldly kingdoms have been terrible because terrible men have been kings. In Christ's kingdom, we will finally be free to live in complete freedom. That freedom will be much greater than anything we have experienced as American citizens.

Why is this so? Well, just look at the King!

↑ CONSIDER OUR SHARED FUTURE WITH ISRAEL IN ISAIAH 44:1-5.

# "BY ORDER WILL ENJOY A PERFECT UNION"

BEHOLD, HOW GOOD AND PLEASANT IT IS WHEN BROTHERS DWELL IN UNITY! (PSALM 133:1)

(From The Preamble) *"in Order to form a more perfect Union."* Our unity is found in our diversity, but that diversity must allow truth to reign. Our union is built upon the presence of justice, peace, defense, the good of all, freedom, and the blessings of prosperity that follow. Our constitution is the order that is meant to promote all of these blessings. We also see the existence of these same pursuits in the Kingdom of Christ. it's no wonder we have a strong foundation in our country! Certainly, that union has been tested (especially in The Civil War), but by God's grace, we have survived.

(In The Kingdom) *"by order will enjoy a perfect union."* Order will exist in the Millenium, but not by the will of the people. Christ will rule with "a rod of iron" (as mentioned three times in the book of Revelation). His believing subjects will gladly serve under him. The unbelieving subjects will be made to serve at his pleasure. Above all, unity will be enforced. This unity will be glorious; finally, we will have a King who always looks after the good of his subjects. Corruption will not exist under Christ. We all will know exactly what we are to do, and we will do it. Your neighbor will care about your well-being; there will not be a "bad part of town"; we will not need a police force to keep the peace; trust will be in abundance.

Does this sound good to you? It's coming! And for all who believe in Jesus Christ, a role given by the King will be yours! I am looking forward to the day when I will enjoy his order, in unity with you all.

↑ PLEASE READ ISAIAH 32:1-8.

# "ESTABLISHED BY HIS JUSTICE"

HE SHALL NOT JUDGE BY WHAT HIS EYES SEE, OR DECIDE DISPUTES BY WHAT HIS EARS HEAR, BUT WITH RIGHTEOUSNESS HE SHALL JUDGE THE POOR, AND DECIDE WITH EQUITY FOR THE MEEK OF THE EARTH; AND HE SHALL STRIKE THE EARTH WITH THE ROD OF HIS MOUTH, AND WITH THE BREATH OF HIS LIPS HE SHALL KILL THE WICKED. (ISAIAH 11:3B-4)

(From The Preamble) *"establish justice."* It means "to put in place those people or institutions that make right decisions." As a result of this establishment, we have justice on many levels. This includes local, district, state, and national courts. At their best, they uphold the law of the land. Teens, in all the right ways, we need justice. When we do what is right, the law is in our favor, and it protects us from those who are lawless. A nation without justice is a nation ripe for destruction.

(In The Kingdom) *"established by his justice."* Indeed, the King will rule with a rod of iron. As you read from Isaiah 11 today, you will notice that the King is full of the Spirit, which equips him to perfectly judge, without the need of help from others (though he will use us, for his purpose and glory). He does not rely on his senses (we certainly do, but he does not, as we read in Isaiah 11:3). The Spirit-led King will do what is right in everything. What a blessing for all who rejoice in his rule!

Some will not rejoice in it. The human heart can be so foolish, and as the Millenium comes to a close, many will rebel. The King's final act of justice will be to vanquish the unjust one to that eternal place of judgment – the Lake of Fire. When Satan's fate is fulfilled, justice will reach its conclusion. Christ will forever be King, and we will know him for eternity as the One who vanquished sin forever. Amen!

↑ THE JUST KING IS COMING TO REIGN. READ ABOUT IT IN ISAIAH 11:1-9.

## "INSURED BY HIS SOVEREIGN TRANQUILITY"

"I HAVE SEEN HIS WAYS, BUT I WILL HEAL HIM; I WILL LEAD HIM AND RESTORE COMFORT TO HIM AND HIS MOURNERS, CREATING THE FRUIT OF THE LIPS. PEACE, PEACE, TO THE FAR AND THE NEAR," SAYS THE LORD, "AND I WILL HEAL HIM." (ISAIAH 57:18-19)

(From The Preamble) *"insure domestic Tranquility."* Stated another way, "We will make sure there is peace inside of our borders." It is what motivated Abraham Lincoln to go to war with the South. He knew that "united we stand; divided we fall." It is also why these current days are scary. The mayhem that has accompanied recent presidential elections are a direct attack on domestic tranquility. The same is true for the disrespect and abuse poured upon law enforcement. In the past, we have been a nation based upon principles higher than ourselves. Peace is lost when truth is ignored.

(In The Kingdom) *"insured by his sovereign tranquility."* As king, Christ will rule this world, and he will bring an undisputed peace to earth. The coming Antichrist will unite the world, but he will bring a false peace, a peace that is not based upon the will of God. The peace of Christ is always given to those of us who are saved, as we now have a restored relationship with the Father. In the Millenium, believers "shall go out in joy and be led forth in peace; the mountains and the hills before you shall break forth into singing, and all the trees of the field shall clap their hands" (Isaiah 55:12).

Teens, we can pray for world peace! However, those who understand the prophecy of the Bible will recognize that world peace is at least 7 years away (the Rapture and the Tribulation must come first).

Do you believe in peace? More specifically, do you believe in the God of peace? He is the only One who can offer it for eternity.

🡅 CHECK OUT ISAIAH 55!

# "PROVIDED FOR BY HIS PERFECT DEFENSE"

BUT THERE THE LORD IN MAJESTY WILL BE FOR US A PLACE OF BROAD RIVERS AND STREAMS, WHERE NO GALLEY OF OARS CAN GO, NOR MAJESTIC SHIP CAN PASS. FOR THE LORD IS OUR JUDGE; THE LORD IS OUR LAWGIVER; THE LORD IS OUR KING; HE WILL SAVE US. (ISAIAH 33:21-22)

(From The Preamble) *"provide for the common defence."* If a nation is to survive, it must do everything in its power to protect itself. Teens, don't be fooled; there are *many* nations that would just love to see our nation destroyed. Yes, we have allies (for which we should be grateful), yet the hearts of wicked men desire power over freedom. This desire is not limited to certain groups of terrorists or religious fanatics. The USA must have a good military in place, or else it could be conquered by a number of opportunistic nations. Keep this in mind: Satan's plan is to throw this whole world into chaos, leaving us with the belief that his solution (the Antichrist) is our only hope. If America falls, the door may be wide open for the devil to make this move. It's a sobering thought!

(In The Kingdom) *"provided for by his perfect defense."* Psalm 46 is a great song that describes Christ's work of provision in the Millenium. Verse 9 tells us, "He makes wars cease to the end of the earth; he breaks the bow and shatters the spear, he burns the chariots with fire." His rule is so complete that we will not need a military! Again, Isaiah talks about Christ's kingdom in Isaiah 2:4, "He shall judge between the nations, and shall decide disputes for many peoples; and they shall beat their swords into plowshares, and their spears into pruning hooks; nation shall not lift up sword against nation, neither shall they learn war anymore." A peace that is so perfect, in which we can turn weapons into farm equipment? Wow!!!

Teens, all who know the King as Lord and Savior are going to live in these days. May God stir rejoicing in your hearts!

↑ SEE WHAT ISAIAH 2:1-5 HAS TO SAY.

# "PROMISED BY HIS FULFILLED WELFARE"

HOW BEAUTIFUL UPON THE MOUNTAINS ARE THE FEET OF HIM WHO BRINGS GOOD NEWS, WHO PUBLISHES PEACE, WHO BRINGS GOOD NEWS OF HAPPINESS, WHO PUBLISHES SALVATION, WHO SAYS TO ZION, "YOUR GOD REIGNS." (ISAIAH 52:7)

(From The Preamble) *"promote the general welfare."* Our government exists for the good of the people, and the Constitution is in place to make sure this happens. When we hear the word "welfare" today, our mind takes us to a system that exists for the poor. It is a system that is often abused. Yet our founding fathers used this word in reference to the good of the citizens. Our good is not dependent upon having lots of money, or an amazing job, or all the toys that we can get. The privilege of American citizenship is the reality of unconditional freedom. We live in this land to take care of one another (to love your neighbor as yourself), so that we may thrive as "one nation, under God."

(In The Kingdom) *"promised by his fulfilled welfare."* In Christ's Kingdom, the King will rule with the good of His subjects in mind. Ezekiel 34 likens his rule as a shepherd over his sheep. The sheep will thrive under the goodness of the Ruling Shepherd, as he knows all of their needs. Just look how joyful the people will be to live under the welfare of the King: "The voice of your watchmen – they lift up their voice; together they sing for joy; for eye to eye they see the return of the LORD to Zion. Break forth together into singing, you waste places of Jerusalem, for the LORD has comforted his people; he has redeemed Jerusalem." (Isaiah 52:8-9).

God has a way of making things good, doesn't He? We will better understand the word "welfare" in the Kingdom. God's goodness is unsurpassed. The millennial government will finally be for the good of the people, and it will be for the glory of the Lord!

↑ LET'S READ ISAIAH 52:1-12.

# "AND SECURED BY THE BLESSINGS OF LIBERTY TO HIS SUBJECTS"

For I will pour water on the thirsty land, and streams on the dry ground; I will pour my Spirit upon your offspring, and my blessing on your descendants. (Isaiah 44:3)

(From The Preamble) *"and secure the Blessings of Liberty to ourselves and our Posterity."* For nearly two and a half centuries, we have enjoyed the blessings of liberty. We are a free people. In spite of attacks from the inside and the outside, we have endured. America, let us remember that God has shed His grace on Thee! I consider myself among those who believe that our posterity will continue with two conditions: one, if we place ourselves under God's authority, and two, if the Constitution is both honored and held in the highest regard.

(In The Kingdom) *"and secured by the blessings of liberty to his subjects."* With Christ as King, we have freedom. Truly, in spite of living in this great country, we cannot experience the kind of freedom we will have in the Millenium. For 1,000 years, we will not be limited by rules which make life difficult to live. No more taxes (!); no more laws that require us to support the government so that it can survive; no more "Republicans vs. Democrats"; no more insecurities about the intentions of our leaders; no more lies from the media; no more failed promises from politicians. Liberty, at its fullest, is offered in the Kingdom.

To a degree, Israel was enjoying the blessings of liberty in Isaiah's lifetime. Yet he knew that their liberty was only temporary, and that Israel will only experience the complete blessing of being a liberated nation when Christ takes the helm. What a tremendous privilege that we also will known as those who belong to the Lord (Isaiah 44:5).

🠉 PLEASE READ ISAIAH 43:25 - 44:5.

## "DO LIVE UNDER THE RULE OF CHRIST IN HIS KINGDOM"

FOR THE LORD WILL HAVE COMPASSION ON JACOB AND WILL AGAIN CHOOSE ISRAEL, AND WILL SET THEM IN THEIR OWN LAND, AND SOJOURNERS WILL JOIN THEM AND WILL ATTACH THEMSELVES TO THE HOUSE OF JACOB. (ISAIAH 14:1)

(From The Preamble) *"do ordain and establish this Constitution for the United States of America."* The words of our Preamble are powerful, but unless they are put into effect, they are just words. Since actions speak louder than words, our forefathers fought for the right to govern themselves according to their new Constitution. This makes me proud to be an American! I hope you feel the same way. Our nation is far from perfect, but it could never be perfect in the first place. When you think about our nation, don't turn a blind eye to our sins; but also don't forget about our blessings. Indeed, "God shed His grace on Thee!"

(In The Kingdom) *"do live under the rule of Christ in his Kingdom."* What a wonderful privilege! I already belong to him – he bought me with his blood – but one day, I will also live in the days of his earthly reign. To live as a subject under this reign will be glorious. His kingdom will bridge the time between the seven-year judgment of this world and the eternal state. Isaiah 65 tells us that we will rejoice in this day. Jerusalem will be our capital. People will live for a very long time. The work of our hands will thrive. Animals won't be carnivorous. We will finally live in harmony. So, let us say, "Thy Kingdom come!"

As we wrap up this series, here is a conjectured view of "The Preamble of the Kingdom." It states, *"We, the People of the Kingdom of Christ, by order will enjoy a perfect union, established by his justice, insured by his sovereign tranquility, provided for by his perfect defense, promised by his fulfilled welfare, and secured by the blessings of liberty to his subjects, do live under the rule of Christ in his kingdom."*

↑ READ ISAIAH 65:17-25. WHAT GREAT VERSES!

## RECLAIMING BIBLICAL WORDS

FOR TRULY, I SAY TO YOU, UNTIL HEAVEN AND EARTH PASS AWAY, NOT AN IOTA, NOT A DOT, WILL PASS FROM THE LAW UNTIL ALL IS ACCOMPLISHED. (MATTHEW 5:18)

Civilizations have languages. Languages are based on words. As a father, I marvel how my children began to learn words. Sometimes Lisa and I taught them words, but in most cases, they simply began to copy us (just like you did when you were running around in diapers!).

Civilizations also have a way of processing words. Through the centuries, some words have remained true to their original meaning, while others have been altered considerably. Some words belong in languages of a higher, more educated society; some belong to the common folk. Some words disappear when a language is lost in history. Some words are slang, and some are blasphemous.

God's Word is made up of many words, yet we still call it "The Word". His Bible is perfect, timeless, and unified, so it rightly is given a singular description. Jesus tells his listeners that the Law (referring to the Scriptures) is so sure, even the little dot on the letter "i" will come to pass! How wonderful is that? If people would believe the words of Matthew 5:18, they would be in awe of the glorious truth found in the Bible. Everything written will be accomplished!

The next series of devotions will bring our attention to many significant words found in the Bible. I will focus our attention on a specific list of words. They are words that have been undermined by our society.

If we are to take God's Word seriously, we need to view the words of the Bible as holy in nature. Let's reclaim them together!

🡅 "WISDOM" AND "THE WORD" ARE VERY MUCH CONNECTED. READ PROVERBS 2.

# RECLAIMING THE WORD AMEN

AND EZRA BLESSED THE LORD, THE GREAT GOD, AND ALL THE PEOPLE ANSWERED, "AMEN, AMEN," LIFTING UP THEIR HANDS. AND THEY BOWED THEIR HEADS AND WORSHIPED THE LORD WITH THEIR FACES TO THE GROUND. (NEHEMIAH 8:6)

Amen! We hear it at the end of a prayer; when we give thanks before a meal; or in response to something that moves us in a church service. For a Christian, it is an important word.

Why do we say "Amen"? What does it mean? Where did it come from?

The root of the word *Amen* means "to build up or support." Related terms include "faithfulness", "trust", and "firm". In everyday language, it is associated with a statement that is true. Add it all together, "Amen" simply means, "So be it". With that said, when you hear the word or speak it for yourself, replace "Amen" with "So be it," and consider what that means in your situation. It may help to shape or redefine your thinking.

"Amen" is the kind of word that can only be associated with truth as referenced in the Bible. It's a word that we often use quickly, and in doing so, we forget its power. However, when uttered by the wise and thoughtful, it is a word that connects us to believers from all generations of history. We boldly say, "So be it!" to both the blessings and curses of God; to His mercy and wrath; and to His grace and judgment. "Amen" is not limited to the pleasant moments alone; the Bible teaches us that it encompasses all that we consider positive or negative. Best of all, "Amen" is a word that is owned by Christ. "For all the promises of God find their Yes in him. That is why it is through him that we utter our Amen to God for his glory" (2 Corinthians 1:20). See why we add "In Jesus' Name" to our "Amen" at the end of a prayer?

🡅 READ 2 CORINTHIANS 1:15-23.

## RECLAIMING THE WORD GOD

AND AS SOON AS WE HEARD IT, OUR HEARTS MELTED, AND THERE WAS NO SPIRIT LEFT IN ANY MAN BECAUSE OF YOU, FOR THE LORD YOUR GOD, HE IS GOD IN THE HEAVENS ABOVE AND ON THE EARTH BELOW. (JOSHUA 2:11)

God's name is uttered all the time, for better or for worse. It's wonderful when we hear that "God loves you," and "God is so good to me, though I don't deserve it." It's terrible when we hear phrases like "Oh my God (or Gosh)" and "God, what is wrong with you?"

When we overuse any word in our language, it has a way of losing its meaning. For many, the name "God" is simply the name of a higher power (real or fictitious).

When people call me by name, they are not thinking that the name *Michael* means "Who is like God?". Yet that is the definition of my name. We do the same with God – we downgrade it to a title that is designated to Him, like we do with our own names. By doing this, we lose the value of the meaning.

But if you were Rahab, you would see God in a different light. In Joshua 2:11, she recognized Him as a deity – a holy being far greater than herself. In fact, He was the God above all Gods, the One who ruled both the heavens and the earth. In her world, there were many gods. The gods of her city were false gods, and her only hope was to plea for mercy and grace from the God of Israel. He spared Rahab and her family; when Joshua fought the battle of Jericho, her wall did not "come a'tumblin down!"

The careful Christian will be slow to utter God's holy name. He has the power to give life, and to take it away. Dare I speak His name in vain?

↑ CHECK OUT THE IMPORTANCE OF GOD'S NAME IN PSALM 20!

# RECLAIMING THE WORD LOVE

So now faith, hope, and love abide, these three; but the greatest of these is love. (1 Corinthians 13:13)

What is the definition of love?

In my life, I have "loved" the following:

1. Stuffed-crust pizza
2. Peanut butter pie.
3. The Pittsburgh Steelers.
4. Kayaking.
5. My wife and our children.

So, teens, which one have I really loved? Hmmm... I'd better answer carefully, right?!! Definitions are so important. If my love for pizza is the same as my love for my wife, we've got a big problem!

In our culture, the word *love* has been grossly mishandled. Both in quantity (the word is used far too often) and quality (our view of love is often lacking), we have lost the value of its meaning. So let's focus again on the "greatest of these" in 1 Corinthians 13. In this context, love is referred to as "agape" in the Greek language. Agape love knows know bounds. It's unselfish in action. It's not trying to get the best for itself. Agape love is so brilliant, glorious, and pure, that we know it must come from somewhere outside of ourselves! Jesus taught us about agape love when he died for our sin: "By this we know love, that he laid down his life for us, and we ought to lay down our lives for our brothers" (1 John 3:16). More than anything else, he exemplified love.

*"God, help me to reclaim this love in my life!"*

↑ READ 1 CORINTHIANS 13. IN CHRIST, WE CAN KNOW TRUE LOVE.

# RECLAIMING THE WORD PURE

WITH THE MERCIFUL YOU SHOW YOURSELF MERCIFUL; WITH THE BLAMELESS MAN YOU SHOW YOURSELF BLAMELESS; WITH THE PURIFIED YOU SHOW YOURSELF PURE; AND WITH THE CROOKED YOU MAKE YOURSELF SEEM TORTUOUS. (PSALM 18:26)

Several years ago, my brother Andy accepted the position of associate pastor at a church not far from me. He asked me to give a "pastoral challenge" during his installation service. It was a privilege for me to speak at this special time in his life. As I prepared my short message, I asked myself what I would personally need to hear as a pastor. I came up with three "remembers." I challenged Andy to remember "humility, purity, and charity."

Why purity? Because my brother and I both know that Satan is taking pastors out of the ministry at an alarming rate. When a person on the street hears the title "pastor", it often brings up feelings of distrust. Too many pastors have forgotten to pursue purity; now they are living the rest of their days with ruined reputations.

We have forgotten that purity is not limited merely to bottled water, the soap we use to wash our hands, or the standards set in place for products sold in stores. Purity is also not limited to the realm of sexuality. First of all, purity *is* related to holiness; the two go hand-in-hand. Purity is a big deal to God, who knows that we can achieve it in His power and grace.

Teens, being pure starts with our thoughts. Let Philippians 4:8 guide the way: "Finally, brothers, whatever is true, whatever is honorable, whatever is just, whatever is pure, whatever is lovely, whatever is commendable, if there is any excellence, if there is anything worthy of praise, think about these things." By God's grace, embrace purity!

↑ TAKE YOUR TIME TO READ PSALM 18 TODAY.

# RECLAIMING THE WORD HOLY

AS OBEDIENT CHILDREN, DO NOT BE CONFORMED TO THE PASSIONS OF YOUR FORMER IGNORANCE, BUT AS HE WHO CALLED YOU IS HOLY, YOU ALSO BE HOLY IN ALL YOUR CONDUCT, SINCE IT IS WRITTEN, "YOU SHALL BE HOLY, FOR I AM HOLY." (1 PETER 1:14-16)

If ever there was a word that needs to be reclaimed, it's the word "holy". It is a word that deeply matters to God (holiness is His most recognizable characteristic). Whatever matters to God should matter to us, right? To be *holy* is to "be separate"; and in relation to believers, we are to be separate from sin. Holiness deals with all aspects of the Christian life. We'll focus on our speech in this devotion.

Many years ago, we looked at a group of words during a youth group meeting. The words included nouns such as cow, guacamole, Toledo, moley, and Moses. I asked what they all had in common. Incredibly, one of our boys knew the answer immediately. They were expressions that people used with the word "holy" serving as the adjective.

Teens, why would we use such expressions? In part, because we have heard them uttered in our presence. But also, because "no human being can tame the tongue" (James 3:8).

Does this give us license to freely run our mouths, including the vain use of the word *holy*? Absolutely not! It's true - no *man* can tame the tongue, but *God* can certainly tame it!

*Holy* is one of the most important words that will ever exist. We need to be serious about our speech. May we use holy words! Heed the warning of Jesus Christ: "I tell you, on the day of judgment people will give account for every careless word they speak" (Matthew 12:36).

↑ PLEASE READ MATTHEW 12:33-37.

# RECLAIMING THE WORD CHURCH

I HOPE TO COME TO YOU SOON, BUT I AM WRITING THESE THINGS TO YOU SO THAT, IF I DELAY, YOU MAY KNOW HOW ONE OUGHT TO BEHAVE IN THE HOUSEHOLD OF GOD, WHICH IS THE CHURCH OF THE LIVING GOD, A PILLAR AND BUTTRESS OF THE TRUTH. (1 TIMOTHY 3:14-15)

Church. Is it the building? Perhaps it's the Sunday meetings that nice people attend? Or is it a religious group of followers that has existed for centuries? If we shot an arrow, none of these answers would directly hit the mark. Words from the Bible are too precious to guess their meaning, so let's figure out the real definition of *church.*

Literally, a church is a meeting of "called out ones". It's a congregation gathered for a special purpose. Universally, God's church includes all believers who have ever lived in the current age (from the ascension of Christ to the present). Locally, it's a body of believers who make up one of many family groups. "Family" is a key word associated with church, as the true church is made up of God's sons and daughters.

You know what I think would be wonderful? It would be wonderful if we defined the gathering of the church as God's weekly family reunion.

Picture God telling us this: *"Come on out for another family gathering this week! All My kids are invited! It will be a time to worship Me. I just love your worship in spirit and truth. It causes Me to pour out my blessings upon you! You will get to sing. You will discover more about your life and freedom as My child. You will learn how to run away from every sinful thing that will hurt you. You will get to grow with others who are just like you. And best of all, I'll be there to see you! I love my time with you. Promise Me you'll be there! And don't forget that my Son loves you dearly – you're his bride. We can't wait to see you again!"*

🡅 CHECK OUT 1 TIMOTHY 3:14-16. THE CHURCH IS SO ESSENTIAL!

## RECLAIMING THE WORD LORD

THEREFORE, GOD HAS HIGHLY EXALTED HIM AND BESTOWED ON HIM THE NAME THAT IS ABOVE EVERY NAME, SO THAT AT THE NAME OF JESUS EVERY KNEE SHOULD BOW, IN HEAVEN AND ON EARTH AND UNDER THE EARTH, AND EVERY TONGUE CONFESS THAT JESUS CHRIST IS LORD, TO THE GLORY OF GOD THE FATHER. (PHILIPPIANS 2:9-11)

Jesus Christ is Lord! By definition, this means that Jesus is "supreme in authority; the controlling one". A lord is a master, which means Jesus is the Master. Teens, how do you feel about that? Is it ok to have him as your master?

Having a master changes our view of life, doesn't it? We Americans tend to think that we are self-sufficient. *"Who needs a master? I am free! I control my own destiny, and no one is going to tell me otherwise!"* Yet think this through with me. Right now, at this very moment, there is something that is controlling you. What is it? Money? Success? Having that special relationship with a boy or girl? Having as much fun as you can get out of life? Looking for the next time you can get drunk or high on drugs?

If I asked you about matters of faith, you might say, "I am a believer". But if I asked you about having Jesus Christ as Lord, what would you say? Is God really allowed to have authority over us? According to Philippians, yes! In fact, we read that Jesus is the master of all – over the angels, the saints in heaven, those who are alive on this earth, those who have died (both saved or unsaved), and even over the devil himself. Every single one of us is destined to a position of humility. We will all bow at the name of Jesus, for he is Lord.

As for me, I can tell you that I will gladly bow down. He is my Lord and my Savior. Can you say the same? How will you bow down before him?

↑ ACKNOWLEDGE HIM AS LORD! READ PHILIPPIANS 2:5-11.

# RECLAIMING THE WORD CHRISTIAN

So Barnabas went to Tarsus to look for Saul, and when he had found him, he brought him to Antioch. For a whole year they met with the church and taught a great many people. And in Antioch the disciples were first called Christians. (Acts 11:26)

So... how many Christians do you know? Hopefully a lot!

I find that it most discouraging when we see a person of stature or popularity claim to be a Christian, yet they live their lives like the the rest of the world. What a terrible testimony! Many people are turned away by the hypocrisy of sinning Christians. Teens, if we claim to be saved, then we need to be authentic in our faith.

Being a Christian means that we have a restored relationship with the Creator. Christ is the One who made that possible. I can become a Christian when I believe the truth, the whole truth, and nothing but the truth. As one who was not a Christian, I was lost, in darkness, and the enemy of God. Make no mistake - I fully deserve hell. Someone would need to pay the ultimate price to get me back. Thanks be to God, His Son did just that! One night at our Vacation Bible School, I was encouraged to simply repent and believe (which I did when I was 8), and now I am His! I will gladly carry the title of *Christian* until I die.

Be careful of those who claim to be Christians, yet live unaffected by the truth. To a degree, being known as a Christian is popular today; for many, it is like being a part of a club or social group. If someone claims to be a Christian, ask them: "How do you know that you are truly a believer?" If you only hear about their good works, then they are fooled. But if you hear about the blood of Jesus covering their sin, giving them redemption and life – praise God for with your sister or brother! A true Christian knows that he is saved by Christ alone.

🡅 THE CONTEXT OF "CHRISTIANS" IS FOUND IN ACTS 11:19-30.

# RECLAIMING WORDS IN YOUR LIFE

Let no corrupting talk come out of your mouths, but only such as is good for building up, as fits the occasion, that it may give grace to those who hear. (Ephesians 4:29)

The words that we say are very important. *"It's just words, man!"* won't cut it when we have a sit down with God one day and explain why we chose the words that we spoke. Remember, we are responsible for our actions, and our actions include what we do, what we say, and what we think. Just pondering this causes me to think about the need to control my tongue.

Growth as a Christian is not about a life of "Don't do this!" and "Don't do that!" Thankfully, it's about "Do this instead!" Ephesians 4:29 is a great verse to help us with the "instead" of our lives. Rather than using words which lack meaning, let's use meaningful words. Also, rather than use words which are worthless altogether (curse words, dirty words, vain words, etc.), let's use words that build each other up. "How can my words help you?" should be the primary thought of our conversations with each other.

When I go to the dentist and need work done, I might need a shot of Novocain. I cringe even as I write this, since I've had plenty of work done to my teeth! But I'm thankful for the shot, as it would have been awful to get the work done without it.

Teens, I believe we sometimes give ourselves a shot of Novocain to the brain as it pertains to our words. We've lost track of their power. I encourage us all to think hard about what we are saying, and reclaim a speech that is pleasing to the Lord. By God's grace, we can do it!

↑ GOD TAKES OUR WORDS SERIOUSLY. LOOK AT LEVITICUS 24:10-23.

## THE PIT OF DESPAIR

WRETCHED MAN THAT I AM! WHO WILL DELIVER ME FROM THIS BODY OF DEATH? THANKS BE TO GOD THROUGH JESUS CHRIST OUR LORD! SO THEN, I MYSELF SERVE THE LAW OF GOD WITH MY MIND, BUT WITH MY FLESH I SERVE THE LAW OF SIN. (ROMANS 7:24-25)

*"Oh God, I am so miserable! I cannot bear this pain! I promised you that I would not fall into this sin, and yet here I am. Oh, how awful I feel right now! I hate myself. I cannot imagine what you think of me at this moment. I call myself a Christian, yet I went ahead and did the unthinkable. Oh God, I feel so sick! I just want this to end. I can't believe myself... how did I ever let this happen! I'm such a hypocrite. If people knew who I really was, I would have no friends. I want to throw up!*

*"How will I escape? Will my good works be enough for You to accept? They say that time heals wounds, yet I have been down this road before, and now, I feel worse than ever. How can I make things right this time? This is so terrible! All of my friends, and my family, and my church, and my relatives... they all will be so ashamed of me once they discover what I did. Why do they have to know? This is so bad - I just want to end it all.*

*"I don't know what else to do, other than to throw myself at Your feet. So that is exactly what I will do, and I'm doing it right now. Please, please forgive me! As bad as I feel, I know I have truly offended You first of all. That scares me the most. I look to You for mercy, for grace, and for help. Rescue me from my pit of despair. I can't find my way in this darkness. Lord, I need you! Please save me, God! Without You, there is no hope."*

↑ THERE IS AN ESCAPE FOR ALL WHO ARE IN THE PIT OF DESPAIR! READ PSALM 69 TODAY.

# I DON'T GET WHAT I DESERVE!

BUT I HAVE TRUSTED IN YOUR STEADFAST LOVE; MY HEART SHALL REJOICE IN YOUR SALVATION. I WILL SING TO THE LORD, BECAUSE HE HAS DEALT BOUNTIFULLY WITH ME. (PSALM 13:5-6)

What do you deserve? How does your answer affect your thinking? Let's look at two different ways:

One way: *"What did I do to deserve this? I so don't need this garbage right now! I am a good person, yet now I have to deal with this problem in my life. I have done nothing to earn it. There is enough going on in my life, and now I have this additional stress put on me. I can't handle this! I despise the people that are hurting me this way, and I hate the circumstances that I have been placed in. God, You knew all this would happen, and You did nothing to stop it! Why do I deserve this?!!"*

Another way: *"What did I do to deserve this? I know myself – I am such a failure at times, and I have some serious struggles with sin, and I fall on my face a lot. Yet, I still have so much going for me, like good health, a family that loves me, and friends that support me. I look out the window and see God's goodness in His creation. He cares for all of my daily needs. Best of all, he sent His Son to die in my place so that I could be with Him forever. Why do I deserve this?!!"*

I don't get what I deserve – thank God for that! There is a word for this reality; it's called *mercy*. I thank God that I don't get what I deserve, for *I know what I truly deserve*. Titus 3:5 says it this way: "he saved us, not because of works done by us in righteousness, but according to his own mercy, by the washing of regeneration and renewal of the Holy Spirit."

↑ READ PSALM 13!

## HOW DO YOU KNOW?

But what does it say? "The word is near you, in your mouth and in your heart" (that is, the word of faith that we proclaim); because, if you confess with your mouth that Jesus is Lord and believe in your heart that God raised him from the dead, you will be saved. (Romans 10:8-9)

Not long ago, God gave me the opportunity to speak to a man in need about his salvation. I was thankful for this chance, for I had been recently learning how to better speak with people about Jesus Christ. When "Carl" told me he was a Christian, I asked him, "How do you know that this is true?" He told me that he was saved by the blood of Jesus. He went on to explain how the Lord got a hold of his life when he was 17 years old. One day, he was drinking himself silly. The next day, he visited the bar, took a sip of his whiskey, and couldn't stomach it.

Though it's not always the case, I sensed that his testimony was true. We helped him on his way, praying that it would make a difference.

When you meet someone for a brief period of time, it can be hard to conclude if a person is really a Christian. Asking a professing believer, "How do you know that you are saved?" is a great way to get to the heart of the matter. So many people respond by telling you all the good they have done in their lives (or good that others have done for them). When that happens, we have an opportunity to help them see the truth. Our works cannot save us (see Ephesians 2:8-9). But if they can look you in the eye and confess a salvation based upon the blood of Jesus? Well then! Now you have some proof!

In order to get accurate answers, don't be afraid to ask pointed questions. Too often, we take people at their word when they say that they are Christians. *"How do you know?"* is a great question to help us to discover the truth.

↑ CHECK OUT ROMANS 10:8-13.

## THE GRACIOUS, OMNISCIENT LORD

OH THAT THEY HAD SUCH A HEART AS THIS ALWAYS, TO FEAR ME AND TO KEEP ALL MY COMMANDMENTS, THAT IT MIGHT GO WELL WITH THEM AND WITH THEIR DESCENDANTS FOREVER! (DEUTERONOMY 5:29)

If you could look down the corridor of history with the power to keep bad things from happening, what would you do? Maybe some would take the keys away from their loved one before they got into that car accident. Maybe some would counsel their friend about the trouble they would painfully discover by dating the wrong person. Maybe some would try to convince their parents to stay together.

Naturally, this causes us to wonder about God and all that He allows. Before the people entered into the Promised Land, the Lord told Moses to give this second generation of Israel a review of what He expected. They agreed to obey Him; however, God knows everything, so He knew that they would quickly fall away. He knew that Israel would turn to idols once they settled in the land. He knew they would eventually reject Him and ask for a king. He knew that His beloved nation would one day split. And yes, He knew that they would be taken captive and sent to a faraway land.

Why would God allow this? Could He have put His foot down before it all happened? Absolutely! However, think about this: "If God decided to start over by destroying rebellious Israel, where would we be today?" No Israel means no Jesus. No Jesus means no salvation. So, with His Son in position as the center of all history, the LORD chose grace for His children. He knew that everything would fit exactly according to plan. In a sinful world, this includes all the horrible things that have happened and are to take place. He hates all that is evil, but He allows for it, because He is the gracious, omniscient Lord.

↑ PLEASE READ DEUTERONOMY 5:22-33.

# WANTED: MY OWN PERSONAL GOD

HAS A NATION CHANGED ITS GODS, EVEN THOUGH THEY ARE NO GODS? BUT MY PEOPLE HAVE CHANGED THEIR GLORY FOR THAT WHICH DOES NOT PROFIT. (JEREMIAH 2:11)

WANTED:

MY OWN PERSONAL GOD.

JOB DESCRIPTION:

***-He needs to be available whenever I call on him for help.***

***-He needs to forgive me of my sins at all times, but he needs to punish others for the sins committed against me.***

***-He needs to give me a life that is healthy and prosperous.***

***-He needs to provide me with a spouse that will always understand me.***

***-He needs to take away everything in life that causes me pain.***

***-He needs to regularly remind me just how much he loves me.***

***-He needs to give me a long life, full of happiness and fun times.***

***-He needs to take me to heaven when I die.***

***-He needs to be my friend, no matter what.***

COMPENSATION:

***My (conditional) loyalty and affection.***

When we turn "God" into a "god", we are involved in idol worship!

READ ABOUT GOD'S HATRED FOR IDOL WORSHIP IN EZEKIEL 8.

## CONFESS YOUR SINS TO ONE OTHER

THEREFORE, CONFESS YOUR SINS TO ONE ANOTHER AND PRAY FOR ONE ANOTHER, THAT YOU MAY BE HEALED. THE PRAYER OF A RIGHTEOUS PERSON HAS GREAT POWER AS IT IS WORKING. (JAMES 5:16)

This morning, I sat down with a small group of guys. We took turns talking about things that we needed prayer for in our lives. One of the fellas admitted to falling away from his exercise regime, which was affecting his weight. I really admired his confession (and have to admit that it made me chuckle, since he shared this confession with us inside of a donut shop). This friend is lighter than I am; I wish that I had his weight "problem!"

I left the small group wondering, "Why are Christians so convinced that confessing sin is the scariest thing we can do?" Somehow, we dupe ourselves into believing that other people around us will never understand, or perhaps they will look at us as despicable creatures. This is just ignorance on our parts, really. Hiding sin is never the answer; instead, James tells us that confession and prayer lead to healing. Do I believe this, or not?

Being a Christian doesn't mean that we'll never sin. However, being a Christian means that we have the power to overcome sin. It's a beautiful thing to know that sin no longer has a hold on us! Yet, we need to remember that God's plan includes using His children to help each other in our times of need. I tell you about what is going on, and you pray for me; you tell me what is going on, and I pray for you.

James finishes his letter with this awesome verse: "let him know that whoever brings a sinner back from his wandering will save his soul from death and will cover a multitude of sins" (James 5:20). Amen!

🡅 PLEASE READ JAMES 5:13-20.

## YOU CAN'T OUTGIVE HIM

AND THE KING MADE THE SILVER AND GOLD AS COMMON IN JERUSALEM AS STONE, AND HE MADE CEDAR AS PLENTIFUL AS THE SYCAMORE OF THE SHEPHELAH. (2 CHRONICLES 1:15)

The king named above was Solomon, and because of his humility and obedience, he was blessed in the early days of his reign. Can you imagine things being so good in your town that silver and gold were as common as stones? Unbelievable!

For God, money is not an issue. Simply put, He owns everything. So why do we have such a problem in giving back to Him what is already His? Honestly, our giving problem reveals a lack of faith. In our weakness, we believe that we must have complete control over our wealth. By doing so, we fail to live out our faith. Somehow, we think we will be better off if we keep our money to ourselves. Yet truly, we lose far more than we gain in this selfish mindset.

When dealing with our personal finances, we must allow God to lead us. When is the last time we asked, "God, what do You want me to do with this money that came *from You*?".

Teens, it doesn't matter one bit whether or not you have a lot or a little. Give out of the abundance of your heart, and watch the Lord work. It will make you say, "Whoa!" every single time. He owns it all anyway, but He is watching and waiting for us to respond in faith to His promises.

Trust the Lord. You can't outgive Him!

↑ READ 2 CORINTHIANS 9:6-11. THESE ARE GREAT VERSES ON THE TOPIC.

## UH-OH! THE STORY WAS ABOUT ME!

THEN DAVID'S ANGER WAS GREATLY KINDLED AGAINST THE MAN, AND HE SAID TO NATHAN, "AS THE LORD LIVES, THE MAN WHO HAS DONE THIS DESERVES TO DIE, AND HE SHALL RESTORE THE LAMB FOURFOLD, BECAUSE HE DID THIS THING, AND BECAUSE HE HAD NO PITY." NATHAN SAID TO DAVID, "YOU ARE THE MAN!" (2 SAMUEL 12:5-6)

Have you ever walked into a conversation that you thought was about someone else, only to realize it was about you? Sometimes those conversations are negative, which makes it all the worse. Talk about a moment of humility. Awkward!

After King David committed adultery, lied about it, and murdered a man to cover it up (yikes!), the prophet Nathan showed up at his door one day. God led Nathan to share an account, and it completely convicted David. It also led to some very serious consequences. You'll get to read about this in 2 Samuel 12.

Today, I want to encourage you to listen. When a story includes a person that made the wrong choice, consider this: in God's eyes, maybe you are the main character of that story.

Honestly, I became a Christian when I discovered that "you are the man!" When I became a believer, I thought that the gospel was being shared with the visitors in class that Monday night at Vacation Bible School. When I realized that I was the one who put Jesus on the cross (indeed, I was "the man"), I repented of my sin and asked for forgiveness. This did not happen until it became personal for me.

Nathan's story of the sinner *was* about me. However, the story of the sinner saved by grace *is* about me. Thank You, God!

↑ PLEASE READ 2 SAMUEL 12. NOTICE THE CONSEQUENCES, BUT ALSO NOTICE THE FORGIVENESS.

## PRAYING OVER THE LONG HAUL

ASK, AND IT WILL BE GIVEN TO YOU; SEEK, AND YOU WILL FIND; KNOCK, AND IT WILL BE OPENED TO YOU. FOR EVERYONE WHO ASKS RECEIVES, AND THE ONE WHO SEEKS FINDS, AND TO THE ONE WHO KNOCKS IT WILL BE OPENED. (MATTHEW 7:7-8)

There is a man that I loved very much, a man that I prayed for over the course of many years. There were days when I believed he was saved; he certainly had a knowledge of the gospel. And there were days when I had to wonder, since he had an upbringing that easily could have led him to believe he was saved by works.

Not long ago, this man died. I'd like to believe that he was saved, but only God knows that answer.

In the years that I prayed for him, I eventually came to the place where I prayed, "Thy will be done." I recognized that God knew the state of his soul, and He also knew how to answer my prayers. I learned to work on building my relationship with this man, showing him what Christ looked like by my actions, and I continued to "pray without ceasing."

When you are praying for someone over the long haul and do not see the results you hope for, this "asking-seeking-knocking" thing often feels old. "Is it really worth it?", I sometimes wondered. And then my "oh, so patient God" reminds me that He works in His own timetable. He is in no hurry. He uses an oven, not a microwave.

The verbs in the verses above are continual in nature. "Keep asking, keep seeking, keep knocking". Don't give up. Leave the results with God, who is glorified by your holy persistence, and who is changing you, no matter the outcome of your prayers.

↑ CHECK OUT MATTHEW 7:7-12. KEEP PRAYING!

## THAT PERSON

Bless those who persecute you; bless and do not curse them. (Romans 12:14)

*"Lord, I find myself angry at him again. I feel like I am at the point where I can hardly look him in the eye. He is so critical and judgmental, and he does not know when to keep his mouth shut! I call him my friend, yet I feel like we are miles apart. How can he act like this and get away with it? It just makes me so frustrated!*

*"Yet here I am, and you remind me of what I must do. So today, I ask you to help me, again. Help me to pray for him. I know from your Word, and from the personal experiences that You have given me, that prayer will change my attitude, regardless of whether or not he changes.*

*"And God, please help me to love him by my actions. I know that things are not always easy for him, and that I also need love when I act unlovable. Father, I know that You love him and are working on him. As Your child, I am a work in progress, so please help me to display the kind of patience that You show to me every day.*

*"By Your grace, I can succeed in being the man You want me to be, and also the friend that he needs me to be. Your Son was offended many times over, and he never sinned once. Since it is Your Spirit who lives inside of me and gives me strength, may I be just like Jesus. By Your grace, I can do this. In Jesus' Name, Amen."*

↑ READ HOW DAVID HANDLED HIS ENEMY IN 1 SAMUEL 24.

# I DON'T KNOW WHAT TO DO! (BY CORY FEHR)

ASK, AND IT WILL BE GIVEN TO YOU; SEEK, AND YOU WILL FIND; KNOCK, AND IT WILL BE OPENED TO YOU. FOR EVERYONE WHO ASKS RECEIVES, AND THE ONE WHO SEEKS FINDS, AND TO THE ONE WHO KNOCKS IT WILL BE OPENED. (MATTHEW 7:7-8)

I don't like to brag, but there's something I'm really good at. It's losing stuff. Most of the time, it's just misplaced, but I still have no idea where it's at. Keys, wallet, phone, remote, water bottle; I've even lost the dog about a dozen times. What's worse is what I'm not good at. It's finding things. It doesn't matter how slow I go, or if I retrace my steps. My wife is just about always the one who saves the day. I've learned that it's not magic, though. I look too fast. I expect it to just show up in front of my eyes. Even though I think I'm looking, I'm not really putting forth that much effort.

Probably the biggest thing that eludes me is how to best handle life's challenges. I've been doing ministry for 30 years, and sometimes I just expect to be wise and have my act together. Here's what I've learned: because I'm human, I'm not really that wise. No one is. I desperately need help.

Look at three things that get repeated twice in the verses above. Really, would you be willing to read it again a little slower? I'll wait. ⍰ Ask, Seek, Knock. I've got to pray, and really humble myself before God. I've got to seek God's help in His Word. There's no quick looking for answers. I've got to slow down in my life. Even ask people for advice. That's what a humble person does. That's really seeking and knocking. That's when God really opens the door and makes us wise for life. We live in a culture that wants fast answers and solutions and then get back to doing what we want. Our walk with God isn't fast food. It's a slow, home cooked meal. Nothing better or more satisfying!

🡅 CHECK OUT MATTHEW 7:7-12!!

# AUGUST

## THE UNBORN: WHAT DO THEY SAY?

"WHEN MEN STRIVE TOGETHER AND HIT A PREGNANT WOMAN, SO THAT HER CHILDREN COME OUT, BUT THERE IS NO HARM, THE ONE WHO HIT HER SHALL SURELY BE FINED, AS THE WOMAN'S HUSBAND SHALL IMPOSE ON HIM, AND HE SHALL PAY AS THE JUDGES DETERMINE. BUT IF THERE IS HARM, THEN YOU SHALL PAY LIFE FOR LIFE, EYE FOR EYE, TOOTH FOR TOOTH, HAND FOR HAND, FOOT FOR FOOT, BURN FOR BURN, WOUND FOR WOUND, STRIPE FOR STRIPE." (EXODUS 21:22-25)

When is a person really a person? For several decades, this has been a controversial debate. Are we a person when we are born? Is it when we have developed to the point that we can live outside of the womb? Is it at the first heart beat? Is it at the moment of conception? Can we even know the answer? Perhaps we should think about those verses in Exodus for a bit...

I'm grateful when we gain political ground in the fight for the lives of the unborn. I believe that this is the result of fervent prayer by godly people. But with that said, do changes in our laws really affect what people believe?

What do they say about the unborn? Of course, it all matters who "they" are. If we are talking about worldly people, they believe you have every right to be happy, as long as it doesn't hurt others. When the others include an unborn baby, it becomes easier to dismiss the unborn as a recognized group of people. When they say that we need to love others for who they are, and that we are not to judge their actions, then who are we to say that abortion is wrong? Who are we to say that the mother does not have a choice?

This is the wisdom of the world. As long as this way of thinking prevails, the unborn are in constant danger of losing their lives.

🡅 A COOL STORY ABOUT AN UNBORN BELIEVER - READ ABOUT JOHN THE BAPTIST IN LUKE 1:39-45!

## THE UNBORN: WHAT DOES GOD SAY?

FOR YOU FORMED MY INWARD PARTS; YOU KNITTED ME TOGETHER IN MY MOTHER'S WOMB. I PRAISE YOU, FOR I AM FEARFULLY AND WONDERFULLY MADE. WONDERFUL ARE YOUR WORKS; MY SOUL KNOWS IT VERY WELL. (PSALM 139:13-14)

Psalm 139 is the answer to "What Does God Say?" about the unborn. It is also one of my favorite psalms!

Abortion is not new. As cursed beings, we do not create new evil and wickedness; no, we just repackage what has been done since the fall of man. In all likelihood, countless babies had been aborted before this Psalm was even penned. A disdain for God's laws leads to a disdain for human life.

As you read Psalm 139 today, notice that Creator God is completely involved in the process of our development. No wonder we all look different, and act different, and think different, and maybe even smell different! When it comes to God's creation of us, we never see the same human being twice.

Also, we are taught that God's law protects the unborn (Exodus 21:22-25 makes this extremely clear). And He chooses the path of the unborn before they see the light of day (see Jeremiah 1:4-5). Our lives are precious to God, regardless of the direction a life may take.

Oh, how the Lord is so wonderful! To think that He knit and wove me together, and He called me His own before I was ever born? All I can say is "Wow, God! You are so amazing!"

Truly, the Father's hand is upon the life of the unborn.

↑ NOW GO AHEAD AND READ PSALM 139!

## THE UNBORN: WHAT DO YOU SAY?

For he delivers the needy when he calls, the poor and him who has no helper. He has pity on the weak and the needy, and saves the lives of the needy. From oppression and violence, he redeems their life, and precious is their blood in his sight. (Psalm 72:12-14)

I hope we can all agree that the unborn would fall under the category of "needy". In Psalm 72, a good king looks out for the needy. King Jesus most certainly does this, we know!

We have many kinds of needy people in our midst. Those needs may include the realm of the physical, mental, emotional or spiritual. For the unborn, their needs are "all of the above." If you have the opportunity to experience an ultrasound, you will recognize the neediness of the life inside. God deeply cares for those who are rely on others with their lives, and He commands us to do the same.

Teens, can you also see just how needy you are? God cares so much for us! It is only reasonable that we care about the things He cares about Himself. So, what if we looked at the unborn as a picture of our own neediness? Think about it: we could not live without His protection. We could not live unless He was constantly providing for our needs. We could not live if we were left alone to ourselves. We could not live unless we were nurtured by Him.

When we reject the unborn, we speak volumes on what we really believe about the Creator and His creation. How dare we lift our hands against those who need our help? Abortion is nothing less than a matter of life and death to Him.

As already asked in the title above, "What do you say?"

↑ READ PSALM 72.

# JUDGING: WHAT DO THEY SAY?

JUDGE NOT, THAT YOU BE NOT JUDGED. (MATTHEW 7:1)

It used to be John 3:16, but Matthew 7:1 appears to have taken over as the most quoted verse of the Bible. It is short, it is no-nonsense in nature, and it is our attempt to keep people off our backs when we make certain decisions.

How often have we heard this verse? How often have we *said* this verse? Do we even know that it is a verse from the Bible? When quoted forcefully to us, it seems like we have no choice but to back down from our position. No one wants to be a hypocrite, right? Deep down, everyone realizes that we have a real problem with sin. We falsely think that we need to get everything in order in our own lives if we are allowed to judge others, but we know that will never really happen.

People use whatever means necessary to excuse sin. Often, that turns into the act of taking biblical verses out of context. Twisting God's Word just enough to make it fit our circumstances helps us to live with a less guilty conscience.

Do you smoke? *"Don't judge me! You have your own problems with cheating on tests."* Did you go too far with your boyfriend? *"Back off! You will be judged for the way you swear all the time."* Do you eat too much? *"How can you judge me when I caught you looking at pornography on your phone?!!"* Misunderstanding Matthew 7:1 gives others the "out" from needed accountability.

There is more to be learned about judging than in Matthew 7:1 alone!

↑ READ MATTHEW 6:25-7:5. THEN MEDITATE UPON THE COMPASSION OF JESUS IN THE CONTEXT OF MATTHEW 7:1.

## JUDGING: WHAT DOES GOD SAY?

AND WHY DO YOU NOT JUDGE FOR YOURSELVES WHAT IS RIGHT? (LUKE 12:57)

What? Is this verse actually telling us to judge? Doesn't the Bible say, "Do not judge"? Well, which is it? If you look up the word "judge", you will find that it is used many times in the Bible. Sometimes we learn that we are not supposed to judge, and sometimes we are told to go ahead and judge. Most of the time, the word is associated with an action on the part of God. It does us well to remember this fact!

The word "judge" means "to make a decision." As we look at the times this word is used in Scripture, we come to understand that judging concerns moral decisions (as opposed to "should I wear the white or black socks today?"). When you think about it, we make judgments all the time. The real question is not *if* we should judge, but *how* we should judge. There is a wrong form of judgment (as referred to in Matthew 7:1), and there is a right form.

Here is a simple way to know the difference between what is the right way and the wrong way to judge. When we judge ("make a moral decision") based upon *what God says,* we are judging correctly; when we judge based upon *what we believe,* we are judging incorrectly.

Think about the following verses in 1 Corinthians 6, and consider the privilege and responsibility of judging: "Or do you not know that the saints will judge the world? And if the world is to be judged by you, are you incompetent to try trivial cases? Do you not know that we are to judge angels? How much more, then, matters pertaining to this life?" (1 Corinthians 6:2-3).

🡅 GOD USED NAHUM TO ANNOUNCE JUDGMENT ON NINEVEH. READ ANY OF THE 3 CHAPTERS, OR READ THE WHOLE BOOK.

# JUDGING: WHAT DO YOU SAY?

BUT THE LORD SITS ENTHRONED FOREVER; HE HAS ESTABLISHED HIS THRONE FOR JUSTICE, AND HE JUDGES THE WORLD WITH RIGHTEOUSNESS; HE JUDGES THE PEOPLE WITH UPRIGHTNESS. (PSALM 9:7-8)

In most cases, the word "judge" and its related terms in the Bible are associated with the actions of God. He is the supreme "Decision Maker" when it comes to matters of His creation. Don't be mistaken - every one of us will meet the Great Judge at the time of our death. Hopefully He will judge you as righteous! He will do so if your advocate is named Jesus Christ.

Teens, by the authority of what God says in His Word, I tell you that we have the responsibility to tell someone when they are wrong. We also have the same responsibility to do this in love and compassion. But again, don't miss out on the fact that we are allowed (even commanded) to point out sinful behavior.

People usually hate it when they are told that they are wrong. But perhaps it will be the best thing you could ever do for them. As sure as it is an act of love when I tell my kids, "You are wrong to go play in the road!", it is also loving when you tell your friends, "You are wrong to do something that is disobedient to the Lord." When you lovingly judge sin in the life of another person, you are showing grace.

I challenge you to reconsider the whole issue of what it means to judge. Think about judging from the biblical perspective. If you do, you will knowledgeably serve well. "My brothers, if anyone among you wanders from the truth and someone brings him back, let him know that whoever brings back a sinner from his wandering will save his soul from death and will cover a multitude of sins" (James 5:20).

↑ READ PSALM 96!

## HATING: WHAT DO THEY SAY?

FOR WE OURSELVES WERE ONCE FOOLISH, DISOBEDIENT, LED ASTRAY, SLAVES TO VARIOUS PASSIONS AND PLEASURES, PASSING OUR DAYS IN MALICE AND ENVY, HATED BY OTHERS AND HATING ONE ANOTHER. (TITUS 3:3)

A new twist on an old word has taken place in recent times. The word "hate" has been given an additional title of "hater". In everyday conversation, you may discover that there are a number of accused haters in this world. Some of these supposed haters are professing Christians. Consider the following examples:

***THE ELDERLY MAN WHO PRAYS OUTSIDE OF AN ABORTION CLINIC.***
***THE LADY WHO SUGGESTS THAT ALCOHOLISM IS NOT GENETIC BY NATURE.***
***THE NEW BELIEVER WHO CONDEMNS GAY MARRIAGE.***
***THE WIFE WHO CALLS PORNOGRAPHY A SIN.***
***THE PASTOR WHO TEACHES ABOUT THE ROLES OF HUSBAND AND WIFE.***

No one wants to be called a "hater". It places a stamp of disapproval upon us. It suggests that we are behind the times. It denotes that we lack love and feeling for others. Eventually, it may even dismiss us as being relevant or necessary in our society.

Indeed, we must recognize that hatred itself is not beyond us! Titus tells us that it was a big problem before we met Christ. We have no business returning to it, since we were saved from it (Titus 3:4-7). However, not all hatred is sinful. I challenge you to consider what God tells us about His hatred, so you can know the difference.

"They" would have us to believe that all hatred should be eradicated from our lives. But are they right?

↑ CHECK OUT TITUS 3:1-8.

## HATING: WHAT DOES GOD SAY?

"I HAVE LOVED YOU," SAYS THE LORD. BUT YOU SAY, "HOW HAVE YOU LOVED US?" "IS NOT ESAU JACOB'S BROTHER?" DECLARES THE LORD. "YET I HAVE LOVED JACOB BUT ESAU I HAVE HATED." (MALACHI 1:2-3A)

What did Esau ever do to deserve God's hatred? Maybe you're thinking, "Wow, God, what is Your problem with him? Oh sure, he had some sin issues in Genesis, but You are the God who forgives, right? So why are you hating on him? That's some serious anger toward Esau right there. Why are You so mean? Where is the love? There's some real favoritism going on here for Jacob. How could you be so unfair, God? I never knew You to be a hater!"

If Malachi were written today, I could see people responding like that. Even if Esau was a mass murderer (and he wasn't), the God of our making is not allowed to hate in any shape or form. But perhaps it would do us good to know what hate means before we go on judging God, don't you think? As surely as love is often expressed in the Bible as a choice, the word *hate* is simply the opposite – it is "not to choose". The focus of this hatred isn't on God's feelings, but upon His will.

So let's look at Malachi again. God chose Jacob, not Esau. This was clear from the day these twins were born. And Esau would father the nation of Edom, who hated Israel and was a thorn in their side. Yet the focus is not on Esau, but upon Jacob. The Lord said, "I have loved *you*" (my emphasis). "*You* are my chosen – not Edom, not Moab, not Assyria, not anyone else. Compared to you, all others are unchosen (hated)."

By the way, as Master of this universe, the Lord has every right to love or hate as He so chooses. If that offends us, then it is time to take a step back and figure out who really is in charge.

↑ READ PSALM 97, ESPECIALLY VERSES 10-12!

# HATING: WHAT DO YOU SAY?

HATE EVIL, AND LOVE GOOD; AND ESTABLISH JUSTICE IN THE GATE; IT MAY BE THAT THE LORD, THE GOD OF HOSTS, WILL BE GRACIOUS TO THE REMNANT OF JOSEPH. (AMOS 5:15)

Psalm 119 is the longest chapter in the Bible. This chapter mentions "hate" several times in its verses. As David expresses his thoughts and feelings about God's law, he sees fit to express his hatred toward sinful thinking (vs. 113), sinful speaking (vs. 163), and sinful doing (vs. 104, 128). Thinking, saying, and doing are all actions in which mankind is held accountable. I am guilty of hating in all of these ways.

What do you say? Are we allowed to hate anyone? I believe Matthew 5 solves that question. "You have heard that it was said, 'Love your neighbor and hate your enemy.' But I tell you: Love your enemies and pray for those who persecute you, that you may be sons of your Father in heaven" (vs. 43-45). Jesus says, "No!" to hating your enemy, so no, we ourselves cannot hate anyone. However, he says "Yes!" to hating sin. Since mankind is the carrier of sin, we must hate the sin inside of us. Can you see the difference between the two (sin and sinner)?

Teens: choose to love the unbeliever. Share with them our great need for Christ, since we all are guilty of breaking God's law, and we deserve hell. Tell them how God intervened in history to offer life in Jesus Christ. Choose not to get involved in their sin; decide to love them with compassion and grace in spite of their sin.

With this kind of love, you can trust that the Lord, the God of hosts, will be gracious to you!

↑ READ AMOS 5:6-15. NOTICE HOW "HATE" IS USED IN THIS CONTEXT. MAY IT SHAPE YOUR THINKING ON WHAT WE ARE TO HATE.

# RELIGION: WHAT DO THEY SAY?

For you have heard of my former life in Judaism, how I persecuted the church of God violently and tried to destroy it. (Galatians 1:13)

At one time, Paul the Apostle was Saul the Pharisee. The apostle had a faith based upon a relationship with God. The Pharisee had a religion based upon no relationship with God.

Saul was ultra-religious. In the eyes of his peers, He was "the man" (a "Pharisee of the Pharisees"). Christians were petrified of him, since his life's goal was to kill them all. You would think that a man so studied in the Bible would know that Jesus was the Promised One. But Saul, like countless others, was completely fooled by the Evil One.

In one of his later letters, we read that Paul never found satisfaction outside of Christ ("But whatever gain I had, I counted as loss for the sake of Christ", Philippians 3:7). People today are no different. They will never find what they are looking for if they reject the Son of God.

However, when we ask the unsaved to consider Christ as the source of life, many recall their past experiences, and conclude that "religion" just does not work for them. If a church does not emphasize that the gospel offers reconciliation (a "restored relationship with the Lord"), then eventually they will just walk away.

When religion is the focal point, church becomes a place to perform a ritual with little to no significant meaning. Unbelievers can easily find something better to do. And most do; our nation has far less church goers than ever before.

↑ GOD HIMSELF HATES WORTHLESS RELIGION! READ ABOUT ISRAEL'S PROBLEM WITH IT IN AMOS 5:21-27.

# RELIGION: WHAT DOES GOD SAY?

RELIGION THAT IS PURE AND UNDEFILED BEFORE GOD THE FATHER IS THIS: TO VISIT ORPHANS AND WIDOWS IN THEIR AFFLICTION, AND TO KEEP ONESELF UNSTAINED FROM THE WORLD. (JAMES 1:27)

When I read this verse, I think, "Of course! This makes sense. Why wouldn't we choose to care for the orphans and the widows?" But for the Jews who heard these words, it would have been a real punch in the stomach. Why? Because they weren't doing it!

The Pharisees were a very religious sect of Jews in the days of Jesus. In order to be holy, they had a crazy amount of rules to follow. Their rules were supposedly based upon the commands of the Old Testament, but by the time you read and tried to follow all of the fine print, you would have been far from actually knowing the purpose of God's original commands. The Pharisees actually shunned the thought of doing anything like helping the needy. How sad!

Unfortunately, Israel had a history of unacceptable religion. God's people went through the motions of their sacrifices, their feasts, their offerings, their holidays, etc., all while missing out on a relationship with God. He hated this worthless activity! Just start digging into what the Lord said to His people when He spoke to them through their prophets. God hated their religion; it was meaningless to Him.

As a Christian, the only way to impress God through religion is to take care of people that are generally neglected by our society, and to keep away from sin (as read in the verse above).

Can you do this if your heart does not belong to Him?

🡅 GOD'S ANGER AT ISRAEL'S RELIGION IS FOUND IN HOSEA 6:4-11.

## RELIGION: WHAT DO YOU SAY?

THE SACRIFICES OF GOD ARE A BROKEN SPIRIT; A BROKEN AND CONTRITE HEART, O GOD, YOU WILL NOT DESPISE. (PSALM 51:17)

The word *religion* has not always had a negative connotation or meaning, but in today's world, it does. A number of churches have made it easy for people to hate religion. Rather than expressing the joys of being found in Christ, these churches will focus on the fear of breaking rules. Does this sound like a church you want to attend?

I'm guessing there may be some "religion-only" people in our own churches. They come, find their favorite seat, sing the hymns and / or praise songs, put some money in the offering plate, listen to what they enjoy from the message, and pat the pastor on the back when they leave. But hear this – all of it is worth *nothing* if the heart is not alive in Christ! When an unbeliever comes to offer his worship to the Lord, he remains an unsaved person who simply performs a religious act.

Would you think about yourself today? Whether it is attending church, or saying some prayers at home, or supporting a local charity, or reading your Bible, why do you do it? What motivates you? If you are hoping that your actions will impress God enough to punch your ticket into heaven, you need to know that they won't! That's not how God works. *He wants a relationship with you, on His terms.*

Teens, let's drop the thinking that "Christianity = Religion". It's so much better than that! Jesus told us, "I came that they may have life and have it abundantly" (John 10:10). Amen!

🡅 THE APOSTLE JOHN FOCUSED ON THE RELATIONSHIP OF THE CHURCH IN HIS SHORT LETTER OF 3 JOHN.

# HELL: WHAT DO THEY SAY?

SHEOL AND ABADDON LIE OPEN BEFORE THE LORD; HOW MUCH MORE THE HEARTS OF THE CHILDREN OF MAN! (PROVERBS 15:11)

Hell. Since the Bible recognizes the reality of it, then hell must be real.

"What do they say?" If you decided to poll your friends about its existence, what would they tell you? That could be interesting!

Many people believe that it is a fictional place, created in order to scare us into believing the Bible. Some believe in the presence of hell, but see it as a place for really bad people (like the terrorists of today). Some have downgraded the word to a curse for the hard circumstances we have to face in life (ex. "I'm going through hell right now with my parents"). If a person deals with a particularly difficult experience, they may call it "hellish" in nature. Some find it to be funny in jokes, and some make light of it in song. The word is certainly used a lot outside of a biblical context. We may unknowingly use it ourselves when we utter the word "heck" (consider this: in God's view, is it really better to say "what the heck?" instead of "what the hell?").

One thing's for sure: Hell is not a popular word when referred to by it's original meaning: the destination for sinners. Americans do not like to think about being responsible for our actions before God the Judge. So hell has been dismissed as non-existent, non-eternal, and unnecessary.

I think you know that we cannot afford to be wrong about hell, no matter "what they say."

↑ PLEASE CAREFULLY READ MARK 9:42-50.

# HELL: WHAT DOES GOD SAY?

FOR YOU WILL NOT ABANDON MY SOUL TO SHEOL, OR LET YOUR HOLY ONE SEE CORRUPTION. (PSALM 16:10)

When we study what God teaches us about the existence of hell, we read in the Old Testament that *Sheol* refers to the grave. While this is true, it is more than just a burial plot. When Christ came to the earth, furthered our understanding of Sheol, and how it directly ties to hell. Hell is a place of separation, of torment, of fire, and of great anguish.

Psalm 16:10 was quoted by Peter in the book of Acts. Specifically, the context of Acts 2:25-28 concerns Jesus Christ. Why would Jesus himself have to deal with death and hell? Let's think for a minute. Was there ever a time that he was separated from God? Did he deal with the torment of God's wrath against sin? Was his body buried in a tomb for three days? Psalm 16 and Acts 2 are direct references to the death, burial, and resurrection of Jesus Christ!

The book of Revelation also teaches us about hell. At the end of the book, we see that hell will be cast into the Lake of Fire. What's the difference between the two places? When an unbeliever dies, the body goes back to the ground, but the soul goes to hell. At the final judgment, the soul and body is once again united for eternity in the Lake of Fire. This is the most awful of all realities that could ever exist.

I trust you will not think any of this is a joke. However, if you do, Jesus has a non-fiction story for you. If you trust that Jesus tells the truth, then you will believe the story about the rich man and Lazarus. God Himself would never joke about something as serious as hell.

↑ SO READ ON ABOUT THE REALITY OF HELL. GO TO LUKE 16:19-31.

# HELL: WHAT DO YOU SAY?

When I saw him, I fell at his feet as though dead. But he laid his right hand on me, saying, "Fear not, I am the first and the last, and the living one. I died, and behold I am alive forever, and I have the keys of Death and Hades." (Revelation 1:17-18)

AC/DC is still a popular classic rock band, and one of its greatest hits is a song called "Hells Bells". Ever heard the song? I heard it many times growing up in a public school (usually on the bus ride). It's not the first song written about hell, and it makes light of just how terrible it will be to live in eternal darkness.

Teens, Satan loves it when we do not take hell seriously. He thinks it's great when we dismiss our sin as bad, but not damning in nature. He is quite content when people believe in heaven and not hell, since they believe in a God of love but not a God of judgment. The devil is the master of distraction. He is the enemy of all who preach the reality of hell and the certainty of its destination for unbelievers.

The account in Luke 16:19-31 tells a different story. The rich man desperately wanted out of hell. He would have even been happy for one drop of cool water to hit his tongue. That relief never came.

Here's the thing – like the rich man, we deserve hell. Listen, teens: WE. DESERVE. HELL. "We" includes both you and I! When God has done everything in His power to save us and we still spit in His face by rejecting His Son? Yes, we deserve hell. When the rich man died, he recognized in full that he got what he deserved. He did not go to hell because he was rich. No, it had everything to do with not believing the truth about his soul... a soul that still suffers in torment, and always will. Please, may this not be the case with your soul!

🡅 GOD IS MERCIFUL! REPENT OF YOUR SIN! DON'T BE LIKE THOSE YOU WILL READ ABOUT TODAY IN ISAIAH 30:8-17.

## CORRUPT SPEECH: WHAT DO THEY SAY?

AND THE PHILISTINE SAID TO DAVID, "AM I A DOG, THAT YOU COME TO ME WITH STICKS?" AND THE PHILISTINE CURSED DAVID BY HIS GODS. (1 SAMUEL 17:43)

I remember being so thankful the day I finally graduated from my public high school. I believed that I would now be leaving a world of cursing classmates. After spending a couple weeks at my first job (a fast-food restaurant), I started to work at a food processing plant close to home. It took one day on the job to learn that I did not leave any of that cursing behind. In fact, I heard far more swear words in those five years at the factory than I ever did with my classmates. It was shocking.

When we swear or curse, we wield our tongue in a powerful way to communicate what is utterly worthless. God takes no pleasure in unholy speech. He hears all that is said (how easily we forget this truth!). He is righteous, and the unrepentant one who uses foul language will be held guilty.

Your friends or family may be in the habit of using corrupt speech. They may try to convince you that it doesn't matter; just "don't swear around the wrong people." But really, how ignorant can we be?

When "they" curse, they are revealing their lack of faith in the One who knows and hears everything. It was our sin that put Jesus Christ on the cross. That sin includes our thoughts, our words, and our deeds. This is a humbling thought! May our language reflect the One who made us.

↑ SAUL LOST HIS SENSES AND WENT ON A MURDEROUS CURSING RAMPAGE IN 1 SAMUEL 20:24-34.

# CORRUPT SPEECH: WHAT DOES GOD SAY?

LET NO CORRUPTING TALK COME OUT OF YOUR MOUTHS, BUT ONLY SUCH AS IS GOOD FOR BUILDING UP, AS FITS THE OCCASION, THAT IT MAY GIVE GRACE TO THOSE WHO HEAR. (EPHESIANS 4:29)

When we approach the Bible for answers to the questions of life, it is important that we understand the meaning of the words found within. For instance, consider the words "swearing" and "cursing". We often define them as one and the same – "using language that is offensive to the listener." However, the Bible would define swearing as "a vow to carry out an action given by the speaker"; and cursing as "a promise to bring negative consequences upon the hearers." God did both to the nation of Israel.

With that in mind, how does the Bible address corrupt speech in today's culture? Many of our impure words deal with parts of the body, whereas ancient civilizations in the Bible would disrespect others by using words which compare people to animals (like dogs). Either way, God commands us to "let no corrupting talk come out of your mouths."

Look again at the verse above. Has any four-letter word ever helped to build someone up for his or her benefit? Of course not. It is worthless! God desires purity in all aspects of our lives. Foul language is nothing less than ungodliness of the mouth.

Finally, let's consider James 3:2: "For we all stumble in many ways. And if anyone does not stumble in what he says, he is a perfect man, able also to bridle his whole body."

↑ CONSIDER THE SUBJECT OF CORRUPT SPEECH IN PSALM 109:17 AND PROVERBS 10:31. MAY GOD HELP US TO WATCH OUR MOUTHS!

# CORRUPT SPEECH: WHAT DO YOU SAY?

LET THERE BE NO FILTHINESS NOR FOOLISH TALKING NOR CRUDE JOKING, WHICH ARE OUT OF PLACE, BUT INSTEAD LET THERE BE THANKSGIVING. (EPHESIANS 5:4)

In these recent days, God has been teaching me the truth of Ephesians 4:22-24. It tells us "to put off your old self... and to put on the new self." When it comes to our speech, something needs to replace the foul language that is used. We often rely on our own efforts to put an end to sin in our lives, and when we fail, we become discouraged and right back in the same hole.

So, what if we replaced filthiness, foolish talk, and crude joking with words of thankfulness? If you obey God's command in Ephesians 5:4, then this is the course to take.

In order to put off worthless talking, begin by being thankful in your thoughts. Think about the many ways you can be thankful during the day. If you take this seriously, you will lose count of the ways – there is so much to be thankful for in one day alone! As thankful thoughts begin to flood your mind, they will naturally make their way out of your mouth. Little by little, the four-letter words will simply leave a bad taste in your mouth, and you will have no desire to speak them. This can happen to you, even in you struggle mightily in this area.

By the way, as you rid yourselves of corrupt speech, you will find that others will grow in their respect for you. It's a great side effect!

What do you say? Are you willing to control your tongue? As surely as God knows when we sin, He also knows when we choose to do what is right. In His Spirit, you can always express thankfulness. A thankful heart is so much better than a mouth of corruption!

↑ PLEASE READ EPHESIANS 4:29-5:2.

# GOSSIP AND RUMORS: WHAT DO THEY SAY?

THE WORDS OF A WHISPERER ARE LIKE DELICIOUS MORSELS; THEY GO DOWN INTO THE INNER PARTS OF THE BODY. (PROVERBS 26:22)

How do we differentiate between "gossip" and "rumors"? Here are simplified definitions for both:

**Gossip** - Spreading nasty information about a person for the purpose of hurting him or her (ex. "Did you know that _______ failed his biology test yesterday?").

**Rumors** – Spreading uncertain information about a person for the purpose of hurting him or her (ex. "Did you hear that _______ might be pregnant?").

Like two wicked siblings, both are linked together. They wreak havoc; they are often unchecked; they are always damaging.

I imagine you have heard your share of gossip and rumors. Too many of us thrive on them. It's so easy to get enticed by their "delicious morsels". But these morsels will cause spiritual food poisoning – a sickness that leaves us wishing we had never eaten dinner in the first place. Sadly, gossip and rumors never digest well.

As you consider this devotion and the conversations you have with your friends, keep track of the amount of times that gossip and rumors come to the surface. If you keep company with those who are not interested in the truth, you will certainly keep company with those who will hurt others with their words.

Woe to the whisperer! He is sick, and he is contagious!

READ PROVERBS 26:17-28. CAREFULLY CONSIDER EACH VERSE.

## "GOSSIP AND RUMORS: WHAT DOES GOD SAY?"

So also the tongue is a small member, yet it boasts of great things. How great a forest is set ablaze by such a small fire! And the tongue is a fire, a world of unrighteousness. The tongue is set among our members, staining the whole body, setting on fire the entire course of life, and set on fire by hell. (James 3:5-6)

Make no mistake – our tongues are dangerous!

Gossip and rumors pour forth from a lying tongue that is out of control. You will read more about it in James 3 today, but the tongue is known for its boasting and cursing, and "it is a restless evil, full of deadly poison" (vs. 8). Yuck!

The Lord knows just what kind of damage is done when we spread gossip or tell a rumor. Do a search on how many times the Bible addresses these words, and you will see that it has always been a serious issue. Consider a small sample of verses that deal with these two sins: "An evildoer listens to wicked lips; and a liar gives ear to a mischievous tongue" (Proverbs 17:4). "A fool's mouth is his ruin, and his lips are a snare to his soul" (Proverbs 18:7). "You shall not spread a false report. You shall not join hands with a wicked man to be a malicious witness" (Exodus 23:1).

On the flip side, watch how a controlled tongue keeps the rest of the whole body in check. Try it! See what trouble you avoid when your tongue is silent. It's quite amazing! And mimic those who commit themselves to speaking truth. They also are quite amazing!

Teens, may your tongue always be held in check. You can do it!

↑ NOW, IT'S TIME TO READ JAMES 3:1-12.

## GOSSIP AND RUMORS: WHAT DO YOU SAY?

YOU SHALL NOT GO AROUND AS A SLANDERER AMONG YOUR PEOPLE, AND YOU SHALL NOT STAND UP AGAINST THE LIFE OF YOUR NEIGHBOR: I AM THE LORD. (LEVITICUS 19:16)

To my shame, I can recount times that I spread gossip and rumors. Immediately, my heart was convicted, and I wished that I had kept my big mouth shut. I know how much I hate it when I am on the wrong end of these sins, so why would I turn around and do it to others? May the Lord help me to do what is right with my tongue.

What is the result of gossip and rumors? That verse in Leviticus is a bit of an eye-opener. In the context of Leviticus 19, several individual commands are given. It may seem that the commands are separate and detached from each other; however, God's holy decrees are always unified. One type of sin easily leads to a different sin altogether. In Leviticus 19:16, we see that spreading slander is linked to endangering your neighbor. That's right – gossip and rumors are life-threatening.

Teens, can gossip and rumors lead to bullying? You know they can! And can bullying lead to fights? It often does! And can fights lead to injuries, even death? Across our nation, violence is on the rise, and indeed, so are the deadly consequences.

Yes, there is a real and ugly connection between our sinful mouths and actions. So, before we spread gossip and rumors, consider these questions about your words: "Are they true?"; "Will they help others?"; "Would I want this spoken about me?"; "Have I prayed about my words today?"; "Am I being slow to speak and quick to listen?"; "Does it please God, who is listening in?".

🡅 SOME OF GOD'S LAWS TO CONSIDER ARE IN LEVITICUS 19:11-19.

## OUR BODIES ARE THAT IMPORTANT TO HIM

For I know that my Redeemer lives, and at the last he will stand upon the earth. And after my skin has been thus destroyed, yet in my flesh I shall see God, whom I shall see for myself, and my eyes shall behold, and not another. (Job 19:25-27a)

At the time of this writing, all three of my kids were sick (a combination of fevers, vomiting, coughing, congestion, etc. Oh, what fun!). My wife and I are praying for them to get better, for their sakes and for ours! Their sickness has me thinking about how much the Lord really does care for our bodies.

The Bible has challenged my thinking about what God thinks of our bodies. In my younger years, I placed too much emphasis on the importance of my body, and not enough focus upon my soul. As I grew in my faith, I came to assume that our souls were far more valuable than our bodies. Though there is a certain amount of truth to the latter, it led to a wide swing in the pendulum of my thinking... so much so that I considered my body of little worth.

Then I started discovering verses like the ones above. Job stated his conviction that *in his flesh* he would see God. Yes, his own flesh! Not just a brand new body given to him at the end of time, but his original body restored. By the way, Job has been dead for thousands of years... yet God has the power to give Job an uncursed body that will never again be affected by sin! How amazing is that?

May our focus be upon the transformation of our souls, but never forget that God cares about the uniquely created body He gave to you. He made it, and He will claim it in the end.

↑ CHECK OUT JOB 19:21-29!

# BUT I WAS FOLLOWING HIM, OFFICER!

BECAUSE OF THE VIOLENCE DONE TO YOUR BROTHER JACOB, SHAME SHALL COVER YOU, AND YOU SHALL BE CUT OFF FOREVER. (OBADIAH 10)

Do you know anyone who was pulled over for speeding, while following someone else who was also speeding? I've been pulled over for breaking the speed limit just once in my life (and yes, it was my fault), but I've also heard of people who have received fines when they were not the first one in line. They can cry "No fair!" all day long, but it does not change the harsh reality of the ticket. Speeding is wrong, even if we are not the leader of the pack.

The prophet Obadiah pronounced bad tidings against a nation called Edom. The Edomites were actually relatives of Israel; their forefather Esau was the brother of Jacob (one of the fathers of Israel). Sometime in history (many scholars believe it was at the fall of Jerusalem in 586 B.C.), the Babylonians captured Jerusalem. Edom itself swept in and took advantage of Babylon's victory. At their weakest moment, Israel was knifed in the back by their relatives. How terrible!

God dearly loves Israel, and Obadiah reminds Edom that He will never forget what happened. They are held fully responsible, despite the fact that they were only on "clean-up duty".

Sin is sin – it does not matter if we are first in line, or second, or third. We are responsible for our actions! God holds us accountable, and if we remain unrepentant, no excuse will get us out of "paying the fine."

🡅 READ THE VERY SHORT BOOK OF OBADIAH TODAY.

# HOW EASILY FOOLED

AS WE HAVE SAID BEFORE, SO NOW I SAY AGAIN: IF ANYONE IS PREACHING TO YOU A GOSPEL CONTRARY TO THE ONE YOU RECEIVED, LET HIM BE ACCURSED. (GALATIANS 1:9)

If you wanted to fool a child into doing something that was not good, how would you accomplish that goal? Adults with evil intentions have all kinds of ways to trick kids into doing things against their will. Sometimes, it is the offer of a special gift. Sometimes, it is the promise that the child will be better off if they listen to their advice. Sometimes, they use threatening words to scare a child into submission.

As the author of all wickedness, Satan controls those who are wicked. He is the master of fooling people into doing what he desires. Above all, he does not want to see sinners come to know Christ as Savior. So he will use anything and everything at his disposal to twist the truth of the gospel. This includes false religion.

Satan has used countless false religions to fool the human race. People were created to worship, so the devil sets up a system of belief that allows people to worship anything but God. Allah, Buddha, the earth, ourselves - just not God! If our worship is focused upon God, his next step is to distort it, by focusing his efforts on twisting the truth. Many churches have been fooled into thinking that there are multiple ways a person is saved (ex. you are saved by faith and works together; you are saved if you were baptized as an infant; you are saved if you can speak in tongues; etc.).

Paul was serious when he wrote Galatians 1:9. Don't be fooled by Satan and his servants. You are saved by believing that Jesus Christ died for your sin. He did it all! We simply need to believe.

CHECK OUT PAUL'S MESSAGE ON SALVATION: ACTS 17:22-34.

# DON'T FORGET!

AND HE SAID TO THEM, "THUS SAYS THE LORD, THE GOD OF ISRAEL: I LED YOU UP FROM EGYPT AND BROUGHT YOU OUT OF THE HOUSE OF SLAVERY. AND I DELIVERED YOU FROM THE HAND OF THE EGYPTIANS AND FROM THE AND OF ALL WHO OPPRESSED YOU, AND DROVE THE OUT BEFORE YOU AND GAVE YOU THEIR LAND." (JUDGES 6:8-9)

I have a big poster board card of encouragement sitting in the corner of my office. The card is from a wonderful group of my former teens! It helps me to remember just how much all of my teens mean to me, and that I have an incredible youth group.

I also have a desk drawer that is full of encouraging notes, pictures from my kids, and other cool mementos that remind me of how lucky I am. I have a big frame of pictures hanging on my front wall, telling me that it is great to be a dad. I have a gold ring on finger, reminding me of the life I share with my faithful wife. I have another printout of a picture of Lisa and I holding Lydia, just minutes after she was given to us in China.

My office holds many clues to God's goodness in my life. They also call me to always be thankful, to not live for myself, and to not take things for granted.

I am struck by the number of times God calls upon Israel to remember Egypt. Israel was to never forget what God did when he led them out of slavery to the Promised Land. Sadly, they forgot many times over. We can learn from them by not following their example.

Look around and remember! I'll bet you can find many clues of His faithfulness in your life.

🡅 CHECK OUT PSALM 105. IT CALLS UPON ISRAEL NOT TO FORGET.

# WALKING ON LEVEL GROUND

TEACH ME TO DO YOUR WILL, FOR YOU ARE MY GOD! LET YOUR GOOD SPIRIT LEAD ME ON LEVEL GROUND! (PSALM 143:10)

In my lifetime, one of the most defining floods in our area occurred in the September of 2011. A friend and I went hiking a couple days before the flood hit. The hike itself was quite an educational experience for me. Before we went on our trip, I thought I liked hiking. Once I was finished, I realized that I never really knew the definition of hiking in the first place. My previous hikes had all taken place in state parks. This hike was on a trail with a backpack and overnight stay in the woods.

I got a lesson in what real hiking is all about! I was soooo sore. And I was so thankful that we left for home when we did; the road was closed just hours after we finished.

As I ponder the verse in Psalm 143, I think back to that hike and the excitement I felt for level ground. Climbing upwards meant the joy of the gorgeous view, but it also left us weary from the necessary exertion. Walking downwards meant going in the right direction, but it also left us prone to stumble. Level ground meant a steady pace and a careful walk. The chances of getting hurt were far less.

David was having a tough go of it in Psalm 143. The psalm does not have a "subtitle" tying it to a specific time in his life (as some of his psalms do), but we can tell that he is tired of being chased by his enemies, and he is struggling with hope. He needed level ground. Who does David depend upon to lead him on that kind of ground? The Holy Spirit. The Spirit is good. He knows how to lead us, and our walk is sure when it is guided by him.

↑ CHECK OUT PSALM 37:23-40 TODAY.

# SURRENDERING, BUT NOT GIVING UP

HE WHO STAYS IN THIS CITY SHALL DIE BY THE SWORD, BY FAMINE, AND BY PESTILENCE, BUT HE WHO GOES OUT AND SURRENDERS TO THE CHALDEANS WHO ARE BESIEGING YOU SHALL LIVE AND SHALL HAVE HIS LIFE AS A PRIZE OF WAR. (JEREMIAH 21:9)

In Jeremiah 21, the LORD is giving the last king of Judah an option: leave and live, or stay and die. Though Zedekiah is warned many times by the prophet, he would not listen to Jeremiah. It cost him his life. Jerusalem fell to Babylon in 586 B.C., and the king was assassinated.

Jeremiah's prophetic ministry not only covered Zedekiah's life, but also a few kings before him. One of the former kings was Jehoiachin, his nephew. He was also an evil king. However, it is interesting to note that Jehoiachin surrendered. The details are very limited, but he seemed to go down without a fight. Decades later, well after the fall of Jerusalem and the deportation of many Jews, Jehoiachin's name shows up at the end of 2 Kings. He had been exiled and in prison for 37 years (!), but a new king of Babylon released him to sit at his table for the remainder of Jehoiachin's days. This is an incredible turn of events!

Think of what Jehoiachin would have went through. Captured kings were usually not treated well. Those kept alive were for the purpose of existing as living trophies by the conqueror. Jehoiachin not only remained alive, he thrived in his final days.

Teens, you may have to surrender one day. Do not fear; all who know the Lord have the Lord for eternity. Based upon this truth, I pray you will never give up. Think about Jehoiachin. How many times could he have taken his own life? I'm not sure, but he stayed alive... and found hope at the end of it all.

🡅 READ JEREMIAH 52:24-34.

# OUR SECOND CHANCE

JESUS STOOD UP AND SAID TO HER, "WOMAN, WHERE ARE THEY? HAS NO ONE CONDEMNED YOU?" SHE SAID, "NO ONE, LORD." AND JESUS SAID, "NEITHER DO I CONDEMN YOU; GO, AND FROM NOW ON SIN NO MORE." (JOHN 8:10-11)

All of us know what it is like to get in trouble. All of us have felt the consequences of doing the wrong thing. All of us have been embarrassed by our sinful actions.

In John 8, we read about a woman who was caught in the act of adultery. She made the decision to twist the laws and boundaries of marriage. Adultery happens when one married person tries to cleave to (meaning "become one with") another person outside of his or her marriage. It is wrong. It's also rampant in our culture, popularized on TV and movies, and has left many families in chaos. The Pharisees were correct to recognize that the adulterous woman was worthy of death. However, when they brought the woman to Jesus, there were no pure motives involved. John 8:6 says that they were looking to catch the Teacher in a religious trap.

How silly of them! Didn't they know that Jesus cannot be trapped? No, they did not, for they were blinded by their own sin and selfish ambitions. In a most marvelous response, Jesus writes on the ground (perhaps words of conviction?) and makes a statement that left them speechless: "If any of you is without sin, let him be the first to throw a stone at her." Bam! Busted! They could not respond, so like a dog with his tail tucked between his legs, they dropped their stones and ran off.

Teens, can you relate? Like the woman, we were found guilty. But in Christ, we were forgiven. Let us never take our second chance for granted! In Christ, let us go and sin no more.

🡅 CHECK OUT JOHN 8:1-11. IT'S SUCH A GREAT STORY!

## LOVING HIS LOVE!

THE LORD YOUR GOD IS IN YOUR MIDST, A MIGHTY ONE WHO WILL SAVE;
HE WILL REJOICE OVER YOU WITH GLADNESS; HE WILL QUIET YOU BY HIS LOVE;
HE WILL EXULT OVER YOU WITH LOUD SINGING. (ZEPHANIAH 3:17)

How tender! How affectionate! How sweet to be embraced by the Lord God! Israel was His special people, and Jerusalem His special city. Indeed, judgment was coming (it came just decades after Zephaniah wrote this verse), but He would never permanently reject His own. God's love for His people is everlasting.

Today, His people are called "the bride of Christ." Likewise, how sweet this is. Jesus has called us to be his own forever. The old hymn, "I Am His, and He Is Mine", states it this way: "Loved with everlasting love, Led by grace that love to know; Gracious Spirit from above, Thou hast taught me it is so! O, this full and perfect peace! O, this transport all divine! In a love which cannot cease, I am His, and He is mine."

For those who have never known God's love, sin is the wall that keeps us apart. For those who are His, sin is what keeps us from enjoying His love at the deepest level. Sin invites us to unfulfilling relationships. Jesus invites us to a love that knows no limits.

Think about the sweetest relationship possible - just the two of you, wrapped in each others arms, enamored with one another as you look each others eyes, having not a care in the world, totally lost in time and space. THIS, my friend - THIS is a picture of what life can be in a loving relationship with your Creator.

Teens, run into His arms and discover the power of His love for us.

🡅 SEE GOD'S LOVE TO JERUSALEM IN ZEPHANIAH 3:14-20.

# IF YOU CHOOSE TO SIN, YOU CHOOSE TO SUFFER

THERE IS SEVERE DISCIPLINE FOR HIM WHO FORSAKES THE WAY;
WHOEVER HATES REPROOF WILL DIE. (PROVERBS 15:10)

"If you choose to sin, you choose to suffer." I heard this phrase the other day from a well-known pastor on his radio program. I heard it right after having a discussion with the father of a prodigal child. Sin and suffering is exactly what this dad is dealing with in life right now.

How sad when a Christian lets go of his Father's hand and runs off to embrace sin! How grieving to the Holy Spirit who lives inside the believer who chooses wickedness over righteousness! How offensive to our Savior when we mock his sacrifice and follow the ways of the devil!

Sin causes suffering, and the end result is death. Only the very deceived soul cannot see the connection here. Many wonder why they lack peace, contentment, hope, and joy, while simultaneously practicing the same things that Jesus died for in their place. Peter told the believers, "If you suffer, it should not be as a murderer or thief or any kind of criminal, or even as a meddler." (1 Peter 4:15). There is enough suffering on this earth, let alone bringing more upon ourselves by choosing sin.

Teens, God's ways are so much better. Do you believe it? And He chose to teach us those ways in His Word, through the power of His Holy Spirit and the example of His Son.

I pray you will choose to obey!

↑ READ PROVERBS 15, AND THINK ABOUT THE CONTRASTS OF RIGHTEOUSNESS VS. WICKEDNESS.

# WHEN LIFE GETS HARD... WHO ARE YOU? (BY ANDY SHANKS)

THEN HIS WIFE SAID TO HIM, "DO YOU STILL HOLD FAST YOUR INTEGRITY? CURSE GOD AND DIE." (JOB 2:9)

His camels? Stolen. His oxen, servants, and children? Killed. His body? Riddled by disease. Basically, there was no one and nothing left for Job. His wife's suggestion seemed to be the only logical conclusion: "Curse God and die." After all, what else was there to do?

In the darkest days, and in the loneliest times, *who are you*? What will you do? Who will you turn to? Where will you seek refuge? This, my friends, is when integrity is essential.

Integrity is defined as "having strong moral principles." As Christians, those principles are grounded in God's Word, and they are developed as we walk with Him.

Put yourself in Job's shoes for a moment. Think about the amount of integrity that he had, the strength of his faith, and his evident love for God. In spite all that happened, he chose to stand firm and not give up.

Now consider your own life. On a scale of 1-10, how would you score your integrity? No matter the score, how can you grow in integrity? It begins with what you are doing at this very moment - you are spending time with God! But it must not stop there. If spending a regular time with God is the foundation for integrity, then the application is the structure. Apply what you have read, and stay in communication with Him (prayer) throughout your day.

If you want to stand up in this sin-cursed world, especially when times get tough, you must pursue your growth in integrity.

🡅 TO LEARN THE CONTEXT OF THIS STORY, CHECK OUT JOB 1 AND 2.

# SEPTEMBER

# NEW BEGINNINGS

IN THE BEGINNING, GOD CREATED THE HEAVENS AND THE EARTH. (GENESIS 1:1)

In one sense, time is vast in nature. Exactly how long has this world been around? How many years do we have on this earth? When will I get married, or have my first child, or finally get to retire? In those cases, time is anyone's guess - we are carried along by a wave that has no end in sight.

In another sense, time is conclusive. As fun as that party was, time brought it to an end. As you persevere, time will finally give way to the day of your graduation. As you take a test, time often ends before you are finished. And unless the Rapture happens during our lifetime, your time on earth will result in your death. Our last day on earth reveals if time was our friend or our enemy (at that point, we all go to a timeless eternity - heaven or hell).

God is not bound by time. He is, He was, and He is to come. The very first verse of the Bible states that He is above and before time. When we read "in the beginning", we learn that this refers to the start of all things that are related to time. Time has no hold upon the One who created its reality and presence.

We'll be looking at some "new beginnings" this month as we study our Bible. Every new beginning in the Bible points to the new beginning for creation. Believers will see the day when our planet will be given a fresh start; it will no longer suffer under the curse of sin. Praise God!

I pray that you will have a good "new beginning" to another school year, and that your time will be God-centered and Christ-focused.

🡅 "EL OLAM", THE NAME OF OUR ETERNAL GOD! READ PSALM 90 TO LEARN MORE ABOUT HIS EVERLASTING NATURE.

# NEW BEGINNINGS - ADAM

So God created man in His own image, in the image of God he created him; male and female he created them. (Genesis 1:27)

New beginnings call for faith. God designed all of humanity to live in faith. However, most people do not place their faith in God; instead, He is replaced by faith in something else.

Recently, I watched my daughter and son take steps of faith as they started a new year at school. Very soon, I will begin piano lessons with an 8-year old girl. I drive around an old truck with nearly 190,000 miles on it. These acts take a certain amount of faith – a belief that the unseen will turn out for the best. But those acts of faith simply include me as a member of humanity. Only saving faith brings me to God.

You would think that Adam wouldn't have to practice faith in the Garden, right? Seriously, God was always with him in a beautifully perfect environment. Yet God provided Adam with an opportunity to take a step in faith. Tragically, he chose a step of sight. Adam's failure proved disastrous to us all. He did not take God at His word, and he ate the forbidden fruit. We live with those consequences daily.

Immediately, there was a new beginning to the beginning – Adam and Eve would start all over again on a cursed planet. However, only time stands in the way of that final new beginning. One day, we step into an uncursed eternity! "We will see him as he is", we are told (in 1 John 3:2). Jesus, who is "the last Adam" (1 Corinthians 15:45), is the one who makes all things new.

Life with him is worth every new beginning I must face here on earth.

↑ TAKE YOUR TIME AND READ ROMANS 5:12-21.

## NEW BEGINNINGS - NOAH

I ESTABLISH MY COVENANT WITH YOU, THAT NEVER AGAIN SHALL ALL FLESH BE CUT OFF BY THE WATERS OF THE FLOOD, AND NEVER AGAIN SHALL THERE BE A FLOOD TO DESTROY THE EARTH. (GENESIS 9:11)

Talk about a new beginning! God had just finished judging the world through a cataclysmic flood. This flood changed everything. We see evidence of it all over the earth.

I want to direct your attention on two points today: Noah's incredible faith, and God's necessary judgment. Think for a minute about an earth that was cursed, but still glorious. This earth was not hydrated by rain, but as best as we can tell, it had a canopy of water, both in the sky above and the ground beneath. These conditions allowed individuals to live for many centuries. Now, God tells Noah that it is going to rain (which has never happened before), and the ground will burst forth with water (which also has never happened). So Noah went and built a boat like no other, taking God at His word. What faith!

Noah did this because God *needed* to judge the world. Man's sin was fully out of control. Of the millions of people in existence, only Noah and his family were good. So the Lord did what He had every right to do – He poured His wrath out upon the wicked. The flood is proof of His destruction. Many months later, the Lord would provide a new beginning by commanding Noah to do what He told Adam: "Be fruitful and multiply" (Gen. 9:7).

God is not afraid to bring judgment upon those who disobey, but He also offers a fresh start to those who repent. As long as a sinner still draws breath, there is hope for a new beginning.

↑ DISCOVER WHAT THE BIBLE SAYS ABOUT NOAH AND THE BUILDING OF THE ARK BEFORE THE FLOOD – READ GENESIS 6:9-7:10.

# NEW BEGINNINGS - ABRAHAM

NOW THE LORD SAID TO ABRAM, "GO FROM YOUR COUNTRY AND YOUR KINDRED AND YOUR FATHER'S HOUSE TO THE LAND THAT I WILL SHOW YOU." (GENESIS 12:1)

Read that verse again. When you do, insert your name in Abram's spot. Would you do what Abram did?

Teens, I want to share with you a great concern of mine. I grieve the fact that teenagers heavily rely on their friends to make decisions. I don't lay the blame with you alone – it is happening with the generations ahead of you, as well. It is a mentality of dependence. *"If my friends aren't doing it, then neither will I!"* When we solely depend upon our friends, we learn to rely on people (who we can see) to make the major decisions in life, rather than God (whom we cannot see), who alone is trustworthy. The long term effect is a life lived empty of faith. That kind of life cannot please God (Hebrews 11:6).

Listen, teens. Our reliance upon our friends or family will only drive us to permanently rely on people to meet our needs. This is nothing less than slavery.

Abram (later named Abraham) was called to begin a life by trusting God in the unseen. In no place do we read about Abraham consulting his friends about leaving home. Because he said "Yes!", God gave him a new beginning. He became the "beginner" of the nation of Israel. The Bible teaches us about the importance of this beginning; our Savior would one day be born as a descendant of Abraham.

What a legacy! What a faith!

↑ THE BEGINNING OF ABRAHAM'S STORY IS IN GENESIS 12:1-9.

# NEW BEGINNINGS - ISAAC

THEN ISAAC BROUGHT HER INTO THE TENT OF SARAH HIS MOTHER AND TOOK REBEKAH, AND SHE BECAME HIS WIFE, AND HE LOVED HER. SO ISAAC WAS COMFORTED AFTER HIS MOTHER'S DEATH. (GENESIS 24:67)

By the time we get to Genesis 24, we have a grown-up Isaac, the miracle child of his ancient parents, waiting for a marriage of his own. Would he ever find the right woman? Genesis 24 gives us the answer. Rebekah not only gave Isaac a new beginning, but also a chance to begin again after the loss of his mother, Sarah.

So, how would you like to marry someone from another country you had never met? Let's just take a stroll back several thousand years, before there was Facebook, Snapchat, Twitter, and even something called e-mail (it really does still exist!). When Isaac met Rebekah, they had never communicated before in their lives. When she arrived in the land of Canaan, Isaac knew she was going to be his wife, period!

Here would have been some of my worries: "What if she can't cook? What if she is on the wrong side of pretty? What if she is 7 feet tall? What if she is the nagging type? What if she hates kayaking?" Funny thing is, none of that really mattered. The one qualification she needed was to be part of Isaac's bloodline (this would keep Isaac from marrying a woman of a pagan nation).

Marriage is an event of new beginnings! Isaac and Rebekah got married with the understanding that they would learn to choose each other, for better or for worse. It took faith, and it worked.

Perhaps a wedding is in your future! If so, may this new beginning be with one who loves God wholeheartedly.

↑ READ REVELATION 19:1-10. IT IS THE MARRIAGE OF ALL MARRIAGES.

# NEW BEGINNINGS - JACOB

AND ISRAEL SAID, "IT IS ENOUGH; JOSEPH MY SON IS STILL ALIVE. I WILL GO AND SEE HIM BEFORE I DIE." (GENESIS 45:28)

You might not know this, but the name *Israel* was given to the man Jacob (the son of Isaac and the grandson of Abraham). Israel means "he struggles with God." What an appropriate meaning for the man who struggled with God for so much of his life. Jacob bore twelve sons, who became the twelve tribes of Israel. If you knew the man, you would never believe he would have been given a new beginning! His story is nothing less than a narrative roller coaster.

Did you ever have a computer or phone that needed to be fixed multiple times? That would be the technology version of Jacob. His default setting was deception – over and over, he chose to trick rather than to treat. So God allowed him to be far away from home and experience the ugly side of marriage. His wives included two sisters and two maidservants. Many years later, he made it back home, but his sons rebelled by living lives that were out-of-control.

Can you believe that God would change Jacob's name to Israel, the future name of His holy nation? By all accounts, this man was a failure. But oh, how God works in mysterious ways! When it seemed Jacob was doomed to finish his days in misery, he discovers that his son Joseph is alive, and God lovingly gives this ancient father peace in the end.

Jacob finishes his days knowing that God is gracious beyond his wildest dreams. How amazing! What a new beginning! As long as we draw breath, we are not beyond the hope that the Lord can do something wonderful with our lives.

↑ JACOB'S SURPRISE NEW BEGINNING (A TRIP TO EGYPT) IS FOUND IN GENESIS 45:21-46:7.

## NEW BEGINNINGS - MOSES

THEN HE SAID, "DO NOT COME NEAR; TAKE YOUR SANDALS OFF YOUR FEET, FOR THE PLACE ON WHICH YOU ARE STANDING IS HOLY GROUND." (EXODUS 3:5)

Moses – the man who began a life as a hunted baby, and a prince of Egypt, and a shepherd in the wilderness, and the deliverer of Israel, and the mediator of God's covenant to His new nation. Moses – a man of many new beginnings!

Not that Moses had it all together, mind you. The Bible makes it clear that he struggled with faith; he had a real anger issue; and he murdered an Egyptian (!). But God is all about perseverance, and His patience is legendary. He did a mighty work in an unwilling man.

Moses is recognized as one of the most important figures in Israel's history. He died with this epithet on his undiscovered tombstone: "And there has not arisen a prophet since in Israel like Moses, whom the LORD knew face to face, none like him for all the signs and wonders that the LORD sent him to do in the land of Egypt, to Pharaoh and to all his servants and to all his land, and for all the mighty power and all the great deeds of terror that Moses did in all the sight of Israel" (Deuteronomy 34:10, 12). God changed Moses in so many ways! His multiple beginnings give us so much hope.

Teens, if you are reading your Bible, perhaps you are picking up on the fact that God can use anyone! We cannot possibly fail in such a way that is beyond HIs ability to overcome. He has only one requirement: a surrendered heart. Imagine if we just quit telling ourselves that we are beyond hope, but started listening to His voice, which calls us to a life of purpose and worth. He did it with Moses – He can do it with you.

↑ MOSES'S NEW BEGINNING AS A LEADER IS FOUND IN EXODUS 4.

## NEW BEGINNINGS - ISRAEL

The time that the people of Israel lived in Egypt was 430 years. At the end of 430 years, on that very day, all the hosts of the LORD went out from the land of Egypt. (Exodus 12:40-41)

How do nations begin? Israel began as a tribal group of people in Egypt, but left that country as a nation. You probably know the story of the Red Sea crossing, but if not, read Exodus 14. Shortly after this incredible miracle, Israel would receive their "constitution." God gave them His law, based on the 10 Commandments. After 430 years in Egypt, God's people were finally free!

I'm not sure how far back you can trace your family history, but I'll pretend that I can go back to the late 1500's A.D. That would be around 430 years ago. Now, let's really use our imagination here. Jacob "Shanks" would have come down with the rest of his 12 sons and family to join Joseph "Shanks" and wait out the long drought. We stayed in the area and multiplied on the earth (sorry, poor world!). Now, in the early 2000's, there are millions of those Shanks' people running around. For whatever reason, the U.S. government does not like it, so if you are a Shanks, you become a slave. But God raised Moses "Shanks" up to deliver us. We cross our nearby river and head for the Promised Land (the beaches of Florida sound good to me!).

Alright, enough silliness! Here's the point: *We cannot overstate the significance of Israel in the role of history.* Nations that have ruled as superpowers get the attention of the world (such nations in the Bible included Assyria, Babylon, Persia, and Rome). But no other nation has ever produced the Savior of the world. And one day, the nation that began with signs, miracles, and wonders will be the nation that is ruled for 1,000 years by her King of kings and Lord of lords.

↑ A NEW BEGINNING AT THE RED SEA CROSSING. READ EXODUS 14!

# NEW BEGINNINGS - JOSHUA

HAVE I NOT COMMANDED YOU? BE STRONG AND COURAGEOUS.
DO NOT BE FRIGHTENED, AND DO NOT BE DISMAYED, FOR THE LORD
YOUR GOD IS WITH YOU WHEREVER YOU GO. (JOSHUA 1:9)

Joshua was a grizzly old vet – he marched out of Egypt 40 years ago with the rest of his kin and served as Moses' right hand man. He would now lead the next generation of Israel into the land God had promised for them. It was a time of great conquest for Israel; the Lord gave them victory after victory over the corrupt nations that once occupied their newly acquired territory.

When we look at this verse in its context, we see that God commanded Joshua to have courage in leading the armies forward to battle. He would also need courage in presiding over the nation as they began to settle down for the first time in their short history.

The timeless truth in Joshua 1:9 is that God is also with every Christian, as well. His presence is complete: He is both near us ("I will never leave you nor forsake you" - Hebrews 13:5) and inside of us ("When the Spirit of truth comes, he will guide you into all the truth" - John 16:13).

As with Moses, we see the Lord use another servant of His that is well advanced in years. But Joshua was up for a new beginning, for he had remained faithful, even when his brethren were rebelling against God.

Our age is not an issue for Him in the least; He is with us, and is willing to use us. So teens, be strong! Be courageous! Don't be afraid! "The LORD is my light and my salvation; whom shall I fear? The LORD is the stronghold of my life; of whom shall I be afraid?" (Psalm 27:1).

JOSHUA'S NEW BEGINNING IS IN THE BOOK THAT BEARS HIS NAME. READ JOSHUA 1.

# NEW BEGINNINGS - THE JUDGES

AND ALL THAT GENERATION ALSO WERE GATHERED TO THEIR FATHERS. AND THERE AROSE ANOTHER GENERATION AFTER THEM WHO DID NOT KNOW THE LORD OR THE WORK THAT HE HAD DONE FOR ISRAEL. (JUDGES 2:10)

There are times when new beginnings are not good. A new beginning might just mean a discovery of a life-altering disease. It may mean becoming pregnant outside of marriage. It may mean not being accepted to the college you hoped to attend. It may mean a personal decision to do something that will destroy your life – like taking drugs, or viewing pornography, or cheating on your spouse. Yes, new beginnings are not always good (in fact, many people are fooled into thinking that receiving Christ as Savior means sunshine and roses all of the time. Not so! Satan hates that new beginning. As a believer, he will now fight against you for the rest of your days).

Israel chose the new beginning of worshipping idols. It's hard to believe how quickly this happened after their 40 years of wandering in the wilderness. Their Idol worship led to slavery; they repented and cried out to God; and He delivered them in His mercy. Yet the following generation would return to idol worship. Crazy! Unbelievably, God never gave up. Imagine if He did say to Israel, "We're done here! I'm starting a new beginning Myself. You are now history." God tested Moses with this thought, but Moses passed the test, trusting that God would not let His name be profaned in the destruction of His people.

So, ask yourself this: What have I began to do this new school year? Why am I doing it? Does it please God? How will it make a long-term difference? Have I prayed about it? May your new beginning not be one that you'll regret, dear ones!

↑ THE "CLIFF NOTES" VERSION FOR JUDGES IS FOUND IN JUDGES 2.

# NEW BEGINNINGS - THE KINGS

THEN ALL THE ELDERS OF ISRAEL GATHERED TOGETHER AND CAME TO SAMUEL AT RAMAH AND SAID TO HIM, "BEHOLD, YOU ARE OLD AND YOUR SONS DO NOT WALK IN YOUR WAYS. NOW APPOINT FOR US A KING TO JUDGE US LIKE ALL THE NATIONS." (1 SAMUEL 8:4-5)

Unfortunately, the book of Judges opens up another chapter of poor beginnings for Israel. There came a time when the nation grew tired of having judges over them, so they sought out a king. Is it wicked to have a king rule a nation? No, not at all. One day, King Jesus will rule the nations! However, notice the primary reason the elders wanted a king. Israel wanted to be "like all the nations." God's nation was called to be a holy, set apart unto Him, but Israel wanted to blend in. This upset Samuel, but God told him to listen to the people (even though they were ultimately rejecting Him as king. How foolish of Israel!).

I suspect we'll see the day when we no longer have a president as the leader of our land. We are not Israel, nor can we expect the same blessing and curses found in the Bible that are given to Abraham's descendants. But as we continue to reject the truths that have made us "One Nation, Under God", we will be subjected to a new beginning as a nation; we will face the terrible consequences of rejecting God as Lord of all. Nations rise and fall... and a fall is inevitable when a nation follows other gods.

The vast majority of kings hurt Israel, starting with King Saul. But God called his faithful followers to seek Him, and He enabled them to thrive in the worst of times.

No matter what happens in our nation, we can do the same! In freedom or in slavery, we can live for the Lord. That's the power we have through Jesus Christ, our one true King.

CHECK OUT 1 SAMUEL 8. HOW DOES IT RELATE TO US TODAY?

## NEW BEGINNINGS - DAVID

AND HE SENT AND BROUGHT HIM IN. NOW HE WAS RUDDY AND HAD BEAUTIFUL EYES AND HE WAS HANDSOME. AND THE LORD SAID, "ARISE, ANOINT HIM, FOR THIS IS HE." (1 SAMUEL 16:12)

The second king of Israel was a man of God's choosing! Completely opposite from the people's selection of Saul, God chose David upon the condition of his heart (1 Samuel 16:7).

Our society is enamored with stature and looks. However, good leaders are known for their character. The best looking people in the world cannot lead us with their beauty or strength. There must be something more! With David, that "something more" was his heart for God. He gave his nation a new beginning; not only was he their first righteous king, he would become the standard for the kings of Israel to follow.

David also starts a new beginning as it relates to Jesus Christ. How is that so? Well, I'm glad you asked! It's a great story. With Abraham, a new race of people began. With David, a special line in that race would be established. In David, the lineage of kings would make its way to the Savior, born about 1,000 years later. Genealogies are a big deal in the Bible – two of them are in Matthew 1 and Luke 3. Both of these specific genealogies point to Jesus as the rightful king; they date from his parents back to Abraham (in Matthew) and and Adam (in Luke).

At one point, David wanted to build "a house" (the temple) for the Lord. God gave him some better news –He would build a lineage from his family. And believers in Christ are saved Jesus is "the son of David!"

"Thank you, O Lord, for new beginnings. We praise you for the grace you poured out on David. It's a beginning that led to our salvation."

FOLLOW THIS SPECIAL GENEAOLOGY IN MATTHEW 1:1-17.

# NEW BEGINNINGS - THE DIVIDED KINGDOM

AND WHEN ALL ISRAEL SAW THAT THE KING DID NOT LISTEN TO THEM, THE PEOPLE ANSWERED THE KING, "WHAT PORTION DO WE HAVE IN DAVID? WE HAVE NO INHERITANCE IN THE SON OF JESSE. TO YOUR TENTS, O ISRAEL! LOOK NOW TO YOUR OWN HOUSE, DAVID." SO ISRAEL WENT TO THEIR TENTS. (1 KINGS 12:16)

Kings Saul, David, and Solomon ruled the nation of Israel, then a civil war took place. Only three kings into the kingdom period, and things were a major wreck. Now, ten tribes made up the north, and two were in the south. When we take a good look at our own civil war, it's easy to see how we could have ended up as two nations (thankfully, in His sovereignty, God did not allow it to happen). But He did allow the break-up of Israel. In fact, he told the king of Judah to leave the rest of the nation alone. For us, that would be like God telling Abraham Lincoln to let the South do its own thing (where would we be today if that happened?).

Our own nation needs a new beginning. Wouldn't you agree? What a mess! Is it possible that we have lost the purpose for why we exist as the United States? Any nation that recognizes the supreme position and authority of God has hope. Even one of the most wicked nations in history was given a chance to remain because it saw the need to repent and begin anew (read about it in the book of Jonah). But when a nation rejects Him and chooses pride over humility, it's over (read about this same nation in the book of Nahum).

Why does our nation remain on the map? Only God can answer that question. Here's a better question: Why do believers exist in this nation? We can answer that one: it's to be a light in the world. That purpose is timeless, no matter what happens to the United States. Our highest calling is to glorify God. When we understand this role, it prepares us for any new beginning we are called to face.

🡅 THE BREAKUP OF THE KINGDOM – READ 1 KINGS 12.

# NEW BEGINNINGS - THE EXILE

AND AS THE LORD TOOK DELIGHT IN DOING YOU GOOD AND MULTIPLYING YOU, SO THE LORD WILL TAKE DELIGHT IN BRINGING RUIN UPON YOU AND DESTROYING YOU. AND YOU SHALL BE PLUCKED OFF THE LAND THAT YOU ARE ENTERING TO TAKE POSSESSION OF IT. (DEUTERONOMY 28:63)

Can I tell you something? I'm afraid! I've read history books about nations that turn their back on God. I've heard of leaders who have done their own thing and hurt or killed their people. I know that Satan hates Christians, and he is always looking for ways to bring us down. I see how a mob can quickly form against a common enemy, and their enemy is often the one who wants what is peaceful and godly. I've read the book of Habakkuk in the Old Testament, and I read that the LORD is not afraid to use terrible nations to take out ones like our own. God's justice is swift and complete, wiping away sin by means of calamites such as floods, droughts, plagues, and the like. In this nation, we are so full of sin, giving people the freedom to abort the unborn, celebrate the degradation of marriage, and pursue the worship of countless idols.

Where is Babylon? Where is Persia? Where is Rome? Where are the other historical empires that raised their fists against Heaven? Oh yes, many of their descendants have survived, but these nations have been dismantled or destroyed. Are we next? I am afraid for us! Will we be taken over, and enslaved, and tortured, and killed? We have offended the Almighty God – how long will He withhold His judgment? I am afraid for us! We deserve the new beginning of slavery.

*"Oh God, please have mercy! Please, have mercy on us!"*

🡅 JEREMIAH LAMENTS THE NEW BEGINNING OF ISRAEL AS CAPTIVES OF BABYLON. READ ABOUT IT IN LAMENTATIONS 1.

## NEW BEGINNINGS - THE RETURN

THUS SAYS CYRUS KING OF PERSIA: THE LORD, THE GOD OF HEAVEN, HAS GIVEN ME ALL THE KINGDOMS OF THE EARTH, AND HE HAS CHARGED ME TO BUILD HIM A HOUSE AT JERUSALEM, WHICH IS IN JUDAH. WHOEVER IS AMONG YOU OF ALL HIS PEOPLE, MAY HIS GOD BE WITH HIM, AND LET HIM GO UP TO JERUSALEM, WHICH IS IN JUDAH, AND REBUILD THE HOUSE OF THE LORD, THE GOD OF ISRAEL – HE IS THE GOD WHO IS IN JERUSALEM. (EZRA 1:2-3)

A pagan king, who just took over control of the civilized world, told the Jews that they could go back home... no strings attached. In fact, they were to go back home, worship God, and rebuild a temple for Him. This is stunning news! Finally, the captives would be free.

The Jews had been driven from their homeland for the appointed 70 years (as Daniel recognized in Daniel 9). The time had come for a new beginning in the land. Another generation of Israel would have the chance to make things right. God had not given up on them; He had kept His promise to bring them back.

How about you, dear prodigal son (daughter)? Are you driven away from everything that is good because you did everything that was bad? Told to leave home and never come back? Sitting in prison because you chose sin over a life surrendered to God? Rejected by your peers because you are pregnant? Tossed aside because you can't seem to overcome your drug addiction? Yes, make no mistake – you deserve the exile and captivity. And so do I! Ah, but you are still living; yes, you are still breathing. This means that *there still must be hope for you.* And look ahead! Jesus stands there, with his arms wide open, saying, "Oh sinner, come home! Oh sinner, come home!"

Dear sinner, it's time to come home. Enjoy a new beginning of grace!

🡅 CHECK OUT THE CONNECTION OF 2 CHRONICLES 36:15-23 AND EZRA 1:1-4. ISRAEL COMES HOME... WHAT A WONDERFUL GOD!

# NEW BEGINNINGS - JESUS CHRIST

JESUS SAID TO HER, "I AM THE RESURRECTION AND THE LIFE. WHOEVER BELIEVES IN ME, THOUGH HE DIE, YET SHALL HE LIVE, AND EVERYONE WHO LIVES AND BELIEVES IN ME SHALL NEVER DIE. DO YOU BELIEVE THIS?" (JOHN 11:25-26)

Teens, life is full of new beginnings. The devotions this month are a snapshot of that reality. Israel itself is a picture of new beginnings. Sometimes those starts were the results of being blessed, and sometimes they were the results of being cursed. My hope and goal is to get us to a point where we are not afraid of new beginnings; we always have the need to be transformed (Romans 12:2).

The fact that we can begin again is because of Jesus Christ. If he did not arrive on the scene and save us from death, our only possible beginning would have been at the point of our conception. After this, the minute we first sinned against God would have been the minute we were doomed to eternal separation from Him.

Christ himself is the Creator of new beginnings (he tells us that "I am making everything new!" in the book of Revelation, as the Millenium finally makes way for the Eternal State).

The Bible teaches us about two important comings of Christ (two "new beginnings"): the first coming was as a baby over 2000 years ago; the second as our victor when the Tribulation comes to a close. Both comings change everything. History was changed his first time around; when he comes again, the kingdoms of this world will become the kingdom of our Lord and Savior, King Jesus.

"O God, life begins with You! We praise you for Your Son, who is both the Alpha and the Omega."

↑ LOOK AT THE NEW BEGINNINGS FOUND IN ISAIAH 42:1-9.

# NEW BEGINNINGS - CHRISTMAS

SHE WILL BEAR A SON, AND YOU SHALL CALL HIS NAME JESUS, FOR HE WILL SAVE HIS PEOPLE FROM THEIR SINS. (MATTHEW 1:21)

There are rare moments in time when the incredible happens in our lives. When it does, we are so blown away that nothing else matters. At a graduation, the high school senior feels the freedom of finally... being... done! At a marriage proposal, the fiancée gasps when her loving husband-to-be slips that gorgeous diamond on her finger. At their wedding, the husband looks at his bride and cares about nothing else in that moment of time. She has enraptured him with her beauty and radiance! At the birth of a child, time stands still as a new life is held in the arms of both mom and dad. They are blessed beyond words to know that they have received a living gift to nurture and love.

When considering Christmas as a new beginning, take a minute and remove your personal experiences from your mind. Take away the presents, the meals, the family, and whatever else you may have enjoyed in the past. When Jesus was born, the world generally missed it. But for those who knew he came, it was pure amazement and joy. Ponder those who were there. Mary and Joseph: *"How can this be? The Son of God, in our arms? Unbelievable!"* The Shepherds: *"Let's check this out! Hurry... it's him! We've got to tell everyone! He's here!"* The Wise Men: *"We worship you, O Holy Child! Here are our gifts, to recognize the great King that you are!"* Simeon and Anna: *"We made it! After all these many years, our eyes have seen the One!"*

The Apostle John said it this way: "In the beginning was the Word... and the Word was God" (John 1:1). The new beginning is "God with us!"

🡅 IMMANUEL – "GOD WITH US" – PROPHESIED MANY CENTURIES AGO. READ ISAIAH 7:10-14.

## NEW BEGINNINGS - JOHN THE BAPTIST

JOHN APPEARED, BAPTIZING IN THE WILDERNESS AND PROCLAIMING A BAPTISM OF REPENTANCE FOR THE FORGIVENESS OF SINS. (MARK 1:4)

We know very little about Jesus and his growing up years. We might be surprised just how uneventful these years turned out to be. We catch a glimpse of a unique time when his parents lost him on a trip to Jerusalem (oops!), but the Bible doesn't go into other details about Jesus as a child or teenager. In fact, we need to wait until he is 30 years old before Christ began a recorded ministry. That was God's plan for His Son; it was also His plan to use the cousin of Jesus as his forerunner.

When we consider what it takes to transport our president to a certain location for a gathering, we know that it takes an announcement and preparation for that city to host him. Important people have forerunners; they make it known that these VIPs are coming to see you. As the forerunner of Jesus, John's mission was to prepare hearts to hear Jesus. Remember, his miraculous birth was only known to a select few. John proclaimed a message that should have sounded familiar to the Jews that knew their history – the Promised One had come to save them. Sadly, evil won the day, and John's ministry came to an end when he was beheaded by Herod.

In my opinion, one of John's best lines is this: "He must increase, but I must decrease" (John 3:30). That is humility defined. Oh, if only we would live by that motto! More of him, and less of me! Too soon, John left this world; in spite of his death, he had done his job to the fullest. The new beginning of Jesus as Savior to the world was introduced by this faithful cousin. May it be that we would also do all that we are asked by the heavenly Father. "He must increase, but I must decrease!"

JOHN THE BAPTIST IS WRITTEN ABOUT IN THE APOSTLE JOHN'S GOSPEL. READ JOHN 1:19-42 TODAY.

# NEW BEGINNINGS - CHRIST'S MINISTRY

SEEING THE CROWDS, HE WENT UP ON THE MOUNTAIN, AND WHEN HE SAT DOWN, HIS DISCIPLES CAME TO HIM. (MATTHEW 5:1)

The authors of the gospel books (Matthew, Mark, Luke, and John) wrote to specific audiences. The writing was purposeful and Spirit-led (indeed, all of Scripture is "inspired by God"). In Matthew, Jesus formally began his years of preaching in what we know as "The Beatitudes." At the famous "Sermon on the Mount," those gathered waited in great anticipation to hear from the Teacher. And what they heard was so different from what they had been hearing. It was words of freedom, peace, comfort, and hope!

In his ministry, Jesus had the amazing knack of saying the very opposite of what was expected. There were times when you can picture his followers with incredulous looks, mouths wide-opened, trying to tell this extraordinary rabbi that he had trounced the common beliefs of the people (again!). But isn't his style just one of a million things that makes Jesus so awesome?!! The Son of God had come to fulfill the law, and he did it by offering grace. Amazing! His three years on earth would be marked by constant opposition, yet he healed, and loved, and taught, and comforted, and challenged, and condemned, and cried... and eventually, he won!

Teens, read the stories of changed lives in the gospels. You may just find that you will be changed, too!

🡅 THOSE FAMOUS BEATITUDES ARE IN MATTHEW 5:1-12.

## NEW BEGINNINGS - CHRIST'S MIRACLES

AND BEHOLD, SOME PEOPLE BROUGHT TO HIM A PARALYTIC, LYING ON A BED. AND WHEN JESUS SAW THEIR FAITH, HE SAID TO THE PARALYTIC, "TAKE HEART, MY SON; YOUR SINS ARE FORGIVEN." (MATTHEW 9:2)

Which is harder? To forgive sins, or to heal the paralyzed? The paralyzed man in Matthew 9 had his body miraculously healed; however, there was a day in the future that his body died. The Christian has his soul forgiven; because of this, there will never be a day that his soul will die. How incredible it would have been for those privileged to see this man get up and walk! And still, the religious leaders were far more concerned about their laws. What a tragedy!

When we read about the miracles of Jesus, we find them linked to the presence of faith. In God's holy wisdom, He insists that no miracle would occur in Christ's lifetime without evident faith found in the believing participant. *"Jesus, I can't see what's about to happen to me, but I believe in you nonetheless!"* This is the kind of faith that moved him to perform miracles time and again.

The Bible is entirely true, which means all the miracles in the Bible took place. But still, many demand "to see it and believe it." What if the man on his mat lived that way? What if he said, *"Jesus, you're a nice guy and all, but I have to see you do something in front of me first. In fact, please just 'wow' me for a bit, then we'll talk about all my sin and my need for salvation."* You and I both know the man would have missed the chance to be saved, both in body and in soul.

Christ's miracles showed us that Jesus is God, but the real beginning for the healed man was found in the forgiveness of his sin. Praise God for the greatest of all miracles: His salvation!

🡅 JESUS HEALS THE PARALYTIC IN MATTHEW 9:1-8.

# NEW BEGINNINGS - CHRIST'S CHARACTER

I AND THE FATHER ARE ONE. (JOHN 10:30)

What a short but powerful verse! And the enemies of Christ hated him for it. To them, the claim was complete blasphemy. Ultimately, they failed to successfully refute the deity of Jesus, for everyone witnessed his miracles, and the crowds were following him.

Never before had anyone so perfectly displayed such flawless character. Grace and truth were found completely fulfilled in the Son of God. He knew exactly when to pronounce judgment, and he knew when to have mercy. He extended grace to those who were considered the lowest of society, and his most scathing words were reserved for the self-proclaimed righteous ones. Against all taboos, Christ touched the lepers; he went out of his way to reach a despised and rejected woman; he had dinner with a hated tax collector. He loved the unlovable, even though he knew most people would never understand why. His character would serve as a new beginning for those who later believed; as we are taught about the church in Colossians 3:11, "Here there is not Greek and Jew, circumcised and uncircumcised, barbarian, Scythian, slave, free; but Christ is all, and in all."

There is just no one like Jesus. When you consider how incredible he is, understand that Christ is *one and the same* with God the Father. Jesus made the claim that only he could make: "I and the Father are one." His character is God's character. It always has been, and it always will be.

How does that make you feel about our Savior today?

🡅 PLEASE READ JOHN 14:5-14!

## NEW BEGINNINGS - CHRIST'S SACRIFICE

NOR WAS IT TO OFFER HIMSELF REPEATEDLY, AS THE HIGH PRIESTS ENTERS THE HOLY PLACES EVERY YEAR WITH BLOOD NOT HIS OWN, FOR THEN HE WOULD HAVE HAD TO SUFFER REPEATEDLY SINCE THE FOUNDATION OF THE WORLD. BUT AS IT IS, HE HAS APPEARED ONCE FOR ALL AT THE END OF THE AGES TO PUT AWAY SIN BY THE SACRIFICE OF HIMSELF. (HEBREWS 9:25-26)

When Jesus died on the cross, much of what was prophesied was finally fulfilled. When he rose from the dead, he made all things new. In the three days that Christ was in the grave, his disciples felt lost, scared, and defeated. Wouldn't you have felt the same way?

It's fascinating to think about what happened in the unseen world during the time that Christ was in the tomb. The angels would have known that Jesus conquered Satan when he shouted, "It is finished!" The greatest of victories was complete; the grave held the body for a short time, but the Spirit of Christ was with God the Father.

What was Satan thinking at Christ's death? Did he realize that he had suffered his greatest defeat, or was he fooled into believing that Jesus had lost? Had his pride convinced him that he beat the Lord?

Some of those discouraged followers actually decided to try a new beginning by getting back into fishing. Immediately after his death, their heads were swimming. We are given a chance to see their world when Luke shares a discussion between two followers on a trip to Emmaus. They truly think it's over. When Jesus shows up, he opened their eyes to the purpose and power of his sacrifice. As it says in the book of Hebrews, Jesus took our place – he alone had the ability "to put away sin by the sacrifice of himself."

*"Father, I will never need to pay what Jesus paid for me. Thank you!"*

↑ READ MORE ABOUT CHRIST'S SACRIFICE IN HEBREWS 10:1-18.

# NEW BEGINNINGS - CHRIST'S VICTORY

O SING TO THE LORD A NEW SONG, FOR HE HAS DONE MARVELOUS THINGS! HIS RIGHT HAND AND HIS HOLY ARM HAVE WORKED SALVATION FOR HIM. (PSALM 98:1)

Pennsylvania is known as "The Keystone State". A keystone is that important link that holds an arch together. If you picture the 13 original colonies (which include most of the states that border the Atlantic Ocean), you can visualize how our state is a link to those who live north and south of us along the coast. A lot of transportation along the Atlantic coast travels through this state (thought some of it goes through New Jersey). Because of this, Pennsylvania has many large shipping businesses, located on or near its interstate highways. I have worked for a few of those businesses myself.

Peter quotes the prophet Isaiah when he refers to Christ as stone that connects it all together: "Behold, I am laying in Zion a stone, a cornerstone chosen and precious, and whoever believes in him will not be put to shame" (1 Peter 2:6). The resurrection is the keystone of the life of Christ. Without it, we worship a dead man. But praise God, Jesus is alive! All of history hinges upon the acceptance or rejection of Jesus as the cornerstone.

Peter goes on to talk about Christ's role as a cornerstone in the next two verses (1 Peter 2:7-8): "So the honor is for you who believe, but for those who do not believe, 'The stone that the builders rejected has become the cornerstone,' and 'A stone of stumbling, and a rock of offense.'" To reject the keystone is to trip and fall... forever.

Teens, how about you? Do you believe the gospel? Is Jesus Christ the rock of your salvation? All victories begin with his.

🡅 CELEBRATE CHRIST'S VICTORY IN 1 PETER 2:4-10!

# NEW BEGINNINGS - CHRIST'S ASCENSION

AND WHILE THEY WERE GAZING INTO HEAVEN AS HE WENT, BEHOLD, TWO MEN STOOD BY THEM IN WHITE ROBES, AND SAID, "MEN OF GALILEE, WHY DO YOU STAND LOOKING INTO HEAVEN? THIS JESUS, WHO WAS TAKEN UP FROM YOU INTO HEAVEN, WILL COME IN THE SAME WAY AS YOU SAW HIM GO INTO HEAVEN." (ACTS 1:10-11)

For *most* believers, death will be the final step before we reach our eternal destination. Like everyone else I know, I would prefer to die in my sleep! For *all* believers, the rapture will be the event that takes us to heaven. Some believers will be alive when it happens. In the book of 1 Thessalonians, we are told that the living will be "caught up in the air" to join those who had "fallen asleep" (the believers who have already died). How wonderful for those who will be alive at the Rapture! Whether I am dead or alive, I can hardly wait for that day!

The ascension of Christ marked a new beginning for the disciples. They could hardly grasp what was next as they watched Jesus go up into the clouds. If you think about it, his ascension would qualify as both the saddest and most glorious event ever witnessed after Calvary. God sent two angels to the believers to assure them that Jesus would come back. He will "catch us in the air" at the rapture; then, he will come back a second time to start the age of the millennium. Praise the Lord!

Losing a loved one is one of the hardest new beginnings in life. Some teens are forced to deal with the painful loss of a sibling or parent as teenagers. This is a very hard thing, indeed. However, I remind you of Jesus' promise to his followers before he returned home to Heaven - he promised them the Holy Spirit. With that reality, we live in the truth of Hebrews 13:5: "I will never leave you nor forsake you." Yes!

↑ READ EITHER ACTS 1:1-12 OR 1 THESSALONIANS 4:13-18. HE WILL COME FOR US, AND WE WILL BEGIN ANEW IN HEAVEN!

## NEW BEGINNINGS - THE CHURCH

HE IS THE HEAD OF THE BODY, THE CHURCH. HE IS THE BEGINNING, THE FIRSTBORN FROM THE DEAD, THAT IN EVERYTHING HE MIGHT BE PREEMINENT. (COLOSSIANS 1:18)

For nearly 2,000 years, the church has been in existence! God's new beginning for the world started around 30 A.D., shortly after Christ ascended to heaven. Her importance is found in her relationship to the Savior: she is both his body and his bride.

It's hard for us to grasp the magnitude of the change that occurred with the beginning of the church. A nation made way for a congregation, bound together not by blood nor law, but in spirit and truth. Many a Jew struggled with this religious and historical change. *"Other nations are included? How can this be?"*

Let's bring our thoughts back to our world today. When you hear the word "church", what comes to mind? I think we would be most blessed if we would learn to associate the word "family" with church. In this family, we recognize God as the Father, and we are His sons and daughters (which makes us brothers and sisters!).

In John 4, Jesus looked forward to the new beginning of the church: "But the hour is coming, and is now here, when the true worshipers will worship the Father in spirit and truth, for the Father is seeking such people to worship him" (John 4:23).

What a great day in which we live! May His church glorify Him, and may we see many more sons and daughters added to our number.

🡅 READ EPHESIANS 2:11-22, IF YOU WOULD!

## NEW BEGINNINGS - THE END AND THE BEGINNING

THEN KING DARIUS WROTE TO ALL THE PEOPLES, NATIONS, AND LANGUAGES THAT DWELL IN ALL THE EARTH: "PEACE BE MULTIPLIED TO YOU. I MAKE A DECREE, THAT IN ALL MY ROYAL DOMINION PEOPLE ARE TO TREMBLE AND FEAR BEFORE THE GOD OF DANIEL, FOR HE IS A LIVING GOD, ENDURING FOREVER; HIS KINGDOM SHALL NEVER BE DESTROYED, AND HIS DOMINION SHALL BE TO THE END." (DANIEL 6:25-26)

If someone asked you about how the world would end, what would you answer? I hope you know that you have all the answers you need in the Bible! The church age will make way for the tribulation (7 years), then the millennium will come (1,000 years), then we will arrive home, in eternity (forever years!).

In God, there are no ends. Just let that sink in for a moment. One end is only another beginning. When I consider this, it takes my breath away.

Teens, think about your greatest desires. Remove from your mind some of the best experiences you could have on this earth (marriage, having kids, etc.), and get to the foundation of your hopes and dreams. Do you realize that God made you live forever? Not only that, He made you to desire to live with Him forever. If you are a Christian, you will do just that – you will live with Him for eternity!

The end of the world as we know it is the beginning of life in the presence of God. No more sorrow, no sickness, no pain, and no death. Our new beginning is our final stop – we'll be home! Joy, forevermore.

A final beginning with no end? Bring it on. "Even so, come, Lord Jesus!"

↑ CHECK OUT REVELATION 22. OH, WOW!

# SATAN VS. SILENCE

BE SOBER-MINDED; BE WATCHFUL. YOUR ADVERSARY THE DEVIL PROWLS AROUND LIKE A ROARING LION, SEEKING SOMEONE TO DEVOUR. (1 PETER 5:8)

God has brought this verse to mind many times over the last several months (if God brings certain truths to your attention over and over again, listen up! It's learning time!).

Teens, we are bombarded with a constant flow of information. How many of us actually spend time in silence? I'm not talking about the kind of silence that comes when the Wi-Fi is out for an hour. No, it's the kind of silence that happens when everything else in life is shut out and you can really (and I mean *really*) think. Do you embrace this kind of silence? Have you ever done so?

I'm guessing this is difficult to do, and that kind of silence is rare for you. I know it's rare in my life. I have to fight hard to find times of quietness. My best times are when I make myself get up early for a morning walk and talk with God. I have never once regretted getting up early, in order to make sure that I am listening to God properly.

My times of silence help me figure out how to cut through the deceptions that Satan sends my way. He tries to tell me, *"You deserve people that treat you better, Mike!"* and *"Your wife and kids will understand if you do not spend more time with them!"* and *"Why should you work so hard when others have it so easy?"* These statements reveal a very selfish root problem; the focus is on "me". God tells us that life is not about me. I need to sober-minded and watchful, or the roaring lion will pounce! Taking time in silence to listen to God is one great way to protect yourself from the devil.

CHECK OUT 1 PETER 5:1-11. LISTEN, AND LIVE!

# BROKEN AND CONTRITE

CAST ME NOT AWAY FROM YOUR PRESENCE, AND TAKE NOT YOUR HOLY SPIRIT FROM ME. RESTORE TO ME THE JOY OF YOUR SALVATION, AND UPHOLD ME WITH A WILLING SPIRIT. (PSALM 51:11-12)

What is the worst thing you've ever done? Take a minute to think about it. Were you caught in a certain sin? How public was it? How many people did it affect? Do you still suffer from it today?

King David made a series of decisions that left a terrible trail of consequences. He slept with a married woman. She became pregnant. He lied to her husband. He tried to get him drunk so that he would have sex with his wife, making it look like it was his baby. None of this worked, so he had him killed in battle. The prophet Nathan finally pulled a confession out of David, after months of living in denial. What a terrible course of events! God knew it all, and David's consequences were severe (the baby died shortly after birth; his own children would later hurt and kill each other; he would deal with insurrections to the throne; unrest marked his final years). So messy, yet so unnecessary.

Yet, here is the great difference between David and most of Israel's other kings. In Psalm 51, we see that David's own spirit was broken before God. He prayed to God to renew a steadfast spirit in him, and to grant him a willing spirit. God answered his prayer and allowed the Holy Spirit to remain with him as king. *Broken* and *contrite* are two key ingredients for repentance. In spite of everything, David did know how to repent. No wonder God was so good to him.

So, if you were to write a psalm about the worst thing you did in your life, what would it say? Would it include repentance? "A broken spirit, a broken and contrite heart, O God, you will not despise" (vs. 17).

↑ CAREFULLY CONSIDER TWO VERSES TODAY: ISAIAH 66:1-2.

# THE FAITH OF THE CENTURION

WHEN JESUS HEARD THESE THINGS, HE MARVELED AT HIM, AND TURNING TO THE CROWD THAT FOLLOWED HIM, SAID, "I TELL YOU, NOT EVEN IN ISRAEL HAVE I FOUND SUCH FAITH." (LUKE 7:9)

The world clamors for a superstar, but the world is changed by a man or woman of faith.

When we study history in our modern day, we are often ignorant of the names who have changed it. God is always active in history, and He has used people in whom He delights. These people are men and women of faith (Hebrews 11:6 tells us, "for without faith, it is impossible to please God"). For those of us who are Heaven-bound, we'll meet countless of brothers and sisters whom we never knew by name. I am certain that God honored their faith in Him by changing the course of the world.

The faith of the centurion is one story of such faith – and it's such a terrific story! Jesus himself was amazed. God included this story in His Holy Word; how many lives have been changed because of this man's faith? And how many stories like this exist, only to be revealed in eternity? I look forward to hearing them all.

As I write today, I read about another incredible basketball game played last night by LeBron James. His skill on the court is unmatched. However, LeBron is not changing the course of history, in spite of his basketball heroics. Faithful saints like the centurion are the ones doing so, for their faith is the power God uses in His greatest acts on earth.

↑ READ ABOUT THE CENTURION IN LUKE 7:1-10.

# A PICTURE OF HIS LOVE FOR US (BY EDDIE NEWTON)

BEHOLD, YOU ARE BEAUTIFUL, MY LOVE; BEHOLD, YOU ARE BEAUTIFUL;
YOUR EYES ARE DOVES. (SONG OF SOLOMON 1:15)

Love is so powerful. It can be an extraordinarily strong motivator, perhaps the strongest and purest motivator of all. It can get us to say things we would not normally say, and do things we would not otherwise do. Many have done foolish things in the "name of love". However, love does not only lead us to do foolish things. It can move us to do that which is wise, wonderful, powerful, and good. For example, many first responders and military personnel have been motivated by love for others, country, and family. They have risked their own lives to protect and provide for us.

In the verse above, we see Solomon express his affections for his beloved through a flattering description of her beauty. I can remember when I first started dating the girl that is now my wife. Yes, I was struck by her external beauty at first, but soon discovered the beauty within. As our love grew, it brought us to the point of our wedding. I will never forget standing at the front of the church with eager anticipation of seeing my soon-to-be wife. As the back doors of the church auditorium opened, and I saw her in her wedding dress, I was overcome by her beauty and the delightful thought of spending our lives together. The events of the day were an expression of our love for each other. It was an amazing day, not soon forgotten! However, the primary massage we wanted to communicate that day was not just our love for each other, but God's love for his people (the church). We knew God's love is not a foolish and accidental love, but rather a wise, wonderful, powerful, and good love for his creation. It is a love that will culminate when God the Father presents the church to His Son as a spotless bride. Make no mistake, God loves You!

↑ WHAT A GLORIOUS REALITY! READ JEREMIAH 31:1-6 TODAY.

# OCTOBER

## WHAT WILL YOU DO? (WWYD)

AND NOW, O ISRAEL, LISTEN TO THE STATUTES AND RULES THAT I AM TEACHING YOU, AND DO THEN, THAT YOU MAY LIVE, AND GO IN AND TAKE POSSESSION OF THE LAND THAT THE LORD, THE GOD OF YOUR FATHERS, IS GIVING YOU. (DEUTERONOMY 4:1)

Teens, the day will soon come when you are out on your own! It may be college; it may be marriage; it may be getting an apartment with a new job; it may be moving in with a friend or relative in another town. A move is usually accompanied by many decisions. Many of these decisions are unanticipated; indeed, you may discover there are far more questions than answers in this season of life.

How wise and beneficial it is when we have biblical answers before life's challenges occur! When we lack these answers, we easily find ourselves walking into a minefield. That never ends up good!

Israel's greatest king (King David) actually wrote a chapter in the Bible that is 176 verses long! These verses describe the significance and wonder of God's perfect law. It's a fascinating piece of poetry – each letter of the Hebrew alphabet starts a section of 8 verses, teaching us about both the necessity of and freedom in His commands. David's love for God's Word molded him into a man of tremendous understanding.

Experience is often a great teacher... but can you completely trust experience to teach you all that is right? Only the Bible is perfectly trustworthy! The more you know the Bible, the more you will know the exact answers to the question, "WHAT WILL YOU DO?".

↑ CHECK OUT DEUTERONOMY 4. GOD COMMANDED ISRAEL TO OBEY HIM FOR HER GOOD. MAY YOU ALSO OBEY, AND MAY YOU BE BLESSED WITH WISDOM IN THE TOUGH CHALLENGES OF LIFE.

## MY DRUNK AND SICK ROOMMATE (WWYD)

DO NOT BE OVERCOME BY EVIL, BUT OVERCOME EVIL WITH GOOD. (ROMANS 12:21)

*Your roommate is drunk and has thrown up all over your room. What will you do?*

I can tell you what I would *feel* like doing... I would *feel* like tossing him out of my window! Thankfully, God has taught us not to live by our feelings. There is a better way!

Let's talk about some good ideas on what you can do...

1. *Pray for him. Don't wait – pray immediately! It is hard to hate the people that we pray for – God intended our hearts to love the ones we pray for in our lives.*
2. *Pray with him. By praying with him, you could accomplish a few things here: his respect, his apology, and his accountability.*
3. *Help him clean up (to the best of your ability). This would be a living example of what Jesus did in washing his disciples' filthy feet (see John 13).*
4. *Try to get help for him. Your roommate may be engaged in underage drinking, which is illegal. Have the courage to stand up for what is right, while at the same time being a real friend to him.*
5. *Get out of the situation (if this problem is not resolved). It may be for the night, or for the week, or for good. Frequent drunkenness invites a host of other problems.*

Romans 12 is a good chapter on living a holy life in practical ways. As you read a section of this chapter today, may the Lord help you in dealing with all of your relationships... including your roommate!

↑ CHECK OUT ROMANS 12:9-21.

# CREATION VS. EVOLUTION (WWYD)

FOR HIS INVISIBLE ATTRIBUTES, NAMELY, HIS ETERNAL POWER AND DIVINE NATURE, HAVE BEEN CLEARLY PERCEIVED, EVER SINCE THE CREATION OF THE WORLD, IN THE THINGS THAT HAVE BEEN MADE. SO THEY ARE WITHOUT EXCUSE. (ROMANS 1:20)

*A few weeks into your first semester, a girl in your dorm comes over to your room and asks questions about the validity of the Bible. She just started reading Genesis, and she wonders why people would believe the creation account. She grew up learning facts about evolution, but she's also not convinced that evolution is 100% correct. What will you do?*

Don't be afraid of situations like this! As God leads you, there are a number of things you can share with her. If you become engaged in a "creation vs. evolution" debate, you can trust that the Bible has all the answers you need.

As Christians, we believe in creation because we believe that the Bible is God's truth to mankind. Since God spoke to us, everything He says must be true. Based upon this, we believe that mankind has no excuse to dismiss God's role as Creator of this universe (see Romans 1:20).

God is our Creator. Anyone who says otherwise is choosing to ignore what should be perfectly clear to him or her. We are without excuse!

Evolution is still a very popular, widespread theory. But let's think about this: do we choose to believe the Living God, or do we believe those who are under the curse of sin and death?

We cannot deny it – there is a Creator, and He is Lord of all. But we do not need to stop at that truth. Tell this young lady about what God did for you – He sent His Son to save us. Evolution will not offer that hope!

↑ CHECK OUT ROMANS 1:16-23.

# TWO WRONGS DO NOT MAKE A RIGHT! (WWYD)

GO TO THE ANT, O SLUGGARD; CONSIDER HER WAYS, AND BE WISE. WITHOUT HAVING ANY CHIEF, OFFICER, OR RULER, SHE PREPARES HER BREAD IN SUMMER AND GATHERS HER FOOD IN HARVEST. (PROVERBS 6:6-8)

*It's almost midnight. Your 10-page paper is due tomorrow, and you have just finished the first paragraph. Your roommate had the class last semester; in fact, he still has his paper saved on his laptop! You don't know how you will get this assignment finished on time, and it counts as a full quarter of your class grade. What will you do?*

It's easy to say that we would not cheat... but what if this is a matter of passing your class? What if your roommate would never find out that you downloaded his work off of his computer? What if you had a teacher who could care less about plagiarism? What if this was the only time you've ever cheated... just this once?

Ah, how we love to procrastinate! However, procrastination is just a form of laziness, and it leads to all kinds of compromise. I strongly urge you to be diligent; do not be in the habit of putting things off. Proverbs 6 addresses this issue by considering the ant. When is the last time you laid down in the grass and watched these critters? They are efficient!

If you do find yourself in the situation above, you will need to do your best to finish what you can and turn in the work that was completed. Or perhaps you would be allowed to turn it in later with a penalty to your grade. Either way, you need to flee from cheating. Allow yourself to grow from your failure. Trust that God blesses obedience.

Dishonesty is not an option for Christians! May the Lord help us to learn from our poor choices... and let's remember the ant.

🡅 CONSIDER THE SLUGGARD (PROCRASTINATOR) IN PROVERBS 26:12-16.

# MY PARENTS ARE GETTING DIVORCED: NOW WHAT? (WWYD)

BE STRONG AND COURAGEOUS. DO NOT FEAR OR BE IN DREAD OF THEM, FOR IT IS THE LORD YOUR GOD WHO GOES WITH YOU. HE WILL NOT LEAVE YOU OR FORSAKE YOU. (DEUTERONOMY 31:6)

*Halfway through your college education, you find out that your parents are going to get a divorce. They both want you to finish your education, but you know that you could help your mom if you came back home. What will you do?*

In our nation, the divorce rate is high. Perhaps your parents are divorced. If this is the case, God knows what you are going through, even if your parents' decisions put you in a hard place. Believe me, the Lord sees your hurt and your grief!

1. ***IF GOD LEADS YOU TO CONTINUE ON AT COLLEGE, you now carry the burden of school work, while trying to reconcile the many questions you have about your life ahead. However, getting a good education can help place you in a better position. One day, we all watch the tables turn as we see our aging parents become the needy ones. Who knows? God may use your education to help support them in their greatest time of need.***
2. ***IF GOD LEADS YOU TO GO BACK HOME, you will feel the frustration and disappointment of setting aside your future plans due to your parents' failures. But please know this: people are always more important than things, even when the "thing" is a life-long dream. Your sacrifice will not go unnoticed by the One who sees everything.***

In Ephesians 6:2-3, we are reminded to "honor our father and mother". In 1 Timothy 5:4, we are told that children are to care for their "widowed mother". May the Lord give you wisdom, no matter what happens in your college career. By His grace, you'll do what is right!

↑ ESTHER WAS FORCED TO LIVE HER LIFE DIFFERENTLY THAN SHE COULD HAVE EVER IMAGINED... BUT GOD BLESSED HER! READ ESTHER 8.

# MY JOB AND COMPROMISE (WWYD)

BUT TAKE CARE THAT THIS RIGHT OF YOURS DOES NOT SOMEHOW BECOME A STUMBLING BLOCK TO THE WEAK. (1 CORINTHIANS 8:9)

*You start college with most of your school bill covered, but you know that you really need a job if you are going to attend in the future. You are aware of one job opening; it's a convenience store, only a ½ mile walk from your dorm. They are willing to give you good evening hours, but part of the job is selling alcohol and tobacco products. What will you do?*

Hmmmm... what to do? Many of you will face a dilemma of choosing work with people or products that are less than desirable. I faced a very similar situation myself many years ago. It was not an easy choice.

These are difficult decisions to make! It may be easy to condemn the person that decides to take a job like this, but it is also foolish to turn down a job and rack up a heavy student debt.

The Corinthians needed to deal with a related issue. For them, the question was this: "Should we eat meat offered to idols?" On one hand, the apostle Paul makes it clear that idols are worthless, inanimate objects. Eating the meat would not hurt a believer. But on the other hand, watching believers eat this meat could be a real stumbling block for those who struggle with idol worship. It's kind of like smoking cigarettes around a person trying to kick the habit.

If you take the job, would it become a stumbling block for others? If you don't know, then ask God to show you the answer. Loving others before yourself is an act of obedience - an act that He will bless, and an act that will keep you from possible compromise.

🡅 CHECK OUT THE SITUATION IN CORINTH: READ 1 CORINTHIANS 8:1-13.

# O BE CAREFUL LITTLE EYES WHAT YOU SEE (WWYD)

I HAVE MADE A COVENANT WITH MY EYES; HOW THEN COULD I GAZE AT A VIRGIN?... DOES NOT HE SEE MY WAYS AND NUMBER ALL MY STEPS? (JOB 31:1,4)

*During a Christmas party, you are invited over to watch a movie that you know has pornography. Your parents would not approve... but now that you are on your own, you don't need your parents' permission anymore (right?). What will you do?*

Teens, many graduate from high school and make a real mess of their lives. Wise adults seek to paint an accurate picture of what your life can be like in the future, being mindful to warn you about the dangers of living in sin... however, God also gave us the ability to make choices. And when graduates choose the wrong path, it is often due to a freedom they feel when being away from under their parents' direct authority ("Mom and Dad aren't here... I'm free!").

If you embrace pornography as an adult, it will destroy your life. The effects linked to this widespread evil reach much farther than we could ever imagine. Don't be fooled – both guys and girls are falling for porn's false promises of happiness and pleasure. The godly Job knew how to handle his eyes; he chose not to "gaze at a virgin".

If you find yourself in the situation above, please heed this advice: *don't watch the movie*! Not simply because of what your parents might think, but because God the Father really knows what is best for you!

Perhaps you'll keep in mind that sweet little Sunday School song many of us learned long ago? "O be careful little eyes what you see, O be careful little eyes what you see, For the Father up above is looking down in love, O be careful little eyes what you see!"

↑ JOB TALKS MORE ABOUT HIS WALK OF PURITY IN JOB 31:1-12.

## SHOULD I DATE AN UNBELIEVER? (WWYD)

DO NOT BE UNEQUALLY YOKED WITH UNBELIEVERS. FOR WHAT PARTNERSHIP HAS RIGHTEOUSNESS WITH LAWLESSNESS? AND WHAT FELLOWSHIP HAS LIGHT WITH DARKNESS? (2 CORINTHIANS 6:14)

*Your senior year of college has finally arrived! But you are still not dating anyone. Most of the Christians you know are poor in character; they are not the kind of person you would like to date. However, there is one guy who really likes you, though he is an unbeliever. Last week, he called you and asked you out to dinner. You know his intentions... he has a long-term relationship in mind. What will you do?*

As we consider this scenario, I am reminded of a girl that attended my youth group many years ago. She decided to date a boy, and she ended up getting pregnant. I am quite certain that she never meant to even have sex with him, but she really wanted a boyfriend, and she made many compromises to keep him. How sad this is... but how common!

2 Corinthians 6:14 gives clarity to the type of person we should date. "Do not be unequally yoked with unbelievers" includes dating relationships! As someone who has been married for over 20 years, I can tell you that marriage is both wonderful and challenging. Would our marriage be thriving today if one of us was an unbeliever? Not in the way that God intends a marriage to thrive.

Many so-called "harmless" dating relationships end up as unhappy marriages. Why? One person is alive in Christ; the other is dead in their sin. I know that sounds harsh, but it is the truth, and this truth is meant to keep you free from a life of regret.

Should you date him? No. Be "yoked together" with other Christians!

↑ CHECK OUT 2 CORINTHIANS 6:15-7:1.

## DRUGS FOR A SHORT TIME? (WWYD)

YOU SHALL HAVE NO OTHER GODS BEFORE ME. (EXODUS 20:3)

*Your friend is doing really well in his college classes. However, he is taking a drug that is helping him to stay awake at night. He knows this is not good for his body, but he knows that he can graduate ahead of time if he can keep up the hectic pace. You are afraid for him. What will you do?*

Oh, how easy it is to make compromises for "the greater good". People do it all the time. Let me encourage you to believe something: if you compromise, it is not "the greater good"!

Here's the problem: We easily convince ourselves that God will bless *our* plans. Along with that belief, many of us live by the creed, "The end justifies the means." When we live like this, we view God as a personal "god"; He is simply a heavenly aid that will help me accomplish my dreams. If our plans control us to the point that we would allow drugs to come into our body (which is the very dwelling place of the Holy Spirit), then our plans have become an idol, and a new god has taken a hold of us.

Shortly after the children of Israel left Egypt, the Lord gave them the 10 Commandments. The first one is listed above. We know that there were plenty of false gods in Egypt and the surrounding nations. Do we grasp that the same is true today? Are we above worshipping gods of our own making?

Teens, we cannot put aside what is right for the sake of our own plans! May God give you grace as you communicate this truth to your friend.

↑ WHAT ARE THE 10 COMMANDMENTS? FIND THEM IN EXODUS 20:1-17.

# DO I HAVE TO STUDY? (WWYD)

FOR TO EVERYONE WHO HAS WILL MORE BE GIVEN, AND HE WILL HAVE AN ABUNDANCE. BUT FROM THE ONE WHO HAS NOT, EVEN WHAT HE HAS WILL BE TAKEN AWAY. (MATTHEW 25:29)

*Your college is only an hour away from home. During the first few weeks of your freshman year, you had no problem with coming home to relax. Now, as finals loom, you have three projects due. You are struggling to get passing grades in two classes. You know that most of your friends will be getting together for a party this Saturday night. If you go, you will sacrifice several hours of study time. What will you do?*

As we think about this scenario, we need to recognize that we are dealing with a choice. Parties are fun, but if you attend the party and fail a class, it is your fault... there's no way around it! The choice is yours: will you go and have a great time (short-term happiness), or will you work hard to pass your classes (long-term fulfillment)?

Teens, I know you deal with similar pressures now, but once you are in college, the stakes only get higher.

I believe you know what to do! However, let's consider a parable. In Matthew 25:14-30, Jesus speaks of three servants. Two obeyed the master, one did not. Two made a choice that benefited them for the long-term, one did what he wanted to do for his own purpose (the master called him a "wicked and slothful servant"). Jesus' conclusion on the matter? The rich will become richer, and the poor, poorer.

What will you do? Will you skip short-term happiness for long-term gain? If so, then keep on studying!

🡅 READ MATTHEW 25:14-30.

## GIVING THANKS (WWYD)

REJOICE ALWAYS, PRAY WITHOUT CEASING, GIVE THANKS IN ALL CIRCUMSTANCES; FOR THIS IS THE WILL OF GOD IN CHRIST JESUS FOR YOU. (1 THESSALONIANS 5:16-18)

*Someone comes over to you in a restaurant, right after seeing you giving thanks for your meal. They want to know why the act of prayer is important to you. What will you do?*

What a simple yet powerful way to show others that you are a Christian! I remember when I started to pray before eating lunch in high school. At first, I was afraid of what others would think. But one day, there came a point when God took that fear away, and it gradually became a lifelong habit. And today, our family occasionally receives nice comments when they see us publicly bow our heads and give thanks for our food.

What caused me to start giving thanks for my food in school? I spotted another girl doing it. I didn't know her; in fact, I can't recall even speaking to her, but I could tell that she was a Christian. And I figured that if she could do it, I could do it, too! One day, when both of us are in heaven, I will thank her for the example she gave me.

Praying for your meal at a restaurant is both proper and testimonial! It is a great opportunity to be a part of "Evangelism 101". It is also a great way of combining those three short commands found in 1 Thessalonians 5, so that you can accomplish "the will of God in Christ Jesus for you."

May you have the courage to give thanks, no matter where you are.

↑ CHECK OUT 1 TIMOTHY 4:1-8.

# MY FRIEND IS PREGNANT (WWYD)

BROTHERS, IF ANYONE IS CAUGHT IN ANY TRANSGRESSION, YOU WHO ARE SPIRITUAL SHOULD RESTORE HIM IN A SPIRIT OF GENTLENESS. KEEP WATCH ON YOURSELF, LEST YOU TOO BE TEMPTED. BEAR ONE ANOTHER'S BURDENS, AND SO FULFILL THE LAW OF CHRIST. (GALATIANS 6:1-2)

*You discover that your friend is pregnant. What will you do?*

I remember it clearly. I was talking to my youth pastor after a church service one day, when my good friend came up behind me. She told me through tears that our mutual friend "Tina" was pregnant. I was shocked. This was the first time I came face-to-face with teen pregnancy. Honestly, I wasn't sure what to think of it all. Thankfully, God is gracious and teaches us how to love one another, even in the hardest of situations. This friend would definitely need all the love she could get in the days to come!

Let me share some advice on how to handle teen pregnancies:

***1. Show love for the mother and the baby.*** *She is probably scared (all expectant mothers are afraid, to some degree!). Express love by asking how she is doing; pray for her; and offer her your help.*

***2. Don't condemn her or her boyfriend.*** *The act that brought about the pregnancy was wrong, but God offers forgiveness! If she gives you an open door to share your view on teen pregnancy, be kind and truthful in your response... but make sure you communicate her value as a mother.*

***3. Seek to connect her with responsible adults.*** *She will need to take this journey with someone who has been there and will love her enough to walk with her in the days ahead.*

Remember, we all need grace! Give abundant grace to your friend.

↑ CONSIDER GALATIANS 6:1-10.

## YOU HYPOCRITE! (WWYD)

*If we say we have no sin, we deceive ourselves, and the truth is not in us...*
*If we say we have not sinned, we make him a liar, and his word is not in us.*
(1 John 1:8, 10)

*Circumstances in life have left your new Christian friend doubting that Jesus is really all that he said he is. On top of that, he thinks that most people who attend church are hypocrites and that real Christians would not struggle with sin. He cannot see the power of God in their lives, as it is not clearly evident to him. What will you do?*

I have been called many names in my life (perhaps you have, too!). However, the one I really hate is "hypocrite". In fact, this word bothers me more than any cursing directed at me. When someone swears at you, it hurts... but swear words themselves carry no value. "Hypocrite" suggests that your character is unworthy. Ouch!

Sadly, there are plenty of hypocrites out there, and too many of them attend churches across our land. If a hypocrite is a person who says one thing and lives another, how can we help our friend understand that Jesus is truly the One who changes lives? This is a tough one, but help him consider this fact: we all struggle with sin. A Christian cannot be a person who claims that he or she does not sin (see the verses above).

By acknowledging your own struggle in the flesh, your friend can see your humility. Remind him that a believer in Christ may not be perfect in his actions, but he is forgiven at the cross. This puts the focus on what Jesus did for us. Also, do not ignore the matter at hand – your friend lovingly needs to know that God sees everything. If another believer is acting like a hypocrite, then he or she must answer to the Lord one day. Indeed, we are all responsible for our behavior.

↑ CHECK OUT 1 JOHN 1:5-2:6!

# I'LL SKIP CHURCH FOR A WHILE (WWYD)

AND LET US CONSIDER HOW TO STIR UP ONE ANOTHER TO LOVE AND GOOD WORKS, NOT NEGLECTING TO MEET TOGETHER, AS IS THE HABIT OF SOME, BUT ENCOURAGING ONE ANOTHER, AND ALL THE MORE AS YOU SEE THE DAY DRAWING NEAR. (HEBREWS 10:24-25)

*You moved to a town where the closest thriving church is 45 minutes away. There is another church in your town, but it does not teach the Bible. What will you do?*

Maybe the easy way out would be to just stay home. God would understand, right? You could use the money spent on fuel for other things, like groceries, driving to work, and visits to your parents. Besides, there are other resources you can use to learn more about God (like watching church on TV, reading the Bible at home, listening to podcasts, etc.).

Not long ago, I had a conversation with a friend on the topic of church attendance. She expressed faith in God's blessing upon her through her daily interactions with Christians, accompanied by her devotions and prayer. In her thinking, church was optional.

Is her approach a workable substitute? In a word, "NO!" Why? Staying at home is not God's plan for His people, who make up the church.

Despite all of our shortcomings and inadequacies, God loves it when His children come together. He designed us to be united with one another. Truly, it is impossible for me to become like Jesus if I am trying to do it all on my own. I need a church family. We are nothing less than the body of Christ (read 1 Corinthians 12 to understand this more).

Make the drive. Watch God work. He will bless your obedient heart.

↑ CHECK OUT PHILIPPIANS 1:1-11... VERSES FOR THE CHURCH BODY.

# WHAT COULD POSSIBLY GO WRONG? (WWYD)

WINE IS A MOCKER, STRONG DRINK A BRAWLER, AND WHOEVER IS LED ASTRAY BY IT IS NOT WISE." (PROVERBS 20:1)

*You are two weeks into your first year of college. You get invited to your first party! Your new friend knows that you do not drink, but he wants you to come anyway, even though there will be drinking at the party. He is only one of two friends that you have made so far at school, and they both are going. What will you do?*

If you do go to college, the odds that you will be invited to a drinking party are very high. Most college parties are not known for social drinking, either... getting drunk is often the goal, which can easily lead to other bad decisions that will hurt people.

Being wise and being drunk do not go hand-in-hand, do they? Only a fool rejoices in the drunken moments of his life.

What can you avoid by *not* going to the party? 1. Engaging in underage drinking (which, by the way, is still illegal!). 2. Being in the wrong place at the wrong time and facing arrest. 3. Unwanted pictures of you on social media for all to see. 4. Being viewed as a hypocrite if you are a Christian. 5. Dealing with drugs and/or sexual temptations (also prevalent at many drinking parties). 6. The possibility of being removed from your school. 7. Being involved in a DUI-related car accident. 8. Great disappointment from those who truly love you.

For what it's worth to you, I have abstained from drinking alcohol. Does that make me a better than the next person? No, not at all. Have I regretted not having a beer? Also no, not at all! I have spared myself much pain that comes from being led astray by alcohol.

🡅 CHECK OUT THE WISDOM FOUND IN PROVERBS 23:29-35!

## SPEAK UP! (WWYD)

FOR I AM NOT ASHAMED OF THE GOSPEL, FOR IT IS THE POWER OF GOD FOR SALVATION TO EVERYONE WHO BELIEVES, TO THE JEW FIRST AND ALSO TO THE GREEK. (ROMANS 1:16)

*You are a year removed from high school, and you run into someone you graduated with – a person you did not know well, but shared a few classes together. You catch up, and then she asks what made you so different than many of the other kids in your class. You are a Christian; you know this former classmate is probably not. What will you do?*

Early on in high school, I did not witness as well as I should have. I regret this as an adult today.

Two memories of my failure to witness come to mind. The first is when I wore a Christian t-shirt that promoted a missionary organization. I got asked about the shirt. The girl wondered what the initials of the organization meant. I told her I did not know (which was a lie, and it made me look stupid!). The second memory is on a trip to a choral tryout. One of the boys asked me about the most important thing in my life. I don't remember my answer, but I know that it had nothing to do with Christ. Man, I felt so guilty about that one for many days...

Why was it so hard for me to witness? Because I desperately wanted to be accepted. And in the process, self became more important than God. By his grace, I eventually learned to put Him first, and because of this, I was sharing my faith more and more by the time I hit my senior year. I am thankful I finally learned how to witness.

Teens, speak up! Don't wait until later - people need the Lord *now*. Do not be ashamed of the gospel – it is God's salvation power!

🠉 READ 2 TIMOTHY 2:1-13 TODAY.

## TITHES AND OFFERINGS? (WWYD)

BRING THE FULL TITHE INTO THE STOREHOUSE, THAT THERE MAY BE FOOD IN MY HOUSE. AND THEREBY PUT ME TO THE TEST, SAYS THE LORD OF HOSTS, IF I WILL NOT OPEN THE WINDOWS OF HEAVEN FOR YOU AND POUR DOWN FOR YOU A BLESSING UNTIL THERE IS NO MORE NEED. (MALACHI 3:10)

*You finally have your own apartment! But now you carry the burden of paying for rent, utility bills, some college debt, a car loan, groceries and gas... and feeding your pet hamster! You got paid yesterday, and as you look at your bills, you realize that paying the electric on time means no money to put in the offering plate at church. What will you do?*

"Adulting" can be daunting, to say the least! And when it comes to our finances, if the Lord is not first in our lives, then the giving of a tithe (defined as God's commanded 10%) and an offering (anything above and beyond the tithe) is set aside for our own gain.

Yet check out Malachi 3:10. This verse is in response to the fact that Israel robbed God of tithes and offerings (the previous verses in the chapter tell us how it happened). In spite of their sin, God invites them to obey Him, and by doing so, to watch a blessing pour down. When we take Him at His word, we find that we cannot out-give God!

So yes, you have to pay your bills... but you also need to give to the Lord. It is an act of faith. Both can be done! Take a hard look at your finances. For the sake of the tithe and offering, what can you live without? Be creative! Don't leave yourself without money because of foolish spending. In the situation mentioned above, you may need to humble yourself and ask for help in paying your electric. That's ok! Do the right thing, no matter what. And always remember that God loves a cheerful giver (2 Corinthians 9:7).

↑ CONSIDER MALACHI 3:6-12!

## MARRIAGE – UNDENIABLY GOOD (WWYD)

HE WHO FINDS A WIFE FINDS A GOOD THING AND OBTAINS FAVOR FROM THE LORD. (PROVERBS 18:22)

*You sit down for a study hall at school, and one of your friends asks you to give your opinion about marriage. You know this is a divisive issue, and many around the table have a worldly view. Personally, you know that marriage is from the Lord, but you don't think your classmates will respect your position. What will you do?*

God knows what is best for His creation, and the marriage relationship is the greatest one offered to mankind. Remember, marriage is the original relationship that existed from the beginning! However, as in any good relationship, commitment is involved. And oh, how we often despise the sacrifice that comes with commitment in our culture today.

Look above at the verse. Guys, understand that wives are good! Also, know that God's favor is offered. These are specific benefits from the Lord Himself, promised to a husband. Does this change your thoughts about commitment and marriage, fellas?

The marriage I have with my wife (Lisa) has been full of joys and sorrows. She has taught me so much about myself. There are times when we think so much alike, and then there are times when I have no idea what is going on! God made her in such a way that I would learn *how to be complete* by being united to this lady. There is *no way* another person could do this for me. Just as Adam needed Eve, Mike needs Lisa.

This is the truth, and it is undeniably good!

↑ JESUS TALKED ABOUT MARRIAGE BY TAKING HIS LISTENERS BACK TO THE BEGINNING. READ WHAT HE SAYS IN MARK 10:1-12.

# THANK YOU, UNCLE

For "everyone who calls on the name of the Lord will be saved." (Romans 10:13)

The story of my salvation is the best story of my life. My uncle David was an integral part of it.

I was saved in 1985. Who knows how many times he had shared the gospel in his life before that year. I'm sure it was plenty. He knew that there were many kids that needed to hear it in our week of Vacation Bible School. So he shared the greatest of news with our class - Jesus had come to save us from our sin. And me, being that well-behaved church kid that I was, looked around and thought to myself, "Boy, am I glad that all these other kids are here to listen to this!" (not very humble, huh?!!). Yet, at some point in his time with us, I was struck by the realization that I had never *personally* done what the gospel demanded of me. I had never asked God to forgive me of my sin and receive me as His own. By the grace of God, I went home that very night, knelt on our couch, and repented before the Lord.

At the time I wrote this devotion, David died just a few days earlier. He was loved by many as a man of compassionate and wisdom. He had a strong influence in my life as a family member and church leader, but most of all, he was the one who had a hand in leading me to the Lord. In his final days, he longed for home – which is heaven, for all who do believe in Jesus. David is now there, and he is one of many that I look forward to seeing again.

Everyone who calls upon the name of the Lord will be saved! I am thankful for the uncle who caused me to see this truth.

↑ "EVERYONE WHO CALLS UPON THE NAME OF THE LORD SHALL BE SAVED." PROPHESIED IN JOEL 2:28-32; RECOGNIZED IN ACTS 2:17-21!

## KEEP IT TOGETHER, MAN!

A fool gives full vent to his spirit, but a wise man quietly holds it back. (Proverbs 29:11)

A man of wrath stirs up strife, and one given to anger causes much transgression. (Proverbs 29:22)

There was a time I was reading through the book of Proverbs when I was in my 20's. For whatever reason, I was in a spiritual rut. As I began to read chapter 29, I was not expecting much (I say this to my shame). However, when I got to verse 11 and 22, I was properly slapped in the face. I took my red pen out and underlined these verses, hoping that I would remember my need to overcome anger in my life.

In my immaturity, I would like to believe that venting my anger is the way to go. Somehow, unchecked anger fools us into thinking that I will forever feel better, and those around me will never dare cross me again. That's simply not true! Losing self-control has never worked out for my best. The result has always been regret, time and again.

Self-control requires faith. It means that I cannot take matters into my own hands. Instead, I need to trust the One who will always do what is right. Faith in the goodness of God calls me to take one for the team. If you like baseball, you probably know that getting hit by a pitch is an awful thing, but getting on base helps lead to a score, and scoring leads to victories. Charging the mound usually means an ejection. How does that ever help the team?

Keep it together, man! I say this to the both of us. Unchecked anger has hurt many people in my life, often the ones I love the most. The better alternative is to pray and ask the God of peace to give you the control you need. You will then discover the joy of being wise.

🡅 BE BLESSED BY THE WISDOM FOUND IN PROVERBS 29 TODAY.

# MY WAGES ARE JUST NOT ENOUGH!

NOW TO THE ONE WHO WORKS, HIS WAGES ARE NOT COUNTED AS A GIFT BUT AS HIS DUE. AND TO THE ONE WHO DOES NOT WORK BUT BELIEVES IN HIM WHO JUSTIFIES THE UNGODLY, HIS FAITH IS COUNTED AS RIGHTEOUSNESS, JUST AS DAVID ALSO SPEAKS OF THE BLESSING OF THE ONE TO WHOM GOD COUNTS RIGHTEOUSNESS APART FROM WORKS: "BLESSED ARE THOSE WHOSE LAWLESS DEEDS ARE FORGIVEN, AND WHOSE SINS ARE COVERED; BLESSED IS THE MAN AGAINST WHOM THE LORD WILL NOT COUNT HIS SIN." (ROMANS 4:4-8)

As a youth pastor, I have watched many teens go through the process of getting a job! It's not easy, is it? Just the other day, I heard a former teen proclaim, "I do not like 'adulting' very much!" Yeah, there are days I'm not fond of it either, and I've been adulting for a while now!

You get a job, and you get a (meager) paycheck. Whether it is McDonalds or Dunkin Donuts or someplace else, they are obligated to pay you for your services. When you get your check, your boss does not say, "Here's a present for you!" No, you earned that money! And since you need more money because the check is never for $1,000,000, you go back and work another week.

When it comes to the matter of righteousness, work is not an acceptable form of wages paid to God. In fact, work *cannot* work. Instead, it is the man who offers his faith that is given credit for salvation. Have you chosen works, or have you chosen faith?

Paul makes reference to our need for God's gift in one of the most well-known verses in the Bible: Romans 6:23. Simply put, "WAGES = DEATH" and "GIFT = SALVATION".

Teens, there is just no way that we can pay off the sin debt that is owed. Receive Christ as Savior – he is the necessary payment!

🡅 PLEASE READ ROMANS 4:1-8 TODAY.

## EXPECTING GOD TO ANSWER

At Caesarea there was a man named Cornelius, a centurion of what was known as the Italian Cohort, a devout man who feared God with all his household, gave alms generously to the people, and prayed continually to God. (Acts 10:1-2)

Learning to pray continually is a life-long process! Sometimes, the Bible deals with the amount of prayer (Cornelius lived the instruction to "pray without ceasing", found in 1 Thessalonians 5:17). Sometimes, it deals with the content of prayer (as in the Lord's Prayer, found in the books of Matthew and Luke). But today, let's look at how the Bible deals with our expectancy in prayer.

God answers the prayers of a faithful Christian. Acts 10 captures an incredible moment of early church history by relating the story of Cornelius. He was a Gentile (another name for a person who is not a Jew). Being a Gentile is no big deal, right? Well, on this day, it was a big deal, as Peter would learn something firsthand – a Gentile could be saved in exactly the same way as a Jew. When Peter met up with Cornelius and his family, he shared the gospel, and lives were changed. Indeed, God's good news was for all of mankind – the nation of Israel made way for the age of the church – and there would no longer be a distinction between Jew and Gentile (see Colossians 3:11).

I have no idea what Cornelius prayed in his days before Peter arrived, but God is faithful to answer the one who is faithful to Him.

I'd like to challenge us today to expect God to move in our behalf. May we not be surprised when He answers our prayers! We may not know the outcome of our prayers; however, there will always be an answer. The Bible teaches us that God is moved by the hearts of the faithful.

According to His Word, may we wait in expectation!

READ ABOUT CORNELIUS IN ACTS 10.

## UNDESIRED TEARS

HE WILL SWALLOW UP DEATH FOREVER; AND THE LORD GOD WILL WIPE AWAY TEARS FROM ALL FACES, AND THE REPROACH OF HIS PEOPLE HE WILL TAKE AWAY FROM ALL THE EARTH, FOR THE LORD HAS SPOKEN. (ISAIAH 25:8)

How wonderful to know that God will wipe away my tears! This truth is mentioned more than once as a promise to us. My pain, my suffering, and everything else that is wrapped up in those tears... gently brushed away by the hand of the One who created me!

But would there be other reasons for tears in the presence of God? Let's carefully think about the following situations. What about the believer who spent his whole life chasing the American dream, ending up with a pile of cash, only to leave it behind on this earth? How about the Christian who broke his promise to his wife and ran off with another woman? Or the saved woman who decided that church wasn't really worth her effort? Or the young believer who spent hours entertaining himself, leaving his Bible on a bookshelf, not knowing that he would only live to be 30? Or the old saint who never forgave her friend for hurting her, carrying her bitterness to a bitter end?

The second we die, *everything will be crystal clear*. Heed these sobering words of Paul: "Now if anyone builds on the foundation with gold, silver, precious stones, wood, hay, straw - each one's work will become manifest, for the Day will disclose it, because it will be revealed by fire, and the fire will test what sort of work each one has done. If the work that anyone has built on the foundation survives, he will receive a reward. If anyone's work is burned up, he will suffer loss, though he himself will be saved, but only as through fire" (1 Corinthians 3:12-15).

May we be faithful! May we only shed tears of joy, not tears of regret.

🡅 CAREFULLY READ 1 CORINTHIANS 3 TODAY.

# WHEN FEAR IS A GOOD THING

THE GREAT DAY OF THE LORD IS NEAR, NEAR AND HASTENING FAST; THE SOUND OF THE DAY OF THE LORD IS BITTER; THE MIGHTY MAN CRIES ALOUD THERE. (ZEPHANIAH 1:14)

Have you ever been in the position when you have to make a decision, yet you will lose, no matter what you decide? That's not a fun position! Many Christians feel like they will lose if they choose to talk about topics that may stir up controversy. So we avoid certain subjects, such as God's wrath and judgment. By doing so, we ignore a large part of the Bible.

What do you think? Is biblical ignorance ever a good thing?

Zephaniah spoke about "the great day of the LORD." I'm sure it was not easy for him to write about this subject. Yet he did, even though fear was an overriding theme in his prophetic message. By proclaiming this coming day, Zephaniah included trials and tribulation which had to come. How would you feel if God told you to speak about this subject, knowing the listeners would be angry at you? I would be scared!

Yet fear, when driven by love and grace, is a good thing. God does call us to warn others about the disastrous consequences of sin, even when it seems like it's the hardest thing we can do. He does not desire anyone to die outside of Christ, nor does he find pleasure in bringing wrath upon the wicked. When people fear the wrath that must come, this fear can be used to rescue them from destruction and death.

Teens, remember what Proverbs 1:7 tells us: "The fear of the LORD is the beginning of knowledge; fools despise wisdom and instruction."

↑ LEARN ABOUT THE GREAT DAY OF THE LORD IN ZEPHANIAH 1:14 – 2:3!

# MY PARENTS AREN'T CHRISTIANS

NOW THE LORD SAID TO ABRAM, "GO FROM YOUR COUNTRY AND YOUR KINDRED AND YOUR FATHER'S HOUSE TO THE LAND THAT I WILL SHOW YOU." (GENESIS 12:1)

It can be very difficult as a Christian when your parents are not Christians themselves! It is especially hard for believers in nations that persecute Christians. In these cultures, having your parents against you may mean losing your home and your job. You may be tortured or killed. Thankfully, we are not dealing with that kind of persecution in America (yet), but for those who are suffering, it is painful to know that the ones who gave them birth do not share in their faith.

Abram (later named Abraham) was called to begin a brand new life. He would leave everything behind, which included most of his family. Haran had been their city, but God called them to go to the land of His future people (Israel). Abram obeyed, and God made him "The Father of Many Nations".

Teens, remember that Abram was a human, like us! It must have been hard for him to leave his relatives behind. He was a good man, and I imagine he loved his family back in Haran. Who knows what they understood of Abram's departure to the land of Canaan? However, his obedience would be his greatest testimony and legacy to those he loved. He did what he was called to do, and he trusted God to accomplish His will when he left his relatives behind.

If your parents aren't Christians, the greatest thing you can do for them is to pray for them, and to live in obedience to the Heavenly Father. Your obedience may lead to peace, but it may also lead to division. Regardless, we do know that our Heavenly Father will never forsake us!

READ MATTHEW 10:32-39. MAY GOD HELP US IN LIVING FOR HIM, NO MATTER WHAT HAPPENS TO OUR PARENTS.

## AM I WORTH IMITATING?

Be imitators of me, as I am of Christ. (1 Corinthians 11:1)

A following. Secretly, many of us desire it. How many "likes" on your social media account(s) does it take to make you feel validated? Whether you know it or not, you are asking for a following. How influential are you at school, at home, or at your church? That is another way to be followed. How popular are you in your sport, band, or club? Again, a certain kind of following.

In my weaker moments in life, I have enjoyed the concept of a following. As a pastor, I know that I have the ability and position to be influential. When things have gone well for me, I have been praised for it. But if I don't defer all praise and glory to God, I have a problem. It's like I'm allowing people to believe they should be like me, so they should not be afraid to be one of "my followers!" That is silliness, and that is sin. In biblical accounts, things never went well for those who did not give all the glory to God.

The Apostle Paul was a follower of Christ. He encouraged the Corinthians to "be imitators of me" (1 Corinthians 11:1). However, he was following the example of Christ. And notice that he was not interested in calling Christians to be his disciples. As great as Paul was, he just wanted to be a worthy example, not gather millions of fans.

I don't need followers. I am so prone to sin. I cannot carry the weight of everyone's adoration. It's too much for me to handle. I don't deserve it, anyway. But I know who does... and that's Jesus Christ. He called to many a sinner, "Follow me!"

I "like" the reality of being his follower!

↑ CHECK OUT 1 CORINTHIANS 10:23-11:1.

## THE PROCESS AND THE RESULT

AND THE WORD BECAME FLESH AND DWELT AMONG US, AND WE HAVE SEEN HIS GLORY, GLORY AS OF THE ONLY SON FROM THE FATHER, FULL OF GRACE AND TRUTH. (JOHN 1:14)

Several years ago, I was playing with my daughter Lydia. At the time, she was just learning how to play catch. My goal was for her to see the ball coming, get comfortable using her hands, and enjoy the accomplishment of "the catch." For her first time playing, she did just fine! But I think I learned more from her than she from me on that day. Whenever she would drop the ball, she just laughed. I thought she would get upset and not want to play, but instead, she thought it was fun! It got me thinking about what our play time meant to her. I was interested in the end result, but she was loving the process. The beauty of the process eludes me far too often, as I work hard to "get 'er done" as quickly and efficiently as possible.

Out of necessity, both processes and results go hand-in-hand. So do grace and truth. One cannot do without the other, and Jesus was full ("complete") in both. His truth is completed with grace, and his grace is completed with truth. In Jesus, the two have become one.

I sense in my life that my desire for results focuses heavily upon truth without grace. Grace is often lacking because it involves a process. However, when I do appreciate the process, I remember that my own life is also a process, and that God is working His grace in me. The truth of the result (glorification) rests on the grace of the process (sanctification).

"O God, cause this man to be patient as you work Your will in my life!"

🡅 WE SEE GRACE AND TRUTH AT WORK IN JESUS IN LUKE 5:17-26.

# PAIN, FORGIVENESS, AND FREEDOM

AND PETER REMEMBERED THE SAYING OF JESUS, "BEFORE THE ROOSTER CROWS, YOU WILL DENY ME THREE TIMES." AND HE WENT OUT AND WEPT BITTERLY. (MATTHEW 26:75)

Some time ago, I spoke with my friend. His life has been a series of extreme highs and lows. The journey is wearing him down. He is getting tired, and he has admitted that he wants his life to be over. He is tired of struggling with sin. When we spoke, I knew that I did not have all the magic words to make his pain go away. I did share some thoughts with him, but I understood that my commitment to prayer would be my greatest act of love for him. I encouraged him not to give up the fight, and that God is for us, no matter what happens.

Peter had several days to think about the pain of disowning his Lord. Three times, he had the chance to courageously tell others that he belonged to Jesus. Three times, he did the exact opposite. When he fulfilled Christ's prophecy about his denial, he cried, and cried, and cried some more. Oh, the pain of rejecting the One with whom he spent three amazing years! Peter loved the Teacher who saw him walk on water, who healed his mother-in-law, who taught him only what was true, and who showed compassion to the sick and lame and poor.

But weeks later, Peter is a changed man. Forgiveness will do that! He knew he had been given a second chance, and he was going to make the most of it. I have to believe that Peter looked back and wished he had stood up for Christ at his crucifixion, but a greater truth drove him onward - he was a forgiven man! He would never be the same again.

The next time that you sin, would you remember Peter? In spite of the pain, he found freedom in forgiveness. You can, too!

↑ THE STORY OF PETER'S FORGIVENESS IS FOUND IN JOHN 21:15-19.

## THE BEST COMMUNICATION

No longer will there be anything accursed, but the throne of God and of the Lamb will be in it, and his servants will worship him. They will see his face, and his name will be on their foreheads. (Revelation 22:3-4)

In 1995, I proposed to my future wife. When I proposed, I did not send her a message (that would have been hard, since texting did not exist in 1995!). I did not send her a tweet (though she makes my heart tweet!). I did not even call her so that she could hear my voice. I sat next to her, asked her to marry me, prayed with her, and put a diamond ring on her finger. I tried to communicate as best as possible that she meant everything to me, and that spending my life with her would be one of God's greatest gifts to me on this earth.

Seeing God face to face will be a joy that we can barely comprehend. I can only imagine what it will be like to look at the Father – we "will see his face," as we read in Revelation. I can't wait!

When we think about the face, we realize that all other forms of communication take a very distant second place. Not to say that all other forms of communication are bad; however, if they dominate our lives (and they often do), then we relationally miss out - big time!

Teens, I want to challenge you to live away from the world of "virtual reality." *Communication that takes place in the presence of one another is a powerful.* Why do we settle for less?

Are you willing to set aside social media for the sake of "the best communication?" I pray you will.

READ OF DAVID'S DESIRE TO SEE THE FACE OF THE LORD IN PSALM 17!

## A GREAT TIME TO PRAY

IN THESE DAYS HE WENT OUT TO THE MOUNTAIN TO PRAY,
AND ALL NIGHT HE CONTINUED IN PRAYER TO GOD. (LUKE 6:12)

Many years ago, I had a time where I suddenly woke up in the middle of the night. The Holy Spirit made it clear that I needed to pray for a former teen of our youth group. So I did. To this day, I have no idea how God might have used that prayer. One day, I will find out. For now, I trust that God answered that prayer for His glory.

Teens, I think it is easy to forget that God works the night shift. We lay down and can't go to sleep, or we wake up at 2:00 am and sleep eludes us, or we wake up early while everyone else is in sleeping and have to hang out in our bedroom until it's time to rise. When this happens, what should you do? How often I have failed to remember that God might just be keeping me awake so that I can have some more conversation time together with Him.

Jump on that opportunity to pray! We all know that it can be hard to pray during the busyness of a typical day. Rather than allowing music, your phone, the TV or the computer swallow up this precious time, pray in faith for yourself and for others. Don't be afraid to kneel down next to your bed and fervently, humbly pray. Our amazing God is always ready to hear and answer, even in the latest hours of the night!

↑ READ PSALM 121. "BEHOLD, HE WHO KEEPS ISRAEL WILL NEITHER SLUMBER NOR SLEEP."

## THE TRICKED AND THE TREATED (BY ALF WILKES)

"NOT EVERYONE WHO SAYS TO ME, 'LORD, LORD,' WILL ENTER THE KINGDOM OF HEAVEN, BUT THE ONE WHO DOES THE WILL OF MY FATHER WHO IS IN HEAVEN." (MATTHEW 7:21)

What would you do if Batman showed up on your front step? I mean, the doorbell rings and when you open the front door, there stands Batman. He's got the black suit on with the mask and flowing cape. This happened to me. Really, it did! Batman had come to my door and said, "Trick or treat!" And you know what I did? I gave him candy! OK, so it was actually a little boy dressed in a Batman costume for Halloween.

There are many people who wear masks and costumes each day. And maybe you are one of those people, too. What others see on the outside looks nice, but what is on the inside is anything but nice. Beneath the masks and costumes, these people are hiding all kinds of hurt (like drugs, alcohol, pornography, cutting, and depression).

In 2 Corinthians 11:12-13, the Apostle Paul warns about teachers in the church who "disguise themselves as apostles of Christ." They wore the costume of a follower of Jesus when they were not truly a follower. Paul goes on to say that he is not surprised by this behavior because Satan himself wears different costumes and masks, too. But just because a person – maybe even yourself - claims to be a follower of Jesus, it does not mean that person really is a Christian.

Are you tricking others into thinking that you are a follower of Jesus when you really are not? You go to church, you know how to use the Bible app on your phone, and you even know the right words to say. Disguising yourself as a follower of Jesus will not get you into Heaven. Talk to your youth leader about how you can be assured without a doubt of an eternity in Heaven with Jesus. No costumes allowed!

↑ CONTRAST THE RIGHTEOUS AND THE WICKED IN PSALM 9.

# NOVEMBER

## OF GOD AND HIS CHARACTER

What shall we say then? Are we to continue in sin that grace may abound? By no means! How can we who died to sin still live in it? (Romans 6:1-2)

"I know that I am forgiven, so it doesn't matter if I do something wrong." I heard this very statement not long ago. It came from a girl who wanted to justify her wrongdoing. I was surprised to hear those words come from her mouth; however, the more I thought about it, the more I realized that many live according to this personal belief.

If a person is truly a Christian, continuing in sin makes no sense. It is against our very nature; we are new creations in Christ, given over to life and light. We know that God's grace covers our sin, but we also know that we must fight against the presence of sin in our lives. Christians understand that we grieve God when we sin; it should cause us grief, as well!

If one of your friends tells you that he or she is a Christian, yet lives in sin without the guilt of offending a holy God, then he or she is telling you a lie. A believer cannot go on living in sin. The Apostle John talks about this at length in his letter of 1 John. If we are forgiven, we increasingly hate sin as we grow in Christ. John does not make the claim that we will never sin (see 1 John 2:1). Instead, he points out the difference between those who are forgiven and those who are unforgiven. The Lord knows the difference!

In the quietness of your heart, it is worth asking these questions: "What do I think of my sin? Do I despise it, or am I ok with it? What does that say about me?" God is completely aware of our actions and what these actions say about us.

READ ROMANS 6:1-14!

# OF GOD AND JUDGING PEOPLE (1 OF 2)

DO NOT GRUMBLE AGAINST ONE ANOTHER, BROTHERS, SO THAT YOU MAY NOT BE JUDGED; BEHOLD, THE JUDGE IS STANDING AT THE DOOR. (JAMES 5:9)

In our culture, we have learned to fear the word "judge." If you have been accused of judging someone, it may have stopped you in your tracks. "Who are you to judge me?" is a question that makes us think twice when it comes to our response against sin.

We may not want to talk about what it means "to judge," yet we need to do so. In today's world, there is such a misunderstanding about what it even means! I want to challenge you to look up verses in the Bible that deal with the topic (and if you do, you will find that there are many verses; we are not left wondering what God thinks about it all).

Among His many titles, God is referred to as "Judge" (see the verse above). As we study the Bible, we discover the following: when it concerns matters of right and wrong, He tells us to judge. When it concerns everything else, He tells us not to judge. Really, it's as simple as that.

Does God judge people? Yes. He has to – it is part of His eternal and holy character. As surely as you have to make decisions every day, God also passes judgment (His "holy decisions") upon the actions of people. If we are in Christ, we are judged righteous – we are free by the power of our salvation we have in Jesus! If we are not in Christ, we are judged guilty – we stand convicted in our sin.

How does the Judge find you? Innocent or guilty?

↑ "JUSTIFIED" MEANS "TO BE JUDGED INNOCENT". READ ABOUT JUSTIFICATION IN ROMANS 5:1-8.

# OF GOD AND JUDGING PEOPLE (2 OF 2)

(THEN) A THRONE IS ESTABLISHED IN STEADFAST LOVE, AND ON IT WILL SIT IN FAITHFULNESS IN THE TENT OF DAVID ONE WHO JUDGES AND SEEKS JUSTICE AND IS SWIFT TO DO RIGHTEOUSNESS. (ISAIAH 16:5)

Very often, when we tell people not to judge others, we refer to a certain way that they look, speak, talk, or behave. Is it fair that I look down upon a person who has multiple rings attached to her body, tons of tattoos, spiked fluorescent green hair, speaks with a stutter, and likes to knit sweaters when she is not skiing? Yes, this is a silly example; no, I shouldn't judge her. Why? In spite of what is happening on her "outside," I really don't know the truth about her "inside"!

I remember hearing a story once about one of my favorite Christian authors. He tells a story about landing in an airport and running into an "undesirable" family. He recalled thinking some not-so-nice thoughts about them. Ironically, one of the members of this family recognized him. He came up to the author and told him how much his writing meant to them all! How funny is that?!!

Teens, don't judge upon the outer appearance; yet be ready and willing to judge what is bad as wrong and what is good as right. Satan would have us see *all* forms of judgment as a bad thing. Don't do that! The Bible tells us that we MUST judge in the correct way (John 7:24 is one example of this).

God is the Judge of all the earth. He has every right to judge. He has also given us the ability to understand the difference between right and wrong – this knowledge is found in His Word. Based upon this, and based upon His commands to judge... you can do it! May the Lord lead you to judge in "grace and truth", so that Christ may be seen in you.

READ EXODUS 28:15-30 TODAY.

# OF GOD AND HIS CONTROL (1 OF 2)

WHY SHOULD THE NATIONS SAY, "WHERE IS THEIR GOD?" OUR GOD IS IN THE HEAVENS; HE DOES ALL THAT HE PLEASES. (PSALM 115:2-3)

Does God ever lose control?

If you believe the Bible, then you know that God is in complete control. In fact, there is a word to describe His control; it's called "sovereignty". What root word do you find in this term? That's right; the word "reign." He has complete reign over everything. He is the King of kings and Lord of lords – absolutely nothing happens that He has not decreed.

Psalm 115 brings another reality check on the character of God. Once again, He is not our eternal Santa Claus in the heavens. God "does all the he pleases". Does this offend you? Might you be thinking to yourself, "Well, if that is the case, then why should I do anything for Him? He knows how to take care of Himself, and I want to do the things that make me happy, so why do I need to serve Him?"

For those of us trying to live outside of His reign, let me ask this: How's it going? Are you happy? Are you content? Do you have peace? Do you have rest? You know the answer to these questions, and so do I!

Truly, God does whatever He pleases, and it pleases Him to offer you His grace and life in Him.

And since I am lost without His control, I am going to let Him have control of me.

CHECK OUT PSALM 115!

# OF GOD AND HIS CONTROL (2 OF 2)

THEN JOB ANSWERED THE LORD AND SAID: "I KNOW THAT YOU CAN DO ALL THINGS, AND THAT NO PURPOSE OF YOURS CAN BE THWARTED." (JOB 42:1-2)

If God is in control, why have I watched teenagers whom I know and love (as their youth pastor) deal with the following trials in the course of one year?

- A brother who is in and out of jail.
- A family who left him behind and moved somewhere else.
- A mother who does not understand how much her daughter is struggling with depression.
- A friend who has tried to commit suicide more than once.
- A girlfriend that ditched a guy with no explanation.
- A father who turns to drugs for his answer to pain.
- A couple of young men that lost their lives in a car accident.

Where is God when it hurts? Is He really in control?

Our lives all take different paths, yet the final destination is the same for each and every Christian: Heaven. God proved His complete control over everything when He gave us the Answer of answers – His Son, Jesus Christ. The pain you experience now is for a purpose. God is allowing it for a time. He has not lost control... rather, He is taking care of us, and will do so until the end!

If you are a believer, then take great comfort in this. And if you do not know the Lord, please consider these encouraging words from another one of my teens: "He is always there, always in control. It's just a matter of us choosing to seek Him and trust Him."

↑ GOD CONTROLS ALL OF CREATION – READ ABOUT IT IN JOB 38:1-21.

# OF GOD AND THOSE WHOM HE HATES (1 OF 2)

"I HAVE LOVED YOU," SAYS THE LORD. BUT YOU SAY, "HOW HAVE YOU LOVED US?" "IS NOT ESAU JACOB'S BROTHER?" DECLARES THE LORD. "YET I HAVE LOVED JACOB BUT ESAU I HAVE HATED. I HAVE LAID WASTE HIS HILL COUNTRY AND LEFT HIS HERITAGE TO JACKALS OF THE DESERT." (MALACHI 1:2-3)

Our society has done an effective job in teaching people that hatred is wrong on all accounts. We have placed the title of "Hater" on those who would desire to stand up against sin. Many embrace the belief that a person has a right to live however they choose (as long as it does not hurt others. However, who is the one that decides exactly what hurts others?). This gives people, not God, the position of authority.

Blindly, we have created another god whom we claim to be God, yet this god does not fit the description of God as found in the Bible. We like having a God who is willing to forgive us, bless us, and watch over us. We are also thankful that Jesus came to die for us. We love John 3:16; in fact, we are thrilled to have all those verses that talk about God's love for us!

However, what about the verses that deal with hate? Is Malachi 1:3 suppose to be in the Bible? Does it really describe God? If so, did He change in the New Testament? Does God hate all those who are not accepting of one another? Does He hate "Haters"?

Teens, God is God, and we are not. If He hates something or someone, He is right in doing so. As much as it depends upon us, we need to learn more about the Lord. As we do, His revealed hatred will make a lot more sense to us.

↑ READ ABOUT GOD AND THE UNREPENTANT NATION OF ISRAEL IN HOSEA 9:10-17 (FOCUS ON VERSE 15).

# OF GOD AND THOSE WHOM HE HATES (2 OF 2)

Do I not hate those who hate You, O LORD? And do I not loathe those who rise up against You? I hate them with complete hatred; I count them my enemies. (Psalm 139:21-22)

We cannot emphasize this enough: God is far above us, and as God, He can do whatever He wants to do. We cannot lower Him to our level. He is perfect in all of His ways... even when it concerns the topic of hatred.

In order to know whom God hates, it is important to know what He hates. For starters, we know that God has a complete hatred of sin. How do we know this? Sin is what broke His original relationship with humanity (the fall of Adam and Eve) at the beginning of time. In order to restore this relationship, there was only one thing left for God to do - He had to send His Son to die for that sin. He had to, for there is no other way to satisfy His perfect, necessary hatred of sin.

Now imagine this - God the Father sent His Only Son into the world - the Son that He loves so much, the Son that He has spent all of eternity with together, the Son that He shares absolutely everything with together – and that Son is separated from Him for the first time ever, because of our sin. *Our* sin! How terrible is that? Even more so, imagine this – there are literally millions upon millions of people that refuse to believe that their sin is worthy of death. They will not acknowledge that their sin caused the necessity of His Son's death. They think that they can come up with another way to get to heaven. They refuse to change their minds. They will not soften their hearts.

Now does it make sense why God hates those who reject His Son? To reject His Son is to reject Him!

🡅 DON'T BE FOOLED - THE WORLD HATES GOD. READ JOHN 15:18-27.

## OF GOD'S WILL AND MY HAPPINESS

WHOEVER GIVES THOUGHT TO THE WORD WILL DISCOVER GOOD, AND BLESSED IS HE WHO TRUSTS IN THE LORD. (PROVERBS 16:20)

Does God want me to be happy? It's a good question! The assumed answer is "yes," but if this is true, why is there so much suffering in the world?

For starters, we need to know that "happiness" is usually associated with a temporary state of being, primarily focused upon how we feel. On the other hand, "joy" has a sense of permanency, with a basis on what we know and understand.

We long to be happy, don't we? People do all kinds of things to find happiness. When we are happy, we don't want to lose that feeling. Indeed, God is pleased when we are happy in Him (Psalm 144:15 tells us, "Blessed are the people whose God is the LORD!"). Yet He also knows that happiness is not always devoid of suffering. 1 Peter (a letter that deals with the trials and tribulations of the Christian) makes more than one reference to the blessings of a sufferer.

Ultimately, in the end, all believers will be blessed and joyful in the Lord: "You make known to me the path of life; in your presence there is fullness of joy; at your right hand are pleasures forevermore." (Psalm 16:11). Right now, on this earth, in the presence of sin, we cannot live without suffering. However, this reality does not change God's will for us... and teens, God *always* accomplishes His sovereign will in our lives.

We can be happy in that thought!

↑ GO AHEAD AND READ PSALM 16 TODAY.

# OF GOD'S WILL AND MY HOLINESS

As obedient children, do not be conformed to the passions of your former ignorance, but as he who called you is holy, you also be holy in all your conduct, since it is written, "You shall be holy, for I am holy." (1 Peter 1:14-16)

The Bible tells us so much about who we are to be and what we are to do. God's commands make up His will for our lives, and Philippians 1:6 tells us that God will complete the work that He began in us. The end result is to make us just like His Son, Jesus. By the way, God will never fail in His perfect work; Romans 8:29 tells us "those whom he foreknew he also predestined to be conformed to the image of his Son."

When we consider the character of Christ, I believe that "holiness" defines him above everything else. Why would it be anything different? Jesus is God, and God is holy. Amazingly enough, we also are called to be holy.

When you hear the word *holy*, what comes to mind? Some only know that word in the context of taking God's name and character in vain. Others may picture people playing harps on a cloud. Perhaps you think of those who pray a lot and never miss church?

Simply put, to be holy is to be separate. God is separate from sin, and He expects the same from us. His will is for us to be holy! And here's the great thing about holiness – it leads to joy and happiness. Did you know that? Indeed, God made believers to be happy when we are holy. When we aim for happiness as our primary goal in life, we miss that goal, because we seek to bypass holiness.

"God, lead me in holy conduct. I want to be happy in You!"

↑ PONDER GOD'S WILL AND OUR HOLINESS IN DEUTERONOMY 7:6-16.

# OF GOD AND OUR ETERNAL DESTINATION

For though I am free from all, I have made myself a servant to all, that I might win more of them... I do it all for the sake of the gospel, that I may share with them in its blessings. (1 Corinthians 9:19, 23)

True or False: "God's grace and mercy will allow everyone to get to heaven." What is your answer?

As we read the Bible, we see that God's desire is for all to be saved, though not all will be saved. The gift of eternal life is offered to everyone, yet many reject this gift. Matthew 7:14 tells us, "For the gate is narrow and the way is hard that leads to life, and those who find it are few." As great as God's grace and mercy are to us, countless numbers of people will not accept it.

Is it possible that unbelievers will have a second chance to make things right? Many religions in this world would have us to believe so. However, *you will not find a second chance mentioned in the Bible.* There is no purgatory, no altered state in a next life, no spiritual unity with the universe. The Lord made it completely possible to believe in Him *in this life.* All we need to do is receive the message of His good news - Jesus died for our sins, with salvation based upon our repentance and His forgiveness. He has given us all the time we need to turn to Him, but countless numbers will still say "no!" in the end.

When an unbeliever dies outside of the Lord, everything is made perfectly clear as he or she stands before the Judge of all the earth. All will know that they were given plenty of chances to believe in the gospel, yet they chose not to do so. Because of the decision to reject Christ, all will not go to heaven. Dear one, may this not be your fate!

MEDITATE ON THE FINALITY OF REVELATION 20:11-15.

## OF GOD AND HIS ANGER (1 OF 2)

MOSES HEARD THE PEOPLE WEEPING THROUGHOUT THEIR CLANS, EVERYONE AT THE DOOR OF HIS TENT. AND THE ANGER OF THE LORD BLAZED HOTLY, AND MOSES WAS DISPLEASED. (NUMBERS 11:10)

Oh yes, God gets angry! It happened in the book of Numbers (as His people complained and disobeyed numerous times); it happened all throughout the Old Testament (as Israel proved herself to be a stubborn nation that worshipped many idols); and it happened in the New Testament (as Jesus rightfully flipped the tables of those taking money from the poor). God's patience is legendary... yet it is an attribute that has a limit. When He gets angry, the world shudders in fear and terror!

Is it ok for God to get angry?

Since He is God, and I am not, the real question is, "Who am I to challenge God?" The Lord has His holy reasons to become angry. And honestly, He made us able to get angry, as well. However, remember that we have boundaries for our anger (Psalm 4:4 says, "Be angry, and do not sin; ponder in your own hearts on your beds, and be silent.").

We are made in His image – God gave us the ability to think, to feel, and to decide. This includes the ability to express anger. Our biggest problem is that human anger is usually accompanied by sin. The Lord does not have that problem, since He does not sin. There has never been a time that God has acted wrongfully in His anger.

If I am angered, may it be over the same things that anger the Lord!

🡅 READ PSALM 4 TODAY.

## OF GOD AND HIS ANGER (2 OF 2)

FOR BECAUSE OF THE ANGER OF THE LORD IT CAME TO THE POINT IN JERUSALEM AND JUDAH THAT HE CAST THEM OUT FROM HIS PRESENCE. (2 KINGS 24:20)

Why does God get angry? Well... what makes you angry?

- You see someone bully a kid that cannot defend themselves.
- You hear your friend call you a nasty name to some other people in your class.
- You watch a video of another act of terrorism.
- You discover that money was stolen from your family while you were out of the house.
- You see someone act one way at church, but live totally different at school.

Is it right to be angry at the examples listed above? Yes! We get angry because sin is involved in every one of those situations.

We should be angry at sin. God is angry because of sin. He must deal with all of our sin. A Christian has his sin dealt with at the cross, praise God. The sin of the unbeliever keeps him or her in chains. God's anger remains upon the unbeliever until the moment of repentance.

Ultimately, the Lord will judge sin once and for all. We read about this in the coming 7-year tribulation, the Battle of Armageddon, and the Lake of Fire – the final destination for all who reject Christ. That is serious anger, yet it is righteous anger.

"Father, thank you that Your Son satisfied Your Holy wrath against me! I recognize that I deserve your anger, but I praise you for Your grace. I am saved by the blood of Jesus... the Holy Lamb of God!"

↑ READ ABOUT GOD'S ANGER AGAINST ISRAEL IN 2 KINGS 17:7-23.

# OF GOD AND OUR BELIEF IN HIM (1 OF 2)

FOR THOSE WHOM HE FOREKNEW HE ALSO PREDESTINED TO BE CONFORMED TO THE IMAGE OF HIS SON, IN ORDER THAT HE MIGHT BE THE FIRSTBORN AMONG MANY BROTHERS. (ROMANS 8:29)

"Does God have a choice over who will believe in Him, or is this choice completely up to us?" Ask this to ten different people, and you may get ten different answers!

When it comes to some of the most difficult questions about God and mankind, it helps to draw from those who know and comprehend the Bible well. Godly men and women who have spent a lifetime studying His Word will have much wisdom and understanding. We see their unwavering faith in the Lord, even when He allows trials into their lives.

Romans 8:29 is an incredible verse, yet it uses the word "those" ... and this word reveals that God doesn't "foreknow" everyone.

Some are predestined to be conformed to the likeness of His Son. God alone knows who the "those" are that will be saved. That knowledge is way above my head; yet God has given us His Word, and He knows all things, so I must believe Him.

If you were God, and you had always been around (eternally existing before the beginning of time), would you learn anything new? No! How could you? It's difficult to wrap our minds around this, but God *always* knew those who would believe in Him, for He has *always* known us! That's the beauty behind the word of "predestined" – before the existence of time, He purposed and planned our way back to Him. All I can say to that is "Wow!"

↑ SLOWLY, READ ROMANS 8:28-30. LOOK UP THE BIG WORDS AND CONSIDER WHAT THEY MEAN.

# OF GOD AND OUR BELIEF IN HIM (2 OF 2)

JESUS ANSWERED, "TRULY, TRULY, I SAY TO YOU, UNLESS ONE IS BORN AGAIN HE CANNOT SEE THE KINGDOM OF GOD." (JOHN 3:3)

When it comes to our salvation, there are two important points to consider: God's sovereignty and man's responsibility. Both are necessary and crucial. It is hard to completely understand just how they work together; however, if we trust what God teaches us from His Word, then we trust that both are essential components.

Pertaining to God and His will for those who are saved (His will = His holy choice or decision), let me pose a picture for you. Pretend that I was teaching a Bible lesson to you. During the lesson, I fell over and died. Now it is your responsibility to take care of me, since no one else will help me (which would be sad!). What would you do for me? I would hope you would be nice enough to pick me up off the floor, find a box big enough to place me inside, dig a hole in the ground, and say something about my dashing good looks before I was buried (the last part about my looks is optional). However, if you did none of the above and there was no one else to help me, what could I do for myself? Nothing, right? When I'm dead, I'm dead. There is nothing more that I can do. I cannot even lift one finger to help myself... it's over!

We read in Ephesians 2:1, "And you were dead in the trespasses and sin." Spiritually, there was NOTHING we could do to save ourselves. Dead is dead! So, in order to somehow spiritually come to life (the big word for this is called "regeneration"), we need a Giver of life. He is the one who indeed chose to save us. He even gave us the ability to choose Him after He awakens our soul, knowing we would make that choice to receive Him. Heavy stuff! But here's the point – our belief doesn't depend upon us; it depends upon Him and His perfect will. Amazing!

↑ CHECK OUT 2 THESSALONIANS 2:13-17 FOR MORE ON THIS TOPIC.

# OF GOD AND HIS THOUGHTS ABOUT US (1 OF 2)

HOW PRECIOUS TO ME ARE YOUR THOUGHTS, O GOD! HOW VAST IS THE SUM OF THEM! IF I WOULD COUNT THEM, THEY ARE MORE THAN THE SAND. I AWAKE, AND I AM STILL WITH YOU. (PSALM 139:17-18)

These two verses from Psalm 139 are stunning! This beautiful psalm expresses both the actions and the thoughts of God for us. Incredible!

I've known the truth of Psalm 139 for many years, but every time I read it, I think to myself, "Whoa... no way!" How can this be? God - who is ever watching over the entire universe - actually has thoughts about me? And not only a few thoughts, but countless? Like the uncountable sand at the beach? For me, this is mind-blowing (but believe me, I believe it!).

Sometimes, I try to think about what thoughts God would have for me. I know Him well enough by now that His thoughts are not full of disappointment and frustration. I have earned all of that, but thankfully, He told us that His thoughts are for us. In spite of my sin, He is looking at me with an everlasting love. He does not say, "Mike, what a failure you are! You did it again! How many times have I told you not to _______, yet you did not listen to me! What are you thinking? I've had it with you!" No. Instead, He says, "Mike, do you know just how precious you are to me? Can you even guess what I thought about you today? I think about you all the time! I love you so much, and I will move heaven and earth just to show you! You will always mean more to me than you'll ever know."

It's unbelievable. It's sobering. It's enough to make us weep great tears of joy. He loves us that much!

🡅 GOD'S THOUGHTS TOWARD ISRAEL KEPT THEM FROM TOTAL DESTRUCTION – READ HOSEA 11:1-11 TODAY.

# OF GOD AND HIS THOUGHTS ABOUT US (2 OF 2)

BUT I WILL FOR THEIR SAKE REMEMBER THE COVENANT WITH THEIR FOREFATHERS, WHOM I BROUGHT OUT OF THE LAND OF EGYPT IN THE SIGHT OF THE NATIONS, THAT I MIGHT BE THEIR GOD: I AM THE LORD. (LEVITICUS 26:45)

Leviticus is the third book of the Bible. At this point, Israel is just a "baby nation." Yet the Almighty and all-knowing God sees a rebellious child in the generations to come. In spite of this, He will keep his everlasting promise with His people. His covenant is unconditional, though the terms of it are based on specific conditions: obey, and be blessed; disobey, and be cursed.

God is weaving all of history together based on His promise made in Leviticus. His thoughts have never left the nation that He loves. The church, wonderful and glorious as she is, exists in part to bring the attention of Israel back to her God and her King. The Lord cannot get His mind off of Israel, and He never will. Eventually, the coming 7-year Tribulation will make way for the Kingdom, which He will use for Israel's restoration. He has declared it; it is inevitable.

It is amazing to learn of God's loyal love to His people, even though Israel was stubborn and stiff-necked. And still, with this big picture in mind, he thinks about little ole me. His thoughts cannot be counted, though I have often acted stubborn and rebellious myself. That is sheer, undeserved love right there.

I catch a glimpse of understanding His thoughts when I think of how much I love my three kids as a father. Yet I have my limitations, and I cannot possibly think of them even half as much as God thinks of me. He is so selfless, so forgiving, and so beyond words.

↑ REJOICE IN PSALM 92!

# MY REPUTATION

BUT JESUS ON HIS PART DID NOT ENTRUST HIMSELF TO THEM, BECAUSE HE KNEW ALL PEOPLE AND NEEDED NO ONE TO BEAR WITNESS ABOUT MAN, FOR HE HIMSELF KNEW WHAT WAS IN MAN. (JOHN 2:24-25)

Reputations. We tend to care very much about them. I know I struggle with thoughts about my reputation. As I work hard for my family and my church, I convince myself that no one has the right to say anything negative about me. If they do so, I will stand up for myself. Why? Because my reputation is on the line.

But then I turn around and counsel other people to not worry about their reputations. I see the frustration on their face when people talk poorly about them, and I encourage them to trust God with their feelings and frustrations. I believe this is correct counsel from the Word of God... so why is it so hard to believe myself?

It would be wise to look at how our Savior handled adversity of this kind. In the King James Version of the Bible, we read that Jesus "made himself of no reputation" (Philippians 2:7). He allowed himself to be a servant – the lowest point on the scale of humanity. And in John 2:24-25, he did not allow himself to be concerned about man and his words. In the gospels, we read that both good and bad words were said about Christ. He knew all men, he knew what was in a man, so he chose to entrust himself to the Father.

My advice (to the both of us) about our reputations? "Believe that you can do the same as Jesus did! Entrust yourself to God, He'll take care of it all."

🡅 NEHEMIAH ENTRUSTED HIS REPUTATION TO THE LORD. SOME OF HIS SUCCESS AGAINST THE OPPOSITION IS FOUND IN NEHEMIAH 6.

# TRUE LOVE TAKES TIME

AND THE LORD SAID TO ME, "GO AGAIN, LOVE A WOMAN WHO IS LOVED BY ANOTHER MAN AND IS AN ADULTERESS, EVEN AS THE LORD LOVES THE CHILDREN OF ISRAEL, THOUGH THEY TURN TO OTHER GODS AND LOVE CAKES OF RAISINS." (HOSEA 3:1)

Patience is not a practiced virtue today. Love is perhaps the greatest wonder of life, yet it is not uncommon to hear men and women quickly proclaim their love for their significant other, even if it is only days after their first date. This past week, I heard of a situation where a girl broke up with one guy, started dating her ex-boyfriend a few days later, and got married a few days after that. If you were not aware of this before, that is no way to "find love" ... and there is a 99.99% chance that this kind of marriage will fail.

Teens, true love takes time. Like, lots of time! You absolutely cannot discover how to love a future mate for life in a matter of hours, days, or even weeks. The best things in life are not only worth waiting for, they are also worth developing. Love is one of them. *If you desire to share true love with a special someone, you will not despise patience.*

Consider the patience of God. Even now, He awaits the return of His wife Israel (which will happen in the days of the Tribulation). He went to extreme measures to prove his love (with Hosea, He used a prophet to marry a prostitute as proof of His love. Woah!).

"Love is patient" (1 Corinthians 13). Give it time! And, if you desire true love, then you will love the truth.

↑ READ A LOVE CHAPTER FROM GOD TO ISRAEL – HOSEA 3.

# HIS CHOSEN FAMILY

AND I TELL YOU, YOU ARE PETER, AND ON THIS ROCK I WILL BUILD MY CHURCH, AND THE GATES OF HELL SHALL NOT PREVAIL AGAINST IT. (MATTHEW 16:18)

The Church: His chosen family! She is God's witness to the world. She is His body of believers, His purchased ones, His redeemed children.

Sometimes she is free to worship, under times of peace and prosperity. Sometimes she is under severe persecution, meeting in secret from those who would torture and kill. Sometimes she is large in number, as great masses come together and sing forth their praises. Sometimes she has a few in attendance, yet still every bit as important in God's sight. Sometimes she meets in big buildings, or a house, or an apartment, or even a tent.

Sometimes she shines brilliantly in her community. Sometimes she suffers the shame of inward fighting and sin. Sometimes she is growing in maturity and number. Sometimes she is about ready to shut her doors. Sometimes she is led forward by wise men who love the Lord. Sometimes she is led astray by false teachers who are self-serving.

Sometimes she is full of various age groups, races, classes, and social status. Sometimes she has one unique set of individuals that look and act the same. Sometimes she is under the umbrella of man-made leadership. Sometimes she is congregationally led. Sometimes she wins over her community. Sometimes she thrives in a city or town that would rather not have her at all.

God loves the church! Not just sometimes, but all the time. He loves His chosen family, now and forevermore. She looks forward to the day of her wedding, when she will be with Him for all eternity.

↑ THE CHURCH AS THE BRIDE OF CHRIST: EPHESIANS 5:25-32.

## FAITH: WHAT AN ADVENTURE!

(AND) AS SOON AS THOSE BEARING THE ARK HAD COME AS FAR AS THE JORDAN, AND THE FEET OF THE PRIESTS BEARING THE ARK WERE DIPPED IN THE BRINK OF THE WATER... THE WATERS COMING DOWN FROM ABOVE STOOD AND ROSE UP IN A HEAP VERY FAR AWAY... (JOSHUA 3:15-16)

Man, the Old Testament stories are so awesome! When we think of Israel crossing a body of water, we usually think of the Red Sea. But did you know that another generation of Israel got to experience a similar miracle? The water crossing mentioned above gave them entrance into the Promised Land. What did this miracle look like? Well, think of a few million people (i.e. the population of Philadelphia) crossing a flooded river. Scholars believe that the Lord approximately made a 20-mile path for Israel that day. Wow!

This time around, the people were ready to enter into the land. There was no complaining involved. They knew that getting across a flooding river with that many people and animals would take a miracle. An act of faith was necessary to cross.

Many centuries later, Jesus would also perform miracles based upon his power and the faith of the people. His greatest miracle of all was his resurrection from the dead. Likewise, it takes faith from the unsaved to cross to "the other side."

For the believer, it is impossible to please God without faith. Did you know that God has called us to a life of adventure? His definition of adventure involves the presence of faith. Hebrews 11 talks about "the great cloud of witnesses" – every believer in this chapter gave us an undeniable example of a "faith adventure." Today, they stand blessed.

So ride on, my friend! Embrace the adventure that awaits you.

↑ LET'S READ JOSHUA 3 TODAY!

## IF YOU HAD ONE WEEK TO LIVE

IN THOSE DAYS HEZEKIAH BECAME SICK AND WAS AT THE POINT OF DEATH. AND ISAIAH THE PROPHET THE SON OF AMOZ CAME TO HIM, AND SAID TO HIM, "THUS SAYS THE LORD: SET YOUR HOUSE IN ORDER, FOR YOU SHALL DIE, YOU SHALL NOT RECOVER." (ISAIAH 38:1)

If you keep reading Isaiah 38, you will see that Hezekiah cried years back on to his life. After bitter weeping and praying, the Lord chose to add another 15 years. In those years, Hezekiah experiences God's victory over Assyria (we read about this in Isaiah 37). But we also see him foolishly reveal Israel's riches to messengers of Babylon. One day, Babylon would be back to destroy Jerusalem, taking away these riches as plunder of war.

It makes me wonder: what if you were told that you had one week to live? If the doctor told you that you had seven days left, I'm sure you would be making some plans, right? For me, I would be spending every moment possible with my wife and kids. I would express how thankful I am to my church for what they have done for me, and I would work hard to make sure things were good to go in my departure. I would witness to those people that God has laid upon my heart. As a musician, maybe I would give a final concert. As a lover of kayaking, I would spend a day on the river. I would make sure that my wife was as financially set as possible for the remainder of her days. I would take day trips with the kids that they would never forget. I would even give the dog an extra time of walking and petting!

You know what? This could be my last week right now. If that is the case, then what am I doing today? Am I living like I have decades left on this earth, or am I living with my eternity in view?

Understanding the brevity of life is a focus of the wise.

🠉 READ ISAIAH 38. DESPITE HEZEKIAH'S FOLLY, GOD WAS GRACIOUS.

## LURKING WITHIN

AND SEE IF THERE BE ANY GRIEVOUS WAY IN ME, AND LEAD ME IN THE WAY EVERLASTING! (PSALM 139:24)

As I write this devotion today, our daughter Lydia is undergoing surgery to get rid of a growing infection in her body. It's an infection that came about from another surgery she had one month earlier. It's amazing to think that an unknown infection had been in her for several weeks before it finally manifested itself. One day, Lydia was outside playing soccer for her team, scoring the first goal of her life; the next day, she is running a fever and hurting all over.

Sin is insidious. Like an infection, it begins its dirty work on the inside. The heart is the place where sin finds its operational headquarters. The weak-willed mind follows the orders of the heart, and what is hidden soon comes to light. Sin causes the eyes, the tongue, the hands, and the body as a whole to betray our God and grieve His Spirit.

Sin lurks within, waiting to come out when we least expect it. If I allow my mind to utter swear words, then one or more will certainly make its way to my mouth. If I view pornography, I will eventually act upon my wicked fantasies. If I harbor bitterness to those who are wealthy, I will find ways to take from others what is not rightfully mine.

Our little girl needs surgery to eradicate her infection. David asks God to search him and know him in order to to eradicate any sin lurking inside. Teens, may the Lord help you discover any grievous ways in your life, and may He also lead you in the way everlasting!

SIN WAS LURKING WITHIN THE LEADERS OF ISRAEL. READ ABOUT THEIR SIN AND ITS CONSEQUENCES IN MICAH 3.

# DATING THE DEAD?

SO YOU ALSO MUST CONSIDER YOURSELVES DEAD TO SIN AND ALIVE TO GOD IN CHRIST JESUS. (ROMANS 6:11)

*There she is, the girl of your dreams... laying inside a coffin. They say she is dead, but you know better. Dressed beautifully, surrounded by flowers, ever so still, yet looking so radiant, you ask her to be your girlfriend. She does not reply; you take that as a 'yes.'*

*And off you go - fun times at high school football games, a trip to an amusement park, hanging out at your uncle's pond - it's all good! Granted, you are hauling her around in a casket the whole time, but she is always with you, no matter what. She is yours!*

*Then the wedding bells ring. What an awesome day! All dressed in white, she is rolled down the aisle into your waiting arms. The ceremony, the music, the cake, the dancing - it was all to die for! You carry that bride of yours out to the hearse, where you are whisked away to your honeymoon spot (Death Valley, of course!).*

*And not long into your marriage, you can't believe she is yours - for all the wrong reasons. In more ways than one, it stinks to have her in your life. She just lies around all day. You have to do everything for her! You finally realize that the two of you really had nothing in common all along. Truly, she had been dead since the day you met her.*

What a silly story... or is it? Well, let me ask you this: when a Christian dates and marries an unsaved spouse, what do you think God sees? Spiritually, one of you is alive, and the other is dead. So, "Do not be unequally yoked with unbelievers" (2 Corinthians 6:14).

🡅 KING AHAB MARRIED A "DEAD" WIFE, AND THE CONSEQUENCES WERE DISASTROUS. READ ABOUT HIS AWFUL START IN 1 KINGS 16:29 - 17:6.

# I AM THANKFUL!

YOU HAVE TURNED FOR ME MY MOURNING INTO DANCING; YOU HAVE LOOSED MY SACKCLOTH AND CLOTHED ME WITH GLADNESS, THAT MY GLORY MAY SING YOUR PRAISE AND NOT BE SILENT. O LORD MY GOD, I WILL GIVE THANKS TO YOU FOREVER! (PSALM 30:11-12)

'Tis the season to be thankful! Truly, it's always the season to be thankful, but I am glad that we have a holiday set aside to give thanks with church, family, and friends.

During this Thanksgiving season, I am struck once again by what I don't deserve. I don't deserve salvation, but here I am, a saved man. Also, I don't deserve a wonderful wife, great kids, a loving church, good friends, my health, cool teens in our youth group, and even a faithful dog... but I have them, too! I am an undeserving man, yet here I am, enjoying the benefits of God's grace in my life every day.

I look forward to going to heaven one day, but until then, I want my life to be one that brings praise to the Lord. When I consider Psalm 30:3, "O LORD, you have brought up my soul from Sheol; you restored me to life from among those who go down to the pit," I am reminded that God has given me every reason to live for Him. One day, I will join all the believers who have gone before me to heaven, forever to stand before Him! No matter what happens in this life, I am the Lord's.

It is proper to give thanks, both today and all the days of our lives. Giving thanks brings eternal reality to our temporary stay on this earth.

Teens, I hope you will be a generation that learns the meaning of thankfulness, for it will certainly change your lives. I am thankful – for you, and for our wonderful Lord and Savior, Jesus Christ!

↑ DAVID EXPRESSES THANKS TO GOD IN 1 CHRONICLES 16:7-36.

# HOW QUICK WE ARE TO BLAME!

He has told you, O man, what is good; and what does the LORD require of you but to do justice, and to love kindness, and to walk humbly with your God? (Micah 6:8)

Our church has an annual thanksgiving service the Wednesday night before Thanksgiving Day. One year, we started the service with a short video. As we began to watch it, I realized that it was the same video we saw the previous year. My first thought was not positive: "What is our tech team doing? This is not the right video! Didn't you see the new one I downloaded for this year? Ahhhh!" Then it dawned on me… I was the one who had mistakenly downloaded the wrong video, and the fellas in charge were playing the video I had given to them. So, I got all hot and bothered about something that was my fault all along. Duh!

I am ashamed to admit that I often blame others before I blame myself. It is a sign of pride to believe that I operate above the "fault line". To think that I am usually right is to consider myself better than others. Honestly, I don't want to consider the truth that I struggle with sin. It's easy to blame others; in that way, I am not the one with the problem, and I can go on my merry way without dealing with the changes that need to take place.

But that approach leaves me with another problem. If I don't change, then it is impossible for me to be transformed into the image of Christ. Blaming others leaves me forgetting that God needs to change me if I want to please Him. However, when I am willing to be conformed, I will understand that I am often the one at fault.

"God, help me to do justice, love kindness, and walk humbly with You!"

🡅 THE NATIONS HAVE THEMSELVES TO BLAME FOR GOD'S JUDGMENT UPON THEM. READ JOEL 3:1-8 TODAY.

## NOT YOUR NORMAL THANKSGIVING

AND WHEN YOU SACRIFICE A SACRIFICE OF THANKSGIVING TO THE LORD, YOU SHALL SACRIFICE IT SO THAT YOU MAY BE ACCEPTED. (LEVITICUS 22:29)

What makes a "Happy Thanksgiving!" for you?

I can guess what an "Unhappy Thanksgiving!" might look like. On that special day, you wake up to the smell of... nothing. Downstairs, a piece of bread awaits you. No turkey this day, no stuffing, no cranberry sauce, no pumpkin pie. And the electricity is out, so no football. Your relatives decided to stay home, so no time together. You are way behind on that paper for school, so no free time.

If this sounds like an awful Thanksgiving, I agree!

Could you be thankful for a day like this? Yes, you could! You can if you do not place your gratitude solely on the physical world around you. If you have Christ, you have eternal life, which means you have everything... indeed, you can always be thankful.

In the Old Testament, the Bible tells us that a thanksgiving offering was to be given with certain rules. These rules helped Israel to understand what was acceptable to God. A sincere heart of thankfulness revealed the heart of the giver and pleased the Lord. The worshipper who gave with gratitude was the one whom God would accept and bless. This person did not insist on being having his or her own way; rather, they obeyed willingly, ever thankful for their forgiveness and freedom.

No pumpkin pie? It's ok! Give thanks, with a grateful heart!

READ HOW HABAKKUK WAS GRATEFUL, EVEN WITH THE WORST COMING FOR HIS NATION. READ HABAKKUK 3.

## A DAY THAT IS REVEALING

ONE OF THE CRETANS, A PROPHET OF THEIR OWN, SAID, "CRETANS ARE ALWAYS LIARS, EVIL BEASTS, LAZY GLUTTONS." THIS TESTIMONY IS TRUE. THEREFORE, REBUKE THEM SHARPLY, THAT THEY MAY BE SOUND IN THE FAITH. (TITUS 1:12-13)

Oh, the verses that are in the Bible! Can you imagine being from the island of Crete and reading this rebuke from the apostle Paul? Ouch! And to think that it would be written for us to read for centuries to follow. Wow. What a bad reputation, man!

Reading Titus makes me wonder what Paul would write about us ("Americans are always _______."). I'm not sure what comes to your mind, but I do think that "Black Friday" is extremely revealing. If Paul visited the U.S., he would get a fairly accurate glimpse of our culture on the day after Thanksgiving. We are absolutely driven by the material. We want our stuff, and we will set up tents outside of stores in cold weather throughout the night to get it. Like the running of the bulls in Spain, we will charge the aisles to make sure we are first. We will shove people out of the way to make sure that our item is still in stock. Just ask any Wal-Mart employee what this day is like! Personally, I feel a whole lot safer at home on this day.

Materialism is just another way to satisfy our unhealthy physical desires (called "the flesh" in the Bible). Paul dealt with this kind of idolatry in his day. Somehow, we think we will be happy with things that will eventually rot, be corrupted, and ultimately destroyed. We know this is senseless, but we get sucked up into that kind of thinking nonetheless. How revealing!

Paul writes to Titus about how to handle the Cretans. Could we ourselves be the same kind of people as they were?

↑ WITH THAT SAID, CHECK OUT TITUS 2.

# READ IT CAREFULLY!

"DO NOT MAKE YOURSELVES UNCLEAN BY ANY OF THESE THINGS, FOR BY ALL THESE THE NATIONS I AM DRIVING OUT BEFORE YOU HAVE BECOME UNCLEAN, AND THE LAND BECAME UNCLEAN, SO THAT I PUNISHED ITS INIQUITY, AND THE LAND VOMITED OUT ITS INHABITANTS." (LEVITICUS 18:24)

Not long ago, I read through the book of Leviticus. In one chapter, it mentions that certain seafood is detestable to God (specifically, fish that have a shell, as written in 11:9-12). Several chapters later, it tells us that homosexuality is detestable to God. Based upon apparent contradictions such as this, some people have dismissed parts of the Bible as irrelevant. Sadly, they have chosen not to read it carefully.

Leviticus is part of the Pentateuch, which is the foundational first five books of the Bible. We must keep this in mind as we seek to understand what we read. What do we know about Leviticus itself?

1. **It was written to God's chosen nation, Israel.**
2. **It spelled out the manner of life in which God wanted His nation to live. The primary focus is the holiness of His people.**
3. **Israel is not the church; the nation is governed differently by the Lord as their God (compare this to the church as the bride of Christ).**
4. **We do not always understand the "why" of how God governed His nation many centuries ago. That's ok! Remember, His ways are not our ways.**
5. **We must consider if this book is dealing with physical or moral laws.**
6. **Concerning the church age: We must consider how the Bible handles a law in the New Testament. Is it ongoing (such as "love your neighbor as yourself")? Or has it been fulfilled (like the laws for sacrifices)?**

A careful reading of Leviticus 18 teaches us what Israel needed to know about sexual wickedness. It specifically tells us that homosexuality is detestable to God (vs. 22). The New Testament does not teach us anything to the contrary. So, teens... what should we conclude?

↑ PLEASE CAREFULLY READ LEVITICUS 18:24-30.

# UNHOLY COW!

AND HE RECEIVED THE GOLD FROM THEIR HAND AND FASHIONED IT WITH A GRAVING TOOL AND MADE A GOLDEN CALF. AND THEY SAID, "THESE ARE YOUR GODS, O ISRAEL, WHO BROUGHT YOU UP OUT OF THE LAND OF EGYPT!" (EXODUS 32:4)

July 4, 1776. One of the greatest declarations ever written was signed by men of courage and conviction. After months of discussion and debate, the day had finally arrived - the colonies would no longer endure the oppression of their mother country. A new nation was born: The United States of America.

Now imagine this fictional scenario, if you would. The signers of the document rise up to leave the building and share the news, only to find complete chaos outside in Philadelphia. While the men were working diligently, the citizens of the city switched their allegiance, proclaiming loyalty to the King of England. In fact, they erected a statue of the king on the steps of Independence Hall, pledging their lives to his service. They do this in spite of the hope that lies with a future of freedom.

If this really happened, where would we be today? This fictional account seems utterly ridiculous, as the signers knew they had the support of the majority of people. Yet, when we consider the story of God's people and the 10 commandments, we see that the ridiculous happened. The people forsook their commitment to God when Moses received the Law on Mt. Sinai. Instead, they chose to bow down to an idol they created. This unholy cow led to the death of thousands.

Think about the Christian leaders in your life. If they "disappeared" for a while, where would you be? Would you serve God, or would you worship an idol? Know this: our holy God will not share worship with an unholy cow!

🡅 READ EXODUS 32:19-35 TODAY.

# PEOPLE (BY MEL WALKER)

"...FOR THE SON OF MAN HAS COME TO SEEK AND TO SAVE THAT WHICH WAS LOST." (LUKE 19:10)

If there's one thing that is obvious about the life of Jesus, it's that he loved people. The Lord Jesus Christ concentrated His entire earthly life and ministry on investing in people. The story of Christ's interaction with Zacchaeus is just one account of how He reached out to people.

Humanly, it didn't make much sense to make a man like Zacchaeus a priority. Luke 19:1-10 presents a fairly negative description of him. Verse 2 mentions that Zacchaeus was a "*chief tax collector*" which meant that he was probably quite despised in that culture. He also says that he was "*rich*". Verse 3 records that he was "*of short stature*", or as the old children's song says, he was a "wee little man."

This is where the story of Zacchaeus takes an interesting turn. Verse 4 says that he ran ahead of the crowd of people that were following Jesus and climbed up in a tree just to get a better look at this great teacher and healer. Jesus sees Zacchaeus in the tree and invites Himself to his house, where undoubtedly this hated, wealthy tax collector put his true faith and trust in Jesus (see verses 6-10).

There is an important personal application in the account of Zacchaeus in the Bible. This illustration vividly demonstrates the Lord's genuine love for people – for *all* people, including you and me.

It's important to remember that Jesus' love for people is what motivated Him to die on the cross as a payment for our sins. As John 3:16 says, "*For God so loved the world, that He gave his only Son, that whoever believes in Him should not perish but have eternal life.*"

↑ LUKE ALONE RECORDS THE STORY OF ZACCHAEUS IN LUKE 19:1-10.

# DECEMBER

## WHAT'S KEEPING YOU FROM BELIEVING?

MANY OF THE JEWS THEREFORE, WHO HAD COME WITH MARY AND HAD SEEN WHAT HE DID, BELIEVED IN HIM, BUT SOME OF THEM WENT TO THE PHARISEES AND TOLD THEM WHAT JESUS HAD DONE. (JOHN 11:45-46)

SO THE CHIEF PRIESTS MADE PLANS TO PUT LAZARUS TO DEATH AS WELL, BECAUSE ON ACCOUNT OF HIM MANY OF THE JEWS WERE GOING AWAY AND BELIEVING IN JESUS. (JOHN 12:10-11)

What will it take for you to believe that Jesus died for your sins? What has to happen for you to repent? What more needs to take place to convince you to follow him?

Would Jesus need to do the following:

1. Show up at your doorstep and perform a personal miracle.
2. Make everything that is painful in your life go away.
3. Let you live your life the way you want to live it, and then receive entrance into heaven.
4. Bring vengeance upon all the people who hurt you.
5. Do something amazing for the public, like walk on water, provide a feast from a lunch box, make the blind see or the deaf hear, or raise a dead man to life.

There is nothing more that Jesus needs to do. Nothing! In his life, He performed many signs, wonders, and miracles (including all of the above!), and ultimately conquered death at the cross. Still, there were (and are) many who did not believe.

What about you? What's keeping you from believing?

↑ CHECK OUT JOHN 11:1-44! WHAT AN AMAZING STORY!

## BUILD-A-FRIEND (1 OF 2)

I AM DISTRESSED FOR YOU, MY BROTHER JONATHAN; VERY PLEASANT HAVE YOU BEEN TO ME; YOUR LOVE TO ME WAS EXTRAORDINARY, SURPASSING THE LOVE OF WOMEN. (2 SAMUEL 1:26)

Do you have a "build-a-bear" at home? If not, I'll bet you've heard of them. We have a couple of bears. If you have never been through the experience of the "build-a-bear" workshop, you literally put the thing together – picking an outer layer, filling it with stuffing, placing a heart inside, decorating it with an outfit, etc.

What if you were allowed to "build-a-friend"? What would you want your friend to look like on the outside? What kind of "stuffing" would go on the inside? What kind of character would be in the heart? How would you accessorize your friend? I'm guessing you would want only the best for this friend, inside and out. So would I! Yet we often settle for friends that aren't built well. The seams are torn, the stuffing is coming out, the outfit is ragged, and the heart isn't soft.

Why do we settle? Could it be because we *personally* settle for less than the best? If we are ok with a mediocre "me," then we'll be ok with that kind of a friend.

In the verse above, we read that King David was blessed to have a friend whose love was "surpassing the love of women." In other words, Jonathan chose David over himself, to the point that he would both live and die for his friend. Teens, please listen: in Christ, that kind of friendship is possible. If Christ put us first (which he did), and if he lives in us (and he does in all who believe), then we can be the kind of friend that we ourselves would "build" in others!

↑ DAVID'S LAMENT FOR HIS FRIEND JONATHAN IS IN 2 SAMUEL 1:17-27.

# BUILD-A-FRIEND (2 OF 2)

"A FRIEND LOVES AT ALL TIMES, AND A BROTHER IS BORN FOR ADVERSITY." (PROVERBS 17:17)

Who are your friends? How did you pick them (or how did they pick you)? They say that our friends reveal the kind of person that we are. That's humbling to consider! It makes me wonder: "What are my friends known for? What caused me to gravitate toward them?"

Thinking again about our "build-a-friend" concept, I'm guessing that your "built friend" would be someone close to your age. He would like much of what you like (perhaps the same style of clothes, or the same movies, or the same sports team). She would appreciate your opinion, and not judge you for being different. He would not lead you into trouble. She would know how to have a good time with you. He would support you in your absence. She would spend lots of time with you.

If this would be true, then let me ask you two questions to consider today. 1. Are you that kind of a friend? To be that kind of a friend takes real commitment and sacrifice. It means making some changes to accommodate this friendship. It isn't always easy! But it is worth it - *if* the friend desires God's good for your life (don't commit and sacrifice for someone who will lead you away from God!). 2. What if this kind of friend isn't around? Well, perhaps you should consider friendships beyond your peers. Your friend could be an adult who would serve as a mentor to you. It could be a lonely elderly man or woman who would love your friendship. As a teen, I had many friends who were girls, as most of the guys that I knew were bad news. Your friendships need not be defined by what is physical (like age, social status, etc.).

In Christ, you have more brothers and sisters than you can count!

↑ WHAT DOES FRIENDSHIP WITH JESUS LOOK LIKE? READ JOHN 15:9-17.

## ARE YOU ALIVE?

But God, being rich in mercy, because of the great love in which He loved us, even when we were dead in our trespasses, made us alive together with Christ – by grace you have been saved" (Ephesians 2:4-5)

Some time ago, I heard a story about a man who had fallen into a snowbank from that massive storm that just missed my town. He had been knocked unconscious and discovered many hours later, pronounced dead at the scene. But God was at work, and through His supernatural power, the man was revived! He lost a few fingers and all his toes, but he did not suffer any brain damage. Incredible!

I love stories like this one. It reminds me of the greatest story ever told: The Gospel, a story of life given by the Author of Life to those who were pronounced dead. I believe the Lord allowed this man to experience a death-defying experience so that many of us would stop and consider our own destinies.

I hope that the man is a Christian, or that he will come to Christ as a result of this occurrence. However, the day will come when he will die, and no amount of revival will bring him back. If he indeed is a Christian, his spirit is ever alive, and only time separates him from something far greater than being revived – his resurrection.

Are you alive in Christ? Those who are saved by grace can say "Yes!". As a Christian, death has no power over me.

Dear teenager, eternity is a matter of life and death. May it be that you find life in Christ! I trust in the power of God as I pray for you to believe. "I am alive!" = "I am a Christian!".

↑ JOHN TALKS ABOUT LIFE IN HIS LETTERS. READ 1 JOHN 3 TODAY!

## ARE YOU HUNGRY?

LIKE NEWBORN INFANTS, LONG FOR THE PURE SPIRITUAL MILK, THAT BY IT YOU MAY GROW UP INTO SALVATION – IF INDEED YOU HAVE TASTED THE THE LORD IS GOOD. (1 PETER 2:2-3)

You do not need to teach a newborn how to cry for food. When they are hungry, they have their ways of letting you know (believe me!). If you want to experience this truth, bring your ear plugs and visit the maternity wing of a hospital!

Now that you are no longer a baby, some things have greatly changed, and some things have not. You may not yell and cry for your food (at least I hope not!), but you have your ways of letting others know when you are hungry. It's only natural that you woke up this morning ready for something to eat. The body is made to crave food. It has its ways of letting us know when to eat.

Teens, take a minute and think hard about your own life. Do you crave time with God? Do you desire to read His Word, pray, spend time with Christians, go to church, etc.? Please take time before you answer this question. Many are quick to reply based upon the answer they believe others want to hear. Yet there is no inner desire - no hunger - to have anything at all to do with God.

*A true believer of Christ naturally desires God's food, which is His Word!* She is hungry for God. His natural response is to seek the Lord and to be filled from His hand.

Does this sound strange to you?

If so, are you truly a Christian?

↑ PLEASE READ PSALM 107:1-9.

## ARE YOU THIRSTY?

THE SPIRIT AND THE BRIDE SAY, "COME." AND LET HIM WHO HEARS SAY, "COME." AND LET THE ONE WHO IS THIRSTY COME; LET THE ONE WHO DESIRES TAKE THE WATER OF LIFE WITHOUT PRICE. (REVELATION 22:17)

I woke up this morning with a bloody nose. Why? I shut our bedroom door last night, which means that the humidifier in our living room could not effectively reach me inside of our dry house. I also woke up parched, wishing someone would go bring me some water so that I would not have to get out of bed! Needless to say, I needed water in more ways than one.

"As the deer pants for flowing streams, so pants my soul for you, O God" (Psalm 42:1). As certain as our body needs its share of water, the soul of a Christian needs streams of living water, so that it will thirst no more (consider the story of the woman at the well in John 4). The panting deer in Psalm 42 (today's reading) is not stooping down for a nice little slurp; rather, she is seeking to guzzle down the water as fast as she can, in order to quench her fierce thirst. Marathon runners know this better than the rest of us - after running a race, very little will get in their way as they find something to drink! A strong thirst drives us forward.

Do you thirst for God? Do you want the drink what He offers to you? Is this a natural part of your daily life? If so, nothing will stop you from getting to the living water. He offers it freely.

Dear one, if you are unsaved, did you know that Jesus offers himself as the Living Water? Come to him, and thirst no more!

READ PSALM 42 TODAY.

## ARE YOU SICK?

BUT I, BROTHERS, COULD NOT ADDRESS YOU AS SPIRITUAL PEOPLE, BUT AS PEOPLE OF THE FLESH, AS INFANTS IN CHRIST. I FED YOU WITH MILK, NOT SOLID FOOD, FOR YOU WERE NOT READY FOR IT. AND EVEN NOW YOU ARE NOT YET READY. (1 CORINTHIANS 3:1-2)

OK, so we know that babies need milk, right? Now, what if your mother decided that you would survive on this same milk until the day of your graduation? That would be crazy! How well could you live on milk alone? We all know that milk does a body good, but we were not created to go without eating solid food. Think what life would be like without pizza, hamburgers, blueberries, and skittles? Not good!

The Corinthians wanted to be content with milk alone, and that was a problem. Spiritually, the church was supposed to have graduated from Gerber food. However, that was just not happening. Spiritually, they were content with their milk, they slept in abundance, and they played in their messy diapers (I'm not kidding; read the book!). They were sick in many ways; sin led the Corinthians down a very unhealthy road.

Are you truly a Christian? Let's say the answer is "yes." Yet you do not have a hunger or thirst for prayer, Bible study, fellowship, worship, communion, or any other spiritual discipline. If so, we need to call it as it is - you are sick! You have contracted the disease of sinful living, and now your soul just feels just awful. It's so bad that you have forgotten your natural healthy desire to be fed from the Master's hand. This happens to many Christians – like cancer that tears the body down, sin eventually causes the soul to be only a shell of what it was meant to be.

Dear teen, if you find yourself that sick, please go see the Great Physician - now!

↑ READ 1 CORINTHIANS 5 TO LEARN MORE ABOUT THE SICKNESS OF THE CORINTHIAN CHURCH.

## ARE YOU DEAD?

AND YOU WERE DEAD IN THE TRESPASSES AND SINS IN WHICH YOU ONCE WALKED, FOLLOWING THE COURSE OF THIS WORLD, FOLLOWING THE PRINCE OF THE POWER OF THE AIR, THE SPIRIT THAT IS NOW AT WORK IN THE SONS OF DISOBEDIENCE – AMONG WHOM WE ALL ONCE LIVED IN THE PASSIONS OF OUR FLESH, CARRYING OUT THE DESIRES OF THE BODY AND THE MIND, AND WERE BY NATURE CHILDREN OF WRATH, LIKE THE REST OF MANKIND. (EPHESIANS 2:1-3)

I hope that you do not need to attend a funeral anytime soon. But if you do, what kind of response would you receive from the deceased? Obviously, there would be no response! That person is dead, and there is nothing more that he or she can do in the flesh. Now the earth will claim the body from which it came (as Genesis 3:19 tells us, "for you are dust, and to dust you shall return").

It is hard to picture someone as dead when you see them walking and talking in person. Yet on this planet, there are dead people by the millions. Most will get out of bed this morning, live their lives, and go back to bed tonight. The Bible says that they are dead because of sin. The curse is still upon them; they have not been set free in Christ. If we could just see people the way that God sees them, it would completely change our thinking on how we must reach them.

God is eternal. He is life. And He gives eternal life to all who believe. Those who refuse to believe are dead in their transgressions and sin. The dead who roam on this earth will naturally sin until they die in their sin, where hell awaits. What an awful reality.

There are plenty of fictional shows and movies about "the living dead." Outside of Jesus Christ, this fiction is reality.

Are you dead in your sin?

↑ GOD'S WORDS OF WARNING ARE GIVEN IN WORDS OF GRACE. READ ABOUT HIS GRACE IN EPHESIANS 2:1-10.

## TO JUDGE, OR NOT TO JUDGE? THAT IS THE QUESTION!

I SPEAK AS TO SENSIBLE PEOPLE: JUDGE FOR YOURSELVES WHAT I SAY. (1 CORINTHIANS 10:15)

One night I walked into our youth room and read the following message left on our board: "They tell you to be yourself, and then they judge you." If you have ever felt this way, let me tell you that I am sorry for your pain. No one likes to be judged!

It is really interesting to see how God's Word handles the topic of judging. Some time ago, I studied the word in the Bible, and I found out that *we are told to judge about as much as we are told not to judge.* That surprised me.

When Matthew 7:1 says, "Judge not, that you be not judged," it is telling us that we are not to make decisions based upon man's standards. For example, if I judge that people are ignorant for rooting against the Pittsburgh Steelers, then I am wrong! Indeed, the Steelers do have a lot of Super Bowl rings, but NFL fans are free to cheer any team they so choose. Good luck rooting against my team!

When 1 Corinthians 10:15 says, "I speak as to sensible people: judge for yourselves what I say," it is telling us that we are to make decisions based upon God's standards. For example, if I judge our nation as a country in trouble because we are ignoring God's parameters of marriage, then I am right! I can make this claim based upon what the Bible tells us about marriage.

So teens, be yourselves. But make sure you are yourself in the Lord! The person that does what is right has nothing to worry about; that person is only concerned about what God thinks above anything else.

➜ CHECK OUT 1 CORINTHIANS 2:10-16.

## WOULD IT REALLY MAKE A DIFFERENCE?

"THEREFORE THE LEPROSY OF NAAMAN SHALL CLING TO YOU AND TO YOUR DESCENDANTS FOREVER." SO HE WENT OUT FROM HIS PRESENCE A LEPER, LIKE SNOW. (2 KINGS 5:27)

Imagine if you could have experienced one of the miracles that happened in the Bible. Which one would you choose?

Naaman was the recipient of one of Elisha's many miracles. He humbled himself and followed Elisha's instructions for healing, and this Syrian commander was now no longer a leper. How amazing! Yet Gehazi (the servant of Elisha) felt the need to take advantage of this miracle, extracting money and expensive clothes from the happy commander. By so doing, Gehazi also received another unexpected "gift" – Naaman's leprosy!

Do miracles have the power to make us believe? You would think so, but people in the Bible choose not to believe God, in spite of His undeniable acts of power displayed for all to see. Even Jesus himself, the Savior and King, was rejected by his people, though he performed countless miracles. The world may teach us that "seeing is believing;" however, the Bible proves this to be untrue time and time again.

If you witnessed a miracle, would it really make a difference? Miracles point the way to God, but they do not have the power to make us believe. How many miracles had Gehazi seen from Elisha? It was not enough to lead him to believe. Teens, it is faith, the evidence of things unseen, that leads to salvation. By faith we are saved – by faith we please God – by faith we know, when we cannot see.

Sight is a wonderful gift, but it cannot save our souls. "So faith comes from hearing, and hearing through the word of Christ" (Romans 10:17).

↑ READ THE STORY OF ELISHA, NAAMAN, AND GEHAZI IN 2 KINGS 5.

## HE KNEW IT WAS COMING

THEREFORE, SINCE WE ARE SURROUNDED BY SO GREAT A CLOUD OF WITNESSES, LET US ALSO LAY ASIDE EVERY WEIGHT, AND SIN WHICH CLINGS SO CLOSELY, AND LET US RUN WITH ENDURANCE THE RACE THAT IS SET BEFORE US, LOOKING TO JESUS, THE FOUNDER AND PERFECTER OF OUR FAITH, WHO FOR THE JOY THAT WAS SET BEFORE HIM ENDURED THE CROSS, DESPISING THE SHAME, AND IS SEATED AT THE RIGHT HAND OF THE THRONE OF GOD. (HEBREWS 12:2)

Jesus always knew it was coming. His death, and his death alone, would mean going from heaven to earth to hell. He trusted the Father to take him from hell back to earth and to heaven again. But before this would happen, he would lay aside his heavenly position, be separated from his Father by the sin of the world, and crucified for the ones he loved. He knew it was coming; he is the only one that could bear the weight of what would inevitably occur.

If I was in the place of Jesus? Well... how fast I would have cracked! The unappreciative men that Jesus was given to disciple; the needy people who hung around to see another miracle, get another free meal, or receive another healing; the ignorant, foolish religious leaders who possessed hardened hearts; the rejection of my own family! Putting up with all of this, knowing that my death was coming, though I was completely innocent? Um, I don't think so!

*"Thank you, Jesus my Savior, for following the will of the Father until the end. You knew that the cross was your destiny, but you endured it for my sake. I am alive because of your perfect obedience! I will praise you forever and ever."*

🡅 DAVID FORESHADOWED THINGS TO COME FOR CHRIST IN PSALM 22. PLEASE READ IT CAREFULLY TODAY.

# ANGELS AND THE BIRTH OF JESUS

AND TO WHICH OF THE ANGELS HAS HE EVER SAID, "SIT AT MY RIGHT HAND UNTIL I MAKE YOUR ENEMIES A FOOTSTOOL FOR YOUR FEET"? ARE THEY NOT ALL MINISTERING SPIRITS SENT OUT TO SERVE FOR THE SAKE OF THOSE WHO ARE TO INHERIT SALVATION? (HEBREWS 1:13-14)

Ah, the Christmas season is here! It's been well over 2000 years since his birth, but all who know Jesus Christ as Savior rejoice in this season!

The angels are absolutely incredible beings, created by God even before man came upon the scene (see Job 38:6-7). However, the angels cannot compare to the human race. Why? Because God did not send His Son to save the angels from their sin. People often assume that angels are more important because they are heavenly beings, but this belief is nowhere found in the Bible.

When Jesus came to rescue us, the angels would have marveled. All would have seen the Son willingly leave his Father's side and become the most helpless of creatures – a human embryo. Some were given the privilege of announcing his birth to a group of local shepherds. The angels always do the will of their Lord and King, but this proclamation was one of a kind. God the Son came to die for his enemies? Even the angels themselves must have shaken their heads!

Whether it was Gabriel, or Michael, or other unnamed angels, the Bible teaches us that they never questioned God. They obey, even though they do not have all the answers (see 1 Peter 1:12). What a testimony to us as servants of God.

Many years ago, the angels watched together as the Redeemer lay away in a manger. And today, together with the saints of the Lord, the angels cry out, "Holy, Holy, Holy!".

READ OF ANGELS AND OUR SALVATION IN HEBREWS 1.

## SATAN AND THE BIRTH OF JESUS

AND THE DRAGON STOOD BEFORE THE WOMAN WHO WAS ABOUT TO GIVE BIRTH, SO THAT WHEN SHE BORE HER CHILD HE MIGHT DEVOUR IT. (REVELATION 12:4B)

Satan never rests. We recognize his pride, and not his laziness, as his downfall. The roaring lion is constantly on the move. If God is for it, he is against it. Revelation 12 gives us a unique historical "blip" into what things were like in the unseen world when Jesus was born. What he knew about the first coming of Jesus is something we can only guess at, but the devil is in the business of disruption and destruction. He did not want Christmas to come to pass!

As the evil prince of this world, Satan would have used all his influence over the Roman Empire. It is no coincidence that the Jews suffered greatly in those centuries. He also would have led Herod to decree the murder of baby boys under the age of two, in order to wipe out the living Christmas miracle. The devil hates God, hates his Son, and hates all who follow Him.

He lost at the cross, but that does not stop the Evil One from warring against God's people today. Keep in mind that he has a battle plan against you. During this season, it would mean getting wrapped up in your material desires, not telling others about the true meaning of Christmas, not being grateful for what you have, not thanking God for sending His Son into the world, and whatever else that would cause you to spiritually fail.

Pray that you will flee from Satan, and that you will make this Christmas all about Christ! Indeed, let's celebrate the holidays as "holy" days, for the Holy One was born to save us from our sin.

↑ A SCENE FROM HEAVEN'S PERSPECTIVE IN THE END TIMES, FOUND IN REVELATION 12!

# ISRAEL AND THE BIRTH OF JESUS

AND THE WORD BECAME FLESH AND DWELT AMONG US, AND WE HAVE SEEN HIS GLORY, GLORY AS OF THE ONLY SON FROM THE FATHER, FULL OF GRACE AND TRUTH. (JOHN 1:14)

Four centuries... and nothing. Silence. 400 years of wondering, and watching, and waiting... and nothing. The Jews were a conquered people. Yes, there were occasional revolts and rare victories in those years, but heaven was silent. Had God given up on His people?

Then, chosen ears heard the whispers. A barren woman past her child-bearing years became pregnant. Angels appeared and made an announcement to some shepherds. A star shone in the sky like no other. Wise men came from very far away to little Bethlehem. A virgin conceived by no means of a man. To those looking forward to this day, they were shouts of the miraculous! But to Israel, the signs were mostly unheard. Indeed, the nation slept when their Savior arrived to this earth.

The baby Boy would spend just a little time in Bethlehem before his family fled to Egypt, and then back to his parent's hometown of Nazareth. And he would grow up the son of a carpenter, finally to reveal himself as their Messiah when the time was right. By God's grace, some believed his message - but most of his brethren would not. And so, Israel ultimately rejected their King in his first coming to them.

It will not be so at his second coming. Israel will finally be ready to receive their King! Hallelujah for this! In the meantime, let us ponder our own souls. Are we ready to believe that Christmas is about the coming of our Savior? Or, like Israel in the days of old, are we also unaware of the greatest truth given to mankind?

↑ PLEASE CONSIDER JOHN 1:1-18.

# THE GENTILES AND THE BIRTH OF JESUS

PRAISE THE LORD, ALL NATIONS! EXTOL HIM, ALL PEOPLES! FOR GREAT IS HIS STEADFAST LOVE TOWARD US, AND THE FAITHFULNESS OF THE LORD ENDURES FOREVER. PRAISE THE LORD! (PSALM 117)

Soon, untold millions will celebrate Christmas. Many do it because it is a cultural thing, and some do it in order to praise God for His salvation. A vast majority of those who celebrate Christmas are Gentiles. By definition, Gentiles are simply those who are not Jews. In the Bible, God focuses much of His attention upon Israel (His chosen nation), but make no mistake – His promise of salvation is given to all the peoples!

When Jesus was born, the Gentiles were not looking for his arrival. If anything, his presence was considered a possible threat to Rome (which was the excuse the Pharisees were looking for in order to kill him). But though the world was not looking for the Savior, Jesus opened the door for all to come to him. Much of his ministry was done in Galilee, away from the religious heartland of the Jews. He poured his love and compassion upon the "lesser ones" of society (the women, the sick and feeble, the prostitutes, etc.). His actions were a clear sign pertaining to the thoughts of God toward humanity.

Jesus promised his followers that they would do "greater things" when he left. What happened next? The church began, Christianity exploded, and Gentiles everywhere would receive Christ as Savior. We are both the proof and the grateful recipients of God's grace!

The good news to the world was revealed to Jew and Gentile alike in a stable in Bethlehem. "Praise the LORD, all nations! Extol him, all peoples! For great is his steadfast love toward us, and the faithfulness of the LORD endures forever. Praise the LORD!"

↑ READ IMPORTANT VERSES OF PROPHESY IN ISAIAH 49:1-6.

# BELIEVERS AND THE BIRTH OF JESUS

AND COMING UP AT THAT VERY HOUR SHE BEGAN TO GIVE THANKS TO GOD AND TO SPEAK OF HIM TO ALL WHO WERE WAITING FOR THE REDEMPTION OF ISRAEL. (LUKE 2:38)

Teens, you probably know the Christmas story well enough to recognize some of the main characters. Most of us can name the shepherds, the wise men, and Mary and Joseph. You might have also heard of Zechariah and Elizabeth, who were close relatives of Mary. All of these people believed and experienced the fulfillment of Christ's coming. They also made up a very tiny group of people who knew exactly what was happening on that first Christmas.

But have you ever heard of Simeon and Anna? If "no," you are going to read a wonderful story today!

When Joseph and Mary brought baby Jesus to the temple for the first time, these two older folks were present. God rewarded their faith and belief in Him by allowing them to see the Christ before they passed away. Specifically, the Holy Spirit had revealed this news to Simeon (see Luke 2:26). But perhaps both remembered what Daniel had said about the coming of their King. And not only Daniel about the "when" of his arrival, but Micah about the "where," and Isaiah about the "who" and "how." For the saints in the Bible who willingly studied the Scriptures, there were clues all over the place.

How exciting for Simeon and Anna! And how exciting for everyone who seeks and finds Jesus. In every age, he is the Savior of the world. And one day, he will come again, this time to stay. Let's rejoice in both his first and second coming!

READ LUKE 2:21-38.

## ZECHARIAH AND MARY

AND WITHOUT FAITH IT IS IMPOSSIBLE TO PLEASE HIM, FOR WHOEVER WOULD DRAW NEAR TO GOD MUST BELIEVE THAT HE EXISTS AND THAT HE REWARDS THOSE WHO SEEK HIM. (HEBREWS 11:6)

Zechariah, the father of John the Baptist. Mary, the mother of Jesus. They were related (through Elizabeth, Zechariah's wife). They were righteous. Neither one had children. They were visited by the angel Gabriel, and they responded with fear and wonder. They both were promised a son. Their sons would be given prominent positions and prophetic purposes.

But when these two characters spoke, the comparison ends and the contrast begins. Zechariah wanted proof, while Mary sought understanding. Rather than respond in faith, Zechariah looked for a sign (Luke 1:18 - "How shall I know this? For I am an old man, and my wife is advanced in years."). This is not the first time in biblical history that a child has been born to an old couple. Zechariah would have known this, yet he still asked for something else.

On the other hand, Mary wondered at the miracle of miracles - a baby would be born to a virgin (Luke 1:34 - "How will this be, since I am a virgin?"). This miracle had never happened before, and it is the only time in history that it would ever occur. Gabriel answered her, and she believed! What faith!

This Christmas, remember that God is not asking you to believe the unbelievable. The fact that Jesus was born to the virgin Mary and proclaimed by his cousin John is a fact. Believe it, and you will understand the true meaning of Christmas.

↑ COMPARE AND CONTRAST THESE TWO SAINTS IN LUKE 1:1-38.

## CHRISTMAS AS A TIME TO GROW

AND LET THE PEACE OF CHRIST RULE IN YOUR HEARTS, TO WHICH INDEED YOU WERE CALLED IN ONE BODY. AND BE THANKFUL. (COLOSSIANS 3:15)

I can remember some of my favorite Christmas gifts as a kid. A desk. A keyboard. A silver trumpet. Transformers galore. Sets of football cards. Various games. Lots of books to read. My parents worked hard to give us nice presents, and I appreciate them for it.

I do remember one Christmas, however, where it seemed like I got less presents than I did the previous year. I wasn't very happy about it, and I think I hurt my parents' feelings with my words and actions. The presents themselves were valuable, but the quantity was less than I expected. Maturity needed to take place in my life, don't you think?!!

As time goes on, I hope that you will find the greatest joy in the act of giving at Christmas (if you do not already feel that way). By giving, you are also getting. Giving means getting joy from putting someone else first. It also best reflects what the Father did when he gave His Son to the world.

How is your heart right now during this Christmas season? Think hard for a minute. Are you more mature about Christmas than you were last year? If you do not get what you want, will you be ok with that? Are you looking to bless as many people as you can? Perhaps you have some maturing to do as well, just like I did.

Christmas is a wonderful time to grow, and I hope you experience true spiritual growth this holiday season.

↑ PLEASE CONSIDER COLOSSIANS 3:12-17!

# A NEW HOLIDAY

AND WHILE THEY WERE THERE, THE TIME CAME FOR HER TO GIVE BIRTH. AND SHE GAVE BIRTH TO HER FIRSTBORN SON AND WRAPPED HIM IN SWADDLING CLOTHES AND LAID HIM IN A MANGER, BECAUSE THERE WAS NO PLACE FOR THEM IN THE INN. (LUKE 2:6-7)

Imagine for one moment that you were given a new calendar for Christmas, and it had absolutely no holidays scheduled on it (no Christmas, no Easter, no 4th of July, nothing!). However, with this calendar comes a certain freedom – YOU get to make up holidays for the year! That's right – it's all up to you! So, what special days would you recognize? How many holidays would you give yourself? What would you celebrate?

In a sense, this is what happened once the church began. Jesus Christ changed everything, including what we recognize and celebrate. We have Christmas and Easter because of Jesus, and I believe other morally-minded holidays come from the influence of Christianity (such as Thanksgiving). At some point in history, Christmas would have been a new holiday, right? Christians rightly recognized the incredible significance of "God with us," so they set aside December 25th as a special day to honor the occasion.

In the days of the Old Testament, the Jews were given many holidays as part of their religious calendar. Followers of Judaism still celebrate those festivals today. As God-followers, we would be doing the same if our Savior still had not arrived on the scene. However, Jesus really did change everything, and so we happily celebrate his birth during these holidays.

May your holiday be full of the wonder of "God with us!"

↑ DO YOU KNOW THE CHRISTMAS STORY? READ LUKE 2:1-20 TODAY!

# PEACE

GLORY TO GOD IN THE HIGHEST, AND ON EARTH PEACE AMONG THOSE WITH WHOM HE IS PLEASED. (LUKE 2:14)

This famous angelic proclamation is one that Christians recognize as an incredible Christmas promise. Peace! Ah, just the sound of the word has a way of bringing hope to our souls.

Peace. Do you have it? How would you know if you had it? Well, ask yourself some personal questions. When I take a good, hard look at who I am, what do I think? When I strip away everything on the surface and ponder the essence of my being – my very soul – and allow it to be undistracted, how do I feel? When I think about the moment that I take my last breath and leave this earth, what do I really know for sure?

Peace. It is often accompanied by silence. Silence is a rare commodity today. Silence is something we often fear, as it tends to reveal the great unrest of the soul. Yet how can we hear if we will not listen? How can we have peace if we cannot discern the voice of God? God has His ways, and He is not one to yell over the chaos of our lives. He calls us to be quiet, to welcome silence, and to receive his invitation for peace. Truly, it's amazing what we learn from God when we will just listen...

Peace. It is offered to "those with whom he is pleased." Notice that this is not an offer to every last individual who has lived on this earth. His favor rests on those who will listen. God knows those who will listen. He knows those who will silence themselves to hear. He knows those who will receive the invite to peace. Are you one of them? Do you have peace in your life? Is your soul settled before Him? Dear teen, do you belong to Him?

READ 2 CORINTHIANS 2:5-14. DO YOU HAVE PEACE?

# STARGAZERS

Now after Jesus was born in Bethlehem of Judea in the days of Herod the king, behold, wise men from the east came to Jerusalem, saying, "Where is he who has been born king of the Jews? For we saw his star when it rose and have come to worship him." (Matthew 2:1-2)

Fascinating, those stars. Here since the dawn of time, they shine with a brilliance only Creator God could have displayed. I know very little about their nature, or the constellations, or how many light years away we are from the nearest one not named the sun. But I love to lay on the grass at night and simply stare into a cloudless sky.

Fascinating, those wise men. They knew right away when the star of all stars had appeared in the night. I think we often imagine that this star was the biggest or the brightest in our galaxy. Maybe it was... but if so, how in the world did the world miss it? No, I tend to think that these men were looking for more than meets the eye, and since they were stargazers, God guided them to see His star.

Fascinating, those who seek God. When we humbly ask God to reveal Himself to us, He always draws near. It's the young lady who comes to the realization that she will do anything for the One who loves her so much. It's the young man who knows that he can no longer live for himself, because that's not a life worth living. It's the group of teens who strive to keep one another walking on a path of righteousness, since this is the very path of freedom.

Fascinating, our God. He guided the stargazers of long ago to not miss the event of their lifetime. Indeed, these star-struck wise men would gladly come and worship Christ, the newborn king.

🡅 YES, EVEN THE STAR WAS PROPHESIED! READ NUMBERS 24:15-19.

# THE GIFT THEY DIDN'T WANT

JESUS ANSWERED HER, "IF YOU KNEW THE GIFT OF GOD, AND WHO IT IS THAT IS SAYING TO YOU, 'GIVE ME A DRINK,' YOU WOULD HAVE ASKED HIM, AND HE WOULD HAVE GIVEN YOU LIVING WATER." (JOHN 4:10)

Have you ever received a present that you did not want for Christmas? As soon as you opened the gift, you knew that you would be exchanging it for something else, or re-wrapping it for another Christmas (yes, I unashamedly do that!).

In Hebrews 6, we read of people who were given a gift that they decided to turn down. Why would this be a problem? Because the gift was from God – and if you are wise, you NEVER turn down a gift from God. But these people did, and because of this, there were consequences to be had. Permanent consequences.

Why would we not accept a gift from God? The answer does not reflect well upon humanity – we turn away God's gift because of pride, selfishness, and unbelief. The "I don't need your charity" mentality comes from one source – the Evil One himself. He turned down God's gifted position for him, proudly believing He was better than the Giver. Those who follow Satan's example have done the same thing. They reject the Baby in the manger who saves the world from sin.

The woman at the well in John 4 knew a good thing when she saw it, and so accepted a gift that many others did not want.

Teens, accept the free gift (Romans 6:23). It's a one time offer – and who knows how long you have left to receive it? Those who have received God's gift could never imagine life without him. What a gift of love!

🡅 CONSIDER HEBREWS 6:1-12.

# THE CHARACTER OF JOSEPH

WHEN JOSEPH WOKE FROM SLEEP, HE DID AS THE ANGEL OF THE LORD COMMANDED HIM: HE TOOK HIS WIFE, BUT KNEW HER NOT UNTIL SHE HAD GIVEN BIRTH TO A SON. AND HE CALLED HIS NAME JESUS. (MATTHEW 1:24-25)

Have you ever considered the character of Joseph (the earthly father of Jesus)? The book of Matthew gives us some insight into this godly man. Though we do not know much about his life, we can conclude that he was a great guy. Why? Because...

- *When he found out that his betrothed wife was pregnant (and not by him!), he planned to divorce her quietly. In his noble character, he did not want Mary to be publicly disgraced (Matthew 1:19).*
- *When the angel Gabriel told him that Mary was pregnant by the Holy Spirit, He believed and kept her as his wife (Matthew 1:24).*
- *Though Mary was expecting, he withheld having sexual union with her in the days of her pregnancy. By keeping her as his wife, many would have believed he had been the one to make her pregnant in the first place. His obedience and self-control further reveal that her pregnancy was not of man (John 1:13).*
- *When the angel told him to move his family to other locations for their safety (Egypt and Nazareth), he obeyed (Matthew 2:13, 20).*
- *Every year, he took his family to Jerusalem to worship (Luke 2:41).*
- *He taught Jesus a trade (carpentry).*

The character of Joseph. What a father he was!

↑ READ ABOUT HIM IN MATTHEW 1:18-25 AND 2:13-23.

# A MIRACLE OF MIRACLES

AND THE ANGEL ANSWERED HER, "THE HOLY SPIRIT WILL COME UPON YOU, AND THE POWER OF THE MOST HIGH WILL OVERSHADOW YOU; THEREFORE, THE CHILD TO BE BORN WILL BE CALLED HOLY – THE SON OF GOD." (LUKE 1:35)

I can only imagine what it must feel like for a woman to find out that she is expecting. Though we had two sons born to us, I cannot fully know what my wife felt inside as an expectant mother. Both of these pregnancies were precious days for us!

"I'm pregnant." How happy for the mother who has been waiting for that moment to happen! How sad for the woman who realizes that she must care for a child when she was not expecting motherhood. How unusual for the only lady in history who did not become pregnant by any man - Mary, the mother of Jesus.

Mary wonders, "How in the world am I going to have a baby when there is no man involved?" If ever there was a valid question, this is it! Gabriel tells Mary that the Holy Spirit would "come upon" and "overshadow" her in such a way that she would become pregnant. If a miracle is defined as an act of God that goes against the laws of nature, then a woman getting pregnant without man's help certainly qualifies!

You know what else is miraculous? That God would love someone like me. I cannot thank Him enough that he would send his Son to die in my place. I marvel at the miracle of the birth of Christ; I fall down and worship at the miracle of my own salvation.

↑ ON THIS CHRISTMAS EVE, CHECK OUT GALATIANS 4:1-7.

## THE BIRTHDAY OF THE KING

O LORD, YOU HEAR THE DESIRE OF THE AFFLICTED; YOU WILL STRENGTHEN THEIR HEART; YOU WILL INCLINE YOUR EAR TO DO JUSTICE TO THE FATHERLESS AND THE OPPRESSED, SO THAT MAN WHO IS OF THE EARTH MAY STRIKE TERROR NO MORE. (PSALM 10:17-18)

Merry Christmas, teens!

What would life be like without Christmas? For you and I, December 25th is the day set aside to celebrate the birth of Jesus Christ. His coming cannot be overstated; it is our Savior that makes this "the most wonderful time of the year!"

With that said, I think back to the previous centuries before Jesus was born. There was a time of about 400 years when Christmas did not exist; in fact, God had not directly spoken to His people at all in those years. For the Jews, these centuries proved to be some of their hardest. The Greeks and the Romans had largely kept them trampled underfoot. They were allowed to exist, but only under strong governmental authority. The Jewish religious leaders made life oppressive for the commoner. The promises of a coming King were a distant memory...

Psalm 10 is not a passage we would normally turn to when we think about the Christmas story, but I want to encourage you to read it today. When you do, think about the children of Israel. They lived the harsh realities of this psalm. The wicked were all around them, causing them to suffer many trials and tribulations.

Yet in the Lord, hope springs eternal. "The LORD is King forever and ever; the nations perish from his land" (vs. 16). In the birthday of the King, we find our strength!

↑ CONSIDER PSALM 10, AND CELEBRATE THE BIRTH OF THE KING TODAY!

## NOW THAT CHRISTMAS IS OVER...

JUDGE NOT, AND YOU WILL NOT BE JUDGED; CONDEMN NOT, AND YOU WILL NOT BE CONDEMNED; GIVE, AND IT WILL BE GIVEN TO YOU. GOOD MEASURE, PRESSED DOWN, SHAKEN TOGETHER, RUNNING OVER, WILL BE PUT INTO YOUR LAP. FOR WITH THE MEASURE YOU USE IT WILL BE MEASURED BACK TO YOU. (LUKE 6:37-38)

A while ago, my wife told me about a social media outrage against a woman who posted a picture on the internet. Apparently, she bought and wrapped 100 presents for each of her 3 kids. Yep, that would be 300 presents altogether (don't you wish YOU had her as a mother?!!). She justified it by saying she wanted to spoil her kids once a year. Yeah, I would say that 100 presents each should do the trick.

I don't know how many presents you received this Christmas, but what I do know is that Christmas should be a picture of our eternal reality. God has given us presents beyond count in the riches we have in Christ Jesus (see Ephesians 1:3). Gifts under a tree are nothing compared to the Gift that hung from the Tree.

I want to challenge you to do something special this Christmas. To show the world that you love God and understand that Christmas is about His Sacrifice to us, give one of your better presents to someone else in need. I'll bet that you know who these people are in your life (a poor relative? That outcast at school? The neighbor three houses down?). In heartfelt love, give something away of great value to that person, and watch God bless you incredibly. The Father remembers doing the same thing for you over 2000 years ago.

BE CHALLENGED BY LUKE 6:27-38 TODAY.

# MY CARD SAYS "CITIZEN OF HEAVEN!"

BUT OUR CITIZENSHIP IS IN HEAVEN, AND FROM IT WE AWAIT A SAVIOR, THE LORD JESUS CHRIST, WHO WILL TRANSFORM OUR LOWLY BODY TO BE LIKE HIS GLORIOUS BODY, BY THE POWER THAT ENABLES HIM EVEN TO SUBJECT ALL THINGS TO HIMSELF. (PHILIPPIANS 3:20-21)

One popular commercial today likes to ask its viewers, "What's in your wallet?" Well, if your wallet is like mine, you probably have a few forms of identity. In my wallet, you would find a credit card, a driver's license, a few membership cards, and a picture of my wife. What you would *not* find in my wallet is cold, hard cash! I think my wallet may be allergic to it or something!

If God decided to give His children I.D. cards, they all could be designated by the title "CITIZEN OF HEAVEN." Indeed, Heaven is our home! Nothing can change this wonderful reality.

I have a passport showing that I am a citizen of the United States (for which I am truly thankful). It also shows that I have traveled overseas to both China and Peru. I consider myself blessed to have been to these nations. But my passport reveals my earthly travels alone. One day, I will go to the place that will forever exist – the place I am created for – the place of my heart's desire!

Heaven's identity card is quite amazing. When our time is up and God calls me home, my card will not only prove my citizenship, but it will also grant me a total transformation. When I cross those golden borders, I will be completely purified from sin. Now that is living!

How about you? "What's in your wallet?" Do you have a "CITIZEN OF HEAVEN" card? Will we share citizenship together when it's time to go?

↑ CHECK OUT PHILIPPIANS 3:12 – 4:1.

## SATAN'S LIES ABOUT HEAVEN

BUT THE SERPENT SAID TO THE WOMAN, "YOU WILL NOT SURELY DIE. FOR GOD KNOWS THAT WHEN YOU EAT OF IT, YOUR EYES WILL BE OPENED, AND YOU WILL BE LIKE GOD, KNOWING GOOD AND EVIL." (GENESIS 3:4-5)

We blew it, and he led the way. The devil tempted Adam and Eve with a lie, and we fell for it. There is nothing better than being in the presence of God, yet through our ancestral parents, we chose the lie, and humanity has suffered ever since.

Do you know people who do not have something they want, and because they don't have it, they don't want you to have it, either? That is an accurate description of the devil at the beginning of time. Because of his pride, he was thrown out of God's presence, and he has made it his purpose to try to destroy all that our Lord pronounced as good. And oh, how Satan knows that Heaven is good! He can't stand the thought that the Lake of Fire is his determined end. His trick was to get Adam and Eve into believing his lie – that paradise *must* include a knowledge of what is good *and* evil. Being exactly like God is the way to eternal pleasure and happiness, according to the serpent. This simply is not so, as the two innocent ones soon discovered.

If something is too good to be true, then it is not true - unless God Himself told us that it is true! It's sad that we end up believing so many lies, yet have such a hard time accepting the truth.

Teens, Satan wants you to believe his lies about Heaven for two reasons: first, that you might also suffer his same fate; second, that you will believe your best days are here on earth. I encourage you to forsake his lies. He will not be in Heaven, so why should we believe what he says about it?

🠉 COMPARE SATAN TO THE KING OF TYRE: READ ISAIAH 28:11-19.

## STAY TUNED FOR THE SECOND ACT!

FOR THE LORD COMFORTS ZION; HE COMFORTS ALL HER WASTE PLACES AND MAKES HER WILDERNESS LIKE EDEN, HER DESERT LIKE THE GARDEN OF THE LORD; JOY AND GLADNESS WILL BE FOUND IN HER, THANKSGIVING AND THE VOICE OF SONG. (ISAIAH 51:3)

For a very brief time, Eden was home to our ancestral parents (Adam and Eve). Once they sinned, our hopes were now found in Heaven. Heaven includes both the new heavens (the skies and the universe beyond) and the new earth. The God of wonders has chosen to restore all things; because of this, the new earth will be an "eternal Eden".

How can this be true? If you are like me, you might imagine Eden as a garden of limits. Though the Bible makes it very clear exactly what the Lord created in Genesis 1, I still imagine Eden as being a very tiny part of the whole earth (like the size of a small farm). However, my small imagination is the fault of my little faith! The Bible gives us an area that Adam and Eve lived (in Mesopotamia), but we should also assume that they were not limited to a gated community. God's wonderful creation was sprawling; indeed, the Garden was not small!

The New Earth will have the same qualities. In the verse above, we see life instead of death. A greenhouse instead of a desert. Singing instead of mourning. Gratitude instead of hatred. Isaiah 35:1-2a echoes this truth: "The wilderness and the dry land will be glad; the desert shall rejoice and blossom like the crocus; it shall blossom abundantly and rejoice with joy and singing."

Do you believe what you are reading? Dear teen, I sure hope so! When I think of Heaven, I like to think of it in this way. About the original creation, God says, "This is very good!". About the restoration, God says, "If you liked the first act, stay tuned for the second act!"

CHECK OUT ISAIAH 51:1-16 TODAY.

# THIS HOME IS PERFECT

SURELY GOODNESS AND MERCY SHALL FOLLOW ME ALL THE DAYS OF MY LIFE, AND I SHALL DWELL IN THE HOUSE OF THE LORD FOREVER. (PSALM 23:6)

Home. I long for it when I am away on a lengthy trip. I miss it when I've been stuck at work on a bad day. I remember how precious it is at special occasions, like the holidays.

Home has a special place in all of our hearts. Sometimes there are exceptions – some people in this world are homeless, or have experienced home as an unsafe place. If these ones know Christ as Savior, they will especially appreciate the home they have in Heaven.

It's hard to see Heaven as home when we cannot see Heaven in our world. It seems unbelievable that a place like no other awaits us – a place made special, with us in mind – a place where everything you see and hear and feel will be eternally pleasurable. There is only One who could ever offer this, and He is the One waiting for us at home. It's true! Jesus is preparing a special place at home, for us (John 14:1-3).

Teens, is it too much to imagine that this world, though cursed, is a small picture of what is to come? Each time you experience a happy homecoming, it's just a glimpse of our glorious arrival to Heaven.

If your own home is one of pain and distress, picture the place here on earth where you go to experience peace, safety, and comfort. The Bible teaches us that "in your presence there is fullness of joy." In Heaven, you'll now be at peace, know safety, and enjoy perfect comfort in Him.

When we see Heaven for the first time, we can rightly say, "I'm home!" and "This place is perfect!" I, for one, can hardly wait!!!

READ PSALM 140: "THE UPRIGHT SHALL DWELL IN YOUR PRESENCE."

# WELCOME HOME! (BY CARL PESESKY)

YOU MAKE KNOWN TO ME THE PATH OF LIFE; IN YOUR PRESENCE THERE IS FULLNESS OF JOY; AT YOUR RIGHT HAND ARE PLEASURES FOREVERMORE. (PSALM 16:11)

Have you ever been homesick? Maybe you went to summer camp or a mission trip. I don't know about you, but after a long trip away from home, nothing seems more rewarding than walking in the door of your home. You can chill out on your sofa, eat a home-cooked meal, spend time with family, and even sleep in your own bed. It is so rewarding!

Homesickness can make you feel sad, and it makes you long to be back at home with your family and its comforts. This is a natural response! Believe it or not, we often feel this way about our heavenly home, as well. The Bible describes Heaven as home. As Jesus spoke about His imminent death, he talked about building a "forever" home (Heaven) for those who believe in him as their Savior (John 14:2). Knowing that this world is not our home should truly change our mindset and perspective on life! As we change, we long for our heavenly home.

You have probably heard the catchphrase "YOLO", which means "you only live once." Well, YOLO isn't true, because this life isn't all that we have to look forward to in the future. We have our eternal home in Heaven! We don't have to get caught up in this world, since our lives only last but a moment. The pain, the struggles, the endless pursuit of popularity, and all of the trivial issues in this life are so much less important compared to living for Jesus in the here and now.

May you live for the day when your Savior calls out to you, shouting the words, "WELCOME HOME!"

↑ CHECK OUT JOHN 14:1-4 TO READ MORE ABOUT WHAT JESUS HAD TO SAY ABOUT HEAVEN, OUR HOME.

## SCRIPTURE REFERENCES FOR READING

Genesis 1:1-13 – May 16
Genesis 1:14-31 – May 17
Genesis 2:15-25 – May 2
Genesis 3:1-13 – June 23
Genesis 3:14-24 – May 1
Genesis 6:1-8 – May 3
Genesis 6:9-7:10 – September 3
Genesis 7:11-24 – May 3
Genesis 9:1-17 – May 4
Genesis 12:1-9 – September 4
Genesis 21:1-7 – May 5
Genesis 24 – January 7
Genesis 34 – January 13
Genesis 37 – January 3
Genesis 38 – June 15
Genesis 45:21-46:7 – September 6
Genesis 50:15-21 – March 25
Exodus 1 – June 26
Exodus 3 – May 21
Exodus 4 – September 7
Exodus 12:29-42 – May 6
Exodus 14 – September 8
Exodus 20:1-17 – October 9
Exodus 28:15-30 – November 3
Exodus 32:19-35 – November 29
Leviticus 18:24-30 – November 28
Leviticus 19:11-19 – August 21
Leviticus 24:10-23 – July 20
Leviticus 26:1-13 – May 7
Leviticus 26:14-39 – May 8
Leviticus 26:40-46 – May 9
Numbers 14:26-45 – March 22
Numbers 24:15-19 – December 21
Deuteronomy 1:26-46 – January 14
Deuteronomy 4 – October 1
Deuteronomy 5:22-33 – July 24
Deuteronomy 6 – May 27
Deuteronomy 7:6-16 – November 7
Deuteronomy 34 – March 16
Joshua 1 – September 9
Joshua 3 – November 20
Joshua 5:13-6:27 – March 15
Joshua 23 – January 21
Joshua 24 – May 10
Judges 2 – September 10
Judges 8:22-35 – May 11
Ruth – June 21
1 Samuel 3 – January 8
1 Samuel 8 – September 11
1 Samuel 16:1-13 – January 2
1 Samuel 17 – April 2
1 Samuel 20:24-34 – August 16
1 Samuel 23:7-29 – April 3
1 Samuel 24 – July 30
2 Samuel 1:17-27 – December 2
2 Samuel 2:1-7 – April 18
2 Samuel 7 – April 13
2 Samuel 9 – April 8
2 Samuel 11:1-5 – April 4
2 Samuel 11:6-13 – April 6
2 Samuel 11:14-26 – April 7
2 Samuel 12 – July 28
2 Samuel 15:1-14 – April 9
2 Samuel 16:5-14 – April 5
2 Samuel 18:29-19:8 – April 10
2 Samuel 21:1-14 – April 11
2 Samuel 22 – April 14
2 Samuel 24 – April 12
1 Kings 2:1-12 – April 14
1 Kings 9:1-9 – April 15
1 Kings 11:1-24 – May 13
1 Kings 12 – September 13
1 Kings 16:29-17:6 – November 30
1 Kings 19:1-18 – January 30

Psalm 119:137-144 – February 18
Psalm 119:145-152 – February 19
Psalm 119:153-160 – February 20
Psalm 119:161-168 – February 21
Psalm 119:169-176 – February 22
Psalm 121 – October 30
Psalm 128 – March 6
Psalm 139 – August 2
Psalm 140 – December 30
Psalm 142 – March 24
Psalm 143 – April 6
Proverbs 2 – July 11
Proverbs 3:1-18 – April 21
Proverbs 3:19-35 – April 22
Proverbs 6:1-11 – June 17
Proverbs 8:1-11 – March 7
Proverbs 10:31 – August 17
Proverbs 15 - August 30
Proverbs 18 – March 13
Proverbs 22:17-29 – June 9
Proverbs 23:29-35 – October 15
Proverbs 25:1-8 – June 30
Proverbs 26:12-16 – October 4
Proverbs 26:17-28 - August 19
Proverbs 29 – October 20
Proverbs 31:1-9 – June 14
Ecclesiastes 2 – March 8
Ecclesiastes 7:1-14 – March 20
Song of Solomon 1 – March 12
Song of Solomon 2 – January 23
Song of Solomon 3 – June 10
Song of Solomon 6 – June 16
Isaiah 2:1-5 – July 7
Isaiah 7:10-14 – September 17
Isaiah 9:1-7 – March 3
Isaiah 11:1-9 – July 5
Isaiah 28:11-19 – December 28
Isaiah 30:8-17 – August 15
Isaiah 32:1-8 – July 4
Isaiah 38 – November 21
Isaiah 42:1-9 – September 16
Isaiah 43:25-44:5 – July 9
Isaiah 44:1-5 – July 3
Isaiah 49:1-6 – December 15
Isaiah 51:1-16 – December 29
Isaiah 52:1-12 – July 8
Isaiah 53 – June 24
Isaiah 55 – July 6
Isaiah 57:14-21 – March 2
Isaiah 65:17-25 – July 10
Isaiah 66:1-2 – September 28
Jeremiah 1:1-10 – January 9
Jeremiah 6:9-15 – March 4
Jeremiah 29:4-14 – January 16
Jeremiah 31:1-6 – September 30
Jeremiah 36:20-32 – June 13
Jeremiah 52:24-34 – August 27
Lamentations 1 – September 14
Lamentations 3 – June 20
Ezekiel 8 – July 25
Ezekiel 11:16-25 – June 7
Ezekiel 18:19-32 – April 17
Ezekiel 36:22-32 – February 28
Daniel 1 – January 4
Daniel 2:17-23 – February 29
Daniel 3 – January 11
Daniel 4 – March 14
Daniel 6 – April 20
Daniel 10 – June 27
Hosea 3 – November 18
Hosea 6:4-11 – August 11
Hosea 9:10-17 – November 4
Hosea 11:1-11 – November 15
Hosea 13:14-14:9 – May 30
Joel 2:28-32 – October 19
Joel 3:1-8 – November 25
Amos 5:6-15 – August 9
Amos 5:21-27 – August 10
Obadiah – August 23
Jonah 2 – February 27
Jonah 4 – April 16
Micah 3 – November 22
Micah 6:8-16 – January 25
Nahum – August 5
Habakkuk 1:12-2:20 – June 1
Habakkuk 3 – November 26

Zephaniah 1:1-13 – April 23
Zephaniah 1:14-2:3 – October 24
Zephaniah 3:14-20 – August 29
Haggai – January 20
Zechariah 1:1-6 – January 26
Zechariah 8 – February 23
Malachi 3:1-5 – May 15
Malachi 3:6-12 – October 17
Malachi 4 – April 25
Matthew 1:1-17 – September 12
Matthew 1:18-25 – December 23
Matthew 2:13-23 – December 23
Matthew 4:1-11 – June 11
Matthew 5:1-12 – September 19
Matthew 6:5-15 – July 1
Matthew 6:19-24 – March 28
Matthew 6:25-7:5 – August 4
Matthew 7:7-12 – July 29
Matthew 9:1-8 – September 20
Matthew 10:32-39 – October 25
Matthew 12:33-37 – July 16
Matthew 16:13-20 – March 1
Matthew 22:34-40 – July 2
Matthew 25:14-30 – October 10
Mark 1:1-8 – May 29
Mark 6:1-6 – April 30
Mark 9:42-50 – August 13
Mark 10:1-12 – October 18
Luke 1:1-38 – December 17
Luke 1:39-45 – August 1
Luke 1:46-56 – January 5
Luke 2:1-20 – December 19
Luke 2:21-38 – December 16
Luke 2:41-52 – January 18
Luke 4:1-13 – June 12
Luke 5:1-11 – June 6
Luke 5:17-26 – October 27
Luke 6:27-38 – December 26
Luke 7:1-10 – September 29
Luke 7:36-50 – March 27
Luke 12:13-21 – April 29
Luke 16:19-31 – August 14
Luke 19:1-10 – November 23
John 1:1-18 – December 14
John 1:19-42 – September 18
John 2:29-41 – May 20
John 8:1-11 – August 28
John 8:42-47 – June 2
John 10:7-21 – May 31
John 11:1-44 – December 1
John 13:1-17 – March 5
John 13:18-30 – January 28
John 14:1-4 – Dec. 31
John 14:5-14 – September 21
John 15:9-17 – December 3
John 15:18:27 – November 5
John 17:12-19 – June 28
John 17:20-26 – June 25
John 21:15-19 – October 28
Acts 1:1-12 – September 24
Acts 2:17-21 – October 19
Acts 2:29-41 – May 20
Acts 10 – October 22
Acts 11:19-30 – July 19
Acts 17:22-34 – August 24
Acts 28:1-10 – March 21
Romans 1:16-23 – October 3
Romans 4:1-8 – October 21
Romans 5:1-8 – November 2
Romans 5:9-11 – April 16
Romans 5:12-21 – September 2
Romans 6:1-14 – November 1
Romans 6:15-23 – June 4
Romans 8:28-30 – November 13
Romans 10:8-13 – July 23
Romans 12:9-21 – October 2
Romans 14:19-23 – March 10
1 Corinthians 2:10-16 – December 9
1 Corinthians 3 – October 23
1 Corinthians 5 – December 7
1 Corinthians 8:1-13 – October 6
1 Corinthians 10:23-11:1 – October 26
1 Corinthians 13 – July 14
2 Corinthians 1:15-23 – July 12

Made in the USA
Middletown, DE
18 November 2021

52828049R00248